Kafka's Creatures

Kafka's Creatures

Animals, Hybrids, and Other Fantastic Beings

EDITED BY MARC LUCHT AND DONNA YARRI

LEXINGTON BOOKS
A division of

ROWMAN & LITTLEFIELD PUBLISHERS, INC.
Lanham • Boulder • New York • Toronto • Plymouth, UK

Published by Lexington Books
A division of Rowman & Littlefield Publishers, Inc.
A wholly owned subsidiary of The Rowman & Littlefield Publishing Group, Inc.
4501 Forbes Boulevard, Suite 200, Lanham, Maryland 20706
http://www.lexingtonbooks.com

Estover Road, Plymouth PL6 7PY, United Kingdom

British Library Cataloguing in Publication Information Available

Library of Congress Cataloging-in-Publication Data

The hardback edition of this book was previously cataloged by the Library of Congress as follows:

Kafka's creatures : animals, hybrids, and other fantastic beings / edited by Marc Lucht and Donna Yarri.
    p. cm.
Includes bibliographical references and indexes.
1. Kafka, Franz, 1883–1924—Criticism and interpretation. 2. Animals in literature.
3. Animals, Mythical, in literature. 4. Human-animal relationships in literature. I. Lucht, Marc, 1969– II. Yarri, Donna.
PT2621.A26Z76125 2010
833'.912—dc22   2010011424

ISBN 978-0-7391-4394-0 (cloth)
ISBN 978-0-7391-4395-7 (pbk.)
ISBN 978-0-7391-4396-4 (electronic)

To Dorothy Yarri and the memory of Daniel Yarri,
who both loved animals, especially cats

and

To Dunkel, Chamois, Tiki, and Dusty,
none of whom were convinced they were "just animals"

Contents

Acknowledgments

Preparing a collection of essays such as this involves the efforts of many people. Most important are the authors of the articles. Their insightful scholarship will greatly enhance our understanding of the roles played by animals and other creatures in Kafka's writing. We are grateful for their patience and continued enthusiasm as our volume took form.

We must thank several people who were indispensable to us as we worked on this project. Esther K. Bauer was unsparingly generous with her expertise on Kafka and German literature in general. As a native speaker of German, her linguistic facility proved essential. Our book would not have been possible without her support. Marc Lucht's years of challenging conversations with Gary Steiner about nonhuman animals have served to inspire and guide his thinking both about who they are and how to achieve a proper moral stance with respect to them. Professor Steiner's scholarship is a model of rigorous philosophical reflection on the nature and foundation of our moral responsibility to animals, and his advice about *Kafka's Creatures* proved invaluable. Henry Sussman's moral support and encouragement at the outset gave us the confidence we needed to move ahead with the project, and David Silbey, a widely published historian in our department, provided us with helpful advice about the publication process along the way. Our other departmental colleagues have cheered us on as we worked on the book. Ms. Bobbie Rohrbach and our research assistant, April Batinsey, worked tirelessly to help us find relevant secondary literature and to meet our multiple requests for interlibrary loan materials, and Mrs. Christine Lindahl's secretarial services were of inestimable benefit to us.

We are especially grateful to our editor at Lexington Books, Michael Sisskin, for believing in our work. We want to acknowledge as well all of the other individuals at Rowman and Littlefield who assisted at various stages of the project.

We would also like to acknowledge the thorough work of Patricia Stevenson, who kept the project on schedule. We also want to thank Random House, Inc., for granting us permission to use the quotes of Franz Kafka in our work. And we would like to thank the staff of Fairchild Tropical Gardens for assisting with images from David Fairchild's *Book of Monsters*.

Finally, thank you to all of our family, friends, and colleagues.

A race began in the woods. The whole place was full of animals. I tried to establish order.

—Franz Kafka, *Dearest Father*

CHAPTER 1

Introduction

Marc Lucht

There are few literary authors in whose works animals and other creatures play as prominent a role as they do in Franz Kafka's writing. The presence in his stories of burrowing forest animals, insects, mice, dogs, horses, apes, jackals, leopards, vultures, jackdaws, hares, rats, larks, and even mysterious creatures such as Odradek, the kittenlamb, and weird bouncing balls testifies to Kafka's continuing preoccupation with nonhuman creatures. These creatures speak, sing, investigate, lurk, tumble, scuttle, and tunnel their various ways to the heart of the issues explored in his literature: the nature of power, the inescapability of history and guilt, the dangers and promise and strangeness of the alienation endemic to modern life, the human propensity to cruelty and oppression, the limits and conditions of humanity and the risks of dehumanization, the nature of authenticity, family life, Jewishness, and the nature of language and art.

Nonhuman animals also play an important part in Kafka's letters and diaries. Often he refers to himself as an animal (indeed, in Czech the word *kavka* refers to a jackdaw, a small Eurasian bird belonging to the same genus as the raven), as when he mentions feeling like "a sparrow, practicing [his] jumps on the step."[1] In November 1913, he compares himself to a dog, writing, "At bottom I am an incapable, ignorant person who, if he had not been compelled . . . to go to school, would be fit only to crouch in a kennel, to leap out when food is offered him, and to leap back when he has swallowed it."[2] He also compares himself to a sheep: "I am really like a lost sheep in the night and in the mountains, or like a sheep which is running after this sheep."[3] In an obscure diary entry from the "Night of comets, 17–18 May," in 1910, Kafka writes, "Together with Blei, his wife and child, from time to time listened to myself outside of myself, it sounded like the whimpering of a young cat."[4] Perhaps especially suggestive, given that his grandfather was a kosher butcher, in 1913 Kafka seems to refer to himself as

3

a pig under the knife: "4 May. Always the image of a pork butcher's broad knife that quickly and with mechanical regularity chops into me from the side and cuts off very thin slices which fly off almost like shavings because of the speed of the action."[5] Kafka's diary from August 1914, to take another example, contains an unpublished story titled "Memories of the Kalda Railway." It is unusual for being narrated from the first person. Much of the story deals with the narrator's attempts to defend his wooden hut from some vividly realized rats. Soon the narrator falls ill with a respiratory disorder, symptomatic of which is a cough described by his fellow railway workers as a "wolf's cough." The narrator reports then sitting on a "bench in front of the hut" in order to greet "the train with a howl [and] with a howl I accompanied it on its way when it departed."[6] In this story, illness seems to render the narrator—perhaps an "I" with whom the hypochondriac Kafka identified—less human and more canine.[7] Kafka's preoccupation with animals extended into his dreams. One "disgusting" dream from 1911 involved a dog lying "on my body, one paw near my face. I woke up because of it but was still afraid for a little while to open my eyes and look at it."[8] Many of his story fragments deal with animals and animal imagery.[9] And Kafka the person, of course, is famous for his moral regard for the well-being of animals. After becoming a vegetarian, according to his friend and biographer Max Brod, Kafka visited the Berlin aquarium with a lady, who afterward reported that Kafka had addressed the fish by saying, "Now I can look you in peace. I don't eat you any more."[10] The centrality of animals to his thinking is made plain in a diary entry from 1917, where Kafka reproduces part of a letter he wrote to his then-fiancée Felice Bauer. In the letter he states that his "ultimate aim" is to "strive to know the whole human and animal community."[11]

Exploring multiple dimensions of Kafka's incorporation of nonhuman creatures into his writing, this volume is the first collection in English of articles all devoted to illuminating this important and ubiquitous dimension of his work. The chapters here are written by an array of international scholars from various fields, and represent a diversity of interpretive approaches. In the course of charting the roles played by nonhuman animals and other creatures in Kafka's writing, they help make sense of the literary and philosophical significance of his preoccupation with animals, and make clear that careful investigation of those creatures sheds light upon his core concerns. Thus the chapters in this volume enrich our understanding of Kafka's work as a whole. Especially striking is the extent to which the articles collected here bring into focus as well the ways in which Kafka anticipated many of the recent developments in contemporary thinking about nonhuman animals.

Over the past two decades, the humanities have witnessed renewed scholarly interest in nonhuman animals. Part of the reason for this attention lies in the need to contend with progress in disciplines such as psychology and cognitive ethology. Because of the discrediting of behaviorist assumptions about the impossibility of knowledge about animal mental life, as well as the refining of experimental and observational techniques in the field of animal behavior, exciting—and, for many people, unexpected—discoveries have been made about the rich cognitive, linguistic, and emotional capacities of nonhuman animals. Work with Kanzi, a captive bonobo, to take just one of numerous examples, has prompted a great deal of thinking about the continuities between humanity and other animals. Kanzi (as are other apes, as well as elephants and dolphins) is able to recognize himself in a mirror, suggesting not just awareness but self-awareness. He will remind people of promises they had made to him days earlier. He possesses a rich vocabulary, and seems able to translate human speech in order to convey messages from human speakers to other bonobos who have not learned to understand human speech or other forms of symbolic communication. Kanzi and other apes engage in sophisticated deceptive behaviors, indicating that they are able to think about the mental states of other animals, represent possible futures, and conceive of the connection between their choices and those futures.[12] Probably more surprising than evidence for complex cognitive capacities in primates are the results of observations of birds. Alex, an African grey parrot, showed evidence of abstract thought (comparable in sophistication to human children older than three and a half years), insofar as he could describe shapes, answer questions about relational properties such as "same" and "different," and correctly utilize numbers (up to six) and color labels in multiple and novel contexts. Perhaps even more impressive was Alex's spontaneous development of a numerical concept similar to zero. Thus he seemed to have the capacity to represent not only quantitative magnitudes and properties of objects such as color, but the *absence* of quantity.[13]

What cognitive ethology has taught us is that the mental abilities that so many have assumed to be uniquely human, and that as such have been used to distinguish humanity from the rest of animal creation, in fact are shared among many species. Many nonhuman animals are able to innovate and learn in ways once considered possible only for human beings, to think abstractly and to manipulate complex symbols, to behave with flexibility and self-consciousness, to plan and predict future events, and even to transmit something like culture.[14] As the psychologist and ethologist Douglas Candland notes, human "beings [attempt] to know about themselves by trying to understand the minds of other creatures."

> [But i]nquiring human beings of our day have been taught that among the distinctions between humankind and animal life are, first, the ability to use language; second, the ability to make and use tools; third, a sense of consciousness about oneself; and, fourth, the ability to transmit culture. Each of these distinctions, as is true of all icons

scientific and scriptural, has crumpled and fallen to make dust and detritus. As human beings have come to invest in the study of animal life, they have come to understand also that whatever may be thought to be unique and defining about human beings is also characteristic of other animals.[15]

Discoveries about what animals actually do have not only inspired scholars to attempt to understand the mental lives of nonhuman animals more adequately, but also, as humanity learns that it is not as unique as many have thought, forced them to begin to rethink what it means to be human.

Developments in ethology are not alone in directing scholarly attention to nonhuman animals. A second impetus driving a renewed interest in animals lies in recent developments in philosophy and literary theory. Because of sustained reflection about the functions of limits and margins and the nature of otherness in phenomenology and postmodern thought, scholars have become increasingly aware that the ways in which human beings represent animals, and distinguish ourselves from them, reveal a great deal about how we understand—or perhaps misunderstand—ourselves.[16] The postmodern philosopher Jacques Derrida, for example, suggests the possibility of a "deconstruction" of anthropocentric conceptions of human subjectivity. Such deconstruction would disclose both the arbitrariness of the human/animal distinction and that such a distinction ultimately is founded on human self-interest and self-aggrandizement. Indeed, our biased self-interest helps explain the fervency with which thinkers have searched for criteria, such as rationality, tool use, language use, self-awareness, or culture, according to which one can distinguish humanity from and raise it above animality. For Derrida, deconstruction will show that traditional conceptions of subjectivity are grounded in a "carnophallogocentrism."[17] Since deconstruction will make clear that "any border between the animal and [humanity is in fact] unassignable,"[18] it will generate a renewed sense of what it means to be a subject as well as cultivate a sense of "responsibility toward the living in general."[19] David Wood makes clear what the import of such deconstruction would be:

> Human/animal (or Man/animal), is of course one of a set of oppositions which anesthetizes and hierarchies [sic] at the very same time as it allows us to continue to order our lives. And when man/God was still a good, working opposition, it too could be drawn into the game. What man is to God, animals are to men (and indeed woman to man)—that is, dependent beings. . . . My point is just this: there are no animals "as such," rather only the extraordinary variety that in the animal alphabet would begin with ants, apes, arachnids, antelopes, aardvarks, anchovies, alligators, Americans, Australians. . . . Suffice it to say that Derrida offers a massive project in which the deconstruction

of the subject (that is, the human subject) would be linked to eating flesh, virility, the possession of nature, the privilege of the head and the head of state—the general scheme of dominance condensed in that ugly neologism "carnophallogocentrism."[20]

The demonstration of the conventionality or arbitrariness of the distinction between human and animal would reveal the moral stakes at play in the maintenance of that distinction—we distinguish ourselves from animals ontologically in order to justify our use of them as resources—as well as the connections between the human dominance of animals and patriarchal, aristocratic, oligarchic, and colonialist power structures.

A third impetus for the scholarly turn toward animals is connected with recent interest in environmental ethics, and, since the publication of Peter Singer's enormously influential *Animal Liberation* in 1975, a new sense within the academy that scholarship relating to animal welfare and animal rights is philosophically respectable. Thinkers concerned with environmental ethics and the possibility of moral obligations toward animals have become increasingly willing to argue that human beings are not the only proper objects of moral concern, and have made it clear that the ways in which we treat nonhuman animals bear upon questions of human virtue and disclose the manner in which we constitute ourselves as moral beings. One of the great inspirations of the environmental movement, Aldo Leopold, for example, refers to what he sees as a trajectory of moral progress over the past three millennia. Gradually, he notes, "ethical criteria have been expanded."[21] Whereas once groups such as slaves, women, and foreigners were excluded as a matter of course from the moral community and were seen as undeserving of full moral consideration, the moral common sense of most people gradually has developed to enlarge the scope of the moral community, thereby according moral consideration to incrementally increasing numbers of people and groups. Thus groups such as blacks and women, once denied the possibility of full membership in the (American and European) moral community, are now (at least in theory) afforded moral consideration equal to that of hitherto privileged classes of people. As the environmental philosopher J. Baird Callicott notes, with the movements for civil "rights, human rights, women's liberation, children's liberation, [and] animal liberation," our "moral consciousness is expanding more rapidly now than ever before."[22] Leopold and Callicott argue that because of such expansion, we are in a position now to realize that morality applies not only universally to all human beings, but that we are bound as well by obligations to a much broader range of creatures. These thinkers reject anthropocentric attitudes, endorsing instead biocentric or ecocentric moral thinking, for which the moral legitimacy of conduct would be measured according to its respect for life or the integrity of ecosystems.

The moral reflection engaged in by many thinkers has suggested not only that humanity has obligations toward nonhuman beings, but that the ways in which we treat those beings indicate something about whether we succeed in measuring up to our own possibilities for being. In a discussion of factory farming, for instance, Matthew Scully says, "Pigs and lambs and cows and chickens are not pieces of machinery, no matter how cost-efficient it may be to treat them as such. . . . And when a man treats them this way, he might as well be a machine himself. Something dies in him, too."[23] He claims that human uniqueness lies in part in our moral sensibility:

> [C]ruelty is not only a denial of the animal's nature but a betrayal of our own. . . . We can say here what makes a human being human is precisely the ability to understand that the suffering of an animal is more important than the taste of a treat. . . . [When] we come to see ourselves primarily as consumers and conquerors, then the creatures will mirror that vision, appearing only as commodities, resources, and production units to be governed only by the laws of supply and demand.[24]

The way in which humanity interprets its own nature orients the way in which we represent and comport ourselves with respect to the world around us. For a thinker such as Scully, it is not merely the case that animals make moral claims upon us. According to him, failure to heed those claims certainly constitutes a failure to treat animals as they deserve, but also is a failure to act in accord with our own dignity. Our reduction of animal life to an "array of pests, threats, resources, obstacles, targets, [and] livestock" is a failure to accord to nature the moral consideration due it, and, insofar as we see ourselves primarily as "consumers and conquerors," is a degradation of human dignity itself.[25] As have postmodern thinkers such as Derrida, animal rights advocates have made clear that often the appeal to capacities such as rationality in order to distinguish ourselves from nonhuman animals is motivated by speciesist and anthropocentric bias. We human beings want to think of ourselves as special, and the pretense of "superiority" justifies the will to practical license. Immanuel Kant's moral thought provides the classic example. For Kant, rational beings in virtue of their rationality are dignified, and as such possess an absolute and incomparable worth. Duty requires that one regard them with respect. Nonrational beings, however, are not dignified, possess no inherent worth, and therefore are valuable only relative to the purposes of rational beings. Morally considered, Kant argues, nonrational creatures are nothing but things. If it is important to avoid cruelty toward animals, that is because such cruelty may desensitize us to human suffering and render us more likely to treat other human beings badly.[26] Thus it becomes important to show that animals lack rationality (or other allegedly morally relevant capacities) in order to demonstrate human moral superiority and justify the continuing employment of animals as resources.[27]

Recent reflection upon our relations with our animal others therefore has led to a renewed sense of the continuities between humanity and animality, as well as a rethinking of the nature of the human and the nature of ethics. The chapters here make clear that Kafka anticipated many of these developments. He too was thinking about the problematic nature of a sharp division between human and animal, the ways in which the human treatment of animals all too often amounts to an unjust victimization also degrading to human dignity, and the manner in which a more edified conception of animality sheds light on the conditions and limits of humanity. He also seems to have recognized that the ways in which we represent ourselves as human, and distinguish ourselves from others human and animal, shape our conduct in morally significant ways, and that human comportment with respect to nonhuman animals is closely connected with the manner in which we treat other people. Thus, in addition to illuminating important dimensions of Kafka's writing itself, by demonstrating that Kafka foresaw many of the concerns at play in contemporary thinking about nonhuman animals, these chapters help contextualize that thinking and make a valuable contribution to understanding the history of current debates about the relations between the human and animals.

Margot Norris, for instance, in "Kafka's Hybrids: Thinking Animals and Mirrored Humans," argues that Kafka explores the limits of our ability to appropriate nonhuman points of view, disclosing the essential opacity of animal consciousness. But at the same time, by writing in such a way as to alter and retract the "foundational premises" of human thinking, and by projecting an imagined animal sensibility that "reflects back a subversive and problematic image of the human," Kafka "deconstructs" the human, hinting at a "creatural ontology" and working to undermine anthropocentrism in favor of a more biocentric attitude. This subversion of anthropocentrism, she shows, is of a piece with Kafka's parodies of human rationality, his demonstration of the cruelty of coercive training and the civilizing process, and his exposure of the ways in which humanity debases itself in its treatment of animals. However, even moral appeals to pity for animals, Kafka's writing indicates, may be all too bound up with anthropocentrism, for such appeals can be "enmeshed with a narcissistic strain in humanistic moral philosophy that impels humans to be humane in order to save their own souls." Norris also captures the complexity and risk of reflection about the ethics of humanity's relations to our animal others in relation to Kafka by problematizing the moral legitimacy of the analogy drawn by one of South African author and Nobel laureate J. M. Coetzee's characters between the human treatment of nonhuman animals and the Holocaust.[28] The question of the legitimacy of such analogies is especially relevant and important to think through given Kafka's

Jewishness, his interest in animals, and the interpretive tendency to read some of his animal characters as representing Jews and their alienation.

Hadea Nell Kriesberg, in "'Czechs, Jews and Dogs Not Allowed': Identity, Boundary, and Moral Stance in Kafka's 'A Crossbreed' and 'Jackals and Arabs,'" and Naama Harel, in "De-allegorizing Kafka's Ape: Two Animalistic Contexts," focus especially on the moral stakes at play in Kafka's stories. Kriesberg ties the stories to Kafka's biography, his vegetarianism, and to the historical reality of anti-Semitism in early twentieth-century Prague, and sees in them exhortations for justice toward animals. Harel suggests that literary critics' own anthropocentrism has led them too often to read Kafka's stories as mere allegories, overlooking the dimension of those stories that is about animals themselves. As does Norris, she investigates the historical background informing "Report to an Academy"; Harel thereby isolates Kafka's commentary on the human reduction of animals to the status of victims and the injustice inherent in the maintenance of institutions such as zoos.

Tahia Thaddeus Reynaga approaches the moral implications of Kafka's stories from a different direction. In "Agents of the Forgotten: Animals as the Vehicles of Shame in Kafka," Reynaga argues that Kafka haunts us with his animal characters and other creatures in order to bring us face to face with humanity's alienation from its own heritage. Such alienation has inescapable moral consequences. Through his creatures, which, as they so often are legacies, amount to "prehistory incarnate," Kafka shows how our estrangement from our prelapsarian selves testifies to our loss of immediacy, innocence, and vitality; our fall into impurity; and the impossibility of human redemption. Caught within a no man's land of shame, humanity has rejected its past in favor of "dreams of Heaven," but has no hope of realizing its aspirations. Thus our alienation from the nonhuman world is not only a failure to treat other creatures according to the justice that they deserve. Such estrangement constitutes as well a failure to achieve a proper relationship to our own history—and thus to ourselves. Reynaga's chapter should prompt us to wonder whether facing up to our origins and history more successfully would enable humanity to foster better a morally sound attitude toward animals.

Eleanor Helms develops further the role played by history and tradition in human life and the existential and moral consequences of our alienation from our history. In "The Difficult Task of Being Real: Odradek, the Kittenlamb, and the Historical Individual," Helms notes that Kafka evokes the peculiarities of living "in a world thickly populated by urgent but ephemeral memories, histories, doubts, and possibilities." These forces all too often obstruct our attempts to choose and live authentically. She argues that reflection upon Kafka's creatures in the light of Søren Kierkegaard's analyses of faith and race could help us understand how to cultivate an appropriate relationship to history that would make possible a reconciliation with reality, an overcoming of our estrangement from the world, and the understanding of what authentic choice would be like. She thus employs Kafka's stories to articulate a new conception of the nature of purposive, authentic conduct.

As do Norris, Kriesberg, and Harel, Burkhard Müller, in "Consolation in Your Neighbor's Fur: On Kafka's Animal Parables," sheds light on the ways in which Kafka's writing undermines our anthropocentric sense of human superiority. He argues that Kafka's animal fables ridicule some of the less savory dimensions of human life: our preoccupation with money, our inflated sense of uniqueness, the constant pressure of mortality, the squandering of our limited time in pointless labor, our submission to conventional social norms, and the tragedy of solitude, but also, as Friedrich Nietzsche puts it, the "inevitable uncleanliness" of all "contact between man and man—'in society.'"[29] Kafka's interest in the relation between the individual and society is explored further in two chapters examining his animal stories in the context of crowd theory. Thomas H. Ford's chapter, "Crowds, Animality, and Aesthetic Language in Kafka's 'Josephine,'" notes that psychology traditionally has turned to a conception of nonlinguistic animality in order to clarify the experience of the submersion of individuality in the collective. He argues that Elias Canetti's engagement with Kafka's writing—specifically with the dynamic relating the animal and the temporality of the aesthetic consciousness—prompted him to "break with the understanding of the crowd as 'animal,' in the sense ultimately, and anthropocentrically, shared by crowd theory and psychoanalysis." It is in the music sung by Kafka's mouse character Josephine that we may detect the traces of more edified conceptions both of crowd experience and animal life. As the aesthetic consciousness can destabilize the phenomenal and temporal limits defining the subject, Josephine's singing (and its effects on her audience) points to a "transindividual" dimension of linguistic experience, yet such that Kafka's crowd is no automatic mechanistic system or "phenomenon of total indeterminacy. . . . It is, instead, a capacity—an animal capacity—within human language" itself. Müller too highlights the resources to be found in "Josephine" for a richer conception of language, insofar as the story evokes nostalgia for a primordial unity of language and music.

Andrea Baer, in "Performative Emotion in Kafka's 'Josephine, the Singer; or, the Mouse Folk' and Freud's 'The Creative Writer and Daydreaming,'" investigates a more troubling side of art and crowd dynamics. Baer reads "Josephine" as a meditation on the ways in which social performance is bound up with the "politics of social control and power." She argues that art creates perils both for the individual and for the social fabric. Often characterized as a seductress or deceiver, the figure of Josephine is a reminder to Kafka's readers to be cautious toward "corrupt social and political leaders, but also toward the human need for social and group belonging that may make individuals vulnerable to larger social powers." What is more, through the character of Josephine, Kafka reminds us that we always assume social roles, that "performativity inevitably structures our lives," and highlights the ways in which such bad faith or inauthenticity can invite social and political "irresponsibility." As does Freud, Kafka thus expresses anxiety about the modern convergence of public and private life.

Questions about power come to the forefront in Esther K. Bauer's "The Power of the Look: Franz Kafka's 'The Cares of a Family Man.'" Relating Kafka's story to Jean-Paul Sartre's, Michel Foucault's, and Kaja Silverman's analyses of power and the "look," Bauer argues that the struggle between the family man and the mysterious Odradek constitutes a comprehensive study of the dynamics of power as infecting the search for knowledge and the constitution of identity. According to her, Kafka's story discloses the look as the "site where the search for knowledge and the search for power intersect, and it reveals the key role assigned to the look in the construction of the self and in the definition and protection of the main character's social identity." She deepens her reading of the story by showing that Kafka uses the figure of Odradek to undermine conventional, bourgeois gender distinctions and subvert our egocentrism by inviting us to adopt the point of view of the outsider and regard ourselves from that external perspective. Bauer's analysis can be related to Kant's account of the sound human understanding. Just as Kant holds that aesthetic contemplation helps us transcend our egoistic provincialism by prompting the mind to stretch itself, envisioning and recognizing perspectives other than its own, Bauer shows that Kafka makes clear that such broadening of perspective can be a "first step toward acceptance and tolerance of otherness." Yet whereas Kant argues that we resist intellectual solipsism especially through dialogue with others and by "comparing" our judgments with the "possible judgments of others," Kafka raises the possibility that the appropriation of novel perspectives can occur in response to the confrontation with the elusive and the mysterious.[30] Bauer's chapter invites the question of whether Kafka's undermining of the categories legitimizing and concealing various techniques of constraint, and his exposure of the power dynamics at the core of social relations, could point us toward enriched conceptions of humanity and the humane.

Tom Tyler and Melissa De Bruyker recall once more the attempt to undermine or deconstruct the putative boundaries separating humanity from animality. Oriented by Red Peter's claim to have left behind his life as an ape in favor of a distinctly human life, Tyler, in "Four Hands Good, Two Hands Bad," argues against the division of human beings and apes into separate biological genera. He claims that Red Peter's "anthropomorphic amnesia," while perhaps feigned, nevertheless presupposes a clear division between humanity and apes. Tyler reminds us of the arbitrariness of systems for classifying the natural world, which does not consist in determinate and clearly delimited categories but in "continua" and "infinitesimal, gradual variation." As Norris reminds us as well, establishing "sharp divisions where none exist [is to] entirely miss the point, and import, of Darwin's discovery." Discussing evolutionary theory and recent theories of taxonomy, Tyler claims that arguments for classifying apes as belonging to the genus *Homo* themselves express anthropocentric bias: our "objective should not be to welcome a few new, privileged members into the charmed circle of human affairs." Instead, human beings should be classified, along with chimpanzees, as belonging to the genus *Pan*. Examining his use of rhetorical techniques such as framing and ekphrasis, as well as his focalization techniques, De Bruyker, in "Who Identified the Animal? Hybridity and Body Politics in Kafka's 'The Metamorphosis' and *Amerika* (*The Man Who Disappeared*)," demonstrates the ways Kafka's representations of hybrids undermine the supposedly natural and stable distinction between human and animal. Kafka's hybrids subvert the concept of "humanity," which was "meant to differentiate between human and animal," but has now "become lost in conflicting discourses." De Bruyker clarifies the capacity of Kafka's rhetoric to provoke an experience of hybridity, noting, for instance, that "the structured intertwinement of adjectives and nouns helps the reader realize that the hybrid is a rhetorically created effect." Looking at the seldom noticed figure of the hare in *Amerika*, she uncovers too the role played by "superstitious" elements throughout Kafka's writings and exposes the tension between Judaism and Christianity in the novel.

Chapters by Dean Swinford and Henry Sussman explore the connections between Kafka's stories and the genres of the fantastic, science fiction, and the graphic novel. In "The Portrait of an Armor-Plated Sign: Reimagining Samsa's Exoskeleton," Swinford argues against traditional interpretations of "The Metamorphosis" that deemphasize the insect's actual body. Distancing "Kafka's tale from the phenomenological realm of things and experiences," Kafka's critics too often have "incised" the insect's bodily form from the text, reducing Samsa to a "linguistic and rhetorical cipher" or "linguistic puzzle." Swinford claims that the story is about a bug. Highlighting Samsa's insectoid corporeality, he notes the "power of Gregor's body to signify as icon, image, and motif," and elucidates the ways in which this motif resonates with the literature of the fantastic and both literary and photographic representations of the monstrous and the demonic. Examining parallels between "The Metamorphosis" and David Fairchild's insect photographs in his *Book of Monsters*, Swinford also reminds us of some of the techniques which various representations of insects use to highlight and exaggerate their apparent menace and portray them as threats to human industry. He argues that Kafka's story can be seen as expressing certain views of "the fundamental conflicts between modern work and the natural." Such anthropocentric portrayals of the natural as monstrous are particularly ironic and are worth serious reconsideration,

given the indispensable roles insects and other invertebrates play in the mainte-
nance not only of agriculture but of a functioning biosphere. Oriented by Gilles
Deleuze and Félix Guattari's notion of deterritorialization and Walter Benjamin's
uncovering of key indices of modernity and anticipations of the graphic novel in
The Arcades Project, Sussman, in "Extraterrestrial Kafka: Ahead to the Graphic
Novel," explicates Kafka as the "poet and prophet of deterritorialization." Kafka
is the master explorer of "alienation and displacement" in the modern world. But
Kafka's creatures are not only alien, they are *aliens*. Sussman argues that Kafka's
characters are so strange and the settings of his stories so disorienting that Kafka
actually "trespasses terrestrial limits." Focusing on the "spatial disorientation, the
sordid involution of his architectural settings . . . [and] on the blurred gender lines
on which his human, animal, and mythological creatures interact," as well as on
his "parody of power," Sussman says that Kafka "delineates the hinge between the
global and the extraterrestrial" and explores the manner in which Kafka "swerves
toward the universe of fantastic literature and the graphic novel."

Donna Yarri concludes this collection with an analytical index that cata-
logues the occurrences of animal and creaturely characters in Kafka's stories
and diaries. Entries are organized such that one may search either according to
particular animal or by text. This index should prove to be an invaluable tool for
scholars interested in pursuing further Kafka's employment of animal characters
and imagery.

Kafka's creatures enjoin upon us questions about who *we* are, who *they* are,
and about how our understanding of each informs our treatment of our animal
others. The chapters in this volume make evident the manner in which Kafka's
writing—in its tireless subversion of received images of humanity and human
society, its parody of the categories we so complacently rely upon to tame and
make sense of the world and to elevate ourselves, and its contesting of the ways in
which we think about and treat nonhuman animals—facilitates reflection about
human and animal nature, challenging us to look again, and to reconsider our
all too often unquestioned assumptions about human uniqueness, superiority,
and righteousness. Such rethinking could be a crucial first step toward overcoming the characteristically modern human alienation from the natural world—an
estrangement that is at the same time a self-estrangement, for we are animals
ourselves—and toward envisioning the lineaments of a morally sound "human
and animal community."

Notes

1. From a notebook fragment contained in Franz Kafka, *Dearest Father* (New York:
Schocken Books, 1954), 54.

2. Franz Kafka, *Diaries 1910–1923*, ed. Max Brod and trans. Joseph Kresh and Martin Greenberg (New York: Schocken Books, 1976), 237.

3. Ibid., 237.

4. Ibid., 14.

5. Ibid., 221.

6. Ibid., 312.

7. The entry for *"Erinnerungen an die Kaldabahn"* in *A Franz Kafka Encyclopedia* suggests additional reasons for which Kafka may have identified with the narrator of this story fragment. See Richard T. Gray, Ruth V. Gross, Rolf J. Goebel, and Clayton Koelb, eds., *A Franz Kafka Encyclopedia* (Westport, CT: Greenwood Press, 2005).

8. Kafka, *Diaries*, 136.

9. See, for example, the long story about a white horse from May 1914, and the children who acquire a puppy and subsequently engage in behavior indistinguishable from that of dogs in the fragment titled "Temptation in the Village" (Kafka, *Diaries*, 269 and 287).

10. Max Brod, *Franz Kafka: A Biography*, second edition, trans. G. Humphreys Roberts and Richard Winston (New York: Schocken Books, 1960), 74.

11. Kafka, *Diaries*, 387. It is noteworthy that Kafka refers here to community in the singular rather than the plural.

12. Sue E. Savage-Rumbaugh and Roger Lewin, *Kanzi: The Ape at the Brink of the Human Mind* (New York: John Wiley & Sons, Inc., 1994).

13. Irene M. Pepperberg and Jesse D. Gordon, "Number Comprehension by a Grey Parrot (*Psittacus erithacus*), Including a Zero-Like Concept," *Journal of Comparative Psychology* 119:2 (2005): 197–209.

14. See, for instance, Donald R. Griffin, *Animal Minds* (Chicago: University of Chicago Press, 1992); Luke Rendell and Hal Whitehead, "Culture in Whales and Dolphins," *Behavioral and Brain Sciences* 24 (2001): 309–32; and Diana Reiss and Lori Marino, "Mirror Self-Recognition in the Bottlenose Dolphin: A Case of Cognitive Convergence," *PNAS* 98:10 (May 8, 2001): 5937–42.

15. Douglas Keith Candland, *Feral Children and Clever Animals: Reflections on Human Nature* (New York: Oxford University Press, 1993), 3.

16. For a brief overview of the development on the field of "animal studies," see Cary Wolfe, "Human, All Too Human: 'Animal Studies' and the Humanities," *Publications of the Modern Language Association of America* 124:2 (March 2009): 564–75.

17. Jacques Derrida, "'Eating Well,' or the Calculation of the Subject: An Interview with Jacques Derrida," in *Who Comes After the Subject?* ed. Eduardo Cadava, Peter Connor, and Jean-Luc Nancy (New York: Routledge, 1991), 113.

18. Jacques Derrida, *Aporias*, trans. Thomas Dutoit (Stanford, CA: Stanford University Press, 1994), 37.

19. Derrida, "Eating Well," 112. On Derrida's shrinking back from the possibility of a strong moral commitment to nonhuman animals analogous to the obligations flowing from responsibility to other human beings, see chapter 9 of Gary Steiner, *Anthropocentrism and Its Discontents: The Moral Status of Animals in the History of Western Philosophy* (Pittsburgh: University of Pittsburgh Press, 2005).

20. David Wood, "*Comment ne pas manger*—Deconstruction and Humanism," in *Animal Others: On Ethics, Ontology, and Animal Life*, ed. H. Peter Steeves (Albany: State University of New York Press, 1999). I read *hierarchizes* for "hierarchies."

21. Aldo Leopold, *A Sand County Almanac* (New York: Ballantine Books, 1966), 237. Such historical claims fail to do full justice to the rich ancient tradition of debate about the moral status of animals. On the history of debates about proper treatment of animals, see Steiner's *Anthropocentrism and Its Discontents* and Richard Sorabji, *Animal Minds and Human Morals: The Origins of the Western Debate* (Ithaca, NY: Cornell University Press, 1993).

22. J. Baird Callicott, "The Conceptual Foundations of the Land Ethic," in *Environmental Ethics: Divergence and Convergence*, second edition, ed. Richard G. Botzler and Susan J. Armstrong (New York: McGraw Hill, 1998), 426.

23. Matthew Scully, *Dominion: The Power of Man, the Suffering of Animals, and the Call to Mercy* (New York: St. Martin's Press, 2002), 288.

24. Ibid., 303 and 306.

25. Ibid., 106.

26. Immanuel Kant, *The Metaphysics of Morals*, trans. Mary Gregor (New York: Cambridge University Press, 1991), 443/238.

27. See Marc Lucht, "Does Kant Have Anything to Teach Us about Environmental Ethics?" in *The Challenges of Globalization: Rethinking Nature, Culture, and Freedom*, ed. Steven V. Hicks and Daniel E. Shannon (Malden, MA: Blackwell Publishing, 2007).

28. See especially lesson 3 and lesson 4 of J. M. Coetzee, *Elizabeth Costello* (New York: Penguin Books, 2003). The Nobel Prize winner Isaac Bashevis Singer, who lost family in the Holocaust, complicates the problem of such comparisons as well. Coetzee's analogy echoes Singer's saintly character Herman Gombiner's lament: "They have convinced themselves that man, the worst transgressor of all the species, is the crown of creation. All other creatures were created merely to provide him with food, pelts, to be tormented, exterminated. In relation to them, all people are Nazis; for the animals it is an eternal Treblinka" (Isaac Bashevis Singer, "The Letter Writer," in *The Collected Stories* [New York: The Noonday Press, 1996]). See also Derrida's discussion of the analogy between genocide and the human treatment of animals especially in industrial factory farming, in Jacques Derrida, "The Animal that Therefore I AM (More to Follow)," trans. David Wills, *Critical Inquiry* 28 (Winter 2002): 369–418, 394–95.

29. Friedrich Nietzsche, *Beyond Good and Evil: Prelude to a Philosophy of the Future*, trans. Walter Kaufmann (New York: Vintage Books, 1966), 284.

30. Immanuel Kant, *The Critique of Judgment*, trans. Werner S. Pluhar (Indianapolis: Hackett Publishing Co., 1987), 293–94/160; cf. Immanuel Kant, *Anthropology from a Pragmatic Point of View*, trans. Victor Lyle Dowdell (Carbondale and Edwardville: Southern Illinois University Press, 1996), 128–30/11–12.

CHAPTER 2

Kafka's Hybrids: Thinking Animals and Mirrored Humans

Margot Norris

Human and Animal Mirrors

In J. M. Coetzee's 1999 book, *The Lives of Animals*, a fictional scholar named Elizabeth Costello presents a distinguished lecture on the ethics of the treatment of animals that begins by invoking a piece by Franz Kafka called "A Report to an Academy." This Kafka "story" was itself written in the form of a lecture, an address by an ape-become-human who, asked to give a scientific account of his life as an ape to members of an academy, instead tells the story of his capture, confinement, and "evolution." We know that J. M. Coetzee presented his fiction, *The Lives of Animals*, as a Tanner lecture sponsored by the University Center for Human Values at Princeton University in 1997–1998. In this work he thereby creates a stunning metafictional *mise en abyme*—a potentially infinite enfolding that here has the real-life performance of a narrative enfolding the fictional performance of a narrative enfolding the fictional performance of another narrative. Living author J. M. Coetzee tells members of the academy the story of fictional author Elizabeth Costello telling the story of Franz Kafka's fictional ape-man telling his life to members of an academy. But Coetzee also uses the Kafka piece to allow Costello to make her highly controversial ethical analogy between the massive murder of animals and the massive murders of the Holocaust—an analogy that bitterly offends a Jewish poet in her audience, who protests, "You misunderstand the nature of likenesses; I would even say you misunderstand willfully, to the point of blasphemy. . . . The inversion insults the memory of the dead."[1] Costello's analogy should be controversial because the Holocaust, as Marjorie Garber notes in one of the "Reflections" on the fictional lecture at the end of the work, "is the event beyond analogy, many people say."[2] But as a reading of the Kafka story, the boldness of Costello's critical and

17

interpretive maneuver should be commended—for she reads "A Report to an Academy" against its traditional grain, not as allegory of the assimilated Jew but as an imaginative act of animal witness.

In this interpretive gesture, Coetzee's novelist reads Kafka from the vantage of today's theoretical and philosophical address to animal consciousness and animal intelligence. But Coetzee's focus in *Lives of Animals* retains the social and psychological costs that imaginative acts of witness inflict on human scholars and activists who speak for and on behalf of animals. Kafka's experimental fictions, on the other hand, delve deeply into the obscurity in which animal thought is held, and in the aesthetic and poetic challenges its representation poses to the artist. Kafka offers an interesting test of the fictional Elizabeth Costello's vision: that "there is no limit to the extent to which we can think ourselves into the being of another. There are no bounds to the sympathetic imagination."[3] But I would argue that in spite of their imaginative reach into the realm of animal ontology, Kafka's animal fictions do expose limits in human ability to "think ourselves into the being of another." And it is precisely the contours of those cognitive and representational limits that conjure a sense, if not a glimpse, of the animal unknown (and, perhaps, "unknowable") that lies beyond the cultural human. At the same time, I believe that Kafka's fictions allowed him to participate in nineteenth- and early twentieth-century shifts from an anthropocentric toward a more biocentric philosophical orientation. This allowed him to conduct a creative imaginative exploration of the human-animal divide, one that gives his literary experiments, however imperfect, a historical significance in the realm of intellectual history.

Treating Kafka's animal stories as animal stories—rather than as allegories or fables of the human—departs from most traditional Kafka criticism that, even while it concedes that the animal stories explore states or ontologies of "otherness," nonetheless assumes that their topic is the human being. Paul Goodman in his 1947 monograph called *Kafka's Prayer* gives two Freudian rationales for Kafka's identification of humans and animals—"[First] The beast is a totem, the symbol of unconscious conflicts, especially those centering round the hostile and castrating father and the son's identification with him. [Second] The beast is a literal friend and lover, a form of childish eros that survives in adult consciousness as the theory—I think it is a true theory—that there is a community in all life and a continuum of the libido."[4] Wilhelm Emrich, in his influential 1969 study of Kafka, finds a more metaphysical set of allegories in the animal stories. "The animals are not described, say, on the basis of zoological animal psychology in an effort to give Gestalt to their inner lives," he writes. Instead, the animal tales are read as producing "a situation . . . in which the totality of human existence erupts unveiled; thus, a situation in which the fundamental antinomies of this existence are experienced and reflected."[5] Coetzee's

Elizabeth Costello, of course, would refute this—speculating, as she does, that Franz Kafka could have read and been inspired by Wolfgang Koehler's 1917 monograph *The Mentality of Apes*[6] in producing "The Report to an Academy." Her argument is further supported by evidence that Kafka, like other students and intellectuals of his time, read Charles Darwin, Thomas Huxley, and Ernst Haeckel.[7] In his day, the evolutionary continuity between primates and humans was discussed, if not as established principle then nonetheless as increasingly respectable theory. Kafka's historical and intellectual context readily supports an argument for, rather than against, the contention that his animal stories use the figure of the animal autoreferentially, to gesture to its creatural ontology, rather than as a trope of displacement for the cultural or ontological human. Such a reading of Kafka makes him a prophetic precursor of contemporary critics of speciesism and what Cary Wolfe calls the "linguacentrism" that afflicts even the most progressive cultural criticism. According to Wolfe, much ethical and political discourse in the humanities remains wedded to the notion that the only possible subject is human with the resultant "repression of the possibility of non-human subjectivity."[8]

But with respect to representation it is one thing to speak for the animal, as Coetzee's Elizabeth Costello does, and another to speak as the animal—or, more accurately, to use human language to pretend to speak as the nonhuman animal—as a number of Kafka's narratives do. Kafka wrote at the time of a flowering of avant-garde art, when a number of radical alternatives for representing nonhuman states were becoming available to artists, including those produced by the extreme distortions of rational perspectives and representations found in the art of Expressionism. But by retaining human language as well as recognizable models of rational human thinking as his basic vehicle for conjuring the nonhuman subject, Kafka's representational options are confined to largely negative maneuvers, textual moves that begin with the human and work by a process of alteration, subtraction, and retraction. The textual unmooring or repeal of foundational premises that Kafka thereby produces participates in the philosophical operations that characterize the collection of theories referred to broadly as "deconstruction." One of the major maneuvers produced by this strategy in Kafka's stories is to transform rationality into a site of perversity that allows the fictional animal to speak itself through or as a deconstructed human. In other words, Kafka has his animal figures thinking or speaking through an untenable rationality that gestures toward animal being by acting out the erasure of the signs and markers that attend the human being. This maneuver is particularly in evidence in four Kafka pieces through which one can trace the progressive deconstruction of the human in the interest of recuperating an imagined animal sensibility that in turn reflects back a subversive and problematic image of the human as seen through animal eyes. The four stories that demonstrate this phenomenon—"The Metamorphosis," "A Report to an Academy," "Investigations of a Dog," and "The Burrow"—all employ degrees of hybridity to produce this critical state. The earliest of the stories present a creature in transition between two species, like the devolution of the clerk Gregor Samsa into an insect in "The Metamorphosis," or the evolutionary narrative of Red Peter, the ape turned human. But in the later fictions, the human as a figure is expelled and extruded from an animal consciousness whose hybridization is internalized as a subjectivity that remains trapped in increasingly futile efforts to reason to itself a sense of its environment and its existence.

"The Metamorphosis" and "Report to an Academy"

In the first two hybrid fictions, the animal is represented as a figure of pathos—degraded and victimized—though in both stories this debasement is treated as problematic. By telling these stories from the imagined animal vantage, the animal degradation and victimization is expelled from within the animal subjectivity and transformed into a judgment of a humanity that debases itself in its treatment of the animal. The animal "eyes" and animal "voice" in Kafka's fiction become mirrors in which the human is reflected back to itself in an oppressive and unflattering guise. This alienating animal reflection of the human is presented in the most direct and explicit way in "The Metamorphosis," the most famous of Kafka's hybrid fictions. This is the story of a hardworking salesman, a young bachelor still living at home as the sole support of his parents and sister, who wakes up one morning only to discover that he has been turned into some sort of indefinable insect. But the human clerk Gregor Samsa, subjected to rigorously oppressive working conditions by his firm, exploited by a parasitic family that feeds shamelessly off his labor, and tormented by a self-punishing scrupulosity, is as much a suffering animal before his metamorphosis into an insect as afterward. For this reason one may be justified in reading "The Metamorphosis" more allegorically than the other stories, as a fable of that typological figure of the modern working man whose theatrical counterparts are Arthur Miller's Willy Loman or David Mamet's salesmen in *Glengarry Glen Ross*. Gregor Samsa's progressive animal disorientation and derangement transforms and inverts his environment until the human arena he has always occupied has become thoroughly alien and toxic to him. First familiar food and then a familiar room cease to fit his organism's needs; the spatial configurations of floors, walls, and ceilings become turned upside-down; and the humans of his world become exposed and alienating in their incomprehension, callousness, and final indifference to him and his needs. The sense of otherness that is thereby created is best captured in the aesthetic name for deranged representation: the term "surreal." When Gregor first appears to his family as an insect, his appalled father shoos him back into his room with a stick all the while hissing at Gregor like a venomous snake. "If only he would have stopped making that unbearable hissing noise! It made Gregor quite lose his head," the narrator tells us.[9] Gregor quickly discovers the difficulty of locomotion with numerous legs and the awkwardness of rotating a semi-spherical body, as well as the satisfactions of new abilities he discovers in himself over time: "He especially enjoyed hanging suspended from the ceiling; it was much better than lying on the floor; one could breathe more freely; one's body swayed and rocked lightly; and in the almost blissful absorption induced by this suspension it could happen to his own surprise that he let go and fell plump on the floor."[10] Human nourishment is discovered as inedible and unpotable, and the process of ingestion is different and difficult: "he could only feed with the palpitating collaboration of his whole body."[11] And the insect's disorientation is not only physiological and subjective but finally also ethical, as the story's shift from a human to an animal perspective reveals the human beings in the story—the parents, the sister, the boarders, the charwoman—as lacking compassion or sympathy. Curiously, critics and readers too often also fail to respond kindly to the suffering insect, and thereby align themselves with the malignant humans in the story, the father with his gigantic and threatening shoe soles, and the charwoman who menaces him with a chair. Kafka's friend Max Brod reports a diary entry from November 24, 1912: "Kafka read to us at Baum's 'his glorious short story about a noxious insect.'"[12] One could contend that "The Metamorphosis" is equally an insect's story of noxious humans.

In "A Report to an Academy," Kafka gives the animal voice more direct expression than in "The Metamorphosis" by making the ape the first person narrator of his own story. The ape (who later reveals that he has been given a name he despises—"Red Peter") addresses, at their request, an academy of learned men on the subject of his life as an ape. In his own account, the ape was shot and captured by men on an expedition for Hagenbeck—ironically, the founder in 1907 of the first humane, uncovered, bar-less, open-air zoo near Hamburg, Germany. Indeed, Carl Hagenbeck is memorialized in the *Encyclopaedia Britannica* as the "internationally known animal dealer and trainer who controlled animals by befriending them, emphasizing for spectators their intelligence and tractability rather than their ferocity."[13] Red Peter, the lecturing ape, is surely such a Hagenbeck specimen, though the actual details of his tale appear to lampoon Hagenbeck's humane pretensions. The ape tells how he was shot, put in a cargo cage on shipboard, and tormented by brutish sailors. In desperation he learned to imitate their manners and eventually their speech, and thus was able to go on to become a famous "artiste," an exotic, a cabaret performer. Kafka glosses here turn-of-the-century fascination with exotic fauna and transitional species, "talking" and "thinking" animals and feral humans displayed in traveling circuses and menageries throughout Europe. Yet the status of the ape-man's narrative is extremely ambiguous. Claiming that he has lost all memory of his original animal life, he will tell only the story of his metamorphosis. It is a story curiously told empirically from the inside but rhetorically from the outside, as though the ape were his own zoological specimen, expounding upon himself in the form of the treatise. Red Peter's rational speech performs nothing of the ape's animality but instead foregrounds qualities that identify the human as civilized: rhetorical skill, intelligence, urbanity, self-control, irony. The ape-man tells his audience, "To put it plainly, much as I like expressing myself in images, to put it plainly: your life as apes, gentlemen, insofar as something of that kind lies behind you, cannot be farther removed from you than mine is from me."[14] Red Peter perfectly mimics both his captors and his audience. Postcolonial critic Homi Bhabha's notion of colonial mimicry—what he calls "the desire for a reformed, recognizable 'Other'"[15]—can be invoked to describe the performance of Kafka's ape-man, who from this perspective is less an evolved human than a colonized ape.

These specifically sophisticated qualities of Red Peter's report make it a doubled and troubled performance, for his rhetorical maneuvers to speak of himself as a scientific specimen require a constant disavowal of his mistreatment, suffering, and self-alienation in the interest of masking himself as human, as rational, as a scientist: "A hunting expedition sent out by the firm of Hagenbeck—by the way, I have drunk many a bottle of good red wine since then with the leader of that expedition—had taken up its position in the bushes by the shore when I came down for a drink at evening among a troop of apes. They shot at us; I was the only one who was hit; I was hit in two places."[16] Later we learn that the sailors forced him to learn to drink schnapps from a bottle, a drink that revolted him; the civilized drinking of "good" red wine with his captors and tormentors may remain an act of desperate mimicry. The ape-man's language is full of circumlocutions, antiphrases, and euphemisms for pain, injury, and cruelty, which he rationalizes, or reports as rationalized, in the interest of science and of his own improvement by domestication. Locked in a cage too small for him, he describes how "[t]he whole construction was too low for me to stand up in and too narrow to sit down in. So I had to squat with my knees bent and trembling all the time. . . . Such a method of confining wild beasts is supposed to have its advantages during the first days of captivity, and out of my own experience I cannot deny that from the human point of view this is really the case."[17] The speaking and thinking ape is an "aping" ape, whose adaptive evolutionary strategy resembles animal camouflage, his ability to mask himself as human in order to escape the fate of the caged zoo or circus animal. Red Peter's experience and report is paradigmatic of the politics of domestication, the process of reproducing an internalized version of one species' traits in another. In Kafka's story, the final form of domestication is a real or feigned internalization and acceptance of its costs to his sensate animal being. "The civilized world depends for the most part on the effects of successful training procedures. That is what culture means," Kafka is said to have told his friend Gustav Janouch.[18] In a nod toward Freud's *Civilization and Its Discontents* and its legacy in postcolonial criticism, the ape-man's report dramatizes that becoming human and civilized also requires the disavowal of the brutalities of the civilizing process. Cary Wolfe, invoking theories of mimicry by anthropologist Michael Taussig and by critic Homi Bhabha, writes, "The colonizing power attempts to produce the colonized as a mimetic reproduction of itself, even as a specifically 'native' content must be maintained in that negotiation, if only to justify the necessity of the 'civilizing' work of the colonizer."[19]

Red Peter's performance holds a mirror up to his audience, letting them see their civilized behavior, their collecting of exotic fauna, their scientific zoological researches, even their interest in animal ethology, as the activity of hypocritical oppressors. The ape's animality is inscribed negatively in his talk, in its silences and omissions, in what he cannot or refuses to articulate rather than in what he actually says. Put differently, Kafka has the ape-man's performance exhibit perverse relationships between rationality, science, ethics, power, and authority. Although she likens herself to Kafka's ape-man, Coetzee's Elizabeth Costello excoriates her audience directly, reproaches them for their inhumanity to the animal, and accuses them of cruelty and callousness—a performance that earns her the Jewish poet's offense, her daughter-in-law's wrath, her son's embarrassment, and the general resentment of a violated audience. But the tension in the lecture of Kafka's ape is that he cannot afford an aggressive gesture, an offensive accusation, an uncivil or uncivilized word. Describing how the sailor burned him with the embers of his pipe when he could not learn the schnapps-drinking trick, the ape expresses no anger or resentment: "And to the credit of my teacher, he was not angry; sometimes indeed he would hold his burning pipe against my fur, until it began to smolder in some place I could not easily reach, but then he would himself extinguish it with his own kind, enormous hand; he was not angry with me, he perceived that we were both fighting on the same side against the nature of apes and that I had the more difficult task."[20] Having the animal speak directly of animal pain and agony—particularly in the vernacular of the howl or the shriek—risks a return to the cage. The ape can speak only in the hypocritical idiom of his oppressor, in rhetoric that denies cruelty, suppresses affect, and consigns aggression to irony and antiphrasis—the word that says the opposite of what it means.

"Investigations of a Dog" and "The Burrow"

In his "pure animal stories"—as Wilhelm Emrich calls "Investigations of a Dog" and "The Burrow"—Kafka moves away from the figural hybrid (the salesman turned insect, or the ape turned man), and invests the hybridity purely in the represented thought processes—the welding of human speculative and logical habits with the animal condition of contingency. Like "A Report to an Academy," Kafka's "Investigations of a Dog" is a first-person narration, although, unlike Red Peter's address to the distinguished gentlemen of the academy, in the dog story neither the species nor the interest of the implied listener can be determined. The dog's own species status is somewhat indeterminate since he claims he is now apart from other dogs yet still has sight of them and they of him: "When I think back and recall the time when I was still a member of the canine community, sharing in all its preoccupations, a dog among dogs, I find on closer examination that from the very beginning I sensed some discrepancy, some little maladjustment, causing a slight feeling of discomfort."[21] The story's narration represents a domestic dog's attempt to theorize its phenomenological condition, to understand a puzzling universe in which food mysteriously appears and disappears, and dogs produce eerie music or appear to float in the air. The story's conceit is that humans are invisible to the dog and he is therefore completely oblivious to human agency. He simply does not see that someone puts down a food dish or holds up a tidbit that he snatches as it drops, or that the musical dogs are trained circus dogs, and the floating dogs lap dogs ensconced on the laps of invisible owners. The dog's oblivion to the human allows for a temporal explanation for his indeterminate membership in the canine community. Clearly, he had been part of a litter when young, but eventually became confined in a household where he still sees dogs from time to time, but no longer belongs to a pack, as it were. Yet the dog construes this state of affairs as a kind of hermitage, a scholarly vantage that lends itself to scientific rumination and research. Does the dog know he exists because he thinks about his existence? "Descartes's anthropocentrism is turned on its head," Marjorie Garber says of this story in her book, *Dog Love*.[22] Kafka's narrating dog reports, "Apart from us dogs there are all sorts of creatures in the world, wretched, limited, dumb creatures who have no language but mechanical cries; many of us dogs study them, have given them names, try to help them, educate them, uplift them, and so on."[23] Those creatures, we may suppose, are humans. Thus, indeed, one effect of this story is to turn anthropocentrism inside out, by parodying the world of species narcissism which allows humans to perceive creatures purely from their own cultural vantage. In the mirror of Kafka's story, we recognize ourselves as failing to recognize that we are merely creatures enfolded in an organic universe teeming with myriad life forms that are each to themselves the centers of their universe.

Unlike the ape, whose speech mirrors human beings as disavowed oppressors, the dog simply does not mirror humans at all and represents them as effectively absent, as void, as beneath notice: "For my part, I am quite indifferent to them except when they try to disturb me, I confuse them with one another, I ignore them."[24] Yet this very occlusion, this failure to give the human recognition, functions as the mirror of human anthropocentrism. Domestication is visible to the dog only as incomprehensible effects—as illogical canine behaviors, such as that of the trained or musical dogs, whose tension, misery, and unnatural actions mystify the canine narrator. "[I]t was not so much coolness as the most extreme tension that characterized their performance; these limbs apparently so sure in their movements quivered at every step with a perpetual apprehensive twitching; as if rigid with despair the dogs kept their eyes fixed on one another, and their tongues, whenever the tension weakened for a moment, hung wearily from their jowls," he observes.[25] Because the coercive causes of trained canine behavior are invisible and absent, the dog represents dogdom purely phenomenologically, without recognizing itself or its species as objects of pathos, as victims, or as oppressed. This interesting twist mirrors back to us, as in a photo negative, another aspect of our anthropocentrism. That is the extent to which our pity for animals—the hallmark of Coetzee's animal advocate—is enmeshed with a narcissistic strain in humanistic moral philosophy that impels humans to be humane in order to save their own souls, as Elizabeth Costello suggests.[26]

Instinctual behavior is codified as scientific law in the dog's phenomenological explanations. "My personal observation tells me that the earth, when it is watered and scratched according to the rules of science, extrudes nourishment," he reasons.[27] Being made to "beg" or to stand on its hind legs for food scraps is emptied of degradation when it becomes a pure phenomenon. Food produced by "begging" is simply a variant of the earth-produced food. The dog reasons, "The main part of the food that is discovered on the ground in such cases comes from above; indeed customarily we snap up most of our food, according to our dexterity and greed, before it has reached the ground at all."[28] Further, by conjuring an active animal intelligence, an endless animal curiosity and speculation that parodies scientific thinking, Kafka's narrative gestures toward a de-anthropomorphized conception of animal intelligence and perception. Again and again, the narrating dog represents the strains that domestication places on animal instinct as a conundrum and a paradox: "We are drawn to each other and nothing can prevent us from satisfying that communal impulse. . . . But now consider the other side of the picture. No creatures to my knowledge live in such wide dispersion as we dogs, none have so many distinctions of class, of kind, of occupation, distinctions too numerous to review at a glance."[29] In its parodic evocation of Freud's *Civilization and Its Discontents*, Kafka has the dog produce a mystified treatise on domestication and its discontents, as he tries to understand natural pack animals segregated into breeds and pedigrees, bred for purposes and tasks at times utterly alien to canine interests and needs. Besides parody, the story evokes allegorical interpretation. "Kafka is not at all concerned with securing merely a metaphysical nourishment," writes Wilhelm Emrich of this story, "but with the synthesis of earthly and unearthly existence."[30] But I would argue that in the process of exposing what Cary Wolfe calls the human "under-knowing" of the animal, the story parodies the human reasoning process as itself trapped in producing fictive causes and effects, fictive necessities and contingencies, fictive theories, and fictive laws. Coetzee's Elizabeth Costello raises this very point in her lecture—"I often wonder what thinking is, what understanding is. Do we really understand the universe better than animals do? Understanding a thing often looks to me like playing with one of those Rubik cubes. Once you have made all the little bricks snap into place, hey presto, you understand. It makes sense if you live inside a Rubik cube."[31]

Like all of Kafka's animal stories, "The Burrow" has generally been read as fabular or allegorical. Wilhelm Emrich writes, "In his late story, 'The Burrow,' man's true 'self,' the theme of all of Kafka's animal characters, is meditated upon to the ultimate limit." He then goes on to read the story as the human attempt to construct "a true, absolutely safe and sure existence in the midst of this unsafe earthly world, and what is more, with the earthly means given us."[32] "The Burrow" is one of Kafka's most radical animal stories, one in which he attempts to represent what appear to be the thought processes of a wild animal. The narrator of "The Burrow" is a creature not only with no perception of the human, no reference to culture, but also with no self-consciousness, no perception of itself as animal, and no perception of other animals outside an inchoate food chain. In this wild subterranean animal universe, there is only predation, and the thinking or speaking voice is that of a predator living in a fullness of being. For the burrow's creature, joy is the happiness of gluttony when there is food aplenty, when his stores of meat are copious and it can "walk about among them, play with them, enjoy their plenty and their various smells. . . . There are times when I am so well provided for that in my indifference to food I never even touch the smaller fry that scuttle about the burrow."[33] In this state of satiety and security, predation temporarily ceases. Yet in its imagination, and Kafka endows the creature with imagination, this joy is always conjoined to a concomitant terror, the fear of losing its food and its own life to some ineffable greater predator. The creature's only images of its invisible enemy are fragmentary and metonymic—"in my dreams I often see a greedy muzzle sniffing around . . . persistently"—yet nonetheless terrifying—"suddenly [I] feel the teeth of the pursuer in my flank while I am desperately burrowing away"[34] Consequently much of the animal's energy and intelligence is devoted to defensive calculation and activity, a business rendered by Kafka in a brilliantly de-anthropomorphized version of human paranoia. But its defensive strategies are heuristically doomed, and the animal is eventually driven to a kind of insanity by its inability to reason itself and its existence into security or safety. It is tormented by the contradictory options presented for securing its prey, whether to keep it all in one place where it can guard it, or to disperse it in a way that makes it less vulnerable, but impossible to guard. In a zoomorphic poetic gesture, Kafka endows the subterranean animal with virtually no visual faculty in order to simulate the putative blindness of such creatures as moles. Kafka conjoins this visual blindness with a compensatory obsession with spatiality, which produces repetitive and inconclusive negotiations of direction and of spatial volumes. This obsession leads the creature to become confounded by the most foundational epistemological premises: the principle of noncontradiction, the inability to be in two places at the same time, the conundrum of presence and absence, and the negotiation of inner and outer space. The most fearsome recognition that these philosophical speculations bring to the creature is the possibility of concentric spheres and their concomitant role reversals. In addition to external enemies, the creature must fear internal enemies that live in the inner earth: "Their very victims can scarcely have seen them; they come, you hear the scratching of their claws just under you in the ground, which is their element, and already you are lost. Here it is no avail to console yourself with the thought that you are in your own house; far rather you are in theirs."[35]

Animality is represented textually in this story, not only in its representations of what the creature thinks or in how it thinks, but also in style and rhetoric, in the affective tremors that quicken the prose of the representation. The prose of the rendered animal thought is capable of conjuring the creature's periods of tranquility, when it experiences the joy that comes of carrying "good food in your jaws, to lie down and rest whenever you like, and to nibble an occasional tasty tidbit."[36] When these moments of peace and contentment give way to an ecstatic frenzy of greed and gluttony, the prose accompanies the narration with an accelerated rush and rhythm: "Then I usually enjoy periods of particular tranquility, in which I change my sleeping place by stages, always working in toward the center of the burrow, always steeping myself more profoundly in the mingled smells, until at last I can no longer restrain myself and one night rush into the Castle Keep, mightily fling myself upon my stores, and glut myself with the best that I can seize until I am completely gorged."[37] Kafka is careful, I believe, to empty greed, gluttony, and predation of all human moral valences in this animal story in order to restore them as terms or concepts for bodily and instinctual exigencies. When contentment, greed, and gluttony are followed by a frenzy of anxiety and anguish, the transformation does not gesture toward moral retribution or self-punishment but rather to the affective products of the precarious animal existence. Even in translation from the German—for example, in Willa and Edwin Muir's English version—the feral animal as a locus of desperate mental activity and psychological passion is captured by the rhythms of the prose:

> But it is not so pleasant when, as sometimes happens, you suddenly fancy, starting up from your sleep, that the present distribution of your stores is completely and totally wrong, might lead to great dangers, and must be set right at once, no matter how tired or sleepy you may be; then I rush, then I fly, then I have no time for calculation: and although I was about to execute a perfectly new, perfectly exact plan, I now seize whatever my teeth hit upon and drag it or carry it away, sighing, groaning, stumbling, and even the most haphazard change in the present situation, which seems so terribly dangerous, can satisfy me.[38]

The idiomatic term "kafkaesque," with its connotations of the condition of being caught in a surreal and threatening nightmare world, is here emptied of its cultural references to bureaucracies and institutional mazes, in order to function in Kafka's pure animal fictions as a poetic analogue to an imagined ontological and psychological condition whose teleology is pure survival.

Conclusion

What do these animal stories of Kafka's tell us about the ability and disability of human language and human art to represent the animal from the inside rather than the outside, from an imagined vantage of animal perception rather than human perception? The answer to this question needs to be set into Kafka's larger historical context by recalling that he was writing at a turning point in intellectual history. In the late nineteenth and early twentieth centuries, the relationship between the human and the animal was in the process of being radically reconfigured in the aftermath of Darwinian theory. The "scandal" produced by Darwin extended beyond its blow to the theological dogma of "origin from design" that saw nature as evidence of the designing power of a creator. More intimately, Darwinian theory unsettled the foundations of human superiority in intelligence, reason, and language. This scandalizing effect is epitomized in Darwin's flat assertion in *The Descent of Man* when he wrote, "My object in this chapter is to shew that there is no fundamental difference between man and the higher mammals in their mental faculties."[39] Darwin's collapse of the borders of animal and human intelligence depended on developing a psychological sense of mental function, one that allowed for fluid and non-Cartesian relations between consciousness, knowing, and thinking. Darwin questioned whether animals might not possess analogues to the higher mental processes "in effect"—that is, with powers to demonstrate them practically and intuitively and to perform them, if not articulate them. His notebooks contain such observations as the thought that when dray horses adjust their pace and stance on pulling a load downhill, they exhibit an effective response to gravity and friction. He describes in the *Descent of Man* how polar dogs, "instead of continuing to draw the sledges in a compact body, diverged and separated when they came to thin ice, so that their weight might be more evenly distributed."[40] To Darwin, this suggests canine behavior that exhibits a practical, intuitive knowledge of the relationship between mass, stress, and surface. "All Science is reason acting/systematizing/ on principles, which even animals practically know (art precedes science—art is experience & observation)," he wrote in one of his notebooks.[41]

The resistances to Darwinian notions of continuities between human and animal intelligence, emotions, and even morals—for example, locating human altruism in examples of animal willingness to subordinate its interests to the needs of its species—diffused themselves far beyond the churches to create curious inflections even in the sciences themselves. This may be seen particularly in the field of psychology, and Kafka may therefore be seen as writing at the commencement of two broadly divergent trends in the psychological approaches to mental function that would circumvent and reverse Darwin's model of animal intelligence as continuous with, and qualitatively similar to, human intelligence. While continental developments in the complex and rapidly evolving field of turn-of-the-century psychology should not be reduced to two figures, we can nonetheless usefully typologize this divergence through the coterminous but radically different theories of Freud and Pavlov. Speaking broadly and reductively, we could say that Freudian theory assigned a psychoanalytical model to human beings, giving them a rich, secret, and subversive inner life that underlies, informs, and often disrupts rational thought and civilized behavior. Animals, conversely, were increasingly consigned to behaviorist theories of stimulus response that emptied them of an inner mental or psychic life, and reduced them to largely reactive objects in an environmentally challenging universe. The 1984 *Encyclopaedia Britannica*'s description of "animal behavior" begins with a patently behaviorist premise: "Any animal may be regarded as an agglomeration of interacting and interdependent structures and behaviors that are responses to environmental conditions."[42] One can legitimately characterize these maneuvers of early twentieth-century science as attempts to typologize animal thought and behavior in largely mechanistic and reactive terms while endowing human thought and behavior with a complex and compelling interiority. Such was early psychology's subtle but powerful resistance to the Darwinian attempt to collapse human and animal difference in the model of an intellectual and emotional continuum. Kafka's fictions—like those of D. H. Lawrence—held a ground against that resistance, yet without receiving adequate recognition for that gesture in their own time. Kafka's fictions are probably best known for what we could construe as a form of human ethology that depicts mystified and dazed human beings trying to cope with inexplicable and threatening environmental conditions. The protagonists of his famous works *The Trial* and *The Castle* can plausibly be seen as human-animal victims caught up in environments designed to stupefy and terrorize them—a state of affairs that lends itself readily to theological allegorization. Yet in his nonhuman animal stories, Kafka supplements the environmental challenges that confront his organisms by obliging them to cope not only with inexplicable phenomena and overwhelming instinctual and physical exigencies (like the creature in the burrow) but also with the effect of powerful and oppressive humans in their lives. Kafka therefore presents animal ethology as directed by an intelligent, speculative, quizzical consciousness that imagines for the animal a rich, complex, emotional, and affect-filled inner life. This inner life in several of his animal narrations must be responsive not only to a natural environment but also to a cultural environment, and finally to the effects of human beings upon the animal itself. Kafka speculatively creates for us a poetic analogue of the thinking animal as a hybrid—a creatural consciousness obliged to use human language and some model of human reasoning and logic that in turn is deconstructed. Kafka's fictions of the animal oblige us to see how the very vehicle for imagining animal thought is itself untenable, unsuitable, and impossible for the very "knowledge" it is asked to convey.

Notes

1. J. M. Coetzee, *The Lives of Animals* (Princeton, NJ: Princeton University Press, 1999), 49.
2. Ibid., 81.
3. Ibid., 35.
4. Paul Goodman, *Kafka's Prayer* (New York: Hillstone Publishing, 1976), 260–61.
5. Wilhelm Emrich, *Franz Kafka: A Critical Study of His Writings*, trans. Sheema Zeben Buehne (New York: Frederick Ungar Publishing Co., 1968), 179.
6. Coetzee, 27.
7. Coetzee's own note in *Lives of Animals* cites Patrick Bridgwater as attributing Haeckel and the writer M. M. Seraphim as Kafka's sources for his portrait of the ape. Ibid., 27.
8. Cary Wolfe, "Faux Post-Humanism, or, Animal Rights, Neocolonialism, and Michael Crichton's *Congo*," *Arizona Quarterly* 55:2 (Summer 1999), 115–53.
9. Franz Kafka, *The Complete Stories*, ed. Nahum N. Glatzer (New York: Schocken Books, 1976), 104.

10. Ibid., 115.

11. Ibid., 105.

12. Max Brod, *Franz Kafka: A Biography*, trans. Humphreys Roberts and Richard Winston (New York: Schocken Books, 1970), 128.

13. "Carl Hagenbeck," *The New Encyclopaedia Britannica* IV (Chicago: Encyclopaedia Inc., 1984), 834.

14. Kafka, 250.

15. Homi K. Bhabha, *The Location of Culture* (London: Routledge, 1994), 86.

16. Kafka, 251.

17. Ibid., 252.

18. Gustav Janouch. *Conversations with Kafka*, trans. Goronwy Rees (New York: New Directions, 1971), 57.

19. Wolfe, 138.

20. Kafka, 257.

21. Ibid., 278.

22. Marjorie Garber, *Dog Love* (New York: Touchstone, 1996), 114.

23. Kafka, 279.

24. Ibid.

25. Ibid., 283.

26. Coetzee, 43.

27. Kafka, 288.

28. Ibid., 303.

29. Ibid., 280.

30. Emrich, 187.

31. Coetzee, 45.

32. Emrich, 207.

33. Kafka, 328.

34. Ibid., 325–26.

35. Ibid., 326.

36. Ibid., 329.

37. Ibid., 330.

38. Ibid., 329.

39. Charles Darwin, *The Descent of Man, and Selections in Relation to Sex* (London: John Murray, 1950), 66.

40. Ibid., 75.

41. Howard E. Gruber, *Darwin on Man: A Psychological Study of Scientific Creativity*, together with *Darwin's Early and Unpublished Notebooks*, transcribed and annotated by Paul H. Barrett (New York: E. P. Dutton & Co., 1974), 333.

42. *The New Encyclopaedia Britannica* 2, 804.

CHAPTER 3

"Czechs, Jews and Dogs Not Allowed": Identity, Boundary, and Moral Stance in Kafka's "A Crossbreed" and "Jackals and Arabs"[1]

Hadea Nell Kriesberg

Introduction

Kafka lived in dangerous times, and the *Zeitgeist* of peril was a subtext of most of his literary works. Historically, there was constant political instability through-out Eastern Europe, as well as the particular vulnerability of the Jewish popula-tion. Additionally, we are all, regardless of epoch, heirs to personal trauma—this seems to be a particular characteristic of the human animal. Kafka felt over-whelmed by the numerous battlefronts he faced on a daily basis, including his geography, his religion, and his family. Instead of finding that this connected him to his fellow sufferers, he felt even more estranged. As he notes in the fourth Octavo notebook, "The distance to my fellow man is for me a very long one."[2]

In Prague, Kafka's hometown, as ethnic groups struggled for survival, the two major Western religions existed uneasily together and anti-Semitic resent-ments often served to unify people searching for common ground. The Jewish minority existed in whatever niches they could. Kafka was an educated German-speaking lawyer from a Czech-speaking upwardly mobile, merchant-class family. He felt a misfit in as many ways as may seem possible: an artist in a bourgeois family and society, raised secular but yearning for spiritual answers, a German speaker with a historically Yiddish heritage, a full-time lawyer who considered himself a writer. He did not feel he had a home he could cling to since he was estranged from his father and felt misunderstood by his family. His family re-sented his vegetarianism, since for them meat-eating was a sign of wealth and status. In addition, taller and thinner than his friends and colleagues, he seemed to be at war with his physical self, often following a dangerously ascetic lifestyle. In his biography of Kafka, Ronald Hayman comments: "What he lacked was a sense of rootedness: he seemed to be living off-center in relation to his own identity. He used the image . . . of an acrobat climbing a ladder that's resting not on the ground and not against a wall but only on another acrobat's feet. He felt precariously situated inside his body."[3]

His work was deeply introspective; he was his own subject, often seemingly mulling chapters in his autobiography, writing to ground himself in a hostile territory. In his diaries and letters he many times referred not only to animals, but to himself as an animal (e.g., describing an interaction with a neighbor, he comments, "I felt as if I were a sparrow, practicing my jumps on the step, and she were ruffling my soft, fluffy gray feathers").[4] Using animals as characters was common in the Yiddish folk tales and Hassidic parables Kafka read. In this his practice was in keeping with his own heritage, telling stories so as to arrive at a spiritual epiphany. What is striking about Kafka's animals is that they have a dual role, seeming to speak both as Kafka's inner voice as he meditates on his life and as characters in their own right. In the sixth Octavo notebook, he describes what appears as a most commonplace occurrence, a mouse lured into a trap by a scrap of food, the almost hidden scream of death, the fright of other mice in the area, and their curiosity as they come out to investigate: "There it lay, the dear little mouse, its neck caught in the deadly iron, the little pink legs drawn up, and now stiff, the feeble body that would so well have deserved a scrap of bacon. The parents stood beside it and eyed their child's remains."[5]

This story seems to point us in a direction beyond the autobiographical. Kafka seems to be making a universal statement about children and parents, using the animal as would the author of a Hassidic cautionary tale. This mouse is not just an animal, but someone's child. The story is an occasion for Kafka to reflect upon his own situation, liken it for some reason to an animal's, and, in addition, contemplate the animals' lives as they live them out, for themselves. Just as the Hassidic parables exist in a particular kind of universal timelessness, an abstract place of time and space, Kafka's stories seem both abstract and literal, a physical meeting ground for human and nonhuman animals.

Yet we must constantly keep in mind the historical reality of Kafka's time: he was not speaking metaphorically. A man could go to sleep an employed Jew and wake up the next morning as vermin. A Jew could study at the university and yet find himself called a dog. In German and Austrian anti-Semitic political publications, Jews were frequently referred to as "rats," "mice," "insects," and "vermin."[6] If a person can go to sleep a Jew and wake up transformed into some kind of "vermin," what is to prevent an animal going to sleep a dog and waking up a person? It is as if Kafka took that reality, the ever-present possibility of being referred to as some sort of animal, and pondered what it would be to truly become an animal. This introspective meditation on the nature of being a Jew in Europe at the turn of the century became also an exercise in contemplating what sort of human being one might become if we truly questioned our own identity.

There is a famous tale from the Hassidic master, the Baal Shem Tov, about a king whose palace contained a complex maze that ended with his own quarters in the most inner sanctum. His servants found themselves blocked, unable to approach their hidden king: "While they stood and wondered, the king's son came and showed them that those were not real partitions, but only magical illusions, and that the king, in truth, was easily accessible. Push forward bravely and you shall find no obstacle!"[7] We recognize the idea of obstacles and boundaries here as a theme for Kafka, both in his life and in his work. Kafka biographer Frederick R. Karl notes, "But there was more, something uniquely Kafkan: the need to find in language a home, parents, beliefs, a center of rest, a way to relieve the ever present sense of alienation and marginality in oneself and in everything around one."[8] He felt homeless, out of place, in constant danger of traps and barriers. It was as if he created a place to live inside his own stories. The events there could perhaps resolve some of his dilemmas, just as the Hassidic teaching, properly understood, could answer a spiritual quest.

As well as exploring the Hasidic tradition and Yiddish theater, Kafka also studied Chinese literature. His stories, a blending of the literal and the mythic, remind us not only of Hassidic tales but also of Zen koans, brief questions or parables that often defy logic, but have the goal of giving the spiritual seeker an experiential form of understanding. Kafka wants us, the audience, not to merely read his stories, but to experience them. Joyce Carol Oates notes, "Kafka . . . has become for many of his readers a kind of perpetual riddle, a Zen koan—the ultimate, interior, soul-transforming experience, to 'solve' which would be to 'solve' the problem of existence itself."[9] In this chapter we will explore how two pieces of writing, the fragment "A Crossbreed" and a short story "Jackals and Arabs," reflect some of Kafka's central concerns about self-identity and marginality.

"A Crossbreed": Fragment from the Front

Most of all, Kafka is writing for himself, trying to reconcile his personal predicament—that of a person feeling marginal in his own family and his society—within the larger context of the historic Jewish experience of marginality. One of the ways in which Kafka expresses this sense of personal predicament along with the larger, societal one is his use of first-person narration. The reader knows Kafka is the author, and yet it is left unclear who exactly the narrator is. We can see this technique in "A Crossbreed," a story fragment published after Kafka's death. The story opens thus: "I have a curious animal, half kitten, half lamb. It is a legacy from my father. But it only developed in my time; formerly it was far more lamb than kitten. Now it is both in about equal parts."[10] The German word for crossbreed is *Kreuzung*, which also means "crossroads" or "intersection."[11] During Kafka's life he was many times at a crossroads, feeling torn between his different personae: a secular Jew searching for spiritual answers, a lawyer defending workers and yet employed by the state, a lawyer who was really a writer, a Jew living in an increasingly anti-Semitic Europe, a confirmed bachelor who longed to be married, a son at psychological war with his father, and a man deeply uncomfortable with his physical body.

In German, *Kreuzung,* like the English "crossing," is also used for "cross-breed." A hybrid is the offspring of two different family lines. Kafka might have felt himself to be hybrid; his paternal line was lower working class, including a peddler and a kosher butcher, while his mother's family was of higher class, a heritage which included scholars and professionals. Frederick R. Karl notes the complexity of the societal conflicts with which Kafka was living: "It meant the deciphering of several codes, all of which appeared to contradict each other. . . . We see how Kafka attempted to adjust to shifting realities in his use of halves, of divisions of self into man and beast or man and insect, of bifurcations that always occur with doubles-two assistants, two guards, two pairs, two selves."[12]

Kafka seems not only fascinated with the phenomenon of the hybrid, but also with the question of what it feels like to live as a chimera. He ponders the nature of the separating boundary, whether this line of demarcation is obvious or hidden, whether the division feels fluid or impermeable, if the doubling feels enriching or a barrier to a strong self-identity. Whatever the feelings of the kittenlamb, Kafka presents the other animals as accepting of such singularity:

> From the cat it takes its head and claws, from the lamb its size and shape, from both; from both its eyes which are wild and flickering. . . . Sometimes the children bring cats with them; once they actually even brought two lambs. But against all their hopes there was no scene of recognition. The animals gazed calmly at each other with their animal eyes, and obviously accepted their reciprocal existence as a divine fact.[13]

Clearly we wonder why this animal is a cat joined with a lamb. A cat is a pet, a taboo animal for eating in most Western countries, but lambs are created to be eaten. One of the critical issues for Jews in Europe at this point in history was that of the process of assimilation into the larger society. Perhaps Kafka is mulling the need to become less a lamb (victim) and more a pet (valuable, but still lesser, still a commodity in some sense). Is he seeing himself (or his tribe, the Jews) as a coddled, domesticated animal in his family (or the larger society), a plaything until falling out of favor? There does seem to be another allusion to this shift in role when Kafka notes that the kittenlamb, originally more lamb than feline, has become during its time with Kafka closer to a 50/50 hybrid. In his diaries Kafka will at times present himself as an animal, rather than a human being, as in this entry where he writes about talking with a literary critic he knew, saying "It sounded like the whimpering of a young cat."[14]

In the first sentence, "I have a curious animal," the German *Eigentümliches*, translated as "curious," can mean "strange" or "peculiar." Intrinsic to the idea of a chimera is its very strangeness: such beings are wondrous and new. But this kittenlamb, though strange, has nothing of the feel of the monstrous about it. Historically, these sorts of species crosses have been seen as dreadful portents, something unnatural to be avoided or destroyed. But Kafka's tone throughout this fragment is completely matter of fact. He might be reporting on any interesting occurrence in his neighborhood. This reminds us of both the Hassidic stories and the koans. In addition, it reflects Kafka's acceptance of such fluidity of boundaries. His comment about the animals accepting such a singular creature might also be a veiled critique of our species for making such a fuss over categories.

The root *Eigen*, which means "own" or "separate," can also mean "having a mind of one's own," "unconventional" or "original." So here is the subtext, again, of being different. Perhaps Kafka is writing about his own sense of belonging to none of the categories he was supposed to fit into, a being apart from the various dueling parties with which he lived. We do know from Kafka's diaries, letters, and conversations that he felt uniquely out of place, separate from other people in some indefinable way. In "A Crossbreed" he describes the relationship between the kittenlamb and its family: "It remains faithful to the family that has brought it up. In that there is certainly no extraordinary mark of fidelity, but merely the true instinct of an animal which, though it has countless step-relations in the world, has perhaps not a single blood relation, and to which consequently the protection it has found with us is sacred."[15]

Throughout the fragment it is not clear who the narrator is: it could be Kafka, it could be anyone. Whoever the narrator may be, however, it seems the kittenlamb is protected by belonging to the narrator's family. In the second sentence of the story the animal is described as a "legacy." In the original, the word is *Erbstück*, which can be translated also as "heirloom," since the root *Erb* refers to heredity. And picking up on the idea of inheritance and blood relationships, there is a subtle, perhaps ironic allusion as well. Kafka's refusal to eat meat in a culture where meat eating and butchering was an accepted tradition marked him as different, especially since his own bloodline included a butcher. So this lamb-like creature has found protection from the butcher with a family of butchers. Speaking of his vegetarianism, Kafka said, "My paternal grandfather was a butcher in a village near Stakonitz; I have to not eat as much meat as he butchered."[16]

It is impossible to have the character of a lamb without the subtext of ritual sacrifice, especially when one of the recurring themes in Kafka's life is the clash of religious faiths. Is this the Pesach lamb or the Easter lamb? In alluding to this ambiguity, there is a sense that this curious creature can be both at the same time. With the boundaries erased, it might be possible that a tribe or an individual can be both victim and treasure. Kafka's genius leads us to realize that the different interpretations are all true, that there are several simultaneous levels of ambiguity and allusion. Reading this story calls forth in us a different reaction than if we were attempting to understand plot or dialogue. Thus Pamela Sur notes that "the unforgettable nature and fascination of Kafka's animals stem largely from the fact that they are difficult to explain rationally. . . . The appropriate response of the reader . . . seems to be a kind of non-verbal meditation."[17] It does indeed seem that Kafka is considering the life he has inherited from his parents, a life of insecurity, saved from slaughter by his "special" status as a professional.

Aside from the psychological and societal themes, there is a third one here, that of the relationship between the human species and the animal. On a deeper level Kafka is subtly asking us to think about our ideas of animals as either sources of food or as coddled pets. Is he questioning our tradition that denies them a unique status with us as simply themselves? The language implies this: the word *Eigenwert* means "intrinsic value." *Eigentümliches*, as we have seen, can be translated as "odd," since it carries the root *Eigen*, which means "own" or "separate," as noted above. Contained within the very language is the subtext of the importance of the individual, even an animal.

Kafka contemplated several different ways to end "The Crossbreed," but the first sentence of the last paragraph of the story in the most accepted version reads, "Perhaps the knife of the butcher would be a release for this animal; but as it is a legacy I must deny it that."[18] In the original German, the word translated as "release"—*Erlösung*—could equally be translated as "deliverance," or "redemption." Again, several thoughts seem to be going on in tandem. Kafka is wondering if to be dead would be better than to exist as such a half-breed, if death would be a release from a life of torment. Is Kafka's life as odd man out so painful that death is preferable? He may be implying that the intrinsic value of such a creature (even if half-lamb, normally to be eaten) demands it be allowed to live a normal life span. To use a word as loaded as *Erlösung* for an animal's death implies that this death (and life) matters. The ambiguity of the fragment, the fluidity of the kittenlamb's identity, is part of the magic of "A Crossbreed."

Kafka: The *Mischling*

In *Franz Kafka: The Jewish Patient*, Sander Gilman discusses the term *Mischling*, which describes a person of mixed racial heritage: the half-breed. In pre–World War I Europe, the term was mostly used in a pejorative sense, to describe the offspring of a marriage between a Jew and a Gentile. The implication was that such people were unstable and deficient, unable to satisfactorily live in society since they were neither this nor that. As Gilman notes, Kafka lived in constant state of discomfort with a physical, bodily existence, in a quandary as to how to reconcile what seemed to him to be animal-like needs with an intellectual, spiritual existence. In commenting on "The Crossbreed," Gilman discusses the complexity of a mixed heritage for Kafka: "Is the mixed breed truly human? And why is the narrator suddenly in the position of ritual butcher? Kafka understands his own imagined body and psyche as that of a Mischling who can never become 'normal,' as in this story."[19] In a scene from "A Crossbreed," the narrator sits with the kittenlamb on his lap in a mood of despair: "I happened to glance down and saw tears dropping from its huge whiskers. Were they mine, or where they the animal's? Had this cat, along with the soul of a lamb, the ambitions of a human being? I did not inherit much from my father, but this legacy is quite remarkable."[20]

Kafka here blurs several different sorts of boundaries. There is the border between the lamb and the kitten which enlarges to take in another animal species: "Not content with being lamb and cat, it almost insists on being a dog as well."[21] Perhaps once this sort of lamb has crossed over from being only a lamb (and a kitten crossed over from only being a kitten) to some sort of composite, then maybe the process could just continue. Kafka is implying here that once a fluidity of species boundaries has been achieved by a sort of chimeric double, any combination might be possible (e.g., a kittenlambdog). It does seem that Kafka is implying that once one boundary of identity is crossed, one could become *anything*. Clearly in this image of the confusion of tears, Kafka is thinking over that boundary we consider impregnable, that between the human and nonhuman animal.

Perhaps this kittenlamb, wanting to be a dog, someday will end up "with the ambitions of a man." The word translated as "ambition" is interesting in this context. *Menschenehrgeiz* has the connotation of greed, of striving for acquisitions. This need for property was one of the disagreements Kafka held with his family, and he himself owned very little. There is in this notion of ambition the embedded idea of the conflict between striving for worldly goods as opposed to the more spiritual goals that Kafka saw as his task. This *confusion over tears*: who is crying for whom? The struggle between our physical and spiritual selves is often revealed in our choice of diet. If the kittenlamb stands for Kafka, the theme of what to eat, an endless conflict for his entire life, becomes clear as well. As a human he has the capacity of a carnivore, like the kitten, but chooses to be an herbivore, like the lamb. Kafka wonders which side of his nature is truly "him" and where in nature does he belong. In writing from inside a personal dilemma over eating, Kafka enlarges the scope of his question to the deeper one of what we can permit ourselves to eat, if we want to honor life itself.

From his diaries, letters, and conversations, it was no secret that Kafka was someone at war with what he saw as his animal needs. His diet went beyond that of an ethical statement about eating meat, to the point of masochism. At times he seemed to be in conflict over another sort of boundary, the point at which food outside himself became transformed into his own body. Eating was often an occasion for anxiety and ritualistic behavior, as seen, for example, in his chewing his food over and over a specific number of times before swallowing. He was severely ascetic in all his activities, often eating as little as possible, choosing celibacy for much of his life, spending much of the night writing rather than sleeping, and owning very little. The idea of being physically comfortable was anathema, and yet he was aware that this approach to psychological conflict between the intellectual/spiritual and the physical ultimately solved nothing. In the fifth Octavo notebook, Kafka writes:

> For the eventuality that in the near future I may die . . . let me say that I myself have torn myself to shreds. If my father in earlier days was in the habit of uttering wild but empty threats, saying: I'll tear you apart like a fish—in fact, he did not so much as lay a finger on me—now the threat is being fulfilled independently of him. The world . . . and my ego are tearing my body apart in a conflict that there is no resolving.[22]

Even though Kafka realized that this is a conflict felt by many, he understood that the depth of his personal conflict set him apart. In "A Crossbreed," he asks, "Why is there only one such animal, why I rather than anyone else should own it, whether there was ever an animal like it before and what would happen if it died, whether it feels lonely, why it has no children, what it is called, etc."[23]

Although it is clear that Kafka is writing about the profound sense of alienation he felt from his own body and his own identity, I propose that Kafka is going further than saying he is at war with his own body or in conflict over his animal nature. Rather, he is saying he is some sort of curious hybrid, some sort of human-animal cross. In a letter to Milena, a woman deeply important to him toward the end of his life, he comments on their relationship: "but fundamentally I was still only the animal, belonged still in the forest, lived here in the open only by your grace. . . . I was desperate, really like a stray animal."[24] He describes himself here as an animal who belongs neither in the house nor in the woods, one who is lost or abandoned, not completely wild, not completely tame.

In a meditative fragment from the eighth Octavo notebook he seems no longer to be human or some sort of hybrid but completely animal, a fox:

> I lay on the ground by a wall, writing in pain, trying to burrow into the damp earth. The huntsman stood beside me and lightly pressed

one foot into the small of my back. "A splendid beast," he said to the beater, who was cutting open my collar and coat in order to feel my flesh. Already tired of me and eager for fresh action, the hounds were running senselessly against the wall, the coach came and bound hand and foot, I was flung in beside the gentleman, over the back seat, so that my head and arms hung down outside the carriage. The journey passed swiftly and smoothly; perishing of thirst, with open mouth, I breathed in the high-whirling dust, and now and then felt the gentleman's delighted touch on my calves.[25]

Is Kafka writing *as* the fox, or *is* he the fox? The image of a collar and coat being cut emphasizes this duality. What sort of coat is this fox wearing? A fox is a wild animal; earlier we quoted him writing about the death of a mouse, another wild animal, but one that often lives with people, or in proximity with them, but not as a domestic animal. The creature in "A Crossbreed" is both a cat and a lamb: a lamb is considered domesticated as is a cat, but, unlike a dog, a cat is considered closer to the wild; indeed, it can go wild or feral within a generation if left on its own. In "A Crossbreed," not only is Kafka identifying himself with an animal, even going so far as to say there is no boundary between him and that animal, but the animal he is writing about has aspects of the marginal, the untamable, on the boundary between domestic and wild. In the fragment about the fox, the animal is wild. This is clearly a strange place to be, an almost taboo geography. Writing about this border between the wild and the not quite wild in "Feral Cats in the City," the authors note how we see cats as existing in an ambiguous space between wild and domesticated: "The designation 'pet' generally indicates belonging: a place in the home . . . however, 'putting the cat out at night' signals incomplete containment . . . only a partial domestication. . . . In this respect pet cats are transgressive, breaking the boundary between nature and culture."[26]

Another level of ambiguity in these two fragments involves Kafka's dual role as author and narrator. Even though he more often than not writes in the first person, the distance between himself and his work is ambiguous. In the passage quoted above, the narrator seems to be more fox than Kafka. In "The Crossbreed," the narrator might be Kafka, thinking over the problem of self-identity, but the author stays removed from the narrator. Peter U. Beicken comments on this subtle technique of distancing: "Kafka had created a specific kind of first-person narration; namely, one in which he successfully eliminates the dialectics of the experiencing-I vs. the narrating-I. . . . Kafka, however, reduces the narrating person to an observing entity who perceives events at the very moment of their origination."[27]

As readers we identify on two levels as well, blurring the boundary between author and audience. We identify with the narrator, who is also the person experiencing the story, and thus we experience the story as something happening to ourselves. Kafka often said he used his writing to reconcile him to his life. In a letter to Milena he speaks of the two of them standing "side by side, watching this creature on the ground which is me; but I, as the spectator, am then non-existent."[28] In meditating on his life, trying to accept its complexities, Kafka felt there to be no boundary between his role as the writer and his role as subject-matter.

In addition, another kind of separation, Kafka's vegetarianism, set him apart not only from his family but also most other Jews. He was a Jew unable to eat meat, while meat eating had a historical importance, as the *shehitah* (ritual slaughter) separated Jewish meat from that of Gentiles. Gilman writes that "Kafka sees his eating habits as being linked to who he is, to his sense of self, but also to a marginal world."[29] Thus Kafka was out of step with his own tradition, having empathy for the animals he was supposed to relate to as objects for use. If you are going to eat the lamb, you must not have sympathy for it. In writing about this division relating to an animal as either food or pet, Kafka creates himself as a kind of animal for us to identify with. Again, Gilman on "The Crossbreed": "For Kafka as the writer, an answer to mixed breeds is ritual murder/butchery, but in his own inverted manner of representing this dilemma, this demands that the victim be seen as 'human.' Is the mixed breed truly human? And why is the narrator suddenly in the position of ritual butcher?"[30]

By blurring the boundaries, both between author and narrator and between author and audience, Kafka pulls us inside the fragment or story: we experience the dilemma; we too are both the eater and the eaten. We not only feel empathy for the mouse in the trap, the fox tied up inside the coach, and the kittenlamb sitting on Kafka's lap, but we, along with Kafka, *are* these animals as well. This frisson owes much to the power of Kafka's writing, a power that is difficult to explain rationally. This relates back to his immersion in the Hassidic stories and Zen koans, both of which have the goal of giving the audience a visceral as opposed to an intellectual experience.

"Jackals and Arabs": Taking the Case

This sense Kafka had, of being both insider and outsider, of being a liaison between the animal and the human, is seen in a well-known story, "Jackals and Arabs." This story, along with "A Report to an Academy," was published under the title "Two Animal Stories," in two consecutive 1917 issues of Martin Buber's Zionist journal *Der Jude*. Thus, the Zionist dilemma—continuing to live in Diaspora or immigrate to what was then Palestine—is clearly a major theme in this story. During his life Kafka contemplated moving to Palestine, and toward the end of his life he began to study Hebrew. The European Jews were deeply divided over either following a secular, assimilated lifestyle, or a deeply religious one, unchanged from earlier generations. Historically this divide over time became a split between Western versus Eastern European Jewry.

The setting and simple plot of "Jackals and Arabs" takes place, as do so many of Kafka's works, in an abstract time and place: the timeless present. Again, the narrator talks in the first person, but does not identify himself; as we noted earlier, this device allows the reader to enter the story. What we will do is summarize the plot, then return and go through the story more carefully, examining the original German text to arrive at insights as to the multiple themes Kafka is setting before us.

The narrator finds himself in the desert, along with unidentified companions. Perhaps the companions are us, the readers. He is addressed by the leader of a group of jackals, who says, "I am delighted to have met you here at last. I had almost given up hope, since we have been waiting endless years for you; my mother waited for you, and her mother, and all our foremothers right back to the first mother of all the jackals."[31] Their complaint is that they need to be freed from living with the Arabs whom they hate with a deep tribal hatred; for reasons not made clear, the jackals have found themselves living among others who hate them and whom they hate as well. Furthermore, they complain that these Arabs slaughter their livestock for food in the wrong fashion. A jackal arrives with "a small pair of sewing scissors covered with ancient rust dangling from an eyetooth."[32] They ask the narrator to take care of the Arabs for them: they don't want to get close enough to kill them, so disgusted are they by the Arab presence. The jackals say, "Cleanliness, nothing but cleanliness, is what we want."[33] The narrator and the jackals sit in the grass and discuss the situation, and the narrator expresses caution as to what he can accomplish, given the age-old enmity between the two groups. The head Arab arrives and disparages the jackals: he throws a dead camel at their feet, which they seize on in frenzy. As they ravenously tear the corpse apart, the Arab begins to whip them as they eat, until the narrator takes him by the arm and leads him away.

Already, we are disturbed—by the description of animals whipped as they eat—and by the strangeness of the story in general. One feature especially noteworthy is the circumstance of animals asking for legal representation. This request seems to link the narrator and Kafka in some fashion, since Kafka was a lawyer and perhaps we may assume that the narrator is also a lawyer. We note that not only is the narrator considering the case, but he is treating the jackals as he would any other group of litigants. This role of liaison was a familiar one for Kafka, who was hired by the government's Workers' Accident Insurance Company to intercede on behalf of workers injured on the job. Kafka's friend Max Brod noted that Kafka was very much disturbed by the patience and humility of these workers who had been injured in industrial accidents. "How modest these men are," he said to Brod. "They come to us and beg. Instead of storming the Institute and smashing it to pieces they come and beg."[34]

Let us proceed through the story analyzing key words in the text from the original German. First we will review the general presentation of the narrator's relationship with the jackals, then the specific complaints for which they seek some sort of resolution, and continue on to the larger context of the case they are bringing before the narrator. Here is how the story begins: "I threw myself on my back in the grass; I tried to fall asleep; I could not; a jackal howled in the distance, I sat up again."[35] Kafka begins the story with the narrator in the grass. He is trying to sleep in the grass, not in a tent or even in a sleeping bag as might a person, but right down in the grass like an animal. The word translated as "howl" (*Klagegeheul*) may be closer to "howling complaint," as *Geheul* is "howl," while *Klage* is similar to "complaint." *Klage* can also mean a lamentation (over a loss), as well as accusation. It is often used to mean "lodge a complaint," "to bring action against," "a petition for divorce," and even "bring suit," as well as to moan or wail. Thus the word works on several levels, emphasizing Kafka's work defending the injured. Here the jackals have come to ask the story's narrator to "take their case"; there is the subtle identification of low-ranking factory workers with a group of disparaged animals.

The jackals and the narrator have their consultation in the grass. The jackals have points of view, they reflect on their situation, and they question their situation. They also address the narrator with respect and good manners. Two young jackals grip the man's clothes so that he cannot get up from where he is sitting in the grass: "[T]wo young beasts behind me had locked their teeth through my coat and shirt; I had to go on sitting. 'These are your trainbearers,' said the old jackal quite seriously, 'a mark of honor. . . . Meanwhile, give ear to our petition.'"[36] The original German for "request" is *Bitte*; it is similar to the way in which a waiter might pull out a chair in a restaurant, saying "please." The animals here are acting with courtesy, an echo of the idea of "a mark of respect." Also, he and the elder jackal are in consultation—the narrator is seated, with the other jackals behind their spokesman. The tone is completely matter of fact, the narrator reports nothing strange in this situation; the jackals are petitioners like any other clients. The ease with which the narrator takes on the role of advocate with the jackals illustrates Kafka's sense that the animal is not *the other*, but just another. Again, Kafka is blurring the boundary between the human and the animal and in doing this, implying an ethical stance. Christina Gerhardt comments on this idea of the mutuality of encounter: "In this way, the truth emerges precisely at that moment when the human slides into the animal, when both man and animal are presenced and stand in dialectical tension to one another. The challenge is to maintain a productive balance between them."[37]

The jackals bring two related complaints to be adjudicated: (1) the manner in which the Arabs kill animals so they can be eaten and (2) to intercede for them in a long-standing quarrel with the Arabs with whom they are forced to live. The latter topic seems evocative of an age-old problem for Jews: Diaspora. Clearly, for Jews in turn-of-the-century Europe, to be homeless in Diaspora is a critical, ultimately deadly issue, and this is certainly a strong theme of this story. The jackal elder says to the narrator, "Is it not misfortune enough for us to be exiled among such creatures?"[38] The German word translated as "exiled" is *Verstoßen*, which is closer in meaning to "disown," "repudiate," to be expelled from, to be banished, to be an outcast. In the original, Kafka writes: *Volk verstoßen. Volk* is a nation, a people, a crowd, the masses, with a subtext meaning of colony. As well as the more obvious metaphor for the Jewish Diaspora, there is the inference that the jackals live in a kind of Diaspora as well, but theirs is a forced exile among human beings. In addition to living as a nation of outcasts, the jackals are disgusted by the manner in which these people with whom they are forced to live obtain their food: "They kill animals for food, and carrion they despise."[39] One subtext might be that what distinguishes people from animals is how and what they eat: animals eat other animals, but people need not choose to do this.

As their conversation continues, the jackals become more and more distraught over their situation in living with the Arabs, explaining their torment at being forced to live in a world of filth and contamination, where animals are not allowed to die natural deaths. When the narrator asks what they expect of him, the response is as follows: "And so, sir, and so, dear sir, by means of your all-powerful hands slit their throats through with these scissors!"[40] At which point a jackal trots up with a small scissors "covered with ancient rust" hanging from a canine tooth. The combination of the image of slitting a throat with that of a pair of encrusted scissors is evocative of the argument over kosher slaughter, *shehitah*. Gilman notes: "The Jewish audience would have recognized the allusions to shehitah without any trouble. . . . It is central to Kafka's representation of the jackals that they eat differently from the Arabs. According to their perspective, they eat 'naturally,' consuming carrion, while the Arabs 'murder' their food."[41]

This brief story is becoming very complex with several themes threaded throughout the plot and dialogue. There is the allusion to kosher slaughter as distinguished from non-kosher slaughter. *Shehitah* seems to be another example of the degree to which Jews were separated from their neighbors. Gentile practice was to stun an animal before killing it to avoid killing a conscious animal: this was thought to be a humane practice. According to the Talmud, a rationale for *shehitah* was to prevent the butcher from taking the act of killing an animal lightly, since the animal remained conscious. Another aspect of this practice was that it would make the meat-eaters more aware of the life taken for them.

From a different standpoint, the thinking was that bleeding the animal cleared out the toxins, preparing the meat so that it was safe to eat.[42] The jackals tell the narrator that he has been chosen to end an ancient quarrel between the jackals and the Arabs: "Sir, we want you to end this quarrel that divides the world. You are exactly the man whom our ancestors foretold as born to do it."[43] The word *Beenden* means "to bring to an end," to finish, or complete. This is certainly an allusion to the argument within the Jewish community as mentioned earlier: do we immigrate to Palestine, a secular solution, or do we wait for the Messiah who will initiate spiritual renewal? For the religiously orthodox, the Zionist stance was tantamount to repudiating the Judaic Messianic tradition, and thus a religious failing.

If this is a story with animals as central characters, what else might be going on? There is certainly the allusion to the precarious situation of the Jews, at one moment people, the next called dogs. But there is another meaning as well, related to animals. The head Arab comes over and tells the narrator that the jackals approach every European who arrives at the oasis with the same request, trotting over with the same pair of old rusty scissors, ever hopeful. What are the jackals asking for? They arrive with an allegorical implement of their death at human hands, old, rusty, perhaps covered with ancient blood, the symbol of the ancient quarrel (*Streit*) that is tearing the world in two. I propose that Kafka is actually calling kosher slaughter before the court, asking, how could ritual slaughter really purify anything? Killing is killing, and to say a prayer before causing an animal to die fully conscious is as far from purity as possible. The jackals are very clear when they say to the narrator, "We want to be no more troubled by Arabs; room to breathe; a skyline cleansed of them; no more bleating of sheep knifed by an Arab; every beast to die a natural death; no interference until we have drained the carcass empty and picked its bones clean. Cleanliness, nothing but cleanliness is what we want."[44]

There is an irony to the jackals' plea for purity as Kafka presents it; really, he might be saying, what is the difference between teeth to the throat versus a knife to the throat? Moreover, he seems to be asking if prayer can purify the act of taking a life. Kafka does seem to asking whether an ancient human ritual can meaningfully set the boundary between life and death. The author is seeing this through the animals' eyes. He is their advocate. In this story the animals have the "right" to speak like any other character. At one point a jackal says to the narrator that since they have only their teeth, their language is limited. This is evocative of the question of language for Kafka, writing in German, growing up speaking Czech, with his heritage being the lowly Yiddish. Yiddish, the language of the European Jew, was discredited, a mark of low class. I think that Kafka is drawing a link between the howling lament of a discredited low-class human and that of an animal. In addition, why disparage them for having only teeth when we have teeth as well? There really is something intrepid about these jackals, bringing the scissors, the butcher's knife,[45] the emblem of their very lowness, their "otherness" to every European who comes their way, hoping for a fair hearing. Kafka seems to be saying that it is indeed heroic, their asking, like any human petitioner, for legal help.[46]

As readers, we identify with both the narrator and the jackals, and this was part of Kafka's plan: to have the reader experience the helplessness of being at risk of slaughter. We also need to look at this story in the light of Kafka's vegetarianism. For him, eating animals was immoral. Kosher slaughter did not purify, did not give permission to eat meat. The sin that cannot be purified through ritual is the sin of killing animals and eating them. In this story Kafka is speaking of the jackals (a metaphor for animals) as a disenfranchised population, really at our mercy and yet courageously existing in Diaspora. The fact that the jackals are nonhuman animals instead of human animals should not be held against them. Joyce Carol Oates, in writing of Kafka's work as visionary, notes that "Kafka goes against the entire Western concept of the hero: the brave, isolated, not-to-be-daunted self against all other selves and, of course, against nature, which exists merely to be conquered or at least classified and dissected."[47] In this case, part of Kafka's vision is to see animals not as a part of nature here for our use, but, as other nations, in need of representation by us.

Now let us look at the phrase, "end this quarrel that divides the world."[48] The original German, *Streit* (translated as "quarrel"), again evokes a legal situation, since it means an argument, a feud, or conflict with the secondary meaning being to go to court, or take legal action. *Streit* has the connotation of an argument deeper and more vicious than a quarrel, with the added subtext of a loud commotion. And *Zweit*, from the root *Zwei*, which means two, can be translated various ways, as in "twosome," "going on together," or other variations of two-ness (e.g., workers versus bosses, the secular versus religious). Earlier, in response to the jackals' lament that they live as outcasts, the narrator cautiously refers to an ageless, tribal divide, one that is not easily explained: "'Maybe, maybe,' said I, 'matters so far outside my province I am not competent to judge; it seems to me a very old quarrel; I suppose it's in the blood, and perhaps will only end with it.'"[49] In a discussion of Kafka's narrative stance, using "Jackals and Arabs" as an example, Walter Herbert Sokel comments on the impossibility of mending the divide:

> The jackals misunderstand the comment of the first-person narrator. With "it probably lies in the blood" ("liegt also wohl im Blut") he meant innateness, the fatefulness of the conflict between the jackals and the Arabs. The feud must endure as long as life. It cannot end until death. His has overtones of original sin, of unregenerate creation. There is no way to mitigate such a feud.[50]

As always, Kafka is addressing several themes in this story at once. As well as the issue of slaughter and meat eating, he is asking us to examine our ideas about societal divisions. He is referring to the age-old tribal divide between Jews and Gentiles, as well as alluding to the intratribal conflict between the secular and religious Jews, a conflict which plays out in the argument over Zionism or Diaspora. But when Kafka presents us with a pair of encrusted scissors and a phrase such as "divides the world in two," he is bringing up a separation so global, so deeply ingrained, that it is about more than our societal divisions. I think that for Kafka, this "great divide" is about how we have separated our species (human animals) from all the other species (nonhuman animals). Here is the great war, the ancient tribal argument that "has split the world in two."

Conclusion

If we think about this most basic duality, or "twosome," then Kafka's penchant for creating characters with ambiguous species membership takes on a new dimension. A lamb becomes a kittenlamb, with ambitions of being a dog and even a person. A group of jackals engage a narrator as their legal representative. We are not sure if another narrator is a fox or some sort of fox-human hybrid. In emphasizing the fluidity of the boundary line between us (human animals) and them (nonhuman animals), Kafka is questioning the species boundary itself. He is saying that these two tribes, the human animal and the nonhuman animal, are actually members of the same family and that we are involved in an ancient family feud. In creating animal characters that act as humans, he is asking us to consider animals as similar to other tribes with whom we have a blood quarrel. Central to the plot of "Jackals and Arabs" is the narrator's recognition of the jackals as similar to any other client worthy of respect and consideration.

In questioning this boundary, Kafka throws us headlong into issues of ethics: if species identification is ambiguous, we need to rethink our treatment of these other family members. In "Jackals and Arabs," the jackals tell the narrator that animals should not be killed, even if they are to be eaten, but allowed to die peaceful, natural deaths. This recalls the argument over *shehitah*, in that kosher slaughter is anything but peaceful, compared to being killed after being stunned. Interestingly, though, if we look at this phrase in the original German, "every beast to die a natural death,"[51] we see that the word *Getier* is used for "beast," as opposed to *Tier*. The former can be translated as creature, while the latter word is more commonly used for animal. These two words have different implications. If we are talking about family members, even if several times removed, clearly such creatures need to be allowed to die peacefully.

What gives these ethical questions about the proper treatment of other species such power is Kafka's role here, as he sees it, as a special sort of messenger. In identifying himself as the animal, Kafka saw himself as taking on a tremendous, almost impossible task. He was both an advocate for them and for himself. In "The Crossbreed," the narrator comments that this hybrid creature has found sanctuary with his family, and is part of the narrator's legacy from his father. Following the idea that the division into human and nonhuman animals is an ancient family quarrel, as well as understanding the level of identity Kafka felt with the animals, we see the deeper dimension to Kafka's statement that the kittenlamb is a family member and should not be slaughtered as we slaughter animals. The subtitle to "The Crossbreed" is "A Sport." The German word is the same. Perhaps Kafka is being ironic, suggesting that we play a game with the boundaries between species. Or he might be suggesting that what is a sport to us, playing with a kittenlamb or hunting a fox, a game for us, is deadly for the animals.[52] Thinking back to the fragment where Kafka presents a fox as a narrator, his collar and coat torn apart by the hunter, flung inside the coach next to the other men, it seems to me that Kafka felt himself in an untenable situation. Feeling marginal on so many levels, I think he felt himself to be a misfit in his own species as well: writing to Max Brod in 1912 he notes that he will be visiting the Dresden zoo, where he belongs.[53] If we experience Kafka's role as narrator in this fashion, stories such as that of the kittenlamb or the fox thrown into the carriage become even more heartbreaking and we understand our emotional, often subliminal, response to his work much better.

Kafka saw his task as showing us, through the ambiguities of narration and audience, that he is/we are these creatures that we have placed on the other side of "the great divide." The idea of humans and animals as being tribally related is of course part of evolutionary history, a physical reality. For most people, eating meat is part of our animal heritage, an expression of our being part of nature. Kafka saw this differently. For him, not eating meat came out of a deep sense of kinship. In addition, being vegetarian was not a repudiation of the natural world, but a moral stance since we have the ability to choose what we eat. This age-old question—what separates us from animals?—is both a question of biology and ethics. Barbara Noske comments on the complexity of the human and nonhuman animal border: "Human-animal relations can be approached from two angles: as human history and as natural history. *Seen as natural history* the human-animal relationship is first of all one of ancestry, of biological kinship, since it is from animals that the human species is descended [italics in original]."[54]

Kafka's acute sensitivity forced him to go far beyond where most people go. When he argues as a lawyer for better treatment of animals, he is also arguing on his own behalf. He is defending himself, or another aspect of himself.

Who he really is—that, of course, is ambiguous. In a diary entry he writes, "Always the image of a pork butcher's broad knife that quickly and with mechanical regularity chops into me from the side and cuts off very thin slices which fly off almost like shavings because of the speed of the action."[55] As usual, we can take this statement on several levels; he might be haunted by the image of an animal being destroyed, or he might be metaphorically speaking of his dismantling as a Jew in an increasingly hostile society. He could also be dramatically referring to his sense of himself as an object, someone unable to live with the intensity of his inner conflicts relating to family and occupation. In a diary entry on May 3, 1913, he writes the line, "The terrible uncertainty of my inner existence."[56]

Kafka's sense of himself as *belonging* to another species must have felt like being endlessly flayed alive. It is one thing to have empathy for animals but quite another to feel yourself one of those objects being torn apart.[57] In writing from this ambiguity of species, Kafka forces us to identify with the *other*. He is asking us to literally feel the pain of other species when they are at our mercy. If we do this, Kafka says, we necessarily begin to question our decision to create the divide between human and nonhuman animals.

Notes

1. Frederick V. Grunfeld, *Prophets without Honor: A Background to Freud, Kafka and Einstein and Their World* (New York: Holt, Rinehart and Winston, 1979), 192. A sign posted in a pub by Sudaten Germans in 1899. See Grunfeld for further discussion.

2. Franz Kafka, *Dearest Father: Stories and Other Writings* (New York: Schocken Books, 1954), 108.

3. Ronald Hayman, *Kafka: A Biography* (New York: Oxford University Press, 1982), 81.

4. Kafka, *Dearest Father*, 54.

5. Kafka, *Dearest Father*, 118.

6. Simon Ryan, "Franz Kafka's Die Verwandlung: Transformation, Metaphor, and the Perils of Assimilation," *A Journal of Germanic Studies* 29:1 (February 2007): 1–18.

7. David S. Ariel, *The Mystic Quest: An Introduction to Jewish Mysticism* (New York: Schocken Books, 1988), 12.

8. Frederick R. Karl, *Franz Kafka: Representative Man* (New York: Ticknor & Fields, 1991), 429.

9. Joyce Carol Oates, *New Heaven New Earth: The Visionary Experience in Literature* (New York: The Vanguard Press, Inc., 1974), 267.

10. Franz Kafka, *The Complete Stories*, ed. Nahum N. Glatzer (New York: Schocken Books, 1971), 426–27; Franz Kafka, *Ich habe ein eigentümliches Tier, halb Kätzchen, halb Lamm: Es ist ein Erbstuck aus mein Vaters Besitz* (Stuttgart: Philipp Reclam jun, 1995), 241.

11. I am indebted to David Greene, North Carolina State University, for consultations over the German translations.

12. Karl, *Representative Man*, 3.

13. Kafka, *Complete Stories*, 426–27.

14. Grunfeld, *Prophets without Honor*, 189.

15. Kafka, *Complete Stories*, 426–27.

16. Franz Kafka, *Letters to Milena* (New York: Schocken Books, 1953), 59.

17. Pamela S. Sur, "Civilization Versus the Animal Nature of Human Beings in Franz Kafka and Ernest Weiß," *The Journal of the Kafka Society of America* 16:2 (December 1992): 51–59.

18. Kafka, *Complete Stories*, 427. "Vielleicht wäre für dieses Tier das Messer des Fleischers eine Erlösung, die muß ich ihm aber als einem Erbstück versagen"; Kafka, *Erzählungen* (Stuttgart: Philipp Reclam jun, 1995), 243.

19. Sander Gilman, *Franz Kafka: The Jewish Patient* (London and New York: Routledge, 1995), 20.

20. Kafka, *Complete Stories*, 427.

21. Kafka, *Complete Stories*, 427.

22. Kafka, *Dearest Father*, 109.

23. Kafka, *Complete Stories*, 427.

24. Kafka, *Letters to Milena*, 198.

25. Kafka, *Dearest Father*, 134–35.

26. Huw Griffiths, Ingrid Poulter, and David Sibley, "Feral Cats in the City," in *Animal Spaces, Beastly Places: New Geographies of Human-Animal Relations*, eds. Chris Philo and Chris Wilbert (London and New York: Routledge, 2000), 58.

27. Peter U. Beicken, "Kafka's Narrative Rhetoric," *Journal of Modern Literature* 6:3 (September 1977): 398–409.

28. As quoted in Oates, *New Heaven, New Earth*, 283.

29. Sander Gillman, "Franz Kafka's Musical Diet," *Journal of Modern Jewish Studies* 4:3 (November 2005): 291–308.

30. Gilman, *Jewish Patient*, 20.

31. Kafka, *Complete Stories*, 408.

32. Kafka, *Complete Stories*, 410.

33. Kafka, *Complete Stories*, 409.

34. As quoted in Mitchell J. Morse, "Kafka and the Planing Machine," *Journal of Modern Literature* 6:3 (September 1977): 342.

35. Kafka, *Complete Stories*, 407.

36. Kafka, *Complete Stories*, 409.

37. Christina Gerhardt, "The Ethics of Animals in Adorno and Kafka," *New German Critique* 97, vol. 33:1 (Winter 2006): 159–79.

38. Kafka, *Complete Stories*, 408

39. Kafka, *Complete Stories*, 408.

40. Kafka, *Complete Stories*, 410.

41. Gilman, *Jewish Patient*, 151.

42. See Gilman, *Jewish Patient*, for a full discussion of *shehitah*.

43. Kafka, *Complete Stories*, 409.

44. Kafka, *Complete Stories*, 409.

45. The image of the rusty, blood-covered scissors is also clearly evocative of another practice that separated Jews from Gentiles involving blood—ritual circumcision. A thorough discussion of this can be found in Gilman.

46. We can recall as well the earlier comment from Kafka to Brod, admiring the workers he represented, who came to him with carefully thought-out complaints.

47. Oates, *New Heaven, New Earth*, 273.

48. "Herr, du sollst den Streit beenden, der die Welt entzweit"; Kafka, *Erzählungen*, 182.

49. Kafka, *Complete Stories*, 408.

50. Kafka, *Complete Stories*, 427. "Es muß deshalb warten, bis ihm der Atem von selbst ausgeht, wenn es mich manchmal auch wie aus verständigen Menschenaugen ansieht, die zu verständigem Tun auffordern"; Kafka, *Erzählungen*, 243.

51. Kafka, *Complete Stories*, 409. "[R]uhig soll alles Getier krepieren"; Kafka, *Erzählungen*, 182.

52. I am indebted to Brian Thomas, Duke University, for an insightful discussion of some of these issues raised in "The Crossbreed."

53. As noted in Karl, *Representative Man*, 434.

54. Barbara Noske, *Beyond Boundaries: Humans and Animals* (New York: The Vanguard Press, 1974), 1.

55. Karl, *Representative Man*, 475.

56. Franz Kafka, *I Am a Memory Come Alive: Autobiographical Writings*, ed. Nahum N. Glatzer (New York: Schocken Books, 1974), 82.

57. During the last weeks of his life, unable to talk due to advanced tuberculosis, he wrote on slips of paper. On one paper he wrote, "One must take care that the lowest flowers over there, where they have been crushed into the vase, don't suffer. How can one do that? Perhaps bowls are really the best," and on another paper he says, "How marvelous it is, do you not think so? The lilac—even though it is dying, it still drinks, still sucks in water." So not only did he identify with animals, he could go so far as to feel viscerally for a plant (Kafka, *I Am a Memory*, 246, 247).

CHAPTER 4

De-allegorizing Kafka's Ape: Two Animalistic Contexts

Naama Harel

More than any other Western writer, Franz Kafka repeatedly used nonhuman animal figures in his work. Vermin, mice, jackals, an ape, a mole-like creature, a dog, a vulture, leopards, a tiger, a horse, a marten-like animal, and a half-cat/half-lamb crossbreed all appear as protagonists in his works. Parallel to their salient place in his fiction, nonhuman animals are ubiquitous in Kafka's biographical texts as well. A reading of Kafka's diaries, biographies, and letters exposes a unique concern for nonhuman animals. For example, in a letter to his then-fiancée, Felice Bauer, Kafka wrote that he wanted to explore both human and animal communities, and to discover their basic preferences and wishes.[1] In addition, Kafka was a vegetarian—he refused to eat nonhuman animals' flesh, as his biographer, Ronald Hayman, describes:

> Kafka's vegetarianism may have had one root in revulsion at the idea of his father's father's daily activity—ritually slitting the throats of animals, hacking up their bodies, feeding his family with money earned from butchering. The butcher's knife will be recurrent in Kafka's nightmares, fantasies and fiction; the animal identifications may have seemed, at one level, like a means of making amends to the animals, or, at least, siding with them against slaughterous humanity.[2]

In spite of this prominent characteristic in Kafka's oeuvre and biography, most critics neglect the animalistic aspect of his work, and the representation of nonhuman animals in Kafka's stories is considered a mere allegory to human issues, such as parent-child relations, alienation from modern society, Judaism and Zionism, metaphysical issues, psychoanalytic ideas, and so on. The allegorical approach toward Kafka's poetics has been highly criticized for decades. Unlike typical allegories, Kafka's works have no simple allegorical key, as their literal level cannot be reduced to one specific theme. As Theodor Adorno asserted, in Kafka's work "each sentence is literal and each signifies,"[3] or as Dabney Stuart asserted,

> To ask *what does it stand for?* is to assume, it seems to me, that Kafka's short stories are, in some basic sense, allegories; that there exists, if only one could discover it, a one-to-one correspondence between details in the work and ideas with which one is familiar. This assumption is a mistake; it acts as a barrier to understanding rather than as an aid to it.[4]

Despite the well-established anti-allegorical approach, Kafka's animal stories are still interpreted mainly as allegories. Indeed, all of Kafka's nonhuman figures are anthropomorphized: they talk and behave, or at least think, in human terms. Nevertheless, unrealistic elements do not necessarily render the literal level irrelevant. Kafka's animal stories, in which nonhumans are not described realistically, raise questions on both the nonhuman condition and human-nonhuman relations. The fact that this type of question has rarely been raised is presumably a result of the critics' anthropocentrism. It seems nonhuman animals are not considered significant or interesting enough to stand as the subject of literary works and therefore they are automatically reduced to human issues. The nonhuman animal in Kafka's work has become, as phrased by Carol Adams, an absent referent, "whose fate is transmuted into a metaphor for someone else's existence or fate."[5] Alternatively, I propose reading Kafka's animal stories as representations of nonhuman animals and their relation with humans.

This chapter will focus on one of Kafka's animal stories—"A Report to an Academy" ("*Ein Bericht für eine Akademie*"), penned in 1917. At the core of the story stands Rotpeter, an ape that was captured in Africa and transported to Europe. In order to escape from a certain dismal destiny, Rotpeter decides to become human, first by imitating human beings and later via systematic learning. The entire story is a monologue, which Rotpeter holds in front of academy members who invited him to report on his previous apish life. Like the rest of Kafka's animal stories, "A Report to an Academy" was also considered an allegory for human issues. Rotpeter's transformation was interpreted as an allegory to the assimilation of Jews in Europe,[6] European colonialism in Africa,[7] conformism,[8] a common person who cannot find spirituality,[9] the loss of innocence,[10] the condition and values of humanity,[11] education as a form of brainwashing,[12] or art as inferior imitation.[13] The fact that there are so many different allegorical readings indicates that the story is not an allegory *par excellence*. Additionally, Kafka himself did not consider the story as an animal parable. In a letter to Martin Buber, the editor of *Der Jude*, the journal that published "A Report to an Academy" and "Jackals and Arabs," Kafka requested these stories not to be termed parables but "two animal stories."[14] Relying on historical and scientific contexts, I will discuss "A Report to an Academy" as an animal story, which deals with the animal condition and its relation to the human condition.

Historical Context: The Abuse of Apes

The capture of African apes, as described in "A Report to an Academy," is largely based on historical facts. References to reality, such as names of real places or people, are quite rare in Kafka's poetics. The absence of such indications reinforces the universal scope of Kafka's work. As Marthe Robert claims, Kafka uses anonymity in order to bring out their transcendent quality.[15] However, "A Report to an Academy" is exceptional in this context. Rotpeter was captured on the Golden Coast, Ghana's official name until 1957, and transported by boat to Hamburg. Hagenbeck, the name of the company that captured Rotpeter, was the real name of a leading animal trade company, which was identified in the German-speaking world at the turn of the twentieth century with wild animals.[16] This historical background was indeed mentioned by some of the story's critics,[17] but as a mere anecdote that had no significant effect on their understanding of the story.

The historian Nigel Rothfels devotes a major portion of his book about the development of the modern zoo to Carl Hagenbeck (1844–1913), who established and managed Hagenbeck Company. Rothfels indicates that Hagenbeck generated a revolution in the concept of zoos, as ever since Hagenbeck's time we are told that animals might be better off in zoos than in the wild. However, more than a major change in the imprisonment conditions of the animals, the change concerned hiding the traces of this confinement. The visitors of the huge zoo that Hagenbeck established in Hamburg in 1907 did not see bars and cages, for hidden or natural objects imprisoned the animals.[18] In this context Rotpeter's remark about zoos can be understand ironically:

> When I was handed over to my first trainer in Hamburg I soon realized that there were two alternatives before me: the Zoological Gardens or the variety stage. I did not hesitate. I said to myself: do your utmost to get onto the variety stage; the Zoological Gardens means only a new cage; once there, you are done for.[19]

It seems that Rotpeter is not impressed by Hagenbeck's propaganda. While human visitors in modern zoos might not notice the animals' imprisonment, the animals themselves are acutely aware of it. The most advanced zoo is, in Rotpeter's words, just "a new cage."

After rejecting the zoo option, show business is Rotpeter's only option. This preference is also well-anchored in Hagenbeck's biography. Rothfels tells the story of many apes that at the turn of the twentieth century, like Rotpeter, were captured in Africa and transported to Europe by Hagenbeck delegations. These apes were trained to act like humans, and like Rotpeter they performed alcohol-drinking, cigarette-smoking, hand-shaking, and other human gestures.[20] The main difference between those real apes and Kafka's fictitious ape is, of course, Rotpeter's speaking ability. Carl Hagenbeck was considered a great innovator in the field of animal circuses as well. His taming concept, as declared in his autobiography, employed humane taming methods, which included friendly treatment of the animals and affirmative feedback, instead of dominating them through techniques such as whipping and intimidating.[21]

Several seminal historical studies describe a growing sensitivity toward animals in the Western world since the Renaissance.[22] Hagenbeck's proclaimed policy suited this tendency that disapproved overt cruelty. But this harmless training policy was not applied.[23] In fact, the main innovation of Hagenbeck's zoo and circus was in the concealing of violence and cruelty from the audience. The cruelty was kept from the human eye and the public sphere, yet it still took place. In this context, we can reread the public unease to the exposure of Rotpeter's scars, which at first glance seem to be connected to Rotpeter's nudity:

> I read an article recently by one of the ten thousand windbags who vent themselves concerning me in the newspapers, saying: my ape nature is not yet quite under control; the proof being than when visitors come to see me, I have a predilection for taking down my trousers to show them where the shot went in. The hand which wrote that should have its fingers shot away one by one. As for me, I can take my trousers down before anyone if I like; you would find nothing but a well-groomed fur and the scar made—let me be particular in the choice of a word for this particular purpose, to avoid misunderstanding—the scar made by a wanton shot. Everything is open and aboveboard; there is nothing to conceal; when the plain truth is in question, great minds discard the niceties of refinement.[24]

Hagenbeck's animal businesses were so successful because they corresponded with the audience's sensitivity regarding animal cruelty by hiding the traces of violence. As long as Rotpeter wore his trousers, the scar—which is a trace of the violence—is hidden from the public eye. Its exposure causes unease as it spoils the illusion of humane treatment, which animal trainers were attempting to generate. The audience is displeased as the unentertaining aspect of the entertainment show is exposed.

Although the story contains unrealistic elements, first and foremost Rotpeter's human speech, the story of Rotpeter—as an ape who lived in Africa, was shot and captured by Hagenbeck's hunting delegation, brought by boat to

Hamburg, and there performed human gestures on stage—describes quite authentically an ape experience. For example, Rotpeter's reactions to his imprisonment are typical reactions of captured wild animals—he is panicked and anxious as any other captured wild animal would be.[25] Rotpeter's behavior is defined in the zoological terminology as "stereotypical behavior."[26] He says:

> I am supposed to have made uncommonly little noise, as I was later informed, from which the conclusion was drawn that I would either soon die or if I manage to survive the first critical period would be very amenable to training. I did survive this period. Hopelessly sobbing, painfully hunting for fleas, apathetically licking a coconut, beating my skull against the locker, sticking out my tongue at anyone who came near me—that was how I filled in time at first in my new life.[27]

The fact that captured apes died shortly after capture was a well-known phenomenon in the sciences that evolved at the turn of the twentieth century. The German zoologist Alexander Sokolowsky published in 1908 research that describes the mental lives of apes. His research focused on the death of apes a few days after they were brought from Africa to Europe. Sokolowsky claimed that the apes could not overcome the loss of freedom.[28] The loss of freedom is indeed a central theme in "A Report to an Academy." Rotpeter frequently mentions that his freedom was taken from him forever:

> I fear that perhaps you do not quite understand what I mean by "way out." I use the expression by its fullest and most popular sense. I deliberately do not use the word "freedom." I do not mean the spacious feeling of freedom on all sides. As an ape, perhaps, I knew that and I have met men who yearn for it. . . . No, freedom was not what I wanted. Only a way out; right or left, or in any direction; I made no other demand; even should the way out prove to be an illusion.[29]

Sokolowsky pointed out that after they are captured, apes become apathetic and gloomy and in many cases they hide themselves.[30] This description well fits Rotpeter's description of his first days after the capture, trying to hide himself in a box on a boat sailing to Hamburg:

> So I had to squat my knees bent and trembling all the time, and also, since probably for a time I wished to see no one, and to stay in the dark, my face was turned toward the locker while the bars of the cage cut into my flesh behind.[31]

If freedom is so essential to apes, as Sokolowsky claimed, Rotpeter is no longer an ape after he has been captured. Rotpeter stopped being an ape not as he started to adopt human behavior; he stopped being an ape once his apish freedom was taken from him. Rotpeter describes this nullifying process by using the German phrase *sich in die Büsche schlagen,*[32] which means to disappear.

Elizabeth Costello, the heroine of J. M. Coetzee's *The Lives of Animals,* suggests another historical background for Rotpeter's story. Costello notes that in 1912 the Prussian Academy of Sciences established on the island of Tenerife a station devoted to researching the mental capacities of apes, a station which operated until 1920. In 1917 the psychologist Wolfgang Köhler, one of the scientists working there, published a monograph titled *The Mentality of Apes* describing his experiments. In the conclusion of his report, which describes a research conducted during 1913 to 1917 (five years, as is the period of Rotpeter's training), Köhler wrote:

> The chimpanzees manifest intelligent behaviour of the general kind familiar in human beings. . . . Chimpanzees do not only stand out against the rest of the animal world by several morphological and, in the narrower sense, physiological, characteristics, but they also show a type of behaviour which counts as specifically human.[33]

Kafka published "A Report to an Academy" a few months later. Costello mentions that just like Köhler's apes, Rotpeter was captured in Africa by hunters specializing in the ape trade and transported by boats to a place where he was trained to behave like humans. Costello tells the story of Sultan, who was Köhler's most talented pupil, and suggests that this ape was the inspiration for Kafka when he created the figure of Rotpeter.[34]

These various contexts—Hagenbeck's zoos and circuses as well as the scientific studies of Sokolowsky and Köhler—support the reading of "A Report to an Academy" as a story about an ape who is victimized by human society. While the context of Hagenbeck's company is explicitly given in the text, the other contexts are only suggested. However, the explicit Hagenbeck context promotes the exploration of the implicit ones, as it drives the attention to the literal level of the text and to its factual dimension. The fact that Rotpeter can use a human language exceeds the factual aspect of the story, but it also enables this critical perspective, by allowing the ape telling his own story about nonhuman animals' abuse, a story that is hardly ever heard.

Scientific Context: Darwin's Evolutionary Theory

Darwin's evolutionary theory had an enormous influence on the intellectual climate in the Western world at the turn of the twentieth century. Kafka read Darwin's works at the age of sixteen and soon became an ardent follower.[35] However, unlike Kafka's other intellectual influences, the influence of Darwinian concepts on Kafka's work was hardly explored.[36] While Darwinian motives can be traced in many of Kafka's works, it seems that "A Report to an Academy," which deals with an ape that became a human being in a gradual process of adaptation, is Kafka's most Darwinian work, as some of Kafka's critics noted.[37] Like the afore-mentioned historical context, the Darwinian context also supports a reading that focuses on nonhuman existence and its relation to human existence.

In her book about Darwin's influence on nineteenth-century literature, Gillian Beer compares the concept of evolution to the concept of metamorphosis:

> "Omnia mutantur, nihil interit." Everything changes, nothing dies. Ovid's assertion in *Metamorphoses* marks one crucial distinction between the idea of metamorphosis and Darwin's theory of evolution. Darwin's theory required extinction. Death was extended from the individual organism to the whole species. Metamorphosis bypasses death. The concept expresses continuance, survival, the essential self transported but not obliterated by transformation. In some ways, evolutionary theory looks like the older concept of metamorphosis prolonged through time, transformation eked out rather than emblazoned. Both ideas seek to rationalize change but through diverse means.[38]

As "A Report to an Academy" follows an individual's change from one species to another, it fits the pattern of the metamorphosis narrative, and it was indeed defined as a metamorphosis story by some of its interpreters.[39] Yet, in many other aspects, "A Report to an Academy" is an abnormal metamorphosis narrative, even relative to Kafka's other metamorphosis story—"The Metamorphosis"—and is more applicable to the evolutionary pattern.

First, Rotpeter's changeover does not occur physically, but only mentally, while metamorphosis narratives deal with physical transformation. Indeed, unlike classic metamorphosis narratives, many modern metamorphosis narratives (such as David Garnett's *Lady into Fox* or Marie Darrieussecq's *Pig Tales*) also present a mental change, which the protagonists experience in reaction to physical changes.[40] However, physical changes are still the basis for the metamorphosis. In fact, as the term "metamorphosis" literally refers to a change in shape, Rotpeter's changeover cannot be considered a metamorphic one. Unlike metamorphosis, an evolutionary change is not necessarily concerned with anatomical change.

Second, unlike typical metamorphosis narratives and like evolution narratives, Rotpeter's change is presented as an essential act for his survival, as a reaction to a threat to existence. As Rotpeter declares, he was about to die, and in order to avoid death, he changed his species. The change from an ape to a human being is based on biological grounds since chimpanzees and human beings are evolutionarily very close. In this respect Rotpeter's changeover is distinguished from typical metamorphosis narratives, whereby the biological gap between the original creature and the creature into which he or she had transformed is much larger, and consequently, the biological probability is much smaller. In fact, Rotpeter is a human ape even before he was transformed; the German term for ape is *Menschenaffe*, which means "human-monkey."

Furthermore, unlike typical metamorphosis narratives and like evolutionary descriptions, Rotpeter's change does not occur instantaneously or overnight (as opposed to Gregor Samsa's change, for example), but was a long and gradual process that took years. The Darwinian concept of evolution requires, of course, much more than a few years, but in the social implications of Darwinism the idea of evolution within the individual over a period of a few years is acceptable. Moreover, the transformation in "A Report to an Academy" is from an animal to a human being and not vice versa, unlike most cases of metamorphosis narratives in which species transformation is involved. Eventually, by saying "to put it plainly: your life as apes, gentlemen, insofar as something of that kind lies behind you, cannot be farther removed from you than mine is from me,"[41] Rotpeter creates an analogy between his own change from an ape and the evolution of human beings.

Presenting the difference between humans and other animals as a difference of variable qualities, the Darwinian concept blurs the species barrier between humans and other animals, which is employed by Western culture. As Darwin asserted in *The Descent of Man*, "Nevertheless, the difference in mind between man and the higher animals, great as it is, is certainly one of degree and not of kind. We have seen that the senses and intuitions, the various emotions and faculties, such as love, memory, attention, curiosity, imitation, reason etc., of which man boasts, may be found in an incipient, or even sometimes in a well-developed condition, in the lower animals."[42] The difference between humans and other species is, according to Darwin, a matter of degree, and furthermore, Darwin does not describe it in terms of value. In his book about the moral implications of Darwinism, James Rachels explains:

> Adaptations are not "directed" to any particular end. There is no "more evolved" or "less evolved" in Darwinian Theory; there are only the different paths taken by different species, largely, but not entirely, in response to different environmental pressures. Natural selection is a process that, in principle, goes on forever, moving in no particular direction; it moves this way and that, eliminating some species and altering others, as environmental conditions change.[43]

And indeed, the change from an ape into a human being in "A Report to an Academy" is not described as a positive occurrence. In the last paragraph of the story, which is also the last paragraph of Rotpeter's speech to the academy, he concludes: "As I look back over my development and survey what I have achieved so far, I do not complain, but I am not complacent either."[44] This closure stands in contrast to the concept of progress. In fact, Rotpeter describes his change in terms of progress only once: "That progress of mine! How the rays of knowledge penetrated from all sides into my awakening brain! I do not deny it: I found it exhilarating."[45] However, this utterance is exceptional not only by its content, but by its style as well. The figurative language, which is abnormal in the context of Rotpeter's report, marks the utterance as inauthentic, as a cliché. Apparently, Rotpeter is trying to reflect the expectations of the academy members, and not necessarily his own thoughts. And indeed, right after this description Rotpeter goes back to his previous views regarding his change, using ordinary language: "But I must also confess: I did not overestimate it, not even then, much less now."[46]

Rotpeter does not find his evolution positive; he was not illuminated, and even after he discovered a few aspects of the human experience, he is not enthusiastic about continuing to explore it. He became human because it was his best option to survive: "I repeat: there was no attraction for me in imitating human beings; I imitated them because I needed a way out and for no other reason."[47] Rotpeter states that he managed to reach "the cultural level of an average European," without elaborating upon the specific nature of an average European. However, previously he described his "educational" process:

> It was so easy to imitate these people. I learnt to spit in the very first days. We used to spit in each other's faces; the only difference was that I licked my face clean afterwards and they did not. I could soon smoke a pipe like an old hand; and if I also pressed my thumb into the bowl of the pipe, a roar of appreciation went up between-decks; only it took me a very long time to understand the difference between a full pipe and an empty one. My worst trouble came from the schnapps bottle. The smell of it revolted me; I forced myself to it as best I could; but it took weeks for me to master my repulsion.[48]

Rotpeter, as well as the sailors on the ship, identify smoking, spitting, and alcohol-drinking with human characteristics, which Rotpeter should adopt in order to become human. Here human existence is described ironically, whereby the difference between human beings and apes is that humans smoke, spit, and drink alcohol, while apes do not. Humanity is identifiable in the story by images connected with vice and trickery. Becoming human does not require rational thinking, and certainly not moral virtues, as in his apish life Rotpeter harmed no one, while human beings shot, captured, and tortured him. According to the story, man is not the thinking animal or the creative animal, as often described in

Western culture, but simply the drinking, spitting, and smoking animal. These are the average European skills that Rotpeter acquired. He learned how to speak as well, but unlike these skills, Rotpeter does not mention speaking as a special effort for him—it was just another aspect of imitation, which he does not regard as very significant. The becoming human process is completed when at the end of the report Rotpeter describes an abusive relationship he has with a female chimpanzee. In addition to smoking, spitting, and drinking alcohol, abusing nonhuman animals is also presented as an aspect of human behavior.

"A Report to an Academy" presents an evolution narrative in which an ape evolved into a human being, but this evolution is not described in terms of progress, as expected, but in many ways as a behavioral regression. This description corresponds with Darwin's evolution theory, which is devoid of value judgment. It does not negate the Darwinian concept but only its popularized implications. The story demonstrates how the scientific claim that humans evolved from ape-like creatures does not presume that human existence is necessarily superior to animal existence. As Marian Scholtmeijer claims in her book about the influences of Darwin's revolution on animals' representation in literature:

> Human beings are not only not different in kind from other animals; they are also not sitting at the top of the evolutionary chain of being. There is no chain of being, and all living entities are in the state of equality within the indifferent workings of nature.[49]

Rotpeter as a Symbol, not a Metaphor

Using the above-mentioned contexts enables us to go back to more general interpretations, which do not necessarily focus on the condition of the non-human animal, yet do not neglect it. For example, we can view the story as a part of Kafka's work, which concerns the theme of a world without justice. The concept of punishment for a sin is undermined in Kafka's stories,[50] such as "The Metamorphosis" ("Die Verwandlung"), in which Gregor Samsa awoke one morning and found himself transformed in his bed into a gigantic insect, and in the novel The Trial, in which Josef K., without having done anything wrong, was arrested one morning. Likewise, Rotpeter did nothing wrong, yet he was suddenly shot and captured. While the occurrence in "The Metamorphosis" is totally fantastic and the one in The Trial is at least very odd and improbable, the occurrence in "A Report to an Academy," insofar as it is concerned with Rotpeter's capture, is entirely realistic and rather common. Apes in Africa, as the rest of nonhuman animals in the world, are not protected by a legal system as are humans, and many of them are indeed exposed to a sudden deprivation of their freedom. Josef K.'s last words before his execution were "like a dog!"—he identifies killing without cause, which takes place in public, with the killing of a nonhuman animal.

The philosopher Bertrand Russell phrased the idea of an immanent uncertainty. In the chapter "On Induction" in his book *The Problems of Philosophy* (1912), Russell presents the problem of induction:

> We are all convinced that the sun will rise tomorrow. Why? Is this belief a mere blind outcome of past experience, or can it be justified as a reasonable belief? . . . We have a firm belief that it will rise in the future, because it has risen in the past. If we are challenged as to why we believe that it will continue to rise as heretofore, we may appeal to the laws of motion. . . . The interesting doubt is as to whether the laws of motion will remain in operation until tomorrow. . . . . The man who has fed the chicken every day throughout its life at last wrings its neck instead, showing that more refined views as to the uniformity of nature would have been useful to the chicken.[51]

As a chicken can be slaughtered one day, in contrast with any past experience, so can an ape be shot and captured. The conditions of nonhuman animals well illustrate the idea of uncertainty in both Russell's and Kafka's texts. But at least in the case of Rotpeter, the nonhuman animal's condition is not merely a means to an end; it is not an absent referent. Rotpeter, as a nonhuman animal, is the prototype, the most salient example, for the idea of uncertainty and the absence of a fair system of sin and punishment. He is not a metaphor for innocent victim, but he is the ultimate example of such.

Conclusion

"A Report to an Academy" is not a realistic story, which authentically describes an ape's life. In fact, most of Kafka's works do not purport to be realistic. But from this recognition we cannot conclude that the representation of the nonhuman animal figure, which stands at the core of the text, should be reduced to human figures and themes. Although the story does not reproduce an ape's life authentically, by using historical and scientific intertexts the fantastic scenario has implications and relevance to our real world. These implications include criticizing the human abuse of nonhuman animals and drawing into question human superiority as well as human separation from other animals, apes in particular. In opposition to Carol Adams's "absent referent" concept, in Kafka's poetics the nonhuman animals are "present referents"—their function on a thematic level is inseparable from their function on a literal level.

Notes

1. Franz Kafka, *Letters to Felice*, trans. James Stern and Elisabeth Duckworth, ed. Erich Heller and Jürgen Born (New York: Schocken Books, 1973), 545.

2. Ronald Hayman, *K: A Biography of Kafka* (London: Weidenfeld and Nicolson, 1981), 31.

3. Theodor W. Adorno, "Notes on Kafka," in *Franz Kafka*, ed. Harold Bloom (New York: Chelsea House Publishers, 1986), 96.

4. Dabney Stuart, "Kafka's 'A Report to an Academy': An Exercise in Method," *Studies in Short Fiction* 6 (1969), 413.

5. Carol Adams, *The Sexual Politics of Meat: A Feminist-Vegetarian Critical Theory* (New York: Continuum, 1995), 42.

6. Elizabeth Boa, *Kafka: Gender, Class, and Race in the Letters and Fictions* (Oxford: Oxford University Press, 1996), 158–63; Andreas Kilcher and Detlef Kremer, "Die Genealogie der Schrift: Eine Transtextuelle Lektüre von Kafka's *Bericht für eine Akademie*," in *Textverkehr: Kafka und die Tradition*, ed. Claudia Liebrand and Franziska Schößler (Würzburg: Köningshausen & Neumann, 2004), 63–70.

7. Richard A. Barney, "Between Swift and Kafka: Animals and the Politics of Coetzee's Elusive Fiction," *World Literature Today* 78:1 (2004), 19; Walter Sokel, *The Myth of Power and the Self: Essays on Franz Kafka* (Detroit: Wayne State University Press, 2002), 268.

8. Roy Pascal, *Kafka's Narrators: A Study of His Stories and Sketches* (Cambridge: Cambridge University Press, 1982), 194.

9. Herbert Tauber, *Franz Kafka: An Interpretation of His Works*, trans. G. Humphreys Roberts and Roger Senhouse (London: Secker & Warburg, 1948), 70.

10. Robin Blyn, "From Stage to Page: Franz Kafka, Djuna Barnes, and Modernism's Freak Fictions," *Narrative* 8:2 (2000), 140–41; Helmut Richter, *Franz Kafka: Werk und Entwurf* (Berlin: Rütten & Loening, 1962), 158.

11. Susanne Kessler, *Kafka: Poetik der sinnlichen Welt* (Stuttgart: Metzler, 1983), 20.

12. Patrick Bridgwater, *Kafka and Nietzsche* (Bonn: Bouvier Verlag Herbert Grundmann, 1974), 131.

13. Margot Norris, *Beasts of the Modern Imagination: Darwin, Nietzsche, Kafka, Ernst and Lawrence* (Baltimore: Johns Hopkins University Press, 1985), 68; Sokel, *The Myth of Power and the Self*, 288; Allen Thiher, *Franz Kafka: A Study of the Short Fiction* (Boston: Twayne Publishers, 1990), 82.

14. Hayman, *K: A Biography of Kafka*, 219.

15. Marthe Robert, *Franz Kafka's Loneliness*, trans. Ralph Manheim (London: Faber & Faber, 1982), 5.

16. Nigel Rothfels, *Savages and Beasts: The Birth of the Modern Zoo* (Baltimore and London: Johns Hopkins University Press, 2002), 45–49.

17. Boa, *Kafka: Gender, Class, and Race in the Letters and Fictions*, 159; Ralf R. Nicolai, "Nietzschean Thought in Kafka's 'A Report to an Academy,'" *Literary Review* 26:4 (1983), 557; Norris, *Beasts of the Modern Imagination*, 66.

18. Rothfels, *Savages and Beasts*, 162–76, 199.

19. Franz Kafka, "A Report to an Academy," trans. Willa and Edwin Muir, in *The Complete Stories*, ed. Nahum N. Glatzer (New York: Schocken Books, 1983), 257–58.

20. Rothfels, *Savages and Beasts*, 212.

21. Carl Hagenbeck, *Von Tieren und Menschen. Erlebnisse und Erfahrungen*, edited and revised by Lorenz Hagenbeck (Düsseldorf: Vier Falken Verlag, 1950), 136–39.

22. Harriet Ritvo, *The Animal Estate: The English and Other Creatures in the Victorian Age* (Cambridge, MA: Harvard University Press, 1987); Keith Thomas, *Man and the Natural World: Changing Attitudes in England 1500–1800* (Oxford: Oxford University Press, 1996); James Turner, *Reckoning with the Beast: Animals, Humanity and Pain in the Victorian Mind* (Baltimore: Johns Hopkins University Press, 2000).

23. Rothfels, *Savages and Beasts*, 156–57.

24. Kafka, *The Complete Stories*, 251–52.

25. Michael L. Rettinger, *Kafkas Berichterstatter: Anthropologische Reflexionen zwischen Irritation und Reaktion, Wirklichkeit und Perspektive* (Frankfurt am Main: Peter Lang, 2003), 26.

26. Stephen St. C. Bostock, *Zoos and Animal Rights: The Ethics of Keeping Animals* (London: Routledge, 1993), 88–89.

27. Kafka, *The Complete Stories*, 252–53.

28. Alexander Sokolowsky, *Beobachungen über die Psyche der Menschenaffen* (Frankfurt: Neuer Frankfurter Verlag, 1908), 17–18.

29. Kafka, *The Complete Stories*, 253–54.

30. Sokolowsky, *Beobachungen über die Psyche der Menschenaffen*, 21.

31. Kafka, *The Complete Stories*, 252.

32. Franz Kafka, *Die Erzählungen* (Frankfurt am Main: Fischer Taschenbuch Verlag, 2003), 332.

33. Wolfgang Köhler, *The Mentality of Apes*, trans. Ella Winter (Harmondsworth, UK: Penguin Books, 1957), 226.

34. J. M. Coetzee, *The Lives of Animals* (Princeton, NJ: Princeton University Press, 2001), 27–30.

35. Hayman, *K: A Biography of Kafka*, 26; Klaus Wagenbach, *Franz Kafka: Eine Biographie seiner Jugend 1883–1912* (Bern: Francke, 1958), 60.

36. Leena Eilittä, *Approaches to Personal Identity in Kafka's Short Fiction: Freud, Darwin, Kierkegaard* (Helsinki: Academia Scientiarum Fennica, 1999), 112.

37. Boa, *Kafka: Gender, Class, and Race in the Letters and Fictions*, 158–60; Kilcher and Detlef, "Die Genealogie der Schrift," 61; Norris, *Beasts of the Modern Imagination*, 67; Walter Sokel, *Franz Kafka: Tragik und Ironie: Zur Struktur seiner Kunst* (Munich: Albert Langen, 1964), 383; Thiher, *Franz Kafka: A Study of the Short Fiction*, 82.

38. Gillian Beer, *Darwin's Plots: Evolutionary Narrative in Darwin, George Eliot and Nineteenth-Century Fiction* (Cambridge: Cambridge University Press, 2000), 104.

39. D. B. D. Asker, *Aspect of Metamorphosis: Fictional Representations of the Becoming Human* (Amsterdam: Rodopi, 2001), 58; Kilcher and Detlef, "Die Genealogie der Schrift," 63; Norris, *Beasts of the Modern Imagination*, 66; Sokel, *The Myth of Power and the Self*, 284; Stuart, "Kafka's 'A Report to an Academy,'" 414–15.

40. Naama Harel, "Challenging the Species Barrier in Metamorphosis Literature: The Case of Marie Darrieussecq's *Pig Tales*," *Comparative Critical Studies* 2:3 (2005), 400.

41. Kafka, *The Complete Stories*, 250.

42. Charles Darwin, "The Descent of Man, and Selection in Relation to Sex," in *The Portable Darwin*, ed. Duncan M. Porter and Peter W. Graham (New York: Penguin, 1993), 328–29.

43. James Rachels, *Created from Animals: The Moral Implications of Darwinism* (Oxford: Oxford University Press, 1999), 64–65.

44. Kafka, *The Complete Stories*, 258.

45. Ibid.

46. Ibid.

47. Ibid., 257.

48. Ibid., 255–56.

49. Marian Scholtmeijer, *Animal Victims in Modern Fiction: From Sanctity to Sacrifice* (Toronto: University of Toronto Press, 1993), 56.

50. Pascal, *Kafka's Narrators*, 137.

51. Bertrand Russell, *The Problems of Philosophy* (Oxford: Oxford University Press, 1959), 33–35.

CHAPTER 5

Agents of the Forgotten: Animals as the Vehicles of Shame in Kafka

Tahia Thaddeus Reynaga

> Ignorance is, in fact, man's privilege. Neither God nor beast is ignorant—the former because he possesses all knowledge, the latter because he needs none.[1]

A few years back, somewhere in the environs of Delta, Alabama, a young boy brought down a feral hog, the monstrous size of which was sure to chasten any previous record holders, and yet others came forward with trophy kills to overshadow it. In an area equally remote and conducive to the flourishing of giant game, another hog surfaced, with proportions as large, if not larger, than the specimen from Alabama. Both of these creatures had already met their demises, and so their actual dimensions, not so easily confirmed, were further veiled by reports of hunters keen to promote, and even inflate, their prowess. One beast had even been decomposing for three years prior, so how was an assessor to render an accurate measurement? Fortunately for the public, vested as it is in evidence that Jurassic-sized brutes still crash through the brambles of the American South, photographs had been taken of the fresh kill. In them, this boy poses victoriously with his quarry and now with his quarry's skull, and while the precise dimensions seem to be a bit exaggerated, we may only fault the usual distortion brought about by inconvenient camera angles and lighting, which itself does not amount to deception. Even if it were only that the soil in these parts is particularly rich with nutrients, and that the brooks flow with an especially generous dose of minerals, there is something to be said for feral hogs that total over ten feet from snout to tail. Still, though, the challenges rise up from the locals, and even those in distant cities, where subway cars are five times the size of this supposed giant, question the natural occurrence of such creatures. A farmer, who himself was no stranger to aberrant products of the natural process, summoned all of his experience and wisdom: this feral hog was not feral at all! Surely someone had lavished years of devoted attention on its rearing, and, soft with domestication, it met an unfortunate but purely accidental end; it was only, after all, a lost pet.[2]

So it is that the unbelievable exploit of a young hunter has come to be disbelieved, with little more than transitory fame to haunt him. What was particularly elucidating were the vitriolic comments that had been addressed to the unfortunate boy on the website his father established to celebrate his son's supposed success. While the majority of his detractors decried the hunt itself, one faultfinder fingered the boy's father and his father's father, censuring the patriarchs of this otherwise inconsequential family for the blood lust with which the son had been unmercifully inculcated.[3] And so what likely began as a recreational hunting excursion for father and son came to be a font of shame and global opprobrium for the son condemned to answer for the velleities of the father. Perhaps someday, when the boy has become feeble with age, an enterprising young academic will attempt, with wholehearted sincerity, to resuscitate the hunter's good name and pride. If so, he may find himself, like Kafka's narrator in "The Village Schoolmaster," yoked to an oppressive and inescapable legacy of humiliation. The questionable size of the dubiously feral hog will be as forgotten as the glory of the hunt; only discomfiture and disgrace will remain.

Who, then, shares the plight of the protagonist in Kafka? Who may bear witness to his tribulations, to his futile engagements with the law and the legions of fathers whose collective existence snuffs out his own? Fraternity eludes him (the hunger artist suffers the public's boredom with his art), and women, whose initial appeal is mitigated by the layers of dust encrusted into their finery, reject him (with the rebuff being made even worse by their overall repugnancy).[4] We know how the law isolates him, and legends proffer no elucidating answers ("There remained the inexplicable mass of rock").[5] Mankind, the true protagonist in all of Kafka's works, does not come up against a single foe; not one, but a multitude of devils assaults him.[6] Is there an expiatory God-man who will join in this fate? "The Messiah will come only when he is no longer necessary; he will come only on the day after his arrival; he will come, not on the last day, but on the very last."[7] Even filth, the one constant companion of Kafka's protagonists, "exists for its own sake,"[8] clinging as disinterestedly and as injuriously as a barnacle on a ship's hull.

Animals, however, mark the greatest disappointment in Kafka. This disappointment arises from the recognition that dualisms exist, that there are purifying right and unchallengeable wrong, piety and cynical disbelief, hope and despair, but all that is desirable will always remain beyond reach to mankind, which remains, by its fallen nature, forever unreconciled with the good. Original sin for the protagonist is the albatross that subsumes the place of the cross around his neck. (More appropriately, the visitation of sin upon the son is as seemingly arbitrary and unanswerable as the flight of the Ancient Mariner's crossbow.) The guilt incurred is the same, though, except that there is penance to be done for Coleridge's protagonist, renouncement with the promise of redemptive atonement to follow. Kafka's animals live in pitiful disconnect from their ancestors, too, and on this premise alone one would imagine that they would comfort the protagonists with commiseration, if nothing more. Their inability to save themselves does not rupture them as it does their human counterparts, however; they are not ignorant because they have no need of knowledge. They suffer, it is true, but their malaise is a preexisting condition, and they are nearly comfortable with it: "What corruption is in the law, anxiety is in their thinking."[9] Through their familiarity with anxiety, they underline the protagonist's pathetic lack of preparedness to receive his fate. Improbable as its presence there may be, the animal remains in the synagogue,[10] the leopards endure in the Temple,[11] but Joseph K. is impassively dismissed from the cathedral by the priest, who wants nothing of him.[12]

Thus, there is a great sympathy in Kafka for the maladapted wanderer (only the animals seem habituated to the perpetual state of anxiety in which they are immersed), for him who tours perfunctorily through foreign lands and experiences that really are his own. The "purity and beauty"[13] of Kafka's "failure"[14] lies in the fact it is absolute and as unavoidable as one's own self; to relocate the locus of the tragedy would be to admit of extenuating circumstances, in which case the damnation could not be complete. This is why Gregor Samsa's metamorphosis must happen in the family home, in his bedroom, in his bed, his only personal place and therefore his last refuge.[15] The tragically rare moments of comfort for Gregor come when he sinks into his animal identity, when he relinquishes his hold on his human past:

> so that for mere recreation he had formed the habit of crawling criss-cross over the walls and ceiling. He especially enjoyed hanging suspended from the ceiling; it was much better than lying on the floor; one could breathe more freely; one's body swung and rocked lightly; and in the almost blissful absorption induced by this suspension it could happen to his own surprise that he let go and fell plump on the floor. Yet he now had his body much better under control than formerly, and even such a big fall did him no harm.[16]

The inversion of coordinates here mirrors the inversion of natural states that occurs in the metamorphosis, which ultimately stands as the near-salvific path Gregor is condemned to follow. He liberates his family (and is liberated from them) when he assumes animal form, proving that man, as long as he remains a man, may not achieve salvation in Kafka's work. In arguably the most moving passage in the author's body of work, Gregor's slipping away is presented as a selfless and total outpouring of love for his family:

> He thought of his family with tenderness and love. The decision that he must disappear was one that he held to even more strongly than his sister, if that were possible. In this state of vacant and peaceful meditation he remained until the tower clock struck three in the morning. The first broadening of light in the world outside the window entered his consciousness once more. Then his head sank to the floor of its own accord and from his nostrils came the last faint flicker of his breath.[17]

Evoked here are two highly significant moments of self-sacrifice: those of John the Baptist and of Christ. The former appears as the prophet who must decrease as He must increase,[18] and accordingly, Gregor must die for the family to live. At the same time, Gregor parallels Christ, as evidenced by the fact that he expires at 3 a.m., the inverse of the Holy Hour (3 p.m.), the hour at which Christ died on the Cross; also like Christ, he gives himself over for the fulfilment of others. There is, then, a salvation of sorts that occurs for the Samsa family that is engendered by the wilful sacrifice of Gregor, but as the hour of his death is inverted, so is the nature of the hero's salvific power. Gregor cannot, even with sterling intentions, save his family so long as he remains a son to his father. It is only through his metamorphosis into a scavenging vermin that he achieves what Gregor *qua* son could not: an escape from the bonds of family oppression. In his lesser (animal) state of existence, he manages to slip through the yoke that harnessed him and kept him tethered to his father as a failed son. In throwing off his human form and assuming that of the vermin, he dies a tranquil and sweet death, not condemned because he no longer has any need of salvation. While it is true that a happy ending eludes Gregor (there is no such thing in Kafka), the ending that comes is, in Kafka's terms, the best possible. The passages that follow his death describe the liberation that ensues for the Samsa family. "Now thanks be to God," Mr. Samsa proclaims, crossing himself as Catholics do upon receiving a blessing.[19] The lodgers are summarily dismissed, each family member notifies his or her employer that the day will be taken as a vacation, the decision is made to let go of the bothersome charwoman, and Grete begins her own metamorphosis into womanhood. Even the air, often so putrid and stifling in Kafka's stories, is cleansed: "Although it was so early in the morning a certain softness was perceptible in the fresh air."[20]

What is most notable about Gregor's demise, necessary as it is for the positive denouement of the story, is that it is predicated upon a retrogression. Regarding the evolutionary place of animals in Kafka, Benjamin observes, "the world of ancestors took him down to the animals. . . . They are not the goal, to be sure, but one cannot do without them."[21] As was the case with a number of artists and writers of the modernist era, the primitive signified an unadulterated existence which, though bestial, was nevertheless more immediate and more pure than that experienced by contemporary man.[22] The tragedy that Kafka lays bare time and time again is the disconnect contemporary man suffers from his ancestors; the miserable relations between fathers and sons underline this point. Animals, though "not the goal,"[23] are the extant forms of the ancestral heritage from which he finds himself estranged. Eternal condemnation does not mark them as it does the protagonists, and so while they exist in a prelapsarian state, or perhaps even in a postlapsarian state with the possibility of salvation held out to them, salvation is of no consequence to them. The irony surrounding them may be likened to that of the doorkeeper in "Before the Law," who himself may gain entry as an agent of the law, but who has no need of it precisely because he is its agent. This is all to say that the utter failure of Kafka's protagonists is significantly enhanced by the presence of the animals, which are less the "receptacles of the forgotten"[24] than its agents.

Two short stories in particular elucidate the more nefarious nature of animals in Kafka: "A Crossbreed [A Sport]" and "The Cares of a Family Man." The first concerns the titular creature, both kitten and lamb, which inhabits the family home and fixes itself to the narrator. From the second sentence of the piece ("It is a legacy from my father"),[25] we infer that the crossbreed is somewhat of an unwelcome presence—at the very least, a compromised one—for all things inherited from the fathers in Kafka are of detriment to the sons. The creature has undergone a metamorphosis, having "only developed in my time" into a chimera more evenly split into its constituent personalities.[26] The questions the crossbreed invites go unanswered by the narrator, who in his ignorance of the answers is "confine[d]" to the mere display of his "possession."[27] Yet as we know with Kafka, power is often exerted against the narrators from unlikely sources. As the narrative continues, it becomes apparent that the crossbreed begets much consternation and apprehension. Its fidelity to the family is likely insincere; not unlike a parasite, it gathers protection and sustenance from its keeper, and thus protects its own interests as it pretends to fulfil those of the narrator, who somewhat wistfully reports, "I did not inherit much from my father, but this legacy is quite remarkable."[28] It is only in the last paragraph, however, that the extremism which marks the narrator's relationship to his "pet" surfaces:

> Perhaps the knife of the butcher would be a release for this animal; but as it is a legacy I must deny it that. So it must wait until the breath voluntarily leaves its body, even though it sometimes gazes at me with a look of human understanding, challenging me to do the thing of which both of us are thinking.[29]

Rather than be enhanced by this "remarkable" legacy, the narrator is enslaved by it and in turn shackled to his father, who from another realm reminds his son not so much of his ancestral past, but rather of his disconnect from it, a disconnect exemplified by the narrator's disappointing lack of knowledge about his crossbreed. What is worse, there is no resolution on the horizon, no means by which these two characters, their fates forced upon one another by the omnipotent father, may escape the other. Still, anxiety seems to lie completely with the narrator, who finds himself challenged, even though it is the crossbreed facing extermination.

Kafka advances the despondency of this situation in "The Cares of a Family Man," in which the eponymous figure is doomed to share his house with Odradek, the most primitive of all Kafka's creatures. The etymology of his name remains uncertain, but its implied Slavonic origin suggests a linguistically distant source. His corporal composition is primeval:

> At first glance it looks like a flat star-shaped spool for thread, and indeed it does seem to have thread wound upon it; to be sure, they are only old, broken-off bits of thread, knotted and tangled together, of the most varied sorts and colors. But it is not only a spool, for a small wooden crossbar sticks out of the middle of the star, and another small rod is joined to that at a right angle. By means of this latter rod on one side and one of the points of the star on the other, the whole thing can stand upright as if on two legs.[30]

Odradek is so ancient as to be prehistoric, lacking as he does any physical symmetry, radial or bilateral. His appearance is haphazard, he exists as a collection of remnants of unknown origins, and, as the most burdensome of Kafka's creatures, he is strewn with refuse. He is not, we learn, a "broken-down remnant," but rather "in [his] own way perfectly finished,"[31] the perfect foil to the titular hero of the story, whose distinction as a family man is now challenged, for the rest of time, by this unwelcome inhabitant of his home. As Benjamin points out, Odradek "prefers the same places as the court of law which investigates guilt."[32] Feeling obliged, the narrator speaks to him when he is in his midst, inclined to address him in simple terms, "treat[ing] him . . . rather like a child."[33] Yet this son is the father of the man, and another of Kafka's protagonists is vanquished by a patriarchal legacy, the ancientness of which he cannot even begin to comprehend or approach. He may recognize aspects of Odradek, such as his laughter, "but it is only the kind of laughter that has no lungs behind it. It sounds rather like the rustling of fallen leaves."[34] The conversation ends there, with the narrator having been outdone by the remoteness of his neighbor, a neighbor in physical proximity only, otherwise removed by eons on the evolutionary spectrum.

As with the crossbreed, the family man is defeated by the enduring presence of prehistory incarnate. Odradek, unbalanced by his very nature and purpose, will not die, if we understand death to be an attainment of perfect equilibrium—no further momentum in one direction or another, but absolute rest. The narrator concludes the same: "Anything that dies has had some kind of aim in life, some kind of activity, which has worn out; but that does not apply to Odradek."[35] This existence is not unlike that of viruses, which do not quite approximate life as we understand it to be. Like a viral particle, Odradek requires his family man to serve as a host, observing his presence and giving testimony to it, offering him the means by which he may perpetuate his influence through history (the narrator is aware that his children and his children's children will be afflicted with this creature). Fathers pass Odradek and the crossbreed to the sons like judgment, and the family man is as incapable of breaking the legacy as he is of receiving it. In their sentient presence, these creatures seduce the protagonists into adopting them as legacies to be passed on, and so it is that these "animals" become agents of the forgotten rather than just receptacles of it.

These figures from an unknowable beyond are encountered not in some foreign locale, but rather in the bosom of the family home. This point is critical, for it emphasizes the son's defeat by the father and the citizen's defeat by the law, both of which are failures of an archetypal magnitude. As Benjamin writes, "Once he [Kafka] was certain of eventual failure, everything worked out for him *en route* as in a dream,"[36] and certainly Odradek and his primitive counterpart, the crossbreed, hail from a phantasmagoric dream world where the only certainty is the ruination of the protagonist: "Only this everlasting waiting, eternal helplessness,"[37] as Kafka wrote in reflection of his own despondency.

In a similar vein is "Blumfeld, An Elderly Bachelor," the hero of which is not a family man but a bachelor confronted with two inexplicable celluloid balls that have moored themselves to him. Particularly confounding is the origin of these animate objects; they have not reached Blumfeld through a patriarchal lineage or through the law, as Odradek and the crossbreed have. The failure here, then, is even more extreme, for even in bachelorhood Blumfeld is forced to adopt "the cares of a family man," though with no recourse to the sharing of the burden with progeny.[38] The story begins with him pondering his desire for companionship; a "little dog," he fathoms, could provide him with the company he seeks. Immediately, however, he discredits the suitability of such a pet, for Blumfeld, like many of Kafka's protagonists, has a very modern desire for sanitization. His struggle for cleanliness is, as with the other protagonists, a repudiation of the oppressive code of law that establishes the rule in Kafka's fiction (the law is always marked by decrepitude and filth, accumulated during the eons of its existence). A dog, he admits, would most certainly bring with it the feculence typically reserved for agents of the courts. So, having decided against a dog, Blumfeld makes his way to his room; however,

> [h]e is not prepared for what he sees. For this is magic—two small white celluloid balls with blue stripes jumping up and down side by side on the parquet; when one of them touches the floor the other is in the air, a game they continue ceaselessly to play. . . . They are undoubtedly ordinary balls, they probably contain several smaller balls, and it is these that produce the rattling sound. Blumfeld gropes in the air to find out whether they are hanging from some threads—no, they are moving entirely on their own. A pity Blumfeld isn't a small child, two balls like these would have been a happy surprise for him, whereas now the whole thing gives him rather an unpleasant feeling. It's not quite pointless after all to live in secret as an unnoticed bachelor, now someone, no matter who, has penetrated this secret and sent him these two strange balls.[39]

These celluloid balls are not living creatures, though like viruses, perhaps they self-activate only when in the presence of a host. Their spherical form is the most rudimentary of all these prehistoric visitors, but their substance, celluloid, is a purely modern, industrial product. So it is that these celluloid balls stand beyond the evolutionary spectrum. Their arrival is a disappointment for the bachelor, as he acknowledges that they have come to him decades too late. His anxiety regarding the balls puts him in the company of those perpetual wanderers Joseph K. (*The Trial*) and K. (*The Castle*) and any number of the other protagonists who never seem to be at the right moment in history. It is even more disconcerting that "someone, no matter who, has penetrated" Blumfeld's otherwise unnoticed existence, and he is powerless to rectify his situation; the impossibility of escaping one's fate is the corollary of the perfection of failure in Kafka.[40]

If figures like Odradek, the crossbreed, and these celluloid balls are the harbingers of the narrator's defeat, then it is critical to note how absolute their existence is. The first two, we learn, are prehistoric enough as to be eternal, and the family men recognize that they will long be outlived by these creatures. While there is no necessity for these beasts to pour their essence into progeny (they are potent enough to exact defeat by themselves), the celluloid balls hold within themselves other balls, thus punctuating their power over Blumfeld. Similarly, as written in "The Invention of the Devil," there is a multitude of devils assailing mankind:

> If we are possessed by the devil, it cannot be by one, for then we should live, at least here on earth, quietly, as with God, in unity, without contradiction, without reflection, always sure of the man behind us. . . . Only a crowd of devils could account for our earthly

misfortunes. Why don't they exterminate one another until only a single one is left, or why don't they subordinate themselves to one great devil? Either way would be in accord with the diabolical principle of deceiving us as completely as possible. With unity lacking, of what use is the scrupulous attention all the devils pay us? It simply goes without saying that the falling of a human hair must matter more to the devil than to God, since the devil really loses that hair and God does not. But as long as many devils are in us that still does not help us arrive at any state of well-being.[41]

Vermin teem in Kafka's world, from the "monstrous vermin" (*ungeheuren Ungeziefer*)[42] into which Gregor Samsa metamorphoses to the mice and rats that populate other stories. The most disgusting products of creation are found in the greatest abundance in Kafka—the court officials, the children, the jackals—and their prolificacy mocks the solitude of the protagonists,[43] among whom, even with the family men, there is no virility or worth to be found. The protagonists may be tempted to engage single specimens of the vermin in struggle, but in their large animal societies, they are incapable of defeat, as the doorkeeper before the law warns the man: "If you are so drawn to it, just try to go in despite my veto. But take note: I am powerful. And I am only the least of the doorkeepers. From hall to hall there is one doorkeeper after another, each more powerful that the last."[44, 45]

As challenging as the presence of these animals may be to Kafka's protagonists, there appears in "Jackals and Arabs" a near rapprochement between the two, but, as may be expected, the failure of the union highlights yet again the ever-repeating condemnation by which man will forever be chastised. The narrator, displaced from his homeland in the North and thus travelling as a foreign companion with nomadic Arabs, awakens to find himself surrounded by a "swarming" pack of jackals who petition him as their savior. Here, perhaps, is an alliance about to form between man and beast against the putridity and brutality that characterizes life after the Fall, for the jackals ask that the man from the north end for them

> this quarrel that divides the world. You are exactly the man whom our ancestors foretold as born to do it. We want to be troubled no more by Arabs; room to breathe; a skyline cleansed of them; no more bleating of sheep knifed by an Arab; every beast to die a natural death; no interference till we have drained the carcass empty and picked its bones clean. Cleanliness, nothing but cleanliness is what we want.[46]

Here is a rare instance in which a being other than the protagonist yearns for cleanliness, which translates into a desire for clarity, pureness of soul, and, by extension, proximity to God. Of course, Kafka's men face obfuscation, moral degradation, and the consequences of their fallen state, so it is curious, if not outright suspicious, that the jackals would seek salvation from such a figure. Nevertheless, they must have been pursuing this futile recruitment for some time; ancient Egyptian mythology establishes that jackals and Arabs have danced around one another in legend for thousands of years.[47] As with any number of Kafka's protagonists, the jackals are incapable of saving themselves from what terrorizes them, and they even revolt against the suggestion that they spill blood themselves. Rather, they importune the narrator to slit the throats of his travelling companions with a pair of sewing scissors, which are ceremoniously introduced "dangling from an eyetooth."[48] The feckless jackals have now revealed their impotence, and accordingly, the Arab leader breaks forth and disperses the unsavory creatures. He dispels any hope the man has of his own importance: "So long as Arabs exist, that pair of scissors goes wandering through the desert and will wander with us to the end of our days. Every European is offered it for the great work; every European is just the man that Fate has chosen for them."[49] In this story, the Arabs equate to the animals found elsewhere in Kafka's works, for they appear as remnants of the primitive that have not succumbed to the disconnect experienced by modern ("European") man. In the end, both the jackals and the Arabs comfortably revert to their respective natural states, while the man from the North is left alone once again, assaulted by the repulsive scene before him as the jackals reduce the camel carcass to a mutilated body soaking in pools of blood.[50]

Conclusion

In all these stories, what has been lost—or rather, ruptured—is man's connection to his pure self, a seamless bond he once enjoyed before the Fall.[51] The Arabs evince wisdom commensurate with their primitive needs. The jackals, in spite of their brief forays outside of themselves, easily revert to their natural state. Only the protagonist remains, far from home, unknown and unknowing, forever removed from his ancestors with no possibility of reconciling himself with God. The vitality with which man used to brim is now to be found only in the animals, and in this way, they mockingly remind him of his fallen state. They exude what he used to enjoy, and they do not even have need of God, though they are much closer to enjoying Heaven if they wish than any of the protagonists are.[52] Animals are the extant representatives of man's primitive state, their bestial vitality having once been shared by his ancestors.[53] In his modern incarnation, man is a neurasthenic cipher, forever dispossessed, subject to condemnation as he dreams of Heaven: "Men did not die, but became mortal; they did not become like God, but received the indispensable capacity to become so. . . . Man did not die, but the paradisiacal man did; men did not become God, but divine knowledge."[54] If eternal rest is preferred, man is denied it. He relives "the expulsion from Paradise" *ad infinitum*.[55]

> Consequently the expulsion from Paradise is final, and life in this world irrevocable, but the eternal nature of the occurrence (or, temporally expressed, the eternal recapitulation of the occurrence) makes it nevertheless possible that not only could we live continuously in Paradise, but that we are continuously there in actual fact, no matter whether we know it here or not.[56]

This is Kafka's mortality, a history configured as a circle, in which the expulsion recurs while the possibility of reconciliation is preserved (though never achieved). Herein lies the startling tragedy of his drama, in which mankind reverberates in Limbo with Heaven still in his view. This is, after all, the landscape of Limbo, where salvation thus far denied may yet visit the soul:

> He is a free and secure citizen of the world, for he is fettered to a chain which is long enough to give him the freedom of all earthly space, and yet only so long that nothing can drag him past the frontiers of the world. But simultaneously he is a free and secure citizen of Heaven as well, for he is also fettered by a similarly designed heavenly chain. So that if he heads, say, for the earth, his heavenly collar throttles him, and if he heads for Heaven, his earthly one does the same.[57]

Afflicted with the "indispensable capacity to become [like God],"[58] yet forever expelled from the heavenly realm, man is a wanderer who retains a faded and dog-eared photograph of a home to which he will never return. His original sin has engendered his detachment from his "paradisiacal" core, and his Sisyphean sentence is to bear witness to his own fall, to hear over and again the sentence of his excommunication. The presence of the animals taunts and challenges him, as does the presence of the patriarchs, but whereas the latter is the punishment incurred by the Fall (the expulsion from Eden becomes translated in estrangement from God the Father and therefore all fathers), the former is the consequence of estrangement from himself.

Notes

1. José Ortega y Gasset, "The Self and the Other," in *The Dehumanization of Art and Other Writings on Art and Culture*, trans. Willard R. Trask (Garden City, NY: Doubleday Anchor Books, 1956), 178.

2. For photographs of Jamison Stone and the prize kill seen around the world, I refer the reader to www.monsterpig.com, a website created by Jamison's father, Mike Stone.

3. Official website referencing Jamison Stone and his giant hog, www.monsterpig.com (3 June 2007). Comments section of site now discontinued.

4. Franz Kafka, "Rejection," in *Franz Kafka, The Complete Stories*, ed. Nahum N. Glatzer, trans. Willa and Edwin Muir (New York: Schocken Books, 1995), 383–84.

5. Kafka, "Prometheus," in *Franz Kafka, The Complete Stories*, ed. Nahum N. Glatzer, trans. Willa and Edwin Muir (New York: Schocken Books, 1995), 432.

6. Kafka, "The Invention of the Devil," in *Franz Kafka, Parables and Paradoxes*, ed. Nahum N. Glatzer, trans. Clement Greenberg (New York: Schocken Books, 1987), 119.

7. Kafka, "The Coming of the Messiah," in *Franz Kafka, Parables and Paradoxes*, ed. Nahum N. Glatzer, trans. Clement Greenberg (New York: Schocken Books, 1987), 81.

8. From the diary entry for 7 February 1915. "The filth you will find exists for its own sake; you will recognize that you came dripping into the world with this burden and will depart unrecognizable again—or only too recognizable—because of it. This filth is the nethermost depth you will find; at the nethermost depth there will be not lava, no, but filth. It is the nethermost and the uppermost, and even the doubts self-scrutiny begets will soon grow weak and self-complacent as the wallowing of a pig in muck." Kafka, *The Diaries 1910–1923*, ed. Max Brod, trans. Martin Greenberg, with the cooperation of Hannah Arendt (New York: Schocken Books, 2000), 330.

9. Walter Benjamin, "Franz Kafka, On the Tenth Anniversary of His Death," in *Illuminations*, ed. and intr. Hannah Arendt, trans. Harry Zohn (New York: Schocken, 1969), 132.

10. Kafka, "The Animal in the Synagogue," in *Franz Kafka, Parables and Paradoxes*, ed. Nahum N. Glatzer, trans. Ernst Kaiser and Eithne Wilkins (New York: Schocken Books, 1987), 49–59.

11. Kafka, "Leopards in the Temple," in *Franz Kafka, Parables and Paradoxes*, ed. Nahum N. Glatzer, trans. Ernst Kaiser and Eithne Wilkins (New York: Schocken Books, 1987), 93.

12. Kafka, *The Trial*, trans. Willa and Edwin Muir (New York: Schocken Books, 1995), 221–22.

13. Walter Benjamin, "Some Reflections on Kafka," in *Illuminations*, ed. and intr. Hannah Arendt, trans. Harry Zohn (New York: Schocken, 1969), 145.

14. Benjamin, "Some Reflections on Kafka," 145.

15. We imagine his bed as the only space uncrossed by others, for in his extended adolescence, there is no indication that he has shared it with a woman. Even his room, by virtue of its architectural configuration, is regularly traversed by his family.

16. Kafka, "The Metamorphosis," in *Franz Kafka, The Complete Stories*, ed. Nahum N. Glatzer, trans. Willa and Edwin Muir (New York: Schocken Books, 1995), 115.

17. Kafka, "The Metamorphosis," 135.

18. John 3:30 (New American Bible).

19. The Samsas are a Catholic family, as indicated by the Sign of the Cross they make upon learning of Gregor's death. Kafka, "The Metamorphosis," 136.

20. Kafka, "The Metamorphosis," 137.

21. Benjamin, "Franz Kafka, On the Tenth Anniversary of His Death," 132.

22. A particularly elucidating quotation captures the modernists' turn to primitivism: "Man is, by nature, an unnatural animal, and it requires a suitably primitive art not to distort this nature, but to reveal it." Roger Shattuck, "The Art of Stillness," in *The Banquet Years: The Origins of the Avant-Garde in France 1885 to World War I* (New York: Vintage Books, 1968), 344.

23. Benjamin, "Franz Kafka, On the Tenth Anniversary of His Death," 132.

24. Benjamin, "Franz Kafka, On the Tenth Anniversary of His Death," 132.

25. Kafka, "A Crossbreed (A Sport)," in *Franz Kafka, The Complete Stories*, ed. Nahum N. Glatzer, trans. Willa and Edwin Muir (New York: Schocken Books, 1995), 426.

26. As a being derived from rather disparate sources, the crossbreed is an animal in spite of itself, not unlike any number of Kafka's protagonists. They, too, are compilations of contrary beings—namely, ancient and modern man.

27. Kafka, "A Crossbreed (A Sport)," 426.

28. Kafka, "A Crossbreed (A Sport)," 427.

29. Kafka, "A Crossbreed (A Sport)," 427.

30. Kafka, "The Cares of a Family Man," in *Franz Kafka, The Complete Stories*, ed. Nahum N. Glatzer, trans. Willa and Edwin Muir (New York: Schocken Books, 1995), 428.

31. Kafka, "The Cares of a Family Man," 428.

32. Benjamin, "Franz Kafka, On the Tenth Anniversary of His Death," 133.

33. Kafka, "The Cares of a Family Man," 428.

34. Kafka, "The Cares of a Family Man," 428.

35. Kafka, "The Cares of a Family Man," 429.

36. Benjamin, "Some Reflections on Kafka," 145.

37. Kafka, entry for 15 March 1914, in *The Diaries 1910–1923*, 266.

38. Blumfeld does hope to hand the balls off to Alfred, the slow-minded son of the charwoman, but even in this effort, he is thwarted by the boy's stupidity. Rather, the janitor's daughters, who mirror the balls in their incessant bouncing and impertinence, become the inheritors, an outcome that frustrates Blumfeld. Kafka, "Blumfeld, An Elderly Bachelor," in *Franz Kafka, The Complete Stories*, ed. Nahum N. Glatzer, trans. Tania and James Stern (New York: Schocken Books, 1995), 195–97.

39. Kafka, "Blumfeld, An Elderly Bachelor," 185.

40. Benjamin, "Some Reflections on Kafka," 145.

41. Kafka, "The Invention of the Devil," 119.

42. Kafka, "The Metamorphosis," 89.

43. "It's beyond Blumfeld's comprehension why a creature like this servant should prosper and propagate in this world." Kafka, "Blumfeld, An Elderly Bachelor," 197.

44. Kafka, "Before the Law," in *Franz Kafka, The Complete Stories*, ed. Nahum N. Glatzer, trans. Willa and Edwin Muir (New York: Schocken Books, 1995), 3.

45. On Kafka's absolute loneliness, see his diary entry for 8 January 1914: "What have I in common with Jews? I have hardly anything in common with myself and should stand very quietly in a corner, content that I can breathe." This confession is not so much an admission of loneliness than it is a perception of his subsistence as that of the only individual of a species which does not quite exist. In *The Diaries 1910–1923*, ed. Max Brod, trans. Martin Greenberg, with the cooperation of Hannah Arendt (New York: Schocken Books, 2000), 252.

46. Kafka, "Jackals and Arabs," in *Franz Kafka, The Complete Stories*, ed. Nahum N. Glatzer, trans. Willa and Edwin Muir (New York: Schocken Books, 1995), 409.

47. The ancient Egyptian god, Anubis, is depicted as a man with the head of a jackal, a holy figure who presides over the dead and leads them to the afterlife. "It seems to me

a very old quarrel; I suppose it's in the blood, and perhaps will only end with it." Kafka, "Jackals and Arabs," 408.

48. Kafka, "Jackals and Arabs," 410.

49. Kafka, "Jackals and Arabs," 410.

50. "We are left gazing awe-struck at what we have lost as the jackals, once thrown a piece of 'stinking carrion,' forget everything else and are lashed into ecstasy in pursuit of primitive cleanliness." Peter Stine, "Franz Kafka and Animals," *Contemporary Literature* 22:1 (Winter 1981): 71.

51. To be sure, the Fall of man in Kafka is really a fall man experiences away from himself, with God serving only as a silent witness.

52. Consider again the animal in the synagogue, which slinks through the latticework and makes a home of the temple. The narrator poses the question, with more than a little distress, "Does this old animal perhaps know more than the three generations of those who are gathered together in the synagogue?" The answer is yes, but it has no need of this divine knowledge. Nevertheless, its presence chastens the worshippers, and it is to be noted that the animal "is usually much nearer [to the women] than to the men." In this case and others, women in Kafka tend to be closer to the law, and thus closer to the divine, than men, who occupy the lowest rung of the hierarchy. Kafka, "The Animal in the Synagogue," 57, 51.

53. So it is that the crowds (another kind of nemesis in Kafka) are drawn to the raw animality of the beasts in the menagerie while the hunger artist desiccates in his cage. The throngs fawn in amazement over the wild animals, which present a view into an ultra-natural state of existence, while the hunger artists gives only "a glimpse of what Christian asceticism looks like to a world that has 'forgotten' or evolved beyond it." Kafka, "A Hunger Artist," in *Franz Kafka, The Complete Stories*, ed. Nahum N. Glatzer, trans. Willa and Edwin Muir (New York: Schocken Books, 1995), 276. The quotation is taken from Stine, "Franz Kafka and Animals," 61.

54. Kafka, "Paradise," in *Franz Kafka, Parables and Paradoxes*, ed. Nahum N. Glatzer, trans. Clement Greenberg (New York: Schocken Books, 1987), 29.

55. It has been said that the coming of the Messiah marked the moment at which the circular history of mankind broke open and became linear; it began to move forward toward an end-time. Perhaps this is why Kafka has the Messiah arriving "not on the last day, but on the very last," for his history is of the circular kind, an endless repeat of the expulsion from Eden. Kafka, "The Coming of the Messiah," 81.

56. Kafka, "Paradise," 29.

57. Kafka, "Paradise," 31.

58. Kafka, "Paradise," 31.

CHAPTER 6

The Difficult Task of Being Real: Odradek, the Kittenlamb, and the Historical Individual

Eleanor Helms

Kierkegaard and Kafka each broke engagements to marry, enacting a deliberate (and well-documented) retreat from the world. Though their decisions were to pursue literary vocations, strangely—or perhaps not so strangely—volumes of those writings are dedicated to understanding and overcoming the distance between themselves and the real world. Why did they not choose in reality what each confessed in writing to be the best? Kierkegaard suggests that if he had enough faith, he would have married Regine.[1] For Kafka it seems unlikely that the broken engagement to Felice could have been a matter of faith in the religious sense. Yet in a broader sense, Kafka's interest in marriage and engagements is inseparable from Kierkegaard's description of faith as the paradox of eternity in time that is lived as a synthesis in the individual believer.[2] The problem of faith for Kierkegaard is thus a problem of how to exist as member of a social race and, at the same time, as an individual alone before God.

For both Kierkegaard and Kafka, the problem of faith was inseparable from the personal issue of their broken engagements. In a letter to Max Brod, Kafka writes of Kierkegaard, "It is in fact just as you say: the problem of arriving at a true marriage is his principal concern, the concern that is forever rising into his consciousness."[3] Kierkegaard understands his own broken engagement as an issue of whether or not it is possible for him—together with all his faults—to belong to another person and yet remain focused on his personal vocation as a writer.[4] Kierkegaard concluded he could not do so. Yet he could never put that decision completely behind him, because for Kierkegaard faith means to be able to live one's solitary Christian life among others. In other words, though it might seem that Kierkegaard's broken engagement is an act of faith, renouncing the world for an inward religious life, he himself interprets it as a failure to live up to the requirements of faith.[5]

Kafka's human characters likewise find their relationship to their history and environment problematic, but it may be that there is more hope for the animals. I will explore Kafka's nonhuman characters in terms of Kierkegaardian faith and its opposite, anxiety. Kafka's animals embody Kierkegaardian faith in their confidence in their own goals as well as their trust in the concerns and actions of their social groups. In these ways, Kafka's animals indirectly suggest possibilities for bringing humans—especially the difficult, reflective ones—back to living reality. This return to living existence was just what Kierkegaard hoped to accomplish through faith, and it is what both he and Kafka gave up by breaking off their engagements.

Kafka's Odradek and the kittenlamb, though not properly animals, sketch the shape of the conflict between an individual and history most clearly, and this conflict turns out to be surprisingly like Kierkegaard's description of the individual as race, posited through faith, in *The Concept of Anxiety*. In this way, Kafka's animal stories bring Kafka's conception of the individual human person closer to Kierkegaard's than one might expect, even on the matter of faith. By "faith," however, we must understand Kierkegaard's general definition: a return to immediacy or the present that passes through an encounter with what I will call an impossible object. Such an object—the absolute paradox for Kierkegaard—reflects one's gaze back in a way that first allows one to take one's own existence seriously and so to act decisively and passionately in the moment. Though real animals cannot have faith in Kierkegaard's sense because they never doubt and they lack self-conscious reflection, Kafka's animal characters do embody passionate and decisive action and so come closer to Kierkegaardian faith than Kafka's human characters.

In the section titled "Kafka's Humans: Neither Here nor There," I will introduce selected stories by Kafka as examples of human ambivalence that is the result of being surrounded by too many memories and possibilities—that is, an intense awareness of both past and future. I will then briefly consider some of Kafka's animal stories as a way of understanding how they differ in general from the human characters ("Animals and Their Worlds"). These animal stories provide context for the encounter between the human narrators and creatures in "Cares of a Family Man" and "A Crossbreed," where Odradek and the kittenlamb challenge their respective narrators' own history and identity. I discuss these further encounters in the section "Stranger Cases: Odradek and the Kittenlamb." I will conclude by suggesting that, though neither Odradek nor the kittenlamb succeed in enacting the synthesis of faith called for by Kierkegaard, they do point toward the possibility of such a synthesis when understood together as aspects of Kierkegaardian anxiety.

Kafka's Humans: Neither Here nor There

Several of Kafka's human stories have in common that an individual with a task sets out but is unable to complete his journey. "A Common Confusion" is perhaps the barest structure of this difficulty, where shifting time and space prevent A and B from meeting. In "A Country Doctor," the inability to arrive at a destination is a failure of memory or a conflict between what is remembered and what is present. The doctor remembers something of which he was insufficiently aware in the present (the servant girl and the groom) and returns to save the girl. The urgency of both what is ahead (at the patient's bed) and behind (the girl and groom) means that the doctor is unable to act wherever he is. Since action is only possible in the present, he is simply unable to act. The resulting landscape is a dreamlike present which, since no action is possible, is indistinguishable from past or future. The reader feels that if the doctor would only make a decision, ending his dreamlike passivity, then everything would come into focus.

In "Between Past and Future," Kafka further explores obstacles to decisive action. Yet here the problem is too much activity rather than too little. Here, as elsewhere in Kafka's work (e.g., "Description of a Struggle," "Wedding Preparations in the Country," and "The Judgment"), the adversary is oneself. In "Between Past and Future," the "forces" pressing one in are pseudo-forces, arising just through one's own activity and movement. Similarly, it is the country doctor's activity of remembering that prevents him from acting, pulling him in one direction and then in another. The doctor's own consciousness is engaged in the inevitable activity of anticipation and memory, pulling his attention and emotion ahead and behind. Wherever he turns, he encounters not the pressing demand of each situation but the force of memories competing with a reflected present, so that the force of the present is neutralized and set on equal footing with the past. The urgency of the present is thus misdirected to the past and future. Instead of the present happening vividly and then beginning to fade into the past, all pasts and futures take on the urgency of the present, as in a nightmare, where the worst part is the sense that one must act but cannot.[6]

Humans do have a startling and sometimes uncanny ability to imagine possibilities and even organize the real present according to these imagined possibilities. This unsettling ability can be called "projection" or simply "imagination"; it allows humans to have purposes and projects that go beyond immediate needs and instincts. Many of our most interesting actions aim at some goal that is not present but imagined in the future (e.g., becoming a doctor, having children, moving to a house by the sea, and so forth). At the same time, our actions are influenced by our memories of the past—our history and tradition. History and tradition can appear as our sense of others' expectations, our own habits of mind and body, the language and concepts with which we are familiar, and our specific memories. Future and past, possibility and history, have in common that they are not present, strictly speaking, but they exert an undeniable influence on the present—a kind of pseudo-force. Kafka's genius is his sense of what it is like to live in a world thickly populated by urgent but ephemeral memories, histories, doubts, and possibilities. Since these unreal elements of experience exert a pseudo-force (e.g., a son acting to meet his father's real or imagined expectations), they can motivate or limit actions just like any real force such as a physical barrier or a physical desire. All humans are thus in some ways like the country doctor, with a desire to act but with a host of memories and other possibilities that interfere with the sense of urgency toward the present that is required for decisive action.

The paradox for humans, as I develop it below, is that decisive action itself depends on the past and future; that is, decisive action depends on feeling oneself to have some kind of purpose. Humans want their actions to have meaning beyond the present. It is not enough to focus all one's attention on the present and simply disregard the forces of tradition or repress the desire to integrate one's present activities with more distant, future goals. For humans, to act in the present just means to act with respect to past and future. To be an individual, the human person cannot be separated from having a past history and future possibilities, even though both history and possibility interfere with being a concrete agent in the present. But what would it mean to be able to act in the present?

Animals and Their Worlds

Two of Kafka's animal characters testify that they have no memory.[7] They are therefore able to pursue tasks the only way it is possible to pursue them—in the present. I make two points concerning animals: first, having no memory and therefore no history means that animals are not properly individuals and so are not distinguished from their environments; second, having no memory enables animals to pursue projects decisively and without ambivalence, attaining a different kind of freedom than is generally available to Kafka's human characters.

The animals themselves explain that they do not have a history. Though Kafka's human characters may find themselves facing opponents who are projections of themselves (as in "The Judgment"), the animals tend to be aware in a matter-of-fact, even reassuring, way that they belong to their societies and cannot escape them. This bond is a source of security and assurance just because it is a limit, even an obstacle. In "Investigations of a Dog," for example, the dog narrates his account of trying to become scientific, to ask questions dogs do not ask, such as the source of their food. He is unable to sustain his inquiry, however, because he has no memory and suffers from "inability to keep my scientific aim continuously before my eyes."[8] This inability to concentrate is in the end a source of comfort for him, a kind of guardrail. His instincts keep him tethered to tradition and society; he will not be able to reflect himself out of it toward a private goal as a human might—and often does without meaning to. Despite this obstacle of having no memory, the dog is one of the most wholehearted and earnest characters in Kafka's stories. He commits to his fast, allowing for his own failings, and waits for the truth to arrive. His society discourages his questions, and their company is sometimes painful,[9] but to sever ties with them completely would be impossible. Strangely, when set in contrast to human projects like the country doctor's, it is just the dog's lack of individuality which enables him to engage wholeheartedly in his project. He does not have infinite possibilities, and so he is able to pursue his present project as long as he can—that is, as long as he can bear it in mind. There may be specific obstacles to its completion of his inquiry, including his own memory, but his weak memory means that he will never suffer the broader paralysis of anxiety suffered by Kafka's human characters.

The situation is similar for Josephine, who, the narrator writes, will be saved by forgetfulness. Because mice have no memory and so no history, Josephine's antics could never alienate her from them.[10] Even in devotion to her art, she cannot abandon the ordinary tasks; her demand for distinction and to be excused from regular work is part of her attempt to belong to the mouse society more completely.[11] As the narrator tells it, however, since mice have no history, her disputable interpretation of her own art is unlikely to be caught up and retold by the others: "So perhaps we shall not miss so very much after all, while Josephine . . . will happily lose herself in the numberless throng of the heroes of our people, and soon, since we are no historians, will rise to the heights of redemption and be forgotten like all her brothers."[12] The mouse people's lack of history means Josephine is not properly an individual, and her art will not be distinguished in the end from all of their other activities.

The case is complicated for the burrow animal because his environment is not society but just the burrow. He is certainly unable to distinguish himself from it; if anything, he takes the perspective of the burrow and sees himself as an intruder.[13] Strangely, his disorienting interchangeability of self and environment results in more or less the same difficulty faced by the human characters: namely, the possibility of struggling only against oneself. The burrow animal is not aware of the struggle against himself, but his entire plan of defense depends on guessing the mind of his opponent. Everything stands or falls on whether his enemy knows that he exists, which in turn depends on whether he knows that his enemy exists: "So long as I still knew nothing about it, it simply cannot have heard me, for at that time I kept very quiet, nothing would be more quiet than my return to the burrow; afterwards, when I dug the experimental trenches, perhaps it could have heard me, though my style of digging makes very little noise."[14] Unlike the human, however, the burrow animal trusts to his own defenses—that is, his environment—and trusts that his own lack of awareness of his enemy's existence will save both himself and his burrow.

Where humans are unable to escape their own reflective activities, animals are unable to sustain them (the dog), recognize them in others (Josephine), or they simply began their reflections late enough (the burrow animal) that they cannot become too anxious concerning the infinite possibilities available to them. Simply enough, animals do not have infinite possibilities because their imaginations and abilities to deny their own instincts and their social traditions are limited. Because of these guardrails—lack of imagination, strong instincts, and unified social traditions—that pull them back from the precipice we humans call existential freedom, Kafka's animals are paradoxically free to invest themselves wholeheartedly in their immediate activities. That is, the dog is free to engage in his scientific inquiries; if he goes too far, his instincts or another dog will rescue him. If Josephine's antics are too absurd, she is redeemed in forgetfulness. If the burrow animal's activities put him in danger, he is saved by his own ignorance, which is interchangeable with the ignorance of his enemy. Each character is free to be completely invested in a project. Society and lack of memory may hinder its completion, but not the earnestness with which it is pursued.

The human situation, by contrast, is always overshadowed by possibilities, doubts, and memories. If Kafka is right in his description of the human situation, is it yet possible for humans, like animals, to become decisive, passionate agents? For Kafka, the answer seems to be no. At least, Kafka's human characters do not offer any model for what such a decisive individual might look like. However, I will argue below that Kierkegaard is aware of the same struggle in human reflection between possibility and actuality as well as between history and the present, and yet Kierkegaard is able to say that decisive action in the present is nonetheless possible. For Kierkegaard, the ability to act decisively in the present is nothing other than faith. Though Kierkegaard himself does not profess to have faith, which would have allowed him to marry Regine, he does hold that such faith is possible for humans. Though it might seem that Kafka is unable to accept the possibility of faith, I will show rather that Kafka's animal characters, when understood in terms of their various relationships to their own individuality and to their environments,[15] do create a space for what Kierkegaard calls faith: a synthesis between possibility and necessity.

Kierkegaard: The Race and the Individual

For Kierkegaard an individual only exists as part of a race, and to be part of a race means to have a history. Kierkegaard and Kafka are both intensely aware of an individual's freedom as in tension with tradition, and both see individuality as inseparable—paradoxically—from that tradition. A clean opposition, where one becomes individual by throwing off tradition, is foreign to both Kierkegaard and Kafka. It is impossible to be an individual while lost in a tradition, but it is also impossible to be an individual in complete isolation from any tradition. For Kierkegaard, true freedom reflects this ambiguity. Freedom is the possibility of positing oneself as a self, where to be a self is simultaneously to be an individual and a member of a race.[16] In other words, though being an individual does conflict with belonging to a society, becoming a true self means enacting a unity of these two aspects of oneself—the individual and the tradition.[17]

Kierkegaard claims that this power of positing oneself as a synthesis between individuality and tradition is inextricably entangled with our fear of positing in general and fear of our own freedom. Though we are certainly anxious about being lost to history and anonymous society, we are also anxious about our own power to remove ourselves from society and history by positing ourselves as individuals. Kierkegaard's definition of anxiety is that it is not a fear of any concrete thing but rather a fear of nothing—a fear of the effects of our own fear.[18] On the other hand, this same anxiety about freedom is a true sense of our own possibilities to enact and produce, and rightly used, freedom can be the enactment of a synthesis between what is possible and what is necessary into a new, unified reality. That is, when the individual is actually posited as an individual who is nonetheless a member of a race, the anxiety disappears. Anxiety is the "dizziness of freedom,"[19] but that power of possibility can become a productive synthesis of possibility and necessity in true selfhood.[20]

The strange thing about anxiety is that, although it has no concrete object, it is nevertheless experienced as having some object. Anxiety is not understood consciously as a fear of oneself or of one's own freedom. Instead, the object of anxiety begins to metastasize into a substantive thing of the individual's own creation. In a sense, the object of anxiety truly is a substantive thing as long as one treats it and reacts to it as if it were real, just like the pseudo-forces in Kafka's "Between Past and Future."

To make matters worse, Kierkegaard points out that this problem of anxiety creating objects for itself is compounded through the history of a race, passed on to each new generation. Kierkegaard writes:

> In each subsequent individual, anxiety is more reflective. This may be expressed by saying that the nothing that is the object of anxiety becomes, as it were, more and more a something. . . . All of this *is* only for freedom. . . . Here the nothing of anxiety is a complex of presentiments, which, reflecting themselves in themselves, come nearer and nearer to the individual, even though again when viewed

essentially in anxiety, they signify nothing—yet, mark well, not a nothing with which the individual has nothing to do, but a nothing that communicates vigorously with the ignorance of innocence.[21]

In short, humans are anxious about nothing, but more precisely about possibility. The fear itself is the only substance that anxiety can take on, but since the effects on our emotions, orientation in the world, and actions are real, the object of our fear and the forces those fears exert on us take on the urgency and eventually even the substance of reality.

For Kierkegaard, to posit something can mean to judge it to be true, to recognize it, or simply to relate to it as a unity or a fact. We posit all kinds of things (the world and its reality, perceived and remembered objects, possible courses of action, real or imagined states of affairs), and since we can posit not only what is real but what is possible, we are never sure whether our own activities and their objects are real. Interestingly, this fear of freedom and the ability to posit oneself as an individual that is distinguishable from that individual's environment, history, or tradition is at the same time the ability to lose oneself as an individual. As soon as one's individuality is posited consciously, it is difficult to maintain a relationship to oneself as self rather than as a separate object like any other object of conscious reflection. This strange problem is expressed neatly by Kierkegaard in the comical situation in which Soldin the bookseller asks his wife: "Rebecca, is it I who is speaking?"[22] This inability to distinguish oneself from surrounding objects does not result from a lack of memory as it might for an animal but rather from too much reflection, such that even one's own "I" becomes an object of conscious reflection and so separable from oneself. Unlike the dog in "Investigations of a Dog," the human—especially the human writer or philosopher—has no instincts toward the real to guide her home.

Uncertainty with respect to objects in the world and whether and how they are related to oneself results in a certain indifference and lack of earnestness toward all objects. In fact, we feel somewhat uncomfortable when someone does take objects of the human world seriously, as does the earnest ape in "Report to an Academy."[23] Similarly, Kierkegaard explains that anxiety, as the possibility of freedom, consumes all finite ends and discovers their deceptiveness.[24] Anxiety "weans us away" from finitude.[25] But for Kierkegaard, there must still be some worthy object, some task worth pursuing. Anxiety is not the final word. In Kafka's stories, too, the human characters and the reader remain disturbed by the fact that all goals are reflected back as apparitions. I have argued that the animals' ability to be wholehearted and decisive in a project, though perhaps hindered by instincts or lack of social recognition, is made possible just by these obstacles (i.e., lack of memory, too strong instincts, and social cohesion) as guardrails limiting possibility and focusing energy on the present. Given that humans are constantly engaged in the stubborn, entangling activities of remembering the past and imagining the future, is Kierkegaard right to think that humans can achieve a unity of self and society (or for humans, self and history) that is essential to decision and action in real life? Both Kierkegaard's and Kafka's comments on the value of marriage suggest they would have wanted such a synthesis, if it were possible, for themselves. Is Kierkegaard right to hope, to believe, that such a synthesis is possible for humans, even if not for himself in particular? I will argue that if Kafka's two most unlikely characters, Odradek and the kittenlamb, are interpreted as representing Kierkegaard's two forms of anxiety, they do point toward a possible synthesis that they, like Kierkegaard, do not themselves enact.

Stranger Cases: Odradek and the Kittenlamb

Odradek and the kittenlamb tumble and bound, respectively, into this already strangely populated landscape. They are captivating images in that they have loosed themselves from history, though I will argue that they remain caricatures or echoes of selfhood rather than true unified individuals in the sense of integrated selves. In *The Concept of Anxiety*, Kierkegaard writes that there are two kinds of anxiety, and I suggest below that Odradek and kittenlamb correspond to these kinds: first, anxiety about continuity, history, or necessity—represented by Odradek; and second, anxiety about freedom, individuality, or possibility—embodied by the kittenlamb.

As an inhabitant of the old family house, Odradek has retained the continuity of history but, since he has no purpose, he is unable to die.[26] To have history means to have the structure of direction—to be going *from* somewhere *to* somewhere. Odradek does not have even an etymology to explain his origin and descent, much less a history.[27] A sequence of unrelated events or bare continuity is not a proper history. On the other hand, Odradek is also not an individual, and for just the same reason: an individual has some sort of integrity, which again implies organized activity and projects. Though Odradek resembles an individual in that he is not at home in his environment (the old family house), he is also not capable of being at home anywhere. His reply when asked where he lives is "No fixed abode" and a hollow laugh.[28] We cannot call Odradek alienated, abstracted, or even distinguished from his environment, since he has no interest in belonging to it to begin with. Thus Odradek is not properly an individual (despite seeming a stranger in the family house); neither has he (or is he) a history. Rather, he is raw continuity without any purpose. Though Odradek is not himself anxious about his lack of individuality or history, he produces uneasiness in the human narrator, who imagines him extending endlessly, aimlessly through time: "Am I to suppose, then, that he will always be rolling down the stairs, with ends of thread trailing after him, right before the feet of my children, and my children's children?"[29] The narrator finds the thought of pure, unchecked continuity "almost painful."[30]

Kafka's Odradek embodies Kierkegaard's first type of anxiety: anxiety about continuity. What is so uncanny about the Odradek is not that he is a misfit, though he is that, but that he is so well-rooted in the narrator's family home.[31] To the owner of the family home, Odradek represents an uncanny continuity—likely to outlive the narrator himself[32]—whose continuance in the home is inevitable. There are no new possibilities here, no progress in communication, and no change through time. In these ways, Odradek typifies Kierkegaard's first type of anxiety, the anxiety that comes from a too strong sense of necessity and continuity and that amounts to a form of fatalism.

Kafka's kittenlamb likewise has a complicated relationship with the narrator's past and family history. Though a legacy, the kittenlamb still lacks a history in that it has no future. It is neither predator nor prey.[33] As singular as this creature is, with no blood relation,[34] it manages to make itself almost interchangeable with the narrator. The narrator "cannot help laughing when it sniffs around me and winds itself between my legs and simply will not be parted from me,"[35] but he is even more struck when he sees tears "dropping from its huge whiskers" and asks, "Were they mine, or were they the animal's? Had this cat, along with the soul of a lamb, the ambitions of a human being?"[36]

This kittenlamb is more than an absurd inheritance embodying the absurdity of inheritance or tradition; instead, gazing so long and so carefully at the kittenlamb challenges and changes the human narrator's own identity and sense of belonging. In these ways, the kittenlamb causes the narrator to be anxious about his own separateness—about the possibility of being as separate and lonely as the kittenlamb itself is. The kittenlamb can thus be understood to embody Kierkegaard's second form of anxiety: anxiety about possibility or individuality. The most frightening possibility is that the narrator could sever the kittenlamb's ties to the family at any moment through rejection as well as through "the knife of the butcher,"[37] as its ties to the family are so tenuous. These possibilities of rejection and isolation color all the narrator's activities and reflections.

The kittenlamb, like Odradek, is itself an uneasy synthesis—if it is a synthesis at all and not merely "a sport" (the story's subtitle). If the kittenlamb resembles the Kierkegaardian absolute paradox that results in a synthesis of selfhood for the person of faith, it does so as a caricature or hollow outline, whose impressiveness is more in what it lacks than in what it is. Yet by having neither individuality nor history, Odradek and the kittenlamb each make conspicuous what is missing in a whole self. They suggest the kind of thing a human being ought to be—as a synthesis of history and individuality—by representing pitiful, skeleton caricatures of selfhood. The awkwardness of simply attaching continuity or separation to a being implies that a genuine human synthesis could not be just a combination of tradition and individuality—and yet, as with Kierkegaard's indirect communication, we now know precisely what is lacking. The tensions concerning continuity and separation are not felt by the creatures themselves (though perhaps more so by the kittenlamb) as much as they are by each narrator, who plays the role of the individual in the face of continuity (Odradek) or isolation (kittenlamb), where a synthesis of necessity and possibility, continuity and individuality, is demanded. The conflict felt by the narrator echoes Kierkegaard's insistence that the paradox, though in one sense paradoxical in itself, most properly becomes a paradox in relation to someone trying to comprehend it.[38] In the same way, Odradek and the kittenlamb are themselves impossible objects—impossible in themselves, but also interestingly impossible for their respective narrators to deal with.

Becoming a Self: A Synthesis of Continuity and Separation

Is facing these kinds of impossible objects at all helpful to becoming a real individual who belongs to and has a history? The contrast between the human and animal stories, and more concretely the characters of Odradek and kittenlamb, establish a contradiction between history and individuality. However, unlike Kafka, Kierkegaard thinks that the contradiction between history and individuality can nonetheless be lived out in a genuine synthesis of selfhood. The synthesis can come about when the conflict between the isolated individual and inescapable tradition is no longer denied:

> When we take a religious person, the knight of hidden inwardness, and place him in the existence-medium, a contradiction will appear as he relates himself to the world around him, and he himself must become aware of this. The contradiction does not consist in his being different from everyone else . . . but the contradiction is that he, with all this inwardness hidden within him, with this pregnancy of suffering and benediction in his inner being, looks just like all the others—and inwardness is indeed hidden simply by his looking exactly like others.[39]

If the same unity described in the knight of hidden inwardness is possible for the history and individuality of any human person, then Kafka's caricatures of these two forms of anxiety—the representation of meaningless continuity in Odradek and of pitiful isolation in kittenlamb—need not be the final descriptions of history and individuality. Yet Kierkegaard's solution is counterintuitive: precisely by distinguishing oneself from society so decisively that one no longer has anxiety about being lost among others, one is able to appear as indistinguishable from the rest of the world and so to take one's place in it. Although absolute individuality and absolute continuity with the past are indeed exclusive, once these differences are established in actuality—not merely as possibilities—we no longer need to be anxious about blurring them. That is, once a person recognizes that individuality and tradition not only seem to be but truly are exclusive, apart from the seeming, it paradoxically becomes possible to rest in relations with others without fear of losing oneself as an individual.

This return to relationship is only possible, of course, because the original conflict, though real, is also in part a consequence of anxiety. Put another way, Kierkegaard's absolute paradox is indeed real, but it is real *for humans*; that is, it is a problem for consciousness.[40] The tension between individuality and history is not thereby a problem to be ignored, even if this were possible, but it is important to remember that when one looks objectively for the object of fear, one finds nothing.

Kierkegaard describes the phenomenon of synthesis in *The Concept of Anxiety* with respect to sexuality—which is, of course, relevant to the initial question of broken engagements. Kierkegaard writes that sexuality is the "ultimate point" of synthesis for humans between body and psyche, where two aspects—human nature and animal nature—were held in tension though they hardly existed in themselves. Just at this "ultimate point," the human also becomes like an animal, but not merely so: "Man can attain this ultimate point only in the moment the spirit becomes actual. Before that time he is not animal, but neither is he really man. The moment he becomes man, he becomes so by being animal as well."[41]

Perhaps both Kafka and Kierkegaard are right that there is something essentially interconnected about faith and sexuality: both faith and a healthy relationship to sexuality can enact an end to anxiety through rest in actuality. If we take their conclusion literally and concretely, perhaps the best a human can do after all is to have a family. In the unreceived *Letter to His Father*, Kafka writes, "Marrying, founding a family, accepting all the children that come [is] the utmost a human can succeed in doing at all."[42] Kierkegaard, likewise, sees his own decision to immerse himself in writing as a second-best, perhaps even a cowardly act. He writes: "If I had faith, I would have married Regine."[43] Yet they chose to abandon marriage and pursue writing, and their writing plagued them precisely for its lack of reality. Kierkegaard concludes repeatedly that what is missing in all writing and thinking, and necessarily so, is existence.[44] As discussed above, Kafka's human characters never accomplish their goals because the force that ought to distinguish the real and set it out from possibility and memory is gone. This altered and uncanny modality, such that reflections, projections, and dreams can take on life, substance, and even personality, is part of Kafka's genius as a writer. His own abstraction from reality was the price.

Kierkegaard suggests that the fact of love is not nearly as problematic as its reflection: "The task, of course, is to bring it [sexuality] under the qualification of the spirit (here lie all the problems of the erotic). The realization of this is the victory of love in a person in whom the spirit is so victorious that the sexual is forgotten, and recollected only in forgetfulness. When this has come about, sensuousness is transfigured in spirit and anxiety is driven out."[45] Kierkegaard does not mean that sexuality should be repressed, which would be merely a form of abstracting from it or reflecting on it. Rather, when it is actually posited as spirit or self, the synthesis of body and psyche, anxiety disappears. As with sin (though sexuality is certainly not sin), the anxiety is a result of "fear of nothing," an apparition that vanishes in love. Love is a kind of forgetfulness, and represents a way in which humans can return to being like animals or—as quoted above—become animal at the same time as becoming human. Love resembles indifferent openness (Kierkegaard's aesthetic), since it does not exert its own will, but it has passed through reflection, and its forgetfulness is the result of a decision to act (Kierkegaard's ethical). The lover comes in the end to be very much like Josephine's forgiving mouse people, though (as Kafka notes) the mice do not really embrace Josephine unconditionally. In fact, the warmth of their admiration depends just on it being collective and not an individual decision. As collective, it can never be unconditional, Kafka's mouse narrator insists.[46] In a sense, then, if love achieves forgetfulness, it goes beyond the acceptance even of animals. It is not neutral or passive acceptance but an unconditional choice—a decisive action—made with all the passionate earnestness of freedom. Though the possibility of such a choice produces anxiety, the choice itself displaces it. It is no longer a choice from among many possibilities but simply the real.

Taking Kierkegaard literally when he says that the human person becomes a synthesis only when spirit becomes actual, we might understand the synthesis of history and individuality in freedom quite simply as having a child. We might also say that Kafka's art and Kierkegaard's work were their children, in a metaphorical sense, but the question from the beginning was the relationship between these children of the mind and the real children that play in the real world and make demands on their parents' freedom perhaps even more insistently than art or philosophy. Children, like a synthesis of Odradek and the kittenlamb, embody both continuity and disruption. Without apology or explanation, they continue to live as a concrete fact the impossible synthesis that we ourselves are living. They are one's own paradoxical synthesis of history and individuality existing again, in repetition more uncanny than any memory.

Kafka's animals pursue their earnest tasks without doubt or ambivalence, trusting to the limits set for them by instinct and society. Because they never doubt the reality or necessity of those bounds, they are able to act with a freedom that seems unavailable to humans.[47] But Odradek and the kittenlamb leap over those bounds of nature, instinct, and society, skipping straight to impossibility, and they too continue on without explanation. In each story it is left to the human narrator to wonder what is to become of these creatures, or what he is to become, given that all of this—without explanation—simply is.

There are, of course, other ways to come to terms with one's own existence as both historical and individual, both given by tradition and free, than by becoming a parent. But if Kierkegaard and Kafka are right in their reflections, their art, and their praise of marriage and family, the relation of individual to history must be *real.* Though anxiety, whether with respect to being lost in the continuity of tradition or isolated through the freedom of individuality, properly has no object other than our own human activity of fearing it, it is also no more able to be ignored than Odradek, "rolling down the stairs with bits of thread trailing after him,"[48] leading nowhere in particular but disrupting everything. Likewise, as with the kittenlamb, something is demanded: either the passionate activity of Kafka's animals, the half-hearted efforts of Kafka's humans, or the unconditional acceptance of Kierkegaard's believer. The third option becomes a real possibility only as the human person is faced with some kind of paradox or, as with Kafka's animals, an impossible object. Yet encountering such an impossible object in a way that cancels anxiety does not mean simply denying the existence of conflict; instead, the more real the paradox is allowed to become, the more real the corresponding synthesis can be as well. Even in Kafka's shifting landscapes of reflections, projections, and memories, Odradek and the kittenlamb stand out with their own, singular kind of impossibility. We have only left to wonder whether their difference, considered in this way as a reflection and test of the narrator's subjectivity, is radical enough to be the last step toward a selfhood that is a living relation to past and future even more startling than these uncanny encounters.

Conclusion

If we give weight to both Kafka's and Kierkegaard's claims that they ought to have married their fiancées, such that the highest thing in life is to enact a synthesis between possibility and necessity in real life, and if Odradek and the kittenlamb can be understood as gesturing toward an absent synthesis of possibility and necessity, what exactly are the relevant differences that remain between Kafka and Kierkegaard? Though Kafka criticizes various versions of Abraham in his notes and letters (some of which resemble Kierkegaard's Abraham, others of which seem to be his own imaginative variations),[49] he rarely critiques Kierkegaard's broader project directly. He does note that Kierkegaard has an optimism or "affirmativeness" that Kafka finds inaccessible and at times alarming.[50] I suggest that the most important difference is that Kierkegaard is able to rely on a real, absolute difference between God and humans—that is, a real difference belonging to the individual in actuality—that does not need to be maintained through mental effort and so cannot finally be lost through forgetfulness. Instead, the believer can accept continuity in experience, and not just fragmentation, without fearing that she has lost hold of the world's multiplicity, complexity, and strangeness.

It is difficult, of course, to be always mindful of the absolute difference between God and human beings; for that reason, faith is a task, not a finished achievement.[51] Nevertheless, Kierkegaard is able to trust in a difference that exists in itself, because God is real, and so the Kierkegaardian self is free to enact selfhood as both individuality and continuity without fear of losing that tension and difference. For his part, Kierkegaard would see Kafka's portrayals of life as disjointed and disorienting as just one side of things,[52] as an emphasis on fragmentation at the expense of unity. From Kierkegaard's perspective, Kafka's stories taken together embody the first form of anxiety: anxiety about continuity. Kafka, on the other hand, worries that Kierkegaard's synthesis of possibility and necessity comes too cheaply, as is suggested by the comical example of Abraham trying to move off with all his furniture into eternity.[53] Kafka's most paradigmatic stories most often express a dread of uniformity, institutions, tradition, and even families that is not present in Kierkegaard, despite all they held in common regarding fear of their fathers, anxiety about commitment, disappointment with society, and mistrust of crowds. I have shown that Kafka's animal stories, however, represent more nuanced approaches to both isolation and continuity than many of his other typical stories. The characters of Odradek and the kittenlamb, when considered together as Kierkegaard's two forms of anxiety, open a space of possibility for a synthesis by showing just what kind of synthesis is lacking.

It may be strange to suggest that acknowledging this kind of conspicuous lack can amount to an attainment of what is lacking, but Kafka himself suggests as much with respect to Kierkegaard's Abraham:

> Abraham is laboring under the following delusion: he cannot endure the monotony of the world. Now the fact is that this world is notoriously and uncommonly manifold, which can be put to the test at any moment if one just takes up a handful of World and looks at it a little more closely. Naturally, Abraham knows this too. And so his complaint about the monotony of the world is actually a complaint about an insufficiently profound mingling with the manifold nature of the world. And so it is actually a springboard back into the world.[54]

Can we not say of Kafka what Kafka says of Abraham: that the recognition of a lack is a springboard back to a unity with the world? If so, then both Kafka's and Kierkegaard's comments on the value of marriage can be read as genuine expressions of what they took to be the highest fulfillment for humans, though they themselves failed to achieve it. We could then say of Kafka what he said of Kierkegaard with respect to Regine, "Perhaps in this way Kierkegaard succeeded somewhat against his will, or unintentionally, in reaching his tangential path."[55] Like Odradek and the kittenlamb, both Kafka and Kierkegaard capture our imagination because of what they were, but also because of what they were not. The ways the two authors embody anxiety and loss suggest that they, like Kafka's creatures, may nevertheless open a window toward what remains—for the rest of us—a possibility.

Notes

1. Søren Kierkegaard, *Journals and Papers* V 5664 (*Pap.* IV A 107). Kierkegaard also described breaking his engagement as lack of faith in the possible. See *Journals and Papers* V 5521 (*Pap. III* A 166). (Selections from Kierkegaard's journals can be found in *Søren Kierkegaard's Journals and Papers*, ed. and trans. Howard V. and Edna H. Hong, assisted by Gregor Malantschuk [Bloomington: Indiana University Press, 1978].)

2. Søren Kierkegaard, *The Concept of Anxiety*, trans. Reidar Thomte and Albert B. Anderson (Princeton, NJ: Princeton University Press, 1980), 85; cf. also *Sickness unto Death*, trans. Howard and Edna Hong (Princeton, NJ: Princeton University Press, 1980), 40.

3. Franz Kafka, *Letters to Friends, Family, and Editors* (Zürau, mid-March, 1918), 199.

4. On the relationship between Kierkegaard's engagement and his writing, see Joakim Garff, *Søren Kierkegaard: A Biography* (Princeton, NJ: Princeton University Press, 2007). Kierkegaard himself does not always express his doubts so nobly; instead, he emphasizes his dark inner life that would make it difficult, if not impossible, to share his true self with another person. He writes, "But if I were to have explained myself, I would have had to initiate her into terrible things, my relationship to my father, his depression, the eternal night brooding within me, my going astray, my lusts and debauchery." *Journals and Papers* 5664 (*Pap.* IV A 107).

5. Kierkegaard is commonly thought of as an individualist, but that caricature does not make sense of his positive discussions of history and race in *The Concept of Anxiety* and *Sickness unto Death*, which I will discuss in this chapter. It is also important to remember that the knight of faith in *Fear and Trembling* and the religious person as described in *Continuing Unscientific Postscript* would both be indistinguishable from the outside from their surroundings and even from the aesthete, though of course the inward difference is radical.

6. The situation is similar in "The Great Wall of China," where the people respond with great emotion to news of battles that took place a hundred years ago and remain loyal to long-dead emperors. (All references to Kafka's stories are from *The Complete Stories*, ed. Nahum N. Glatzer [New York: Schocken, 1971].)

7. See Kafka, "Investigations of a Dog" and "Josephine the Singer; or, the Mouse Folk," both discussed below. This is not a biological or empirical claim but a self-description by the characters.

8. "Investigations of a Dog," 315.

9. Ibid., 314.

10. Kafka emphasizes their unity as a social group through the mouse narrator, who describes Josephine as "our singer" (360), and wonders about her gifts in contrast to piping, which "we all know about" (361). The mouse narrator describes the response of the other mice as coming from "the people" (364–65), and "our people" (365–70).

11. See "Josephine the Singer; or, the Mouse Folk," 372. We should contrast Josephine with the hunger artist, who is not noticed at all by the passersby and whose art is not recognized as anything at all. The world changes outside the hunger artist's cage, but Josephine's world can never change.

12. Ibid., 376.

13. He laments that its one weakness is its main entrance—namely, himself. "The Burrow," 322.

14. Ibid., 359.

15. I will consistently use "environment" rather than "history" when referring to Kafka's animal characters, since it is not clear they can have a proper history without a reliable memory or a more human-like self-consciousness. For each of them, their ability to have a history is precisely what is at issue. It may also be that human history is problematic, but I think it would beg the question to use the word "history" with respect to any of Kafka's animal characters, especially Odradek and the kittenlamb.

16. "He is not essentially different from the race, for in that case there is no race at all; he is not the race, for in that case also there would be no race. He is himself and the race." Kierkegaard, *The Concept of Anxiety*, 29.

17. Kierkegaard's own experience of possibility and necessity is clearly rooted in his own experiences with Regine and their engagement. In his journals, he expresses the awful burden of his own power over her, which he articulates as the possibility of giving their relationship any interpretation he chooses. Yet at the same time, he describes the interpretation he does choose—that he has been deceiving her—as lack of faith in God's ability to bring about new possibilities. He writes: "I prefer what I did do; my relationship to her was always kept so ambiguous that I had it in my power to give it any interpretation I wanted to. I gave it the interpretation that I was a deceiver. Humanly speaking, that is the only way to save her, to give her soul resilience. My sin is that I did not have faith, faith that for God all things are possible, but where is the borderline between that and tempting God; but my sin has never been that I did not love her." See *Journals and Papers* 5521 (*Pap. III A 166*), also referenced above.

18. "Frequently the reading of medical case histories can produce an effect related to presentiment . . . there is a certain receptivity so strong that it is almost productive." *Journals and Papers* IV 3992 (*Pap. II A 19*). See also *The Concept of Anxiety*, 49.

19. *The Concept of Anxiety*, 61.

20. Kierkegaard, *Sickness unto Death*, trans. Howard and Edna Hong (Princeton, NJ: Princeton University Press, 1980). "A human being is a synthesis of the infinite and the finite, of the temporal and the eternal, of freedom and necessity, in a short, a synthesis"

(13). Kierkegaard writes that both imagination's infinite possibilities (cf. 30ff) and the fatalism of extreme necessity (cf. 37ff) can disrupt that synthesis. With respect to fatalism and despairing of possibility, Kierkegaard appeals to the difference between humans and animals explicitly: "Personhood is a synthesis of possibility and necessity. Its continued existence is like breathing (*respiration*), which is an inhaling and exhaling. The self of the determinist cannot breathe, for it is impossible to breathe necessity exclusively, because that would utterly suffocate a person's self. . . . To pray is also to breathe, and possibility is for the self what oxygen is for breathing. . . . That God's will is the possible makes me able to pray; if there is nothing but necessity, man is essentially as inarticulate as the animals" (40, 41).

21. Ibid., 61–62.

22. *The Concept of Anxiety*, 51.

23. The ape pursues becoming human with great zeal, which only brings uncomfortably to mind how few human activities are worth pursuing passionately. Instead, we replace earnestness with vehemence, expressed as the manner in which the ape learns to drink from the schnapps bottle and throw it to the side. Cf. 256–57.

24. *The Concept of Anxiety*, 155.

25. Ibid., 160.

26. "Can he possibly die? Anything that dies has had some kind of aim in life, some kind of activity, which has worn out; but that does not apply to Odradek" ("The Cares of a Family Man," 429).

27. "The Cares of a Family Man," 427–28.

28. Ibid., 428.

29. Ibid., 429.

30. Ibid., 429.

31. "He lurks by turns in the garret, the stairway, the lobbies, the entrance hall. Often for months on end he is not to be seen; then he has presumably moved into other houses; but he always comes faithfully back to our house again" (428).

32. Ibid., 429.

33. "[T]he beast knows neither fear nor lust of pursuit" ("A Crossbreed [A Sport]," 426).

34. Ibid., 427.

35. Ibid., 427.

36. Ibid., 427.

37. Ibid., 427.

38. "When the eternal truth relates itself to an existing person, it becomes the paradox. . . . But since the paradox is not in itself the paradox, it does not thrust away intensely enough, for without risk, no faith." Kierkegaard, *Concluding Unscientific Postscript*, 209.

39. *Concluding Unscientific Postscript*, 499–500.

40. "The paradox came into existence through the relating of the eternal, essential truth to the existing person" (*Concluding Unscientific Postscript*, 209). Similarly, in *The Concept of Anxiety* Haufniensis insists that an idol is "nothing" in itself, and yet is nevertheless what a pagan worships: "there is no idol in the world; nevertheless, the idol is the object of the pagan's religiousness" (97). Idol worship is a metaphor for the situation of every spirit in anxiety: "If we ask more particularly what the object of anxiety is, then the answer, here as elsewhere, must be that it is nothing" (96).

41. *The Concept of Anxiety*, 49.

42. Kafka, *Letter to His Father* (New York: Schocken Books, 1966), 99, quoted in John Updike, "Forward," *The Complete Stories*, xiii. Updike notes, of course, that Kafka himself did *not* in fact succeed in doing so. See also Erwin R. Steinbert, "Kafka's 'Before the Law': A Reflection of Fear of Marriage and Corroborating Language Patterns in the Diaries," *Journal of Modern Literature* 13:1 (1986): 133.

43. Kierkegaard, *Journals and Papers* V 5664 (*Pap.* IV A 107), May 17, 1843.

44. Kierkegaard, of course, targets Hegel most directly in his critique, who is all the more comical for thinking that he has captured actuality neatly.

45. *The Concept of Anxiety*, 80.

46. "[N]o single individual could do what in this respect the people as a whole are capable of doing." "Josephine the Singer; or, the Mouse Folk," 365. Also, "perhaps as individuals the people may surrender too easily to Josephine, but as a whole they surrender unconditionally to no one, and not to her either" (370).

47. On this different animal freedom, see "Report to an Academy" (253) and "Investigations of a Dog" (316).

48. "The Cares of a Family Man," 429.

49. See *The Blue Octavo Notebooks*, ed. Max Brod and trans. Ernst Kaiser and Eithne Wilkins (Cambridge: Exact Change, 1991), 54–56, and *Letters to Friends, Family, and Editors* (199–200). Cf. also Robert Arnold Darrow, "Kierkegaard, Kafka, and the Strength of 'The Absurd' in Abraham's Sacrifice of Isaac," MA thesis.

50. "In *Fear and Trembling*, for example—which you ought to read now—his affirmativeness turns truly monstrous and is checked only when it comes up against a perfectly ordinary helmsman. What I mean is, affirmativeness becomes objectionable when it reaches too high. He doesn't see the ordinary man (with whom, on the whole, he knows how to talk remarkably well) and paints this monstrous Abraham in the clouds." To Max Brod, mid-March 1918, in *Letters to Friends, Family, and Editors*, 200.

51. Kierkegaard, *Concluding Unscientific Postscript*, 488–89.

52. Here "A Common Confusion" and "Description of a Struggle" are paradigmatic examples.

53. Kafka, *The Blue Octavo Notebooks*, the Fourth Notebook, 55.

54. Kafka, *The Blue Octavo Notebooks*, the Fourth Notebook, 55.

55. Kafka, *Letters to Family, Friends, and Editors*, 202.

CHAPTER 7

Consolation in Your Neighbor's Fur: On Kafka's Animal Parables

Burkhard Müller

Silence befits Kafka. He resembles a natural phenomenon, a sunset or a rock, about which of course we can talk, like about everything else, but talk will not touch it. It is hard to say nothing at all in front of that which moves you. And silence does not in itself express reverence.

Kafka has encouraged endless talk. It is not the results, whatever they are, that carry that expression of reverence, but its mere quantity, like the stream of picture postcards that testify to the majesty of the Grand Canyon. Kafka possesses, in Goethe's words, the quality of being "important and uninterpretable" (*bedeutend und undeutbar*). That Kafka conveys this sense of importance makes everybody restless; they want at least to try an interpretation. Thus Kafka is probably the world's most interpreted author. Kafka had a premonition that things would turn out that way, and trickily laid out his snares. Who could resist the pull of the "Little Fable"? Who wouldn't fall under the doorkeeper's spell in "Before the Law"? To interpret these texts always means to do the wrong thing: to treat the rock of this prose as if it contained some kind of ore, as if it were a chunk of matter, from which the pure metal of meaning must be extracted. As this smelting procedure did not succeed, the rock was ground down to the gravel of particular opinions. Of course, Kafka was a Jew, and being Jewish shaped his life and his writing. But among all those Jews who have lived and written, only one Kafka has come forth. To insist on Kafka's Jewishness is to misjudge his singularity. Those who want to understand Kafka as a Jew and nothing else mistake the springboard for the jump.

Yet, after these precautionary words, I will try to speak about what I consider to be the summit of Kafka's oeuvre, the three animal parables. It is a summit that cannot be reached in one leap; and I will put in some intermediary stations. As it comprises just a few lines and because it is the very first text in the edition of Kafka's shorter texts, I want to start with "Wish to Become an Indian":

> If only one were an Indian, ready at once and on the running horse, askance in the air, trembling repeatedly in short intervals above the trembling soil, until one let go of the spurs, for there were no spurs, until one threw away the bridles, for there were no bridles, hardly noticing the land ahead as an evenly mowed turf, already without the horse's neck and the horse's head.[1]

This text provides a look at the syntactic material Kafka uses. It is hard to imagine that all this is not merely there (like a natural phenomenon) but was in fact *made*. Kafka has his own very special way of treating German syntax. He always prefers hypotaxis to parataxis. This prose supports incredible spans—mainly because it has a knack for the German subordinating conjunction *wenn*, which will reach further than any other introduction to a clause. Like the queen in a game of chess, it unites the powers of two other figures: like the castle, it moves along the straight path of the temporal clause; and like the bishop, it can also move along the diagonal line of the conditional. It combines the meaning of the English words "when" and "if." Basically, Kafka is an author who, I believe, translates well into other languages, as he goes beyond the peculiarities of any single language; he is not a "German" author in the way of, say, Jean Paul. But whoever translates him has to make up his mind and decide whether he wants to write down "if" or "when," and will lose some of the implications of this semantic ambiguity. The coincidence that results in German turns the mere possibility into the regular case, without really announcing it. Take, for instance, "On the Gallery" ("*Auf der Galerie*"). This text is generated and directed by its first word, *Wenn*, which seems to stretch forever before it is finally answered and completed by *dann*, preparing the ground for the next accord, in an alto voice: "Da—so." After these two figures have complemented and fulfilled each other, nothing is left but the weeping that finishes the text like a river reaching the sea. Kafka is among the large number of German poets that are tone-deaf; otherwise he couldn't make the text sing like this. That *Wenn* in "Wish to Become an Indian" is so powerful that there is no need for the main clause any more; the subordinate clause proceeds like an arrow into the open space, exactly matching the content of what it describes—*schon ohne Pferdehals und Pferdekopf*, riding without a horse, pure wishing in all its glory.

What is the substance of Kafka's writing? It is tricky to pose this question because it leads so easily to one of these particular interpretations. To steer clear of it, I want to resort to another short text (which, as it happens, follows immediately after "Wish to Become an Indian") that cannot possibly be misunderstood, "Refusal" ("*Abweisung*"):

> When I encounter a beautiful girl and ask her: "Be so kind to come with me" and she passes on in silence, she intends to say:

"You are no duke with a high-flying name, no broad American of Indian stature, with eyes horizontally at rest, with a skin smoothed by the air of the lawns and the rivers that run through them. You have not travelled to the big lakes and on them, which are to be found I do not know where. Therefore, I ask you, why should I, a beautiful girl, go with you?"

"You are forgetting that no automobile carries you in long sways through the streets; I do not see the gentlemen of your retinue pressed into their clothes, who, mumbling blessings for you, are walking behind you in an exact semicircle; your breasts are well arranged in their bodice, but your thighs and hips take their revenge for this austerity; you wear a finely pleated taffeta robe that pleased us all well enough last autumn, and yet you smile—this mortal danger on the body—now and then."

"Yes, we are both right, you and me, and in order not to become irrefutably conscious of this fact, let us both, each one of us, walk home alone."[2]

That it cannot be misunderstood does not mean that its implications are not breathtaking: how little men and women can avoid making each other unhappy. They will not avoid it precisely because they expect incomparable happiness from each other. Even so, however, it can be compared; a price tag is being attached to this happiness so that it can be measured. In this duet of man and girl, money is stealthily singing its song. They appraise each other. Conventionally, it starts out with the man's vulnerable wishing. The girl, expecting it, declines in a casual and well-practiced way, saving herself any trouble, as if even uttering the word "No" would be a waste of time, at least for this man. Properly speaking, the dialogue does not even happen, for the rules of this play between the sexes require that the all-important question not be explicitly voiced. Here, too, it is the interaction of *Wenn* and *So* in the first sentence that gives existence to what has only been imagined. What the man desires cannot take place, as he has too little to offer in the way of personal appearance and material resources (both are closely intertwined in the motive of the "American"). The girl pertly makes him understand that she is too good (i.e., too expensive) for him. She thinks that the choice she coolly exercises toward the man, who has accosted her in the street almost at random, will distance her from any semblance of prostitution; the opposite is true. The man in turn responds with a prepared mockery that teaches her about the mistake she makes about her value. That she lacks an elegant appearance is not considered a substantial shortcoming, but only an indication of what she is worth. In truth, only her body matters. With a meanness that otherwise seems reserved for how women treat each other (how astonishing that a man uses such language!), he includes her clothing in his snide remarks;

a venomous compliment targets her "taffeta robe." It is said of men that they undress women with their eyes. This man does the exact opposite: he makes her naked by looking at her dress, starting with the bodice that "arranges" her breasts—as if they needed such an arrangement. Under his scrutiny, her body changes into an amorphous mass like toothpaste in its tube, which, when you squeeze it in one place, makes up for it by bulging in another. The "beauty" that is addressed in the beginning turns out to be rather impersonal; it corresponds with a mark on a scale, like a grade in school; what she gets is a B-. Both are right—that's the terrible thing; both must demand more from the other than they themselves are worth in the marketplace. And for this, they must despise and hate each other. To stay alone for the night seems the merciful solution, for otherwise they would have to confront their quintessential loneliness. Summing up the text's substance in one sentence, it would have to be: The total socialization (*Vergesellschaftung*) of man produces through money (that is always present, even when not mentioned) his total isolation.

Why does Kafka feel so attracted to animals? He puts them at the centre of some of his most important late writings, in a way that connects with the long European tradition of the fable. He starts with the "Little Fable," which is followed in time by the great ones. The ascent is steeper than it seems. I will need one more intermediary station to get there, by discussing the "Report to an Academy" ("*Bericht an eine Akademie*").[3]

Kafka firmly believes that inspiration will be found only when the act of writing is not interrupted, like the casting of a bell. Yet here, he sets out several times— and produces a number of false starts. Only the "Hunter Gracchus" is comparable in this respect. His four different attempts are concerned with varying perspectives. First, Kafka tries the outside narrator, who wants to pay a visit to the transformed ape; he starts, "We all know Red Peter." The text does not continue beyond the encounter with the ape's manager, who forces a dish of eggs upon him—a casual contact like so many others that occur in Kafka's novels. They all disappear in the fables. Red Peter himself does not even show up, the text remains a fragment after one-and-a-half pages. A second attempt, somewhat longer, makes use of a dialogue between Red Peter and a visitor, who very likely is identical with the former narrator: "Sitting here with you like this, Red Peter"; a third start, the shortest one, consists in a letter that breaks off, "Dear Mr. Red Peter."

All that is discarded. The one text that is finally realized presents Red Peter in the first person as "I." It looks as if Kafka resented this solution, as it was the hardest way to do it, but had to acknowledge in the end that it would work out only like this.

Being human seems like a special project here, added on to the animal's basic existence like a saddle put on its back. But the narration has to keep both things present, what has been and what is now: ape *and* man. No gawking from the outside will do. That is what the music hall visitors come and pay to do every night. Yet the "Report to an Academy" is realistic in the sense that it compels the reader to use his visual imagination.

That is why Kafka has chosen a chimpanzee, man's closest relative among the animals. The distance between the two species is so small, it has been suggested, that they might both belong to the same genus. Before the leap can take place, the gap has to be narrowed down as much as possible. The story is told in a straightforward, linear manner, like a metamorphosis by Ovid. As it concerns the mind and not the body, only the person who experienced it may tell it. The narrator, however, has since come a long way, so far in fact, that he now has trouble reconstructing his old identity. What could Red Peter know and say about it? If Kafka ever showed a sign of weakness, it is here. The ape in his apish condition cannot have made the decision to become a human being in a rational, linguistic way; whatever he intended, it must have taken effect differently. Kafka uses the word *Ausweg* ("way out"). The way out for the ape always meant a local situation, a bodily escape. But there must have been the moment when the ape grasped that the way out could no longer consist in the physical option to flee. Instead, he took to something that must be called a rather far-reaching plan for modified behavior. The ape "thought" about this new type of a way out. Yet he thought about it "with his belly," as apes do. "Belly-thinking" has since had a rather questionable career in German language and culture. In its heyday during the 1980s, it stood for some kind of vague sentiment, demanding and lazy in thought, that made a claim of being equal or even superior to the "brainy attitude." Kafka may be credited with having coined this word, long before it became fashionable. Yet the problem stays with him: that the humanized being, even if there remains some memory, cannot express adequately within the bounds of language what it had been like to be an ape; for all language belongs to the realm of man. How do you speak of a dream after you wake up? All waking talk will misrepresent it. Ape and man, dreaming and being awake concern the same living entity. Waking causes the rift that divides what is One. It is a moment of anxiety, violent and precious—and yet it cannot be credibly narrated: when the ape, who has been handed a bottle of booze by the sailors and gulped it down, says "Hello!" all of a sudden, the sailors, raw-cut and good-natured, are rendered almost animal-like. The gap has been minimized—and yet is much too wide.

Nevertheless, Kafka's genius (if we may use this rather vague word in the absence of a better one) asserts itself even when he strives for something that proves impossible. Consider the few lines that mention Red Peter's sexuality. As he remains an ape in body, his lust, too, must turn toward a female ape. He cannot wish to associate with a human woman. That is the last thing we hear about before the report's closing lines; and it is tinged not only by a sense of shame about how inevitably shamelessly he must behave, but also, as it were, by a sense of meta-shame that he feels shamed this way. The sentence reads, "When I return home late at night from a dining party, a scientific meeting or an informal gathering, a little half-trained female chimpanzee is expecting me, and I enjoy her companionship in my apish ways." That sentence is followed by another one: "In daylight, I do not want to see her; for she has the insanity of the confused trained animal in her eyes; only I will recognize this, and I cannot bear it." This apish well-being—how painful it is to listen to it when it is put in language! Dealing with sexuality, Kafka almost always observes restraint. Yet he finds a way to insinuate that all human unhappiness, though not caused by sexuality, is brought by it to the point where it hurts. He who cannot tolerate his nighttime mate in daylight has failed in life. Red Peter, returning from his gentlemen's clubs, quaffing bottles of red wine with the leader of the expedition that caught him, corresponding with the Academy, may lead a life more unhappy than that of a child molester.

The "Report to an Academy," though admirable in itself, may nevertheless be viewed as a stepping stone toward other texts: "Investigations of a Dog" ("*Forschungen eines Hundes*"), "Josephine the Singer; or, The Nation of Mice" ("*Josefine, die Sängerin oder Das Volk der Mäuse*"), and "The Burrow" ("*Der Bau*").

What is it about the fable that makes it so attractive throughout the millennia? It cuts things short. When the fox shows up on the stage, there is no need for direct or indirect characterization; everything has been expressed by the fact that it *is* the fox—the story can start immediately. Of course, the classical fable has a simple and linear plot. As soon as we see the fox, we can be sure that he will try to cheat the raven, and no time is lost in giving us the moral of the story: Do not trust flattery! Kafka's fables are not that short and straightforward. They are short only in comparison to his novels, which are peopled by humans, and what they have to teach us is not easily defined.

Yet Kafka makes extensive use of the fable's most important feature, the ability for abbreviation. The three animals there have a presence that is different from Red Peter's. For Red Peter, improbable as he might be, is represented as some kind of naturalistic phenomenon. You are invited and even compelled to watch him as he raises the bottle of booze and utters his first human word. It is a monstrous picture; yet it is a picture. A picture, by forcing us to acknowledge its reality, fits in with all the long-established reality around it. It is only with the animals of the three fables that Kafka completes the truly fabulous feat of creating a restriction that reaches beyond. The clear-cut pattern of the fable always contained more than meets the eye. Its animals seemed like a mere means to simplify human complexity. But this was achieved only by allowing for a void in visualization between the talking fox we heard of and what we were able to see with our inner eye. The illustrations that originated in the late Middle Ages and early modern times did little to fill this void; their clumsy artwork keeps the secret. What would the animal look like that thinks and feels like a human being and yet remained an animal with all its undiminished qualities? The answer to this puzzle was given only centuries later, in what the cartoon movies did to their animal protagonists. Their artificial lives look as if a bolt of electricity has met the rude woodcuts of the fifteenth and sixteenth centuries. They are truly animated. Kafka would have loved Donald Duck and Wile E. Coyote—not with a completely innocent love, though; he would have chuckled (one might imagine) at the demonic undercurrents that go along with this late success.

The animals Kafka stages gain their abbreviating quality not from this or that single trait of character. Rather, being animals, they possess a quality of reduction as such; and this sets the texts in motion. What is a dog? There is no closeness of kin, and yet he has surrendered as completely to man as no other animal has, in an *emotional* way. This isn't the case with cows, pigs, chickens, even canaries, even though they are wholly dependent on man. Not even the cat compares in that respect. The cat may be called the true winner in the war man has made on nature. The cat is free like a wild animal, but at the same time protected from prosecution and always reliably fed. It inhabits an unfair paradise. We may rightly praise Kafka for having given the cat a wide berth (save for the short and unflattering appearance in "Little Fable"), preferring not to choose this comfortable and, as it were, purring way that leads to the land of the animals.

Dog *loves* man. It is a disgraceful romance. There is no other meaning in life for the dog but his master, which is more than could be said of the master himself. When the dog, as he is accustomed to do, lies at his master's feet and the master starts talking about him, the dog, hearing his name, will understand very well that he is being discussed. But he is incapable of decoding anything else of this conversation, as recognizing his name constitutes the maximum of what he will grasp of human language. In this situation, he will become quite restless; he will appeal to his master, looking for reassurance, pleading with him not to use his incomprehensible powers to do him any harm. It is a very earnest prayer the creature addresses to man, who truly turns into a god in this moment. The faithful, uneasy dog expresses a restriction that transcends itself by growing aware of itself; in this respect, he resembles man in his religious worship.

That is why Kafka chooses the dog. The dog wants to be with us; and there he is, as we touch each other. But the very physical contact accentuates the disparity that is registered by the master with some ironic distraction, by the dog with a sense of discontent that makes him very much like us.

The substance of "Investigations of a Dog" can thus be summed up in a parallel: What the dog is to us, we are to somebody else; by looking down on the dog with a smile, we get an idea of what a sight we might present to a higher being. So Kafka seems to say: Let us have a look at what a dog (who is given, for the fun of it, the complete possibilities of German syntax) will achieve when he does "science"!

Dogs, the text presupposes, are different from all the other animals in a fundamental way. Toward the rest of the animal kingdom they are thus in a position like man. Without being triumphant about it, they consider themselves as the crown of creation; a rather low and sad crown, yet, as the canine narrator notes, a proud one. The narrator speaks in the first-person singular; Kafka has had the experience by now that no other form will succeed. This dog speaks about the other creatures without arrogance; he pities them, as they are restricted to making certain noises and, knowing no community, act as complete strangers to each other. They have received neither the gift of language nor, even more important, the grace of being a "people."

Volk is the central term in the "Investigations" as well as in "Josephine." It is difficult to translate. It contains aspects of "nation," "folk," and "people," but matches none of them completely. The Volkswagen was supposed to be the national car by being the people's car. *Volk* are those who belong together without asking questions about it; by being a *Volk* the dogs (and supposedly the mice) tower over the brute and scattered beasts. Yet the term hardly applies to what dogs and mice really are. For both represent a species in the biological sense, a natural entity, which comprises all individuals that can breed with each other and produce offspring (which, by the way, is true for the lower animals as well). Kafka, however, insists on his *Volk*, and it can make you quite uneasy. For it resembles to an eerie degree the usage of the word by the German fascists, including derived forms like *Volksgemeinschaft* ("national/popular community"), *Volksgenosse* ("comrade"), and *volklich*. Fascism intended *Volk* to mean a historical and yet natural fact, a fate and an obligation they wished to be enthusiastically embraced by every single person, there being no alternative. That is exactly what Kafka has in mind. His *Volk*, too, hovers between nature and history, between the innocence of the species and the rational, political implications of society, combining the worst and most discouraging aspects of these two and omitting their positive sides.

The harrowing idea of the *Volk* marks exactly the point which Kafka's animal protagonists are able to reach in their reflections. It should pose the challenge to transcend it. This, however, never happens. The first person—the singular "I" in the "Investigations," the plural "we" in "Josephine"—functions as some kind of hybrid between a cage and its inmate. Only in the first person is it possible to voice the pain of pressure you feel when your skull is squeezed against a ceiling without having to give a name to the obstacle.

So the dogs are a stand-in for mankind. But there is no seamless allegorical match. The dogs preserve the very most shameful traits of their kind. They greet each other with "intimate hugs" (*innige Umarmungen*)—it seems that human interpretation wins against the empirical dogs, which, as we know, have no arms for hugging. But the sentence is continued by "honourable sniffings" (*ehrenvolle Beschnupperungen*), in human eyes the most revolting feature of canine behavior. The coupling of these two traits casts a doubtful light on every bodily aspect of human expression and emotionality as well. We may also recall "Jackals and Arabs" ("*Schakale und Araber*"), where the jackals address the traveller as "o gentle heart and sweet entrails" (*Du edles Herz und süßes Eingeweide*). The music dogs offend canine morality by walking on their hind legs and uncovering their private parts, without respect for the soul of the little puppy that witnesses it. It is described with disgust. What can it teach us, bipeds that we are? That is left for every reader to decide for himself. Here, Kafka's humor has one of its great moments. He always plays with shame and shamefulness, producing the most horrendous and grotesque results. The greatest happiness for dogs consists in the "warmth of being together" (*warmes Beisammensein*) in the "heap" (*Haufen*). And the protagonist buries his face in his neighbor's fur, the old, limping dog that comes to see him; it already exudes an odor somewhat like a fur that has been skinned (*abgezogenes Fell*). Kafka uses his dogs to uncover the repulsiveness of everything that is social; all intimacy must overcome it like appetite must overcome the faint sense of nausea that is caused by a smelly piece of meat. And how few rewards there are! No dog, that is quite certain, will ever share the tiniest morsel of food with another dog; in this respect, dogs might as well live in complete solitude. They even surpass mere egotism: they snatch away the food even when they are full and even from their malnourished neighbors, not out of greed but for reasons of principle. Which principle could that be? Probably the same one that makes us collect even the tiniest debts of others, although we do not need or even want the money.

The dog's inquiries deal with a subject that, at first glance, seems to be chosen and shaped in an absurd and arbitrary way. He wants to find out how the dogs' food is being produced. Here, all similarities with dogs as we know them, as pets, predators, and scavengers, disappear. Food production is based on "making everything wet," as already the newborn puppies are taught by their mothers; spells, dances, and chants support the procedure, even though it is not entirely clear what exactly they contribute to it. Food subsequently springs up partly from the earth and partly descends from the air, and this in turn partly on a direct path, partly sideways, or even in spirals. The remarkable thing is that the dogs, who do it on a daily basis because they have to, do not have the slightest idea how it happens. One should think that no science is required here; yet such a science does exist, the results of which, however, must be called rather unsatisfactory. Insight is blocked by irresistible forces: The "working of the ground" (which probably alludes to the canine habits of urination) is carried out compulsively, and as soon as a piece of food presents itself, it is greedily snapped up and devoured, thus destroying the scientific object.

But all absurdity vanishes at once as soon as the word "food" is replaced by a different one—"money." Money can justly be called the food of man. The number of people who live on what they directly harvest, gather, hunt, and slaughter is quickly approaching zero. All the others have to buy what they need. They know what money is for, but not what it is. They do not even know that they do not know. A "Lexicon of Ignorance" that was published recently in Germany counts the question "What is money?" among the great unsolved riddles, right next to the Big Bang and the Abominable Snowman. It quotes Alan Greenspan, former chairman of America's Federal Reserve, who never said a word about it while he held office, but now, in retirement, generously shares his ignorance, or rather his insight into his ignorance. That was his Socratic farewell gift to us. Money is the foundation of our lives and yet has a metaphysical tang to it. It is something everybody has to strive for actively, even if nobody quite understands what he is chasing. It provides something for us we do not comprehend, and makes us suffer without explaining how and why. Thus it resembles God. There are university departments of economics and theology, and yet they save no one the trouble of making a living and making sense of it. This it what Kafka means when he comes up with a scientific dog and puts it right in our face as our metaphor. Kafka is cruel.

Literary quality never varies within Kafka's work—for how could you improve what is perfect? Yet there are variations of cruelty. The "Investigations" bypass some of the factors in human life that really hurt. The dog's endeavors fail, his life has been in vain, and the older he gets, the more the range of his plans and inquiries narrows. That certainly is sad. Yet the motive of death is absent. Dogs get old; they can accompany man for what looks even to him like a long time. The details of the dog's old age do not inflict any pain on us that goes beyond what we know all too well, for we experience on a daily basis how our lives are gradually spent and lost. With mice, however, things change; death intrudes.

The text about Josephine does not complain. Nonetheless, the very absence of lamentation can be taken as a symptom. That generations rapidly succeed each other, and that cataclysms and nameless enemies (who even break up Josephine's concerts) cause untold casualties on top of it are taken as natural constants. There is neither reflection nor mourning, but always an inevitable haste that shapes all these lives. Of course, all schools are full of children, but in other schools, they are at least the same children for some time! Not so with mice. Even the emotion about the little ones and their rosy little muzzles is tinged with horror: how many there are, how they never stand still, how they are forever pushed along by what is already the next generation. They cannot be spared the fight for existence; otherwise, they would be killed on the spot.

In the realm of dogs, science had had its place—there had been activities and occupations of all kinds—but they took care of their living in quite a different way—in a way, it might be said, that did not require too much exertion. In the life of mice, all these things are replaced by labor (*Arbeit*) as an absolute necessity, as the demand of need. As though by a pair of tongs, the mice are held in place by the permanent compulsion to work and the permanent threat of death. They are so hard-pressed that they have no leisure to account for their desperate situation. The "Investigations" knew of specialization; there was space for seemingly pointless ways of life as well—the "air dogs," for example. "Josephine" falls back behind that to a much earlier stage of civilization. Her intent wish not to have to work anymore—a wish she thinks is justified by the gift of her art—is denied. Among mice, Neolithic conditions seem to prevail, or at least conditions of the early Middle Ages; no surplus is being produced that could be appropriated and distributed. All mice, though they are conscious that higher spheres exist, are so stooped in their poverty that no exception can be granted, not even if an individual had the best collective reasons. Even societies with a primitive structure make room for the shaman, who combines the jobs of priest, healer, and teacher, and, in exchange for what he does, receives alimentation. The mice cannot afford that. How sadly this primitivity contrasts with the complexity of Kafka's language!

"Josephine," too, even more so than "Investigations," is an analytical text that casts a sharp and almost sociological glance at the existence of a whole *Volk*. All the more terrifying is the tranquility, blindness, and exhaustion that accept the appalling situation. Among the dog people, there was at least enough liberty for the individual, if it observed certain rules, to yield to his private sadness. The narrator in "Josephine," who uses the first-person plural (the singular finds no foothold on these teeming grounds), resembles an otherwise intelligent human with severe organic brain damage, as it is described by Oliver Sacks: so severe is the damage that it precludes even the awareness that it has occurred—that, say, short-term memory or the visual field on the left side has been lost. Instead, a certain spectral equanimity, serenity almost, pervades this elaborate report, some "cheerfulness impossible to kill" (*nicht zu ertötende Munterkeit*), as the text puts it, where childish and elderly traits mix.

In this, the mice have a fate no different from mankind. They complete the predestined circle of their existence, and comply with it. The tradition of the community (which is fiercely guarded, although mice do not practice history as a discipline) is kept up and reproduced by the individual lives that succumb to it. Any single life makes up only a tiny miserable part of it, and yet the individual does not feel this misery; in this way, life acquires a semblance of happiness. It is true of the lives of mice and men alike what Schopenhauer has said about the life of man alone: that as such it is neither long nor short, but gives us a scale by which to reckon the shortness or length of any other state or event. Everybody's lifetime thus acquires the value of the absolute, of absolute scarcity. The life of mice, however, speeds along before our eyes like a film shown in rapid motion;

the notion of scarcity is magnified to a desperate degree, and yet it allows for comic effects as well. Kafka's trick, if it succeeds, can lead us to a sense of pity for ourselves, as we come to understand what poor beings we are, trapped in nature and history, nature bringing us quick death and history making it quicker still.

The "Investigations" as well as the "Singer" that provide the titles of the two stories are progressively diminished in the course of their narratives. In the end, practically nothing is left of them. What did the dog's inquiries yield? Very little—basically an undoglike tendency to brood and withdraw. And how about the singer? Her song, too, decreases; it becomes clear soon enough that it consists of little more than a whistling noise, and even that whistling withers away until it is level with the ordinary mice's whistling at work, possibly lower. As with the inquiries, only an attitude or a gesture remains, touching in its frailty.

"Josephine" is threatened by the misunderstanding of interpreting the story in an allegorical way, even more so than "Investigations." There are two alluring allegories: the mice are Jews; the whistling is art. Both are not entirely wrong; it becomes wrong only when you stop there. Kafka could not foresee what would happen to Jews in his near future—that their life expectancy in the years 1941 through 1945 would dwindle to that of mice, measurable in months and weeks rather than decades. In hindsight, Art Spiegelman has projected the Jewish fate onto the picture of mice. Doing that, he is more concrete, but also more constricted than Kafka. What happened to the Jews can be taken as a terrible premonition of what can happen to historical beings in general. In viewing "Josephine" as a Jewish allegory, one should go one step further and view the Holocaust as an allegory of mankind. This perspective does not impinge on its singularity; it raises it from the state of a particular event to that of a general warning.

If the Jewish allegory errs on the narrow side, the equation whistling = art is stretched too far to be illuminating. That art has to battle the obstacles of practical life, that the artist is loved as well as humiliated, and so forth—all that is quite banal. The subject has been treated exhaustively by lesser poets than Kafka. The text aims at something different: the specific relation of art's achievement to an underlying everyday activity. For art as a whole that includes all its genres and aspects, such an activity cannot be named. But to which type of art does this apply? It has to break loose with considerable effort from what people do anyway without trying too hard; it is always in danger of degenerating into the raw material it had previously transformed. Apparently this applies neither to the visual arts nor to the performing arts, nor to music. For all popular use that is made of these three is of a secondary character. Everybody who croons a pop song, draws a funny picture on a birthday card, or stages a little scene for a carnival event knows that he utilizes, in an undemanding way, something he has received from other spheres; that art in its strict sense has been the source of the stream from which he takes what he needs. Only with one form of art are things reversed:

literature utilizes language, which is truly and primarily owned by everyone. In literature, art must be considered as something that has not been the source, but derived from it. The relation between the whistling of Josephine and the whistling of ordinary mice is that between a poet's and the people's language.

But even that is not enough. Why has Kafka decided to represent a poetical problem in terms of music? To grasp the core of language, he apparently has to transpose it to a place where it loses its potential to communicate and is reduced to mere sound. The particular world of man is converted to the world of mice, which is no less particular. This is how the general conditions of animal and social existence are made perceptible. The particular genre of literature has been converted to the particular genre of music—in order to accomplish what? Which general truth can be brought to light this way? What is the intersection of music and language, their common essence?

Only nostalgia feels it. Nostalgia must be understood here as a productive ability that does not simply wish to return to an older state of things (this state has probably been just miserable), but looks in both directions, to the past and to the future. It sees sunset and sunrise at once. If only music and language would together! And this preferably not in the typical wrestling match of an aria, where the words are swallowed by the music, or a composed song, where the music gets a free ride on the back of the poem. There must have been some primordial home, where the two of them were still undistinguishable from each other, something like the primordial human being in the shape of a sphere about which Plato tells us, before it was sawed apart into man and woman. From this ancient paradise, both music and language moved away, each on its own way: toneless language, dumb music. Music is a motif in all three fables, strong in "Investigations," central in "Josephine," and consistently alluded to in the hissing sound that pervades the second half of "The Burrow." Yet Kafka is at pains to prevent it from entering the realm of audibility. He would never admonish his readers with a lifted finger like Thomas Mann: listen to this, join me! Of course, this music in *Doktor Faustus* was nonexistent as well, and even if it existed, we couldn't hear it because, after all, it is a novel. But that, so to speak, is just a matter of chance—it *could* exist. Kafka's music, by contrast, is at times feeble, like Josephine's whistling, at times powerful like in the music dogs' performance—yet every attempt to imagine its acoustic realization will fail. The seven music dogs produce neither instrumental nor vocal music; they stand above this technical distinction; they bring forth these sounds in their movements as the movements of the stars bring forth the harmony of the spheres. The best way to honor Kafka is to quote him:

> They did not talk, they did not sing, they generally remained silent with an almost embittered quality, but from the empty space they conjured up music. Their lifting and putting down of their feet,

their turning their heads, their running and resting, the positions they took in respect to each other, the dance-like conjunctions they entered, one of them for instance placing his front paws on another one's back and all seven of them carrying out the task in such a way that the first one bore the burden of all the others, or all of them forming intertwining figures with their bodies sneaking closely to the ground, never erring.[4]

It is only with a violent interruption that I stop here; the sentence goes on for a long time. What in world literature compares to these lines? Language itself shares the destiny of the seven dogs: it produces something that is based on a certain activity and course of events, but cannot be exhaustively understood that way. The language Kafka employs attests to the overpowering force of music without giving a hint of what it would sound like—and does so by assuming that quality itself. It plays on syntax like a musician plays on keys and strings; their mechanical properties, however, tell you nothing of the notes that stream forth. It is difficult to describe the effect; the text contains and conveys some kind of mystical experience. Kafka's art may be compared (if you do not consider this metaphor debasing) with a hornet that, trying to break free, bumps against the window pane time and again, and this buzzing and bumping in its modified repetition gives a rhythm to the process. Although the hornet does not succeed in passing through the glass (which is impossible, and impossible to grasp for the insect, for the very reason that the pane is transparent), somebody watching will not fail to notice how blue the sky is beyond the obstacle.

After all this, I do not want to say too much about "The Burrow." The two other texts contain, though weakly, the motive of redemption. To the inquiring dog, once in his lifetime, the music dogs have presented themselves; Josephine receives the consolation that her obstinacy will dissolve one day in cheerful general oblivion. "The Burrow" lacks this motive entirely. Many readers may feel that they cannot bear it. The protagonist, who speaks exclusively as "I" and has no notion whatsoever of its plural, is outlined much less clearly than the dog and mouse. Judging by what he does, you would guess that he was a badger-like animal, although otherwise you get the (rather hazy) impression of a canine being. In any case, he belongs to the large number of nonsocial animals that come together only during the mating season for a short and aggressive encounter; only the females spend some time with their cubs—the males live alone all year round. We may assume that an old bear feels no sadness about it, as this is consistent with his nature. Neither does the text's protagonist voice sentiments of loneliness; social contacts he may have had remain buried deep in the past (perhaps they never occurred at all). His life is dominated by the project of his burrow, which encloses, as a smaller subplot, the preoccupation with his store of food. Yet the fact that he uses such elaborate language to represent his hard, lonely, life-consuming work at such length gives the text a disconsolate note absent in the other two.

To whom does he speak? With dogs and mice, a listener can at least be imagined. The language of "The Burrow," however, proceeds emptily in a space that does not resound or respond. That he should speak at all has an uncanny air, as if it had undergone a strange transformation, turning an unknown liquid into a solid body that is not to be trusted. Kafka always writes in a way that makes things exist that did not exist before, save as a vague mood or atmosphere—as opposed to any type of literature that settles for describing what it sees. This, and not any telling details, comprises what is called the "kafkaesque." In this sense, no other text is as kafkaesque as this one. The contours are given in a fierce manner; yet Kafka does not show things, but calls their names, and there they are. (Just remember the Statue of Liberty in "The Lost One"—"*Der Verschollene*"—that raises a sword instead of the torch!)

"The Burrow" adds even more to this peculiar quality of Kafka's language by talking about things that are expected to be shrouded in complete darkness as if they were clearly visible. No lighting system seems to exist within the burrow (save for some tiny air shafts that have been dug by the wood mice); such a system would have crossed the strict technical barrier Kafka has set up between man and animal. No tool whatsoever is mentioned in the three fables; of the burrow's protagonist we hear that he has no instrument to fix the soil in place but his forehead, which he rams against the ground until he bleeds. All light that is shed on the fortification, which is rendered in great detail, is provided by language alone. That might be the reason, too, that the anatomy of his protagonist is left as vague as possible: we must not see his eyes. He acts as if he could see, which is quite out of the question.

This kind of seeing in the dark supplements a kind of speaking that takes place although it certainly never reaches this loner's throat, turning into sound. Vision and language occur in a space that is physically impossible, so that it may be called, with all due caution, metaphysical. There is, however, a total lack of any liberating aspect with which metaphysics is usually associated. Quite to the contrary, being constrained to the burrow, it becomes something far more oppressive than anything found in the common physical world.

Yet the others do exist. They will appear only in one of three shapes, two of which are strictly imaginary: as prey that is smaller than the protagonist (that a skinned rat occasionally clings to his teeth indicates his considerable size); as competitor of about the same size who has got wind of the gorgeous burrow and could feel the urge to establish himself inside, "somebody of my own kind, somebody able to esteem and value a burrow, some brother of the woods, a lover of peace, but a despicable scoundrel who wants to have his own quarters without building them"—what hatred breaks forth here! And finally, there is the enemy. The others are the fate even of the total loner, just as with dogs and mice, and even more so, but without any of the consolations that these two *Völker* provide for their members, although they cannot help each other much. Socialization in "The Burrow" takes on the form of nagging sorrow exclusively. The two other texts have something like a storyline: in the case of the dog the course of his life in general, from youth to old age; in the case of Josephine the quasi-musical sequence of the motives that follow each other: song, laughing, labor, childhood, paternal protection, fighting and salvation, and coloratura. (Coloratura: that word is repeated so often within a short paragraph that it becomes something of a coloratura in itself.) Of the burrow, by contrast, you get the impression that nothing at all ever happens. How could it? The burrow is there from the very start. And while the other two texts tend to take their respective project, the "investigations" and the "singer," apart playfully, so that they get smaller and smaller, and finally more or less disappear—the burrow always keeps the one note of its undisputed existence. But the accent slowly shifts from pride toward anxiety. The text begins, "I have constructed the burrow, and it seems a success." It begins, that is to say, with a conclusion. The further the text proceeds, the more that word "seems" turns from a mere auxiliary affecting modesty into a true predicate: It *seems* that way, but the appearance is misleading.

Since "The Burrow" sets out with its end, as it were, it cannot have a proper ending. The burrow is futility embodied. How sad is even the happiness it gives! Happiness will be felt most strongly by the owner when he abstains from it. This animal dreams of building a hollow that will envelop the *Burgplatz*, the central fortified place, enhancing it into some kind of egg-like object he can clutch with his claws from the outside. This is how he wants to "reimburse" himself for having to do without the central chamber itself: "And if I had to choose between dwelling in the central chamber (the 'Burgplatz') or in the outer hollow, I would decide in favour of the hollow for all the rest of my life." What Sigmund Freud called *Vorlust*, the "lust before lust," has been stretched here toward eternity, forever excluding lust's actual presence. And things are similar with the burrow's hidden entry, which the protagonist likes to watch secretly from a privileged observation post outside, a hiding of the second degree—even of the third, if you remember that the entry together with its maze-like corridor serves only as a confusing introduction to the burrow proper. Happiness here is removed three times over from him who would be happy.

While "Josephine" has a clear-cut ending, with the concluding motive of oblivion, and while "Investigations" at least somehow stops by mentioning the idea of freedom, "The Burrow" has remained a raw fragment. It breaks off in the middle of a sentence, even in the middle of a subordinate clause. But it does not break off in an accidental way, let alone arbitrarily, as the Romantic school would have it. This ego will build and talk as long as it breathes (for breathing and building are one), always driven by the conviction that the great work has not been completed yet. He will either die from exhaustion, or else be killed by one of the gigantic beings that are active in still-deeper dimensions of the earth, when one of them suddenly breaks through the burrow's walls. In any case, death will reach the protagonist at the only time possible: the unforeseen wrong moment. That we should prepare for a final turn is announced, at about the middle of the text, by the hissing noise. The longer the protagonist listens to it, the more evil it seems. We may assume that it originates from one of the hidden beings that had been briefly mentioned earlier in the text, one of the creatures that are characterized like this: "Even he who fell victim to them will hardly have seen them, they come, you hear the scratching noise of their claws immediately beneath in the ground that is their element, and you are lost." That description fits in with the text's last written word, the relative pronoun *das*—to be more exact, with its last letter, "s." The hissing sound that has long been just a threat springs into the rabid presence of death: It cannot take longer than this split second.

Did Kafka do that on purpose? No, probably not. And yet we must attribute it to him like a great artistic achievement. It seems like the kind of perfection he himself characterizes in his diaries, reluctantly, as it seems: that he only had to write down a sentence like "He went to the window," and it was perfect already. Perfection like that cannot be measured by a literary scale alone; what is literary about it is something like an outer skin. I only want to note this phenomenon, not to explain it. Kafka's fragmentary writing has an inner infinity that baffles everybody who ponders it, and whatever the outcome, it will remain a fragment, too. With a sense of sacrifice and incompleteness, I stop here. As Red Peter finishes his report, "to you as well, gentlemen of the Academy, I only reported."

Notes

1. "Wenn man doch ein Indianer wäre, gleich bereit, und auf dem rennenden Pferde, schief in der Luft, immer wieder kurz erzitterte über dem zitternden Boden, bis man die Sporen ließ, denn es gab keine Sporen, bis man die Zügel wegwarf, denn es gab keine Zügel, und kaum das Land vor sich als glatt gemähte Heide sah, schon ohne Pferdehals und Pferdekopf." (Franz Kafka, "Wunsch, Indianer zu werden." *Die Erzählungen und andere ausgewählte Prosa*, ed. Roger Hermes [Frankfurt: Fischer Taschenbuch Verlag, 2000], 7.) All translations in this article are the author's own.

2. "Wenn ich einem schönen Mädchen begegne und sie bitte: 'Sei so gut, komm mit mir' und sie stumm vorübergeht, so meint sie damit:

> Du bist kein Herzog mit fliegendem Namen, kein breiter Amerikaner mit indianischem Wuchs, mit waagrecht ruhenden Augen, mit einer von der Luft der Rasenplätze und der sie durchströmenden Flüsse massierten Haut. Du hast keine Reisen gemacht zu den großen Seen und auf ihnen, die ich weiß nicht wo zu finden sind. Also ich bitte, warum soll ich, ein schönes Mädchen, mit dir gehen?

Du vergißt, Dich trägt kein Automobil in langen Stößen schaukelnd durch die Gasse; ich sehe nicht die in ihre Kleider gepreßten Herren Deines Gefolges, die Segenssprüche für Dich murmelnd in genauem Halbkreis hinter Dir gehen; Deine Brüste sind im Mieder gut geordnet, aber deine Schenkel und Hüften entschädigen sich für jene Enthaltsamkeit; Du trägst ein Taffetkleid mit plissierten Falten, wie es im vorigen Herbste uns durchaus allen Freude machte, und doch lächelst Du—diese Lebensgefahr auf dem Leibe—bisweilen.

Ja, wir haben beide recht und, um uns dessen nicht unwiderleglich bewußt zu werden, wollen wir, nicht wahr, lieber jeder allein nach Hause gehen."

(Franz Kafka, "Die Abweisung," in *Die Erzählungen und andere ausgewählte Prosa*, ed. Roger Hermes [Frankfurt: Fischer Taschenbuch Verlag, 2000], 8.)

3. All passages from "Report to an Academy" are taken from "Ein Bericht für eine Akademie und andere Texte zu Rotpeter-Thema," in *Die Erzählungen und andere ausgewählte Prosa*, ed. Roger Hermes (Frankfurt: Fischer Taschenbuch Verlag, 2000), 322–37.

4. "Sie redeten nicht, sie sangen nicht, sie schwiegen im allgemeinen fast mit einer gewissen Verbissenheit, aber aus dem leeren Raum zauberten sie die Musik empor. Alles war Musik. Das Heben und Niedersetzen ihrer Füße, bestimmte Wendungen des Kopfes, ihr Laufen und ihr Ruhen, die Stellungen, die sie zueinander einnahmen, die reigenmäßigen Verbindungen, die sie miteinander eingiengen, indem etwa einer die Vorderpfoten auf des andern Rücken stützt und sie es dann alle sieben so durchführten, daß der erste die Last aller andern trug, oder indem sie mit ihren nah am Boden hinschleichenden Körpern verschlungene Figuren bildeten und niemals sich irrten." (Franz Kafka, "Forschungen eines Hundes," in *Die Erzählungen und andere ausgewählte Prosa*, ed. Roger Hermes [Frankfurt: Fischer Taschenbuch Verlag, 2000], 414–15.)

CHAPTER 8

Crowds, Animality, and Aesthetic Language in Kafka's "Josephine"

Thomas H. Ford

In *Barnaby Rudge*, Dickens's novel of the Gordon riots, the energies of urban insurrection and collective disorder appear at their most concentrated in the figure of Maypole Hugh.[1] An illiterate hostler and the bastard son of an executed gypsy and a debauched aristocrat, Hugh becomes the hero of the rioting crowd. He is also animalistic, resembling the horses he lives and works with and in whose barn he sleeps. As his employer states, "That chap that can't read nor write, and has never had much to do with anything but animals, and has never lived in any way but like the animals he has lived among, *is* a animal."[2] And Hugh is never more animal than when he leads the uprising, fused with the dray-horse he rides, appearing as the violent center and "centaur" of a collective storm of bodies.[3] Amid the crowd, Hugh most truly becomes an animal.

This correspondence between collectivity and animality has a long if somewhat subterranean history. Traces of this history can be found in our language, for example, in its wealth of collective nouns for animal groups: a shoal, a school, a herd, a pack, a swarm, a flock, a covey, a brood, a bevy, a pod, and so on. By the end of the nineteenth century this correspondence had acquired a newly scientific focus. The center of the discursive affinity between crowds and animals shifted from the kinds of folk belief drawn on by Dickens in *Barnaby Rudge* to the emerging disciplines of psychology and sociology. For crowd theory—a tradition which runs from Hippolyte Taine through Gabriel Tarde, Scipio Sighele, Gustave Le Bon, and William McDougall to Wilfred Trotter and Robert Park—people cease to behave as individuals when in a crowd. To articulate this loss of the boundaries that keep individuals distinct from one another, crowd theorists turned to animal life. In consequence, collective social forms mark a point of continuity between human and animal worlds for these writers. Le Bon, for instance, writes that "as soon as a certain number of living beings are gathered together, whether they be animals or men, they place themselves instinctively under the authority of a chief."[4] Even more explicitly, Wilfred Trotter set out to investigate "that yearning in us which is identical with the mechanism that binds the wolf to the pack, the sheep to the flock, and to the dog makes the company of his master like walking with God in the cool of the evening"—this is a yearning, we should note, "most evident in man's behaviour when he acts in crowds."[5] Similarly, William McDougall writes that the action of a crowd "in the worst cases is like that of a wild beast, rather than like that of human beings."[6] The pages of crowd theory teem with animals—honeybees, dogs, ants, elephants, sheep, deer, horses, wolves—swarms all taken to figure the experience of great crowds in the cities of modernity.

In *Group Psychology and the Analysis of the Ego*, Freud synthesizes the descriptive claims of crowd theory, citing predominantly Le Bon, Trotter, and McDougall, with the topography of the subject that he had recently elaborated in *Beyond the Pleasure Principle*.[7] But Freud does not directly engage this trope of animality in his analysis of crowds. Crowd theory understands collective social forms to be a biological trait that humans share with other animals. Freud, by contrast, locates the origins of collectivity in the symbolic history of the primal scene, which is rehearsed every time a child is brought up within a family. In this way, Freud historicizes crowd theory: what crowd theory undertook as a kind of comparative zoology is reinscribed in psychoanalysis as the historical hermeneutics of the subject. Freud marks this shift, for example, when he writes, "Let us venture, then, to correct Trotter's pronouncement that man is a herd animal and assert that he is rather a horde animal, an individual creature in a horde led by a chief."[8] With this substitution of "horde" for "herd," psychoanalysis seeks to escape the mythicizing appeal of zoological analogies, and instead sets out to analyze the individual subject in terms of his or her history. The relevant sense of history here is itself invoked by Freud in his account of the threat of death that is suspended by the chief over the members of the collective. But in what follows, I will show that this psychoanalytic turn to history still draws upon an implicit correspondence between the crowd and animal life. This is clear in Lacan, for instance, for whom properly human language is that in which each subject takes up his or her inalienable individuality. Lacan expressly defines this language in opposition to the animalistic language of the crowd. But for Lacan, as for Freud, crowds are always unified by a leader, and specifically by the death with which the leader threatens each individual member of the crowd. Here too, as for Freud, the crowd is always "led by a chief." In this understanding, crowd language, while partially animal, only ever communicates the knowledge of death—that same knowledge understood to inscribe the human subject within the time of history. Thus a latent, secretive anthropomorphism remains in this psychoanalytic reference to the animal. When we understand crowds through this recourse to the individual creature "led by a chief," do we limit, perhaps invalidly, our experience of animal life? And what other types of subject might come to speech in the crowd?

Kafka turns to the relationship between mass life and animality in his story "Josephine the Singer; or, the Mouse Folk," in which he takes this basic metaphor of crowd theory—that in crowds, we are animals—quite literally. Crowd theorists naturalized the language of the masses—the speech of the crowd—by conflating it with the cries of animals. But Kafka denaturalizes and defamiliarizes the voice of the animal by affiliating it to aesthetic discourse. He announces, through the song of a mouse, the connection established in modernity between the language of the crowd and aesthetic language. In Kafka's story, aesthetic discourse involves suspending the communicative function of language; the silence instituted in this way allows the proximity of transindividual language to animal life to be encountered. The language of the crowd resounds with the muteness with which animal life confronts us, we who are individual subjects of speech. The critical force of Kafka's position, I shall argue, is evident in the way it enables Elias Canetti to break with the understanding of the crowd as "animal," in the sense ultimately, and anthropocentrically, shared by crowd theory and psychoanalysis.

"Josephine" is the last story Kafka wrote, and the last to be published during his lifetime. Like many other instances of his late work, it is a first-person narration that circles, ruminatively, a set of enigmatic and quasi-philosophical problems. Here, perhaps more than anywhere else, Kafka's writing converges with the mode of construction of Kleist's stories. Kafka's narrator poses a series of questions which all refer to the difficulty of "the real riddle which needs solving, the enormous influence [Josephine] has" (*ihrer großer Wirkung*).[9] For on the one hand, the effect of Josephine's song is undeniable: "anyone who has not heard her does not know the power of song. There is no one but is carried away by her singing."[10] And yet on the other hand, it is unclear what the source of this great effect actually is, and whether Josephine's singing is in any way remarkable at all. Indeed, it appears that Josephine does not even really sing, for there is no discernible difference between her singing and everyday speech.

Listening to Josephine's song is not a question of understanding; hers is a song that signifies and communicates nothing. In her own opinion, when Josephine sings, "she is singing to deaf ears; there is no lack of enthusiasm and applause, but she has long learned not to expect real understanding, as she conceives it."[11] The significance of her song does not lie in the meaning it carries, for it carries no meaning. It acts rather than states, and the effect of its action is "to awaken the masses."[12] In this sense, the song conditions collective experience and being. Listening to her, the people "are soon sunk in the feeling of the mass, which, warmly pressed body to body, listens with indrawn breath."[13] The narrator names, as the best quality of the people, an "infallible practical common sense" (*untrüglicher praktischer Verstand*).[14] And yet the crowd's absence of understanding (*Verstand*) is one of the most peculiar aspects of the reception of Josephine's singing. The experience made available to the people by Josephine's song marks a clear break with their usual realm of "practical cunning."[15] It lies beyond the concerns and cares of everyday life, residing outside any general hermeneutics of understanding.

Yet if there is nothing to understand in her song, Josephine, when not singing, is quite capable of communication. Her own views on the nature and effect of her singing are stated clearly, and they carry full illocutionary force. She believes, for instance, that her song can rescue the people "when we are in a bad way politically or economically."[16] She makes claims on behalf of the social function of her art. She demands that the importance of her singing be publicly recognized by the people, and that she be accorded a status distinct from the others. The narrator describes the society as one of "a race of workers" (*ein Arbeitsvolk*).[17] But Josephine insists, albeit fruitlessly, that she be released from work: "Josephine has been fighting for exemption from all daily work on account of her singing; she should be relieved of all responsibility for earning her daily bread and being involved in the general struggle for existence."[18] All these claims and demands are asserted by Josephine, and understood by the narrator and by the people more generally. They are articulated within a discursive realm in which differing interests, projects, and beliefs can be shared and coordinated by a determinable set of communicative principles—principles which all discursive participants implicitly accept simply by virtue of participating in this discursive realm, even if only as listeners capable of comprehension. The world of practical understanding—the world regulated by this protocol of communicative speech—is oriented toward collective, public action. Both Josephine and the people are clearly able to accept the conventions and speech practices that govern this shared realm, and to operate within them. Josephine's song, on the other hand, appears to have no place here.

The narrator devotes considerable attention to the endless labor of the people, the projects they undertake, the threats that overhang them, and the hostile world into which they are thrown. Their life, we are told, is one of an inexorable struggle for existence. This struggle is their everyday condition, and also the situation that has shaped their language and which it consequently addresses. Josephine's song creates an aperture to a different type of existence and another mode of temporal experience; she introduces a breath within the struggle, bringing about a collective relief and release. It is the experience of a crowd, but also the experience of a shared dream. If her song serves "to awaken the masses," they awaken not to waking life but to a dream state. The great effect of her singing is such that those listening cannot even pay attention to her song, for they are asleep:

> The real mass of the people—this is plain to see—are quite withdrawn into themselves. Here in the brief intervals between their struggles our people dream, it is as if the limbs of each were loosened, as if the harried individual once in a while could relax and stretch himself at ease in the great, warm bed of the community.[19]

The song awakens the crowd by allowing the limbs, articulations or divisions (*die Glieder*) of individual subjectivity to relax and fade from consciousness. The crowd is not the dream state of the individual, but the bed in which the individual can participate in collective dreaming. Josephine's song opens the experience of the people out into this dream of collectivity.

So Josephine's noncommunicative language of singing is one that is clearly both formally removed and experientially distanced from daily concerns. And yet the difference that enters Josephine's voice when she sings is no real difference at all. Her song sounds the same as her everyday speech. Josephine doesn't so much sing as "pipe," and this "piping" is nothing other than "our people's daily speech" (*Pfeifen ist die Sprache unseres Volkes*).[20] Thus, while "many a one pipes his whole life long and does not know it," when Josephine sings, "piping is set free from the fetters of daily life and it sets us free too for a little while."[21] In this sense, the medium of Josephine's song is the medium of normal communication. It is made up of nothing but the language of the people—language that is normatively oriented toward the horizon of mutual and "infallible" understanding. Josephine's song communicates nothing, and yet it is made up of nothing but communicative language. If her song can be said to contain a kind of music, it is a music "reduced to the least possible trace" (*auf die möglischste Nichtigkeit reduziert*).[22]

For this reason, Josephine's song, the narrator tells us, should not be assimilated into the traditional musical forms of the people, forms which perhaps once composed an organic unity with the lifeworld they expressed:

> Although we are unmusical we have a tradition of singing; in the old days our people did sing; this is mentioned in legends and some songs have actually survived, which, it is true, no one can now sing. Thus we have an inkling of what singing is, and Josephine's art does not really correspond to it.[23]

The difference introduced into language by Josephine's refusal to communicate cannot be understood in terms of tradition, or as the inflection of her discourse by a remnant of an otherwise lost popular art form. Instead, it is a difference dependent on an absence of difference; it is a negated difference, a distinction under erasure, one reduced to nothingness. This is a very recognizable sense of the paradoxical autonomy, the indeterminable difference, of the aesthetic—one which can be traced back to Romanticism, but which was formulated with greatest disciplinary rigor within central European linguistics during the period in which Kafka composed this story.[24] That Josephine's art falls under this rubric is suggested, at least, by the narrator's frequent use of the verb *erheben* to describe Josephine's "lifting" her voice into song—the verb from which *das Erhabene*, "the sublime," is derived. But equally, the narrator is careful to note that this Romantic aesthetic does not adequately encompass the effect of Josephine's singing:

> What drives the people to make such exertions for Josephine's sake? This is no easier to answer than the first question about Josephine's singing, with which it is closely connected. One could eliminate that and combine them both in the second question, if it were possible to assert that because of her singing our people are unconditionally devoted to Josephine. But this is simply not the case; unconditional devotion is hardly known among us.[25]

While Josephine's song is proximate to a Romantic thematic of art, Kafka's story always retains a distinction between the aesthetic framing of her song and the experience to which it opens. The aesthetics of elevation and the sublime rehearsed by Josephine do not lead to her own elevation, to a fetishization of the artist by the public. No Romantic cult of individual genius is in evidence here. Instead, the people remain primary. They refuse to surrender to Josephine, even as they enter the dream of collectivity through her singing.

In his biography of Kafka, Max Brod writes:

> In the last weeks he was meant to speak as little as possible. So he made himself understood through written communications on slips of paper, some of which I possess. Once he wrote: "The story receives a new title. Josephine, the Singer, or, the Mouse Folk. Such or-titles are certainly not very pretty, but here it perhaps has a special sense. It has a something of a set of scales."[26]

Kafka's comment on the story's new title—originally titled simply "Josephine the Singer"—underscores a sense in which Josephine and the people may be viewed as opposing parties. It seems to suggest that the function of the story as a whole might be to mediate or find a balance between their differing interests. Such a balance implies a third position that belongs neither to Josephine nor the people. In this reading, a third party, the implied reader, acts as a fulcrum between the singular name (Josephine) and the collective people. One could point to many analogous three-party schemas in Kafka's work: the European functions as a mediating third term in the dialectic of "Jackals and Arabs," for instance; the absent, invisible emperor stands as a third party to the nomads and shopkeepers in "An Old Manuscript"; or, perhaps most relevant, the public sphere forms the backdrop to the dialectic of persecution in "A Little Woman." To interpret "Josephine" in this way is, in effect, to appeal to an external frame of judgment—to the place of criticism, in the etymological sense of discriminating between two things and coming to a decision. It is to understand reading the story as an exercise of judgment; the scales referred to in Kafka's comment to Brod are taken to weigh up the two alternatives between which we must decide.

But can we assimilate Kafka's scales to this conventional understanding of judgment? Does Kafka not question, at a much more radical level, the norms of mutual understanding and rational consensus implicitly appealed to in such an act of criticism? In *The Trial*, Josef K. visits Titorelli, the painter, where he views a portrait of a judge. Behind the judge rises an allegorical figure that K. at first cannot recognize:

> "It's the figure of Justice," the painter finally said. "Now I recognize it," said K., "there's the blindfold over her eyes and here are the scales. But aren't those wings on her heels, and isn't she in motion?" "Yes," said the painter, "I'm commissioned to do it that way, it's actually Justice and the goddess of Victory in one." "That's a poor combination," said K. smiling, "Justice must remain at rest, otherwise the scales sway and no just judgment is possible."[27]

The figure in Titorelli's painting soon acquires a third identity, that of the goddess of the hunt, so that justice blurs indistinguishably into pursuit, persecution, triumph, and death. In Kafka, the scales of justice are always shadowed by the threat of execution. In law, a death sentence must be carried out as soon as possible. In Kafka, it must be carried out in the moment it is pronounced, as in "The Judgment," in which Georg Bendemann is precipitated into the river still bearing the blow of his father's judgment—"I sentence you now to death by drowning!"—in his ears.[28] In Kafka's writing, death always attends the critical moment, the decisive tilt of the scales, as if the message conveyed by this semaphoric tilt were fatal in and of itself. For the scrambled allegorical attributes of Titorelli's painting suggest the presence of a further god, Hermes, who bears with his winged heels the capacity to deliver a message—"die!"—instantaneously. Through this ironic pun on "hermeneutics," Kafka's overdetermined iconography refers out to the reader and to the theories of interpretation we bring as readers to this writing. K.'s comment that justice must remain at rest suggests a desire to isolate the law from action. K. wants to be able to distinguish between judgment and its realization; he wishes the law to stand separate from its execution. Only then, he believes, can the scales of justice measure truly and tell the guilty from the innocent—the party to which, K. has just declared to

Titorelli, he belongs. In the world of *The Trial*, of course, this is deeply inadequate as an understanding of the law, for in that world, as in ours, the law operates as the very springs of action, and never as a pure realm of disinterested and unmoved contemplation. Titorelli paints the allegorical figure in this way, for instance, because he has been instructed to by the judge. As he says, "I'm just following the wishes of the person who commissioned it" (*meinem Auftraggeber*).[29] Without this commission or task—this message that transmits action because it allows no firm distinction to be drawn between message and action, because it is a message always already caught up in a world of action—Titorelli's paintings yield only stasis. In his free time, as he reveals to K., he paints serial, identical barren landscapes.

The command—this immediate identity of action and message—is the central concept of Elias Canetti's *Crowds and Power*, the concept that links the two themes announced by his title. For Canetti, the defining function of power is to issue commands, while crowds are formed by a peculiar circulation of commands. "Every command consists of *momentum* and *sting*," Canetti writes.[30] He proposes that the role of momentum is to transmit action, so that the ordained task is performed. Momentum is exhausted once this action has been accomplished. But the time frame of the sting is different. It remains, unchanging, as an unassimilable foreign body in the one who has to obey. This intransigent temporality of the sting derives from the threat of death, which Canetti identifies as the vehicle of every command, the bearer of its motive force. This symbolic and potential death, conveyed by the command, lodges in the individual body forever whenever a command is obeyed; it constitutes a nugget of *ressentiment*, never to be eroded. The sting, Canetti writes, "is never lost . . . it remains stored up for ever."[31] Receiving a command leaves a residue of petrified shock in the individual that can only be released when the situation is reversed, and the one who once obeyed the command can now issue it, and compel the obedience of another through the threat of death. The desire to achieve this situation of reversal, Canetti argues, motivates much of what we understand as ambition and careerism, which hierarchical structures, such as exist in armies, are designed to encourage. In this view, history appears as an unending slow transmission of commands through generations. Historical time, the continuous outpouring of the new, is here understood as nothing but the empty medium through which these unalterable symbols of fatality eternally travel. It may take decades, Canetti writes, to pass on the commands one received as a child, but one's life will be determined, in unknowable ways, by the need to retransmit all the commands with which one has been struck, thus freeing oneself from the accumulated stings of subalternity.

Canetti's concept of the command breaks with the way commands have generally been theorized within modern philosophies of interpretation. Hans-Georg Gadamer, for example, attempts to assimilate commands to the hermeneutic understanding that he sees as underlying the human sciences and, indeed, the possibility of historical experience at all:

> To understand the order means to apply it to the specific situation to which it pertains. . . . A person who refuses to obey an order has understood it, and because he applies it to the situation and knows what obedience would mean in that situation, he refuses. . . . [He] is well able to distinguish between understanding and obeying an order. It is possible for him not to obey even when—indeed, precisely when—he has understood it.[32]

Gadamer introduces the hermeneutic primacy of understanding even into the situation of command. But for Canetti, the command is a statement which always transmits the threat of death: to receive a command is, implicitly, to receive a possible death sentence. No matter the extent to which this death is sublimated and domesticated through social structures, it is always present as the horizon of the imperative. So if we accept Canetti's suggestion that every command bears within it this murderous and complete denial of understanding, then the possibility of understanding and not obeying an order is in fact never present. In this way, the command is a kind of "communication" that rests on the possible total destruction of all communicative possibility. Inasmuch as this violent limit to understanding is borne within every command, the structure of command can never be assimilated to the model of understanding, as Gadamer attempts to do. Like Josephine's song, commands are a noncommunicative use of communication; at their core, there is nothing to understand.

Although he nowhere acknowledges this, Canetti's concept of the command derives very directly from his close and lifelong engagement with the work of Kafka. One could offer little better evidence for this than the way the allegorical attributes represented in Titorelli's painting are the very qualities that determine the command: speed, irreversibility, lethality. "In the Penal Colony" presents another likely source for this idea of the imperative judgment as an illegible, incommutable, and murderous utterance. While Kafka's name appears nowhere in *Crowds and Power*, his influence on that text is vital, and the centrality of Kafka to Canetti's analysis of power and collectivity is set out clearly in Canetti's *Kafka's Other Trial: The Letters to Felice*.[33] Kafka's words lie beneath Canetti's conception of becoming animal, for instance; they also confirm his aversion to judgment, and direct his attention to the aspects and postures of power. It is Kafka who, through the song of the animal, allows Canetti to arrive at a concept of the language of the crowd that retains none of the parameters established by the tradition of crowd theory represented by Le Bon. Canetti's notion of command is in similarly sharp disagreement with such twentieth-century theorists of the experience of the crowd as Freud and Heidegger, and consequently with the hermeneutics of historical understanding—psychoanalytic as much as Gadamerian. The significance of the conceptual resources Canetti derives from Kafka can be seen quite clearly by contrasting Canetti's notion of the command with the theory of crowd language developed by Lacan in his synthesis of the Freudian topology of the subject with Heideggerian *Dasein*.

Lacan articulates the Freudian model of the crowd in his argument that a letter always arrives at its destination. In Lacan's schema, the symbolic order guarantees that the letter's address is deliverable, that the letter will always reach its target because that address is an effect of the symbolic order—that is to say, an effect of "the letter" itself. Thus a subject is always oriented, individually, by his or her position within the order of language. There is one exception to this inevitable destiny ordained in the register of the symbolic, Lacan states, and that occurs in crowds. There, one finds instead,

> the communion established between two people in their hatred directed at a common object, with the proviso that this can never occur except in the case of one single object, an object defined by the characteristics of (the) being that each of the two refuses to accept. But such communication is not transmittable in symbolic form. It can only be sustained in relation to this object. This is why it can bring together an indefinite number of subjects in a common "ideal"; the communication of one subject with another within the group thus constituted will remain irreducibly mediated by an ineffable relation.[34]

For Lacan, this "communion" is enabled by a very specific form of communication "not absent in man," a communicative mode homologous to the waggle dance of bees.[35] In making this claim, Lacan refers to Émile Benveniste's "Animal Communication and Human Language," in which Benveniste draws a number of essential distinctions between the waggle dance and human language, concluding that bee communication "is not a language but a signal code."[36] Two distinctions in particular are most relevant for Lacan. First, Benveniste argues that human language is intersubjective; speech is addressed by one subject to another who is deemed capable of replying purely by virtue of the formal structure of being a subject of address. It is in this sense that a letter always arrives at its destination. Bee language, conversely, "lacks the dialogue which is distinctive of human speech."[37] The waggle dance is not uttered by a subject, or addressed to a subject. Secondly, Benveniste argues, "the bee's message cannot be reproduced by another bee which has not seen for itself what the first bee has announced. . . . The bee does not construe a message from another message."[38] Bees, that is, cannot pass on messages; they can only carry them out. Human language, by contrast, can retransmit messages to infinity. In effect, by relating Benveniste's argument to the Freudian model of the crowd, Lacan declares these two characteristics of human language—intersubjectivity and retransmissability—to be inextricably intertwined. Lacan's claim is that the subjectivity inherent to human language should be understood as an effect of the capacity, borne within human language, to pass on messages. For Lacan, such retransmissability is therefore the basic indicator of the existence of a human subject.

Only in the crowd, according to Lacan, do we enter into a paradigm that approaches bee language (i.e., no passing on messages, therefore no individual "human" subjects). There, we are as vulnerable to command as a honeybee. Thus the "communion" of a crowd is established through a pure order language, a language of commands that must be enacted, here and now, in the presence of the object (that is to say, the leader). In the crowd, for Lacan, every statement is an order that must be carried out immediately; it cannot be passed on:

> While a message of the kind described here determines the action of
> the "socius," it is never retransmitted by the socius. This means that
> the message remains frozen in its function as a relay of action, from
> which no subject detaches it as a symbol of communication itself.
> [But] the form in which language expresses itself in and of itself
> defines subjectivity.[39]

From this point, Lacan can determine the structure of the individual subject as being-toward-death on the basis of the necessarily intersubjective nature of properly human language: "I identify myself in language, but only by losing myself in it as an object. . . . What is realized in my history is . . . the future anterior as what I will have been, given what I am in the process of becoming."[40] In the Lacanian argument, the crowd provides the only collective exterior to this intersubjective structure in which each individual leads an historical existence retrospectively oriented by the anticipated standpoint of his or her death. And for Lacan, this exterior, the crowd, is quite explicitly continuous with the life of animals. It is made possible by a form of communication "not absent in man" that conforms to the model provided by the waggle dance of bees. This entails that only in the crowd do we evade the symbolic imperative of individuation that forms our world and regulates our conduct, unconsciously, in everything we do. And we only evade this imperative in the crowd, according to Lacan, by immediately submitting to and carrying out the imperatives issued by the crowd's leader. A command addressed to a crowd is a power-sign; in effect, it is inscribed directly onto the real. No time can elapse between receiving the message and carrying it into action. Like Georg Bendemann, the crowd precipitates itself into obedience and liquid emotion, still bearing the shock of the command in their ears.

It is in this context that we can register the importance of Canetti's borrowings from Kafka. For Lacan, in the crowd, a command immediately determines action because it cannot be passed on. But for Canetti, in the crowd, commands can always be passed on. Indeed, a crowd comes into being as a linguistic form of existence for Canetti once commands cease to stick to and "sting" the individuals to whom they are addressed. Canetti argues that in a crowd commands are retransmitted immediately through the physical density of bodies: everyone passes on every order to everyone else.

> In a crowd a command spreads horizontally. It may originally strike a single individual from above [i.e. from a leader], but, since others like himself stand near him, he immediately passes it on to them. . . . The instantaneous spread of the same command turns them into a crowd. . . . It is only commands that remain isolated which lead to the formation of stings.[41]

Commands are passed on so swiftly they leave no remainder, no "sting," but become pure momentum. And this instantaneous retransmission does not give rise to a symbolic order, for to this extent Lacan's formulation is quite correct: these commands are passed on as "relays of action," not as "symbols of communication itself." There is no symbolic position of subjectivity available within the crowd. And in this sense, crowds need no "common object" through which their "messages" must pass as a necessary point of reference, as Lacan claims. This common object is, if it can be identified anywhere, expanded to the dynamic limits of the crowd itself. There is a crowd—rather than an army, or mere seriality—once this imaginary object-relation is erased by the omni-directional, horizontal, and reciprocal retransmission of commands. This seething rhythm of commands is the language of the crowd.

Canetti's extrapolations from Kafka attune us to the emergence, in "Josephine," of this language of the crowd through the mediation of aesthetic discourse. Josephine's piping assembles great crowds because it is received "almost like a message from the whole people to each individual" (*fast wie eine Botschaft des Volkes zu dem Einzelnen*).[42] The effect of this individual address is to return its hearer to the collective body of the people. So the message passes through two points of individuality, Josephine and the individual listener, but only in order to bring them both, finally, into the crowd. To understand the apparent alternatives of the title—Josephine and the mouse people—as representing a clear opposition between individuality and collectivity is to overlook this sense in which the people is itself composed of individuals until the articulations and divisions of their individuality are released in the crowd, in the communication of collective being.

A minute temporal gap exists between the moment in which the message is heard and the moment when that message dissolves its hearer into the crowd. The singularity of aesthetic experience, Kafka's text suggests, lies in its capacity to stage in this gap an opening to the language of the crowd. Lacan, as we have seen, claims that a retransmitted message can be abstracted from its communicative context in order to serve as "a symbol of communication itself." This possibility, he argues, underwrites the existence of the individual human subject. We can recognize how close this formulation is to that account of aesthetic language, discussed above, which identifies it as the foregrounding of language as such, the purposive bracketing or suspension of communicative purpose. In this sense, the use of communication to symbolize communication itself could serve as a post-Romantic definition of the poetic function. But Josephine's art establishes a passage, crossed in the briefest temporal gap, from this "subjective" and aesthetic suspension of purpose to a nonsubjective experience of collective being in the crowd. "Josephine" confirms that aesthetic language bears within it a capacity to open onto the language of the crowd. It bears that capacity not because it brackets communication but because, in this bracketing, it places itself at the limit of the phenomenal structure of the individual subject, making possible a collective recirculation of commands to which it is itself subject. Rather than confirming the symbolic order, aesthetic language here allows access to a nonsymbolic experience of collective existence, to the dream state of the crowd.

Josephine's song is nothing other than language, somehow set free from the demands of daily life. But her audience—or at least, those who receive the full effect of her singing, that is to say, the crowd—in no way apprehends this language. What they attend to is the silence that her song makes manifest. Josephine is "a mere nothing in voice, a mere nothing in execution" (*dieses Nichts an Stimme, dieses Nichts an Leistung*).[43] Hers is a song "reduced to the smallest possible nothingness." And yet something of this nothing "irresistibly makes its way into us."[44] This irresistible force cannot be located in her song itself; it resides in the silence that her song allows the people to perceive. That is why when, in the proleptic movement with which the story ends, in which the narrator discusses Josephine's death, slipping between past, present, and future tenses, Josephine's individual death does not entail the end of the crowd:

> She is a small episode in the eternal history of our people, and the people will get over the loss of her. Not that it will be easy for us; how can our gatherings take place in utter silence? Still, were they not silent even when Josephine was present? Was her actual piping notable louder and more alive than the memory of it will be? Was it not rather because Josephine's singing was already past losing in this way that our people in their wisdom prized it so highly?[45]

Conclusion

Josephine's death will strip her of all claims to individuality. For Heidegger, the exemplary historicity of *Dasein* is inscribed by its being-toward-death. This position is also foundational for Lacan, for whom a "profound relationship" unites "the death instinct to problems of speech," as well as for the hermeneutics of Gadamer, for whom "all experience is experience of human finitude."[46] But the people of Kafka's story conduct no history: "Generally speaking we ignore historical research entirely."[47] They have memory and futurity, but these temporal horizons cannot be unified for them in the future anterior ecstasis of the death of the present subject. Josephine, upon dying, "will happily lose herself in the numberless throng of the heroes of our people, and soon, since we are no historians, will rise to the heights of redemption and be forgotten like all her brothers."[48] In the space opened by Josephine's piping breath, through which the articulations of the individual are relaxed, we sense a collective time other than that regulated by intersubjective understanding—that is to say, by history and being-toward-death. Historical understanding is possible, Gadamer argues, because the other, the object of our understanding, is bound like us within a finite temporal horizon. It is on this basis, he claims, that we can understand the texts of the past, just as we understand—but need not obey—a command. But crowds are not constituted by this sense of an ending; the crowd lies outside the individuating frame of this kind of historical understanding, and beyond the parameters of our experience of history. Crowd-time informs our present—it comes to speech in the present, for instance, in aesthetic language—but it can never be realized as an aspect of the historical determination of that present. Crowds open the present to a nonhistorical future, a future whose coming is felt like a rhythmic pulse, rather than being anticipated within a hermeneutic horizon of understanding.

When they form a crowd, the people resonate with this silent beat of a different future. As we have seen, the scales structure established by Kafka's title sets up a series of critical expectations that the story systematically denies, and calls for an exercise of critical judgment that the text endlessly defers. That title also marks the people as mice. And yet only once in the story is this mousiness of the people ever mentioned. They are referred to throughout merely as "people" (*das Volk*), not as mouse people or animal people. There is a single exception: when listening to Josephine—or rather, listening to the silence that Josephine's singing makes audible—the crowd is described as sitting "in mouselike stillness" (*mäuschenstill*).[49] Through this silence, this animal muteness, opened by the indiscernible difference introduced into language by the aesthetic, the people encounter the crowded futurity promised to them by their subaltern status and by the threat of death that hangs over them. They are an abundant—proletarian—people, and their multitude is announced in this briefest interval, in the time through which Josephine's song uncovers the difference that separates the being-toward-death of the historical human individual from the rhythmic anticipation of the crowd in the flux of animal life:

from our race come pouring at the briefest intervals [*aus unserem Volke strömen in Zwischenräumen*] the innumerable swarms of our children, merrily lisping or chirping, so long as they cannot yet pipe, rolling or tumbling themselves along by sheer impetus so long as they cannot yet run, clumsily carrying everything before them by mass weight so long as they cannot yet see, our children! . . . without end, without a break, hardly does a child appear than it is no more a child, while behind it new childish faces are already crowding so fast and so thick that they are indistinguishable [*ununterschiedbar in ihrer Menge und Eile*], rosy with joy.[50]

This is a life lived outside the trajectories of death borne in the command. We are directed to it as much through aesthetic language as by the animal forms we encounter as we pass across the threshold separating the individual from crowd. For to cross that threshold is not to leave language behind. To oppose the crowd to the symbolic order that discursively structures the everyday lifeworld, as I have done here, is not to fetishize a nonlinguistic other, or to construct a mythical fantasy of animal alterity. The crowd is no mystical resource of dizzying shock, no phenomenon of total indeterminacy that explodes all the certainties of reason. It is, instead, a capacity—an animal capacity—within human language: a crowd is always, at least in part, a discursive event. The meaning of that event is given to us by Kafka.

Notes

1. Charles Dickens, *Barnaby Rudge* (Harmondsworth, UK: Penguin, 1973).

2. Dickens, *Barnaby Rudge*, 140.

3. Dickens, *Barnaby Rudge*, 671.

4. Gustave Le Bon, *The Crowd: A Study of the Popular Mind* (London: T. Fisher Unwin, 1897), 112.

5. Wilfred Trotter, *Instincts of the Herd in Peace and War* (London: T. Fisher Unwin, 1919), 51, 28.

6. William McDougall, *The Group Mind* (Cambridge: Cambridge University Press, 1920), 45.

7. Sigmund Freud, *Group Psychology and the Analysis of the Ego* (London: International Psycho-Analytical Association, 1922).

8. Freud, *Group Psychology*, 89.

9. Franz Kafka, "Josephine the Singer; or, the Mouse Folk," in *The Complete Stories* (New York: Schocken Books, 1971), 361.

10. Kafka, "Josephine," 360.

11. Kafka, "Josephine," 363.

12. Kafka, "Josephine," 363.

13. Kafka, "Josephine," 364.

14. Kafka, "Josephine," 369.

15. Kafka, "Josephine," 360.

16. Kafka, "Josephine," 366.

17. Kafka, "Josephine," 375.

18. Kafka, "Josephine," 371.

19. Kafka, "Josephine," 370.

20. Kafka, "Josephine," 370.

21. Kafka, "Josephine," 370.

22. Kafka, "Josephine," 370.

23. Kafka, "Josephine," 361.

24. The paradoxes through which Kafka passes in his elaboration of the linguistic difference that characterizes Josephine's singing bear comparison with contemporary documents of Russian formalism, which, at the time of writing of "Josephine," was about to confirm its emergence with the foundation of the Prague Linguistic Circle. Take the "Theses Presented to the First Congress of Slavic Linguists": "there is a function of communication, that is to say, one directed toward the signified, and a poetic function, that is to say, one directed toward the sign itself." This "poetic function" can be understood as the function language has in the absence of a function. As Jan Mukarovsky writes, "The poetic foregrounding of linguistic phenomenon . . . is its own purpose"; Bohuslav Havránek similarly argues, "There is an essential difference between . . . dialects . . . which are always used to communicate something (have a communicative function) and between poetic language which is not primarily communicative." This position can ultimately be traced back to the Kantian formulation of aesthetic purposiveness: the poetic work is at once subject to a determination (its elements are coordinated into a purposive unity), and yet not determined by any purpose. It is the proximity Josephine's art has to Kant, mediated through this contemporary formalism, that justifies its description as Romantic. The nature of Kafka's art—which frames our access to Josephine's song—is, of course, another matter. See "*Thèses présentées au Premier Congrès des philologues slaves*," in *A Prague School Reader in Linguistics*, ed. Josef Vachek (Bloomington: Indiana University Press, 1964), 41–42; Jan Mukarovsky, "Standard Language and Poetic Language," in *A Prague School Reader on Esthetics, Literary Structure, and Style*, ed. Paul L. Garvin (Washington, DC: Georgetown University Press, 1964), 28, 20, 22; Bohuslav Havránek, "The Functional Differentiation of the Standard Language," in *A Prague School Reader*, 15.

25. Kafka, "Josephine," 364.

26. Max Brod, *Franz Kafka: Eine Biographie* (Berlin: Fischer, 1954), 251.

27. Franz Kafka, *The Trial* (New York: Schocken, 1998), 145.

28. Franz Kafka, "The Judgement," in *The Complete Stories*, 87.

29. Kafka, *The Trial*, 145.

30. Elias Canetti, *Crowds and Power* (Harmondsworth, UK: Penguin, 1973), 354.

31. Canetti, *Crowds and Power*, 354.

32. Hans-Georg Gadamer, *Truth and Method* (New York: Continuum, 1997), 333–34.

33. Elias Canetti, *Kafka's Other Trial: The Letters to Felice* (New York: Schocken, 1988).

34. Jacques Lacan, "Seminar on 'The Purloined Letter,'" in *Écrits* (New York: Norton, 2006), 13.

35. Jacques Lacan, "Seminar," 13.

36. Émile Benveniste, "Animal Communication and Human Language," in *Problems in General Linguistics* (Coral Gables, FL: University of Miami Press, 1971), 54.

37. Benveniste, *Problems in General Linguistics*, 53.

38. Benveniste, *Problems in General Linguistics*, 53.

39. Lacan, "The Function and Field of Speech and Language in Psychoanalysis," in *Écrits*, 246.

40. Lacan, "Function and Field," 247.

41. Canetti, *Crowds and Power*, 360.

42. Kafka, "Josephine," 367.

43. Kafka, "Josephine," 367.

44. Kafka, "Josephine," 367.

45. Kafka, "Josephine," 376.

46. Lacan, "Function and Field," 260; Gadamer, *Truth and Method*, 357.

47. Kafka, "Josephine," 366.

48. Kafka, "Josephine," 376.

49. Kafka, "Josephine," 362.

50. Kafka, "Josephine," 368–89.

CHAPTER 9

Performative Emotion in Kafka's "Josephine, the Singer; or, the Mouse Folk" and Freud's "The Creative Writer and Daydreaming"

Andrea Baer

Franz Kafka's later stories have frequently been characterized by their frustration with language's failure to make sense of modern experience. This underscoring of language's lack, apparent in Kafka's own resistance to interpretation,[1] is especially characteristic of his final published work, "Josephine, the Singer; or, the Mouse Folk" (*"Josefine, die Sängerin, oder das Volk der Mäuse"*).[2] Perhaps in part because of its seeming refusal to be dissected and explained, this brief but complex story has received relatively little critical attention. Filled with self-contradictions and irony, "Josephine" points to the dangers of social performance, while at the same time delighting in its own theatricality. As this story invites its audience to consider the performative qualities of everyday life and the complications which it may bring, "Josephine" refers not only to itself as performance, but also to social, human, and emotional experience as such.

The numerous performative frames in "Josephine" underscore the ubiquitous and often deceptively dangerous nature of social performances, which frequently are tied up in the politics of social control and power. The narrative "I," foregrounding the story of Josephine and her song, serves as the diegetic frame through which Kafka tells his tale. Pointing to the artifice of everyday human and social interactions, "Josephine" invites readers to question the roles and the character of the text's key players: Josephine, the narrator, and the story's actual writer, Kafka. By highlighting the paradoxical potentials and perils of performance, Kafka draws attention to the social and personal relevance of performance.

For the mouse folk (who seem far more human than mouse-like), the desire for performance stems largely from a need for social belonging. Josephine's concerts offer individuals a sense of community which is fundamental to a meaningful existence. At the same time, however, her performance contributes greatly to social inequities and injustices. As it suggests the potential danger in social performances, as well as their inevitability, "Josephine" asks readers to be wary of how such theatricality calls upon individual and collective needs for community, leadership, and collective identity. "Josephine" hereby warrants caution toward not just corrupt social and political leaders, but also toward the human need for social and group belonging that may make individuals vulnerable to larger social powers. "Josephine" thus reflects anxieties characteristic of modernity and Western culture that would be profoundly affected by events of the twentieth century, such as the rise of psychoanalysis and crowd psychology and such atrocities as the Holocaust.[3]

That "Josephine" is a self-conscious meditation on the meanings of narrative and performance in relation to affect becomes all the more apparent—and, I would argue, intriguing—when read alongside Sigmund Freud's 1924 essay "The Creative Writer and Daydreaming" ("*Der Dichter und das Phantasieren*").[4] Here Freud argues that the creative writer appeals to his public with a confounding emotional intensity. The reason for the writer's allure, Freud explains, lies in his ability to call upon the unconscious fantasies of his audience, dreams made impossible by a repressed society. The creative writer "creates a fantasy world" in which "he invests large amounts of emotion" (26). Similarly, Josephine's power eludes logical understanding. "[W]e are quite unmusical," the narrator explains, and then continues,

> how is it that we understand Josephine's singing, or, since Josephine denies that, at least believe we understand it. The simplest answer would be that the beauty of her singing is so great that even the most sensitive cannot be deaf to it, but this answer is not satisfactory. (360)

In both texts, the stage and its players are granted incredible degrees of psychological and political influence which, paradoxically, may be resisted but are also inevitable. Kafka and Freud hereby indicate that our personal and social relationship to performance is one of ambivalence: theatricality, fundamental to our social lives, also may threaten the common social good.

Though Kafka's and Freud's works are placed within distinctly different literary and psychoanalytic frameworks, both texts explore performance and narrative as socially and emotionally relevant. Demonstrating narrative self-consciousness alongside warnings about performance, "Josephine" and "The Creative Writer" concern themselves with art and life as social constructs that may at once fulfill and deny our emotional, social, and often unconscious needs for social belonging. As these works ask readers to be wary of social and political authority and control, Kafka and Freud place their audiences before the authors' theatrical stages of writing. Hence, the reader likely finds herself placed in the same position about which she has been warned: that of the passive audience member. Just as our cultural and political leaders and their words may not deserve the public's trust, "Josephine" and "The Creative Writer" suggest that we should approach any performance, story, and its presenters with caution—that is, if such a thing is possible. Precisely because humans are likely to forget the prevalence and artifice of social performance, we must recognize that performativity inevitably structures our lives—on the one hand giving a meaningful shape to human experience, but on the other making possible social irresponsibility and oblivion to social, political, and historical realities.

This chapter begins with a focus on "Josephine" as a self-reflexive performance on theatricality's prevalence, inevitability, and potential dangers. In considering "Josephine," I look to the text's narrative framing, the ambivalent relationship between Josephine and her people, and the secondary staging of the text's narrator and of Kafka himself. I then turn to Freud's "The Creative Writer and Daydreaming" as a kind of mirroring of "Josephine," which similarly points to the cunning and yet desired qualities of performance and performer.

"Josephine, the Singer; or, the Mouse Folk"

Essentially, "Josephine" tells the story of a troubled and persecuted people, the mouse folk, who find solace in the song of their star singer Josephine. As Josephine brings together a collective which, without her, has little to no sense of community or social identity, her persona and her theater have become powerful and mysterious forces. Except for some moments when the songstress performs, the mouse folk appear a powerless and persecuted people with little social interaction and even less social influence. This lack of community and empowerment (both social and personal) is likely the greatest source of the mouse people's worries.[5] The notion of collectivity here is fraught with anxiety and ambivalence, as becomes apparent in the fact that social and performative spaces in this narrative world are inseparable. The mice, audience members like us, suggest that this tale might have something to say about our own culture.

The self-reflexivity of "Josephine" is perhaps most apparent in its narrative layering. Performance abounds in this text: Josephine sings to her public, which responds to her act in dramatic ways; the narrator tells his tale to yet another audience; and Kafka works behind the curtains to create the acts of Josephine, the folk, and its storyteller. Underscoring the ubiquitous and often deceptively dangerous nature of social performances, the numerous performative frames of "Josephine" point to the artifice of everyday human and social interactions. Kafka's work hereby asks readers to question the roles and the character of each of the text's key players: Josephine, the narrator, and the story's actual writer, Kafka.

At the center of these frames is, of course, Josephine, presented to the reader by the unnamed narrator. Because the reader learns about Josephine only through the lens of this storyteller (yet another artist, and the fictional writer of the story), the artist and her presentation exist on two distinct levels: one, Josephine and her singing act; and, two, the narrator and his storytelling. If we wish to take this a step further, we might include Kafka and his reader in yet a third, extratextual production and reception. Building these diegetic levels, "Josephine" is a performance about performance, a self-reflection on art as an aesthetic and a social construction.

The narrative framing of "Josephine" raises questions about the reliability, trustworthiness, and motives of the text's performers. The reader, most likely, will find it difficult to passively accept the storyteller's illogical statements, particularly when the narrator challenges some of his audience's most basic assumptions about Josephine's performance, such as the song's musicality and production of sound. It is thus left up to the reader to decide what she will and will not believe about this text. The ongoing judgments a reader must make about the story and its speaker call attention to the processes of character and narrative construction, be they those of the narrator or of the reader herself. As "Josephine" asks its audience continuously to question the story, the text subtly invites readers to draw connecting lines between the story and their own worlds.

Josephine, the narrator tells us, is the songstress of the mouse folk, a socially marginalized community which fears that its history and its culture are being forgotten and eventually will be obliterated. In the midst of the mice's distress, Josephine's song appears to offer solace and a sense of community when this culture perhaps needs it most. The songstress's stage serves as a gathering place for an otherwise alienated social group: the stage provides a space for the mice to experience emotions of which they are unaware during their everyday lives. In this sense, Josephine's performance may be likened to the Aristotelian notion of theater as cathartic. The singer's art is imbued with emotional meaning as her spectators respond to it in incomprehensible ways.

The appeal of Josephine's song, the narrator implies, lies in the fact that the folk, subjected to so much hardship, is made vulnerable in its longing for community and emotional comforting. "Our life is very uneasy," the narrator explains. "[E]very day brings such surprises, apprehensions, hopes, and terrors" (363). This uneasiness (in the original German *Unruhe*, or disquiet) calls to mind the positive connotations of the *Ruhe* (which translates to both "quiet" and "calm") that may be characteristic of Josephine's song. Quiet, often presented (paradoxically) as a quality of Josephine's concerts, hence appears to soothe. While individuals in this community usually feel isolated from the world and from one another, during these concerts they find refuge, a feeling of physical and emotional intimacy. Each mouse, lost in what Nietzsche might have considered a Dionysian trance, becomes an embodiment of Nietzsche's understanding of tragedy as described in *The Birth of Tragedy* (*Geburt der Tragödie*).[6] The artist

Josephine gives her audience the euphoric experience of losing their selves and returning to the original creative source. Even her opponents become "sunk in the feeling of the mass" (364). Theatricality gives the mice the euphoric sense of melting into the mass, returning to the One, and briefly escaping the pain of everyday life and separation. The mice hereby take part in the enactment of yet another story, that of cathartic release.

Because this experience is one of such great pleasure, Josephine has the power to magically gather together this vermin mass, even though the mouse people (like most modern-day citizens) rarely stop what they're doing.

> And to gather around her this mass of our people, who are almost always on the run and scurrying hither and thither for reasons that are often not clear, Josephine mostly needs to do nothing else than take up her stand, head thrown back, mouth half-open, eyes turned upwards, in the position that indicates her intention to sing. She can do this where she likes, it need not be a place visible a long way off. (364)

But while Josephine and her song, standing in the story's spotlight, appear almost magical, determining the nature of Josephine and of her performance is difficult, if not impossible, for the narrator presents her and her act primarily through negations. Josephine's profound effect on her viewers suggests that her performance possesses a consoling quality that defies explanation, and the narrator's opaque language helps little in explaining the mystery of exactly what her song is. While one would presume that the mice's favorite music would be composed of sound, they consider "tranquil peace" ([s]tiller Frieden) to be their favorite music (360). This sentence is representative of Kafka's love of word play. Does this mean that Josephine's song is an example of such music, or do the mouse folk prefer other musical forms to Josephine's song? The "tranquil peace," or stiller Frieden, that defines music cannot be interpreted simply, as is apparent in the difficulty of translating these two words into English. "Still" could mean tranquil, but might also refer to quiet: is Josephine's act a peaceful sound, or is it perhaps a silent peace? In suggesting that music may be pure silence, the storyteller's ongoing self-contradictions indicate that the world of "Josephine" does not conform to our everyday assumptions.

The storyteller seems to make yet more contradictions when he explains the ordinariness of Josephine's song. While one might think that the everyday and the aesthetic contrast with one another, these qualities appear to coexist in this tale: in some instances the narrator describes Josephine's performance as everyday, while at others he indicates the profundity of her song. The claim that "Josephine's singing, as singing, is nothing out of the ordinary" (361) is first used to criticize her act as undeserving of the reverence it receives. But two pages later, the narrator explains that Josephine "denies any connection between her art and ordinary piping" (362), and for this reason her opponents view her deceptive performance as an imitation of the aesthetic and as unworthy of reverence. A reader then might ask if Josephine's representation of the everyday makes her music worthless, or if that very ordinariness makes it great. As Ann Smock and J. P. Stern have argued, perhaps this very everydayness, by dissolving the boundaries between the mundane and the beautiful, is what makes Josephine's act moving.[7] Perhaps the convergence of the beauty and the ordinary is precisely what the mice need in order to experience life as meaningful,[8] for when Josephine whistles (whistling being the people's everyday language), the "piping is set free from the fetters of daily life and it sets us free too for a little while" (370). Josephine's exaltation of the everyday may expose the beauty of the ordinary that the people usually forget amid their emotional turmoil. The experience of life as beautiful, it seems, offers solace to a normally restless people. If the narrator is suggesting that the everyday is itself beautiful and Josephine worthy of praise, however, why does he go on to imply that she is a fraud?

Josephine's opponents, with whom the speaker partially affiliates himself, recognize that Josephine's song is nothing more than whistling (362). The description of her performance as "piping" (*Pfeifen*) seems to demystify it, since piping is "the people's daily speech" (370), a language that is constantly spoken and that belongs to the mice people's "unreflected habits" (362). And yet the speaker in many moments admires Josephine's song ("Anyone who has not heard her does not know the power of her song. There is no one but is carried away by her singing, a tribute all the greater as we are not in general a music-loving race" [360]), while at others he identifies himself as one of her enemies ("the opposition, with which I too am half in sympathy, certainly admires her no less than the crowd does" [362]).

Though the mouse folk's responses to Josephine might seem to suggest that performance and its reception simply become a refuge for a troubled people, her music (if we dare to call it such) also poses great danger to them, as becomes evident toward the story's end. The enemy has unexpectedly attacked and killed folk members during Josephine's concerts, and "Josephine, who was responsible for it all, and indeed perhaps attracted the enemy by her piping," simply disappears, "occup[ying] the safest place" (371).

As the narrator's claims contradict one another, his language fails to make sense of the mouse folk's reality. But Josephine's performance, despite its muteness, reaches its audience: "a mere nothing in voice, a mere nothing in execution, she asserts herself and gets across to us [the mouse folk]" (367). Here, art seems to exist more in the receptive response to a performance than it does in that performance's physical properties of sound and materiality. Because the people's reactions to Josephine's act are oftentimes so profound, the effects of her performance appear far more important for her audience than are her presentation's actual qualities. As her act, or maybe simply the communal gathering that accompanies it, enables the people to experience vicariously internalized (and perhaps repressed) feelings, she serves a vital collective and individual need for a spiritual leader. Describing Josephine's overwhelming power over the folk, the narrator declares that "anyone who has not heard her does not know the power of her song" (360); "the beauty of her singing is so great that even the most insensitive cannot be deaf to it" (360). Here the narrator seemingly cannot understand the effect of Josephine's song, perhaps because he attempts to understand its impact in terms of logic.

Such an understanding of cathartic art nods its head toward both Aristotle and Freud: art unleashes something within the individual that longs to find bodily expression. Thus, the idea that Josephine's singing is voiceless does not necessitate that her art is meaningless, for at this moment in the story sound is not the only means of expression. This "mere nothing in voice" that is Josephine's performance "rises up where everyone else is pledged to silence" and "comes almost like a message from the whole people to the individual" (367). The song, transcending language, speaks simultaneously to the individual and to the collective. The nonverbal and seemingly transcendent power of this performance suggests that it exists in the realms of the ineffable and the sublime, which, according to Lacan, remain unrestrained by the socially controlled and repressed domain of the symbolic.[9] While entranced in Josephine's performance, the mice, seemingly unaffected by anything other than her song, appear to transcend the everyday world of social confinement and earthly limitations.

While Josephine's message may appear to the mice as liberated from rigid social constraints, it quickly becomes evident that, at least according to the narrator, the songstress's message, unlike Lacan's symbolic one, feeds on individuals' desires to be part of social culture. For to take part in Josephine's concerts is to experience "not so much a performance of songs as an assembly of the people" (367). In Josephine's social realm, thoughts, feelings, and actions inevitably are restrained and influenced by cultural norms. Hence, the song, characterized largely by the mice's reception of it, is intimately connected to the social, the political, and the historical, as well as to the personal and the emotional. The reception and the assessment of Josephine's performance is socially determined by the mice, the narrator, and the circumstances that surround them.

Despite the narrator and the folk's tendency to evaluate Josephine's song, the mice's reactions to the performance are not rational. When the folk gathers to watch Josephine, they appear to enter a trance, a subconscious state in which unexpressed thoughts and emotions rise to the surface. Despite the fact that the folk usually whistle, when Josephine appears, her audience members do not whistle: "it sits in its mouselike stillness; as if we had become partakers in the peace we long for" (363). In their altered and silent state, the people, who long for peace, "sunk in the feeling of the mass, which, warmly pressed body to body, listens with indrawn breath" (364).

Strangely, the sense of peace that the song brings is also characteristic of the people's struggles. The similarities between Josephine's act and the people's everyday experiences of "tumult" suggest such a mimetic quality in her whistling: "Josephine's thin piping amidst grave decisions is almost like our people's precarious existence amidst the tumult of a hostile world" (367). Following Aristotle's notion of the mimetic as cathartic, one reason for the healing effects of Josephine's song may lie in its mimetic qualities. As people witness the externalization of their suffering, they experience a release of that emotion that soothes them.

Josephine presents to her audience their wish to express their pain and to know that they are not alone in their isolation. She does this through an impossible performance of resonance and stillness that may have begun on stage but which continues afterward in the people's social imaginations. The people's vulnerability and intense responsiveness during Josephine's songs suggest that their helplessness makes them more receptive to the potential healing effects of the songstress's performance. During her act,

> [t]his piping . . . comes *almost* like a message from the whole people to the individual; Josephine's thin piping amidst grave decisions is *almost* like our peoples precarious existence amidst of the tumult of a hostile world. Josephine exerts herself, a mere nothing in voice, a mere nothing in exertion, she asserts herself and gets across to us; it does us good to think of that. (367; my italics)

Josephine's whistling, coming to the mice as a message during their present-day struggles in a world of enemies and conflict, "does good." Here the vulnerable mouse folk experience the song as comforting, protective, and powerful.

But at the same time that Josephine's concerts appear to console the mouse community, its unsettled nature may be fed by her act. For the consoling that she offers the people perhaps lures them into a silence that may reflect the very source of their pain: their forgetting of both their pasts and their identity. In this silence, their oral tradition of tales and songs, which serve as reminders of their past ("in the old days our people did sing; this is mentioned in legends and some songs have even survived" [361]), cannot continue. Josephine's quieting effect, rather than being therapeutic, becomes an opium so powerful that even those who oppose her, like the narrator, cannot resist her drug. Even her adversaries "admire[] her no less than the crowd," for "when you take a seat before her, you know: this piping of hers is no piping" (362). It appears to be something far greater than the folk's everyday language. In such moments, Josephine appears to be more seductress than she is nurturing mother or spiritual leader. And as a deceiver, Josephine makes a reading of her song seemingly impossible—her singing, which is also a whistling, is now no whistling at all.

Moreover, Josephine does not always seem to be a protector of the community. At the same time that she lures the people and gives them a sense of well-being, she also endangers them when she brings them together and attracts the enemy through her whistling: "[W]hen such gatherings have been unexpectedly flushed by the enemy and many of our people left lying for dead, Josephine, who was responsible for it all, and indeed perhaps attracted the enemy by her piping" quietly slips away into safety (371).

Moreover, the folk, when threatened, become all the more faithful to Josephine: "And yet it is true that just in emergencies we hearken better than at other times to Josephine's voice. The menaces that loom over us make us quieter, more humble, more submissive to Josephine's domination; we like to come together, we like to huddle close to each other" (366).

In such passages, the allure of Josephine's act suggests that the comfort which the people experience through her song is illusory, for in actuality, her show creates troubles for the mice that Josephine can foresee and escape. The dangerous quality of the songstress's act complicates the idea that it has cathartic effects, implying that her evocation of affect might be in some sense traumatizing for the mice. Her manipulative, childish, and selfish motives again suggest that her act is not simply a means of catharsis that serves the mice. The disservice of her drama is reflected in the unreasonable demands she places upon her audience. For example, "Josephine has been fighting for exemption from all daily work on account of her singing; she should be relieved of all responsibility for earning her daily bread and being involved in the general struggle for existence, which—apparently—should be transferred on her behalf to the people as a whole" (371).

But the storyteller's many questions about the status of Josephine's singing may also call into question his motives for his narration. As Thomas Vitzthum argues in "A Revolution in Writing: The Overthrow of Epic Storytelling by Written Narrative in Kafka's *Josefine, die Sängerin oder Das Volk der Mäuse*," the story's speaker is no more credible than Josephine.[10] He does, after all, belong to those who oppose Josephine, and when she is gone, what will remain is his written account; the only way that we know of Josephine's music is through his inconsistent assertions. As the author of this report, he may decide what the song is, just as he may determine what does or does not qualify as aesthetic. Like Josephine, this "historian" seems to be yet another example of the egotistical artist—both his and Josephine's creative acts have allowed them some degree of control and power over the mouse folk. For just as the speaker records and erases Josephine through the introduction and the obliteration of her in his textual document, he affirms and denies the mice's history in that same instant. In this way, performance becomes about social and political power.

If "Josephine" and its actors continually mislead their audience, how can a reader arrive at any conclusions about the text? While at times the narrator speaks of himself as a fellow citizen of the mouse people (at the story's beginning, for example, he speaks of "our singer," "our life," and repeatedly of the "we" that is affected by Josephine's performance), at others he appears to be an outsider (360). As Vitzthum writes, "[t]hough the narrator identifies himself as one of the mouse-folk, he often seems much too outspoken, knowledgeable, and curious to be counted among their ranks" (271). The narrator's inconsistent use of pronouns similarly raises questions about the speaker's stance as citizen of the mouse people. Compare, for example, Vitzthum's following examples: "unconditional devotion is hardly known among us; ours are people who love slyness beyond everything" (Kafka 365) and "but we do not laugh at Josephine. Many a time I have the impression that our people interpret their relationship to Josephine" (Kafka 365) (Vitzthum 271).[11] "In the first instance," Vitzthum argues, "the narrator sounds like a loving patron of the mouse-folk; in the second, he seems to be regarding them, his people, from afar; and in the third he sounds as if he is setting himself off as a total stranger" (271).

How is one, then, to understand the narrator? Introducing himself as a historian (one could indeed argue that the narrator is male, as I will discuss shortly), the storyteller would like to be perceived as objective, but his endless contradictions make clear that he is far from trustworthy. As Vitzthum and Deborah Harter have argued, by presenting Josephine as the central figure, the narrator deemphasizes his own role in the narration so that he may hide behind the curtains of Josephine's stage,[12] manipulating his audience and portraying his account as a historical fact of this ahistorical people. The narrator's discussion of the status of this song, whether it is music, song, silence, or something else, suggests that his impulse to categorize Josephine's performance stems, at least partially, from his unstated aim to undermine the mice's star entertainer. As Vitzthum argues, "Josefine is precisely what is standing in the way of the narrator's creativity," and for this reason, he wishes to obliterate her (272). But, ironically, Josephine is also what makes it possible for him to tell his story. As the speaker presents Josephine's disappearance and claims that she will be forgotten, he disallows both her erasure from memory and the forgetting of the mice's past, since his writing produces a record.[13] In the story's last line, he asserts that "Josephine . . . will happily lose herself in the numberless throng of the heroes of our people, and soon, since we are no historians, will rise to the heights of redemption and be forgotten like all her brothers" (376). But what, other than a history of the mouse folk, is the narrator writing, and how can Josephine and her singing be forgotten now that it has been recorded and relayed to the reader? While Josephine remains among the undocumented heroes of the mouse folk, her song continues to be heard, seen, and perhaps felt. Her story hereby exists as a phantom narrative, an absent presence defined by negativity.[14]

The ghostliness of Josephine exists alongside the seeming absence of Kafka as author. Though the narrator addresses his reader directly, Kafka maintains the fourth wall separating him and the story. The storyteller thus may be read as a foil for Kafka, who stands behind the façade of the narrative "I." The reader must also become skeptical of Kafka's motives as writer, since he, like the fictional storyteller, plays games with his audience through textual inconsistencies, word play, and a self-reflexivity that hints at the connections between the textual world and that of the reader.

Though the narrator and Josephine express concerns for the mice, their untrustworthy characters suggest that they are most interested in their powerful social positions. The reader, herself an audience member, may depart from this brief text wondering what games Kafka, the ultimate puppet master of "Josephine," is playing.

Josephine and Freud's Creative Writer

In reading Freud's "The Creative Writer and Daydreaming," one might question if among Kafka's games is a staging of Freud's essay. Though I do not mean that Kafka necessarily had read Freud's 1907 essay or deliberately transferred its ideas to "Josephine," I do believe these two texts mirror one another in interesting and multiple ways which are significant to the cultural moments in which they were written. Placed alongside one another, "Josephine" and "The Creative Writer" reflect a modern experience of growing anxiety and ambivalence about the converging of public and private life. Indicating at once fascination with and distrust in the performative, "Josephine" and "The Creative Writer" suggest that performativity has become inescapable in modern life.

"The Creative Writer and Daydreaming" concerns itself with two main questions: from where does the creative writer draw his material, and (of particular interest here) what is the appeal of his stories to his audience members? Freud is intrigued by the creative writer's ability to arouse emotions in individuals who otherwise believe themselves incapable of experiencing such intense feelings. The creative writer, like Josephine, is a performer whose magical effect on his audience seems to elude explanation. The writer's allure lies in the fantasy world to which he gives birth. He "creates a fantasy world" in which "he invests large amounts of emotion" (26). In this sense, "The Creative Writer" speaks to the unconscious minds of his public; it is for this reason that his performance is so powerful.

Because of Freud's interest in the very allure of the creative writer, his paper gives far more attention to reception than artistic production. The creative writer's fictional storytelling, Freud argues, functions for audience members as a projection of their own secretive and repressed fantasies. The listeners' "real enjoyment of a literary work derives from the relaxation of tensions in our mind" (33) as the poet "enables us . . . to enjoy our own fantasies without shame or self-reproach" (33).

Despite the seeming incomprehensibility both of the writer and Josephine, Freud and the narrators of "Josephine" attempt to analyze the power and attraction of these mysterious performers. While Freud's explanation of the creative writer's appeal is clearly more coherent and convincing than that of Kafka's storyteller, a surprising number of Freud's and the storyteller's ideas nevertheless mirror one another.

In presenting Josephine and the creative writer as socially influential hypnotists, Kafka and Freud indicate both the dangers and the possibilities of the many social performances that shape human reality. Though Freud's creative writer is not necessarily cunning and ill-intended, as is the Josephine Kafka's narrator describes, both Josephine and the creative writer share a mysterious and even mystical quality, as their performances speak deeply to their viewers' (potentially harmful) unconscious desires. These texts acknowledge that performance has a profound effect on individuals and society which often goes unrecognized; as Kafka and Freud accept that performance shapes our everyday lives, they express an ambivalence about the collective and its sometimes understandable and occasionally disturbing unconscious desires. On the one hand, Kafka and Freud's works imply an Aristotelian perspective of theatricality and its reception: the stage and its actor offer viewers a cathartic purging of their otherwise unexpressed desires. On the other hand, the texts indicate a more Platonic view: the surfacing of feelings makes viewers blind to reason, and thus vulnerable and yielding to the power of others who often do not have the well-being of humanity in mind. Performance, in these contexts, organizes, and to a large extent controls, society and its members.

"Josephine" and "The Creative Writer" offer neither straightforward praise nor condemnation of the ubiquity of performativity. Both works suggest that audience members who otherwise have no outlet for their unspoken wants and needs may be soothed when art evokes their repressed or suppressed desires. But these texts also present their audiences as somnambulists who, in their need for a strong sense of group identity and belonging, have become socially irresponsible and susceptible to the allure and deceit of corrupt social and political figures. The instinctive desire for social belonging that is evident in "Josephine" and "The Creative Writer" is surrounded by an ambivalence about the value of group identity. (This anxiety would, of course, become crucial to modern culture in the later twentieth century, in the face of events like the Holocaust, McCarthyism, and the Cultural Revolution.)

Whether through Josephine's singing or the creative writer's storytelling, performance in these texts functions as a kind of hypnosis, luring audience members into a trance-like state in which unconscious desires rise to the surface. While Josephine carries about her a much darker aura, both she and the creative writer possess attractive and potentially foreboding qualities which complexly present performance as simultaneously intrinsic to and potentially harmful to human and social life. These texts thus express an anxiety about human emotion, especially when it is manipulated for the purposes of political power and social control, as it would be not much later in Germany's history.

For the individuals of Freud and Kafka's narrative worlds, aesthetic fantasy appears a refuge from fear and anxiety. The mice are transfixed by the emotional power and beauty of Josephine's presence, and because the creative writer's audience listens to him, it experiences reprieve from its own repression. Freud's belief that the creative writer allows one to experience a soothing through fantasy closely resembles the moments when the mice, entranced by Josephine's song, "sunk in the feeling of the mass" (364). The fantasies that the creative writer makes permissible have an incredible psychological power to awaken "one of his major desires," which "harks back to the memory of an earlier experience, usually belonging to his childhood, in which his desire was fulfilled" (29). In this sense an audience's deepest, unspeakable desires seem to be fulfilled. Freud's creative writer, like Josephine, seems to offer his audience a view of its own internal experiences. That psychic representation, like the songstress's act, comforts the audience by enabling both the individual and the collective to experience a release from life's everyday strains, or what Freud would label as repression.

The social angst that affects the psychic and emotional experiences of Kafka and Freud's audiences makes clear that the impact of performance extends far beyond the individual lives and memories of audience members. Human beings are social beings who, psychology contends, share the same basic needs and desires. Yet despite this commonality, according to "The Creative Writer," people believe their fantasies to be abnormal and socially unacceptable, and therefore keep them secret. Because one's fantasies reflect an ego that cannot act upon its impulses, Freud asserts, the individual becomes ashamed of her daydreams and attempts to hide them from others. As a result, the dreamer "thinks he is the only person to construct such fantasies and has no idea that quite similar constructs are widespread among others" (27). Much like the citizens of the mouse folk, Freud's subject experiences a disconnection from the rest of society because she cannot express what she thinks and feels.

This sense of human disconnection, however, is in large part an illusion, for not only do all people fantasize, they also share common desires which are expressed in their individual dreams. Such shared longings are often apparent, Freud explains, in myths which he defines as "distorted remains of the wishful fantasies of whole nations, the *secular dreams* of youthful humanity" (32; italics in original). The mouse folk, similarly, share dreams of returning to childhood and no longer facing the threat of the enemy, and when Josephine performs, these dreams seem realizable.

Most of the time, however, the mouse folk's wishes for community do not seem obtainable to them. Their feeling of separation from one another is apparent in their longing for a sense of camaraderie, as well as in their process of forgetting their past and culture. Ironically, it is this very feeling of alienation, inseparable from the silencing of personal desires, that unites and to a large extent defines the mice. While these individuals' experience of isolation is itself real, their belief that they share little in common with others is largely imagined. Ironically, their individual experiences of isolation ultimately seem to bring the people together, as they search for emotional fulfillment from Josephine's performances. In such moments, "it is as if the limbs of each were loosened, as if the harried individual once in a while could relax and stretch himself at ease in the great, warm bed of the community. And into these dreams Josephine's piping drops note by note" (370). The "harried" (*ruhelos*[15]) individual wants intimacy with the folk, as implied by the image of the people's communal warm bed. This person looks for comfort, not only in dreams (which suggest the unconscious or the unexpressed) but also in a sound that—despite its sometimes noisy and overwhelming qualities—often is calming. Josephine's whistling, whether it is real or dreamed, consoles.

Josephine, like Freud's creative writer, enables the people to fantasize—both individually and collectively—by projecting their own emotions onto her, and the result of this process, one might argue, is cathartic. Envisioning its feelings in Josephine's performance, the audience is relieved of the strain of repressed desires. At the same time that the mice's yearnings seem externalized, they do not have to acknowledge their impossible yearnings as their own. Josephine hereby offers the mice an affective release that is not possible in the everyday world.

The expression of repressed desires that Josephine and Freud's creative writer offer their audiences is intimately linked to childhood memories, needs, and desires. According to Freud, the creative writer's audience are like children, who can distinguish between fantasy and reality during play, but whose pretending is nonetheless emotionally invested and meaningful. Because child's play and poetic creation, through language, share an intimate connection ("the language itself captures the relations between children's games and literary creation" [26]), the creative writer's stories and children's game-like pretending—both performances—function quite similarly. This kind of make-believe is pleasurable for its participants, even if the fantasized events would in reality be experienced as distressing. In play (as in fictional stories), children can confront troubling realities, such as death, while maintaining a sense of security.

But at the same time that Freud's writer can comfort his audience, he, like Josephine, also has the potential to deceive and harm his audience, leading them to maladaptive and neurotic behavior. "When fantasies proliferate and become over-powerful," Freud asserts, "the conditions are given for a lapse into neurosis or psychosis; moreover, fantasies are the immediate mental precursors of the painful symptoms that our patients complain of. Here a broad byway branches off toward pathology" (29). As in "Josephine," the artist can become just as much an agent of pathology as she is one of solace. Kafka's and Freud's shared uncertainty about the value of the performative appears to reflect a simultaneous fascination with and anxiety about emotions and the unconscious, an ambivalence that becomes especially relevant to Western culture with the turn of the century and its social, political, and intellectual developments.

Like the nature of performance, the unconscious in both "The Creative Writer" and in "Josephine" is also closely connected to childhood memories, which lead audience members to experience at once vulnerability and soothing. Freud explicitly points to the connection between the writer's fantasy and individuals' childlike desires: as individuals enter adulthood and leave behind the egoistic stage of childhood, Freud explains, they must give up selfish pleasures in order to function in the social world. Among those pleasures is that of play. Like the members of the mouse folk, Freud's human subject regrettably must leave behind her childhood (and, interestingly, also her mother). To make up for the loss of childhood, individuals replace play with fantasy, since daydreams are far less confined by social constraints.

The storyteller's soliloquy in "Josephine" similarly suggests that Josephine's act may be attractive because it speaks to the mice's emotional needs for social belonging, comfort, and nurturing. Childhood, in both texts, reflects human vulnerability and fundamental emotional needs which adulthood often masks, but which nonetheless may make one susceptible to the ill influence of others. In "Josephine," for example, the mouse folk's longings become particularly apparent when its members, mesmerized by Josephine, experience a return to childhood that is characterized by vulnerability and need for parental support. The mice's unfulfilled emotional needs appear to be rooted in their lost childhoods, and the reason for the community's strong attraction to Josephine's song, the narrator explains, is their way of life: they know no youth (368). Josephine's song offers them something from youth that they lack—the security of a mother figure and the ability to be at once safe, emotionally expressive, and vulnerable. Her singing creates a nurturing space that the mice associate with childhood, "[s]omething of our poor, brief childhood is in it [her singing], something of lost happiness that can never be found again" (370). This is "expressed not in full round notes but softly, in a whisper, confidentially" (370). Freud's creative writer similarly reminds his listeners of the fantasy world of their childhoods:

> [T]he creative writer acts no differently from the child at play: he creates a fantasy world, which he takes very seriously; that is to say, he invests large amounts of emotion in it, while marking it off sharply from reality. Moreover, the language itself captures the relation between children's games and literary creation by applying the word *play* to those of the writer's inventions that need to be linked to tangible objects. (26)

As these passages suggest, both the creative writer and Josephine act as nurturers: they give solace to their audiences by projecting for them unexpressed pains and longings to return to the joy of childhood and the freedom of play. Under the trance of these performers, audience members can forget temporarily the mundane world which, according to Freud, causes suffering through socially imposed (yet necessary) repression. The writer and Josephine thus become parental figures for their spectators, who at times fulfill and at others disserve their children.

Interestingly, the soothing quality of the creative writer's and Josephine's theatricality, as well as the fact that both figures remind their audiences of childhood, suggests a maternal quality in both performance and performer. But while Freud's creative writer takes the characteristically male role of psychotherapist, Josephine's feminine qualities possess their own significance. As Margot Norris and Ruth Gross have convincingly argued, Josephine may be read as both a female and a maternal figure.[16] Norris points to the female stereotypes which the (apparently male) narrator attempts to impose upon. When someone points out to Josephine the folk's common whistling, Josephine presents a "sarcastic and arrogant" smile, "she, who in appearance is delicacy itself, conspicuously so even among our people who are prolific in feminine types" (362), and later, when Josephine stamps her feet, she "swear[s] in most unmaidenly fashion" (364; in the German original, *unmädchenhaft*). Quoting Michael Feingold's preface to his play "Josefine: The Mouse Singer," Norris furthermore writes that Kafka's "narration displays cultural sexual attitudes toward Josephine anthropomorphic enough for Michael Feingold to speak of 'her virtually feminist bitterness when mouse-males treat her as a mere love object.'"[17] Gross similarly points to the patronizing and even fatherly tone of the narrator in "Josephine" (6), arguing that the storyteller's "style is that of a possessive spokes*man* of his people. . . . He is speaking from the standpoint of a center and this center is always man" (63; italics in original). Male authority and its preservation, Gross suggests, are at stake in the narrator's account of the songstress. Gross's reading of Josephine's representation as holy mother/seductress, particularly when put in dialogue with Vitzthum's claim that the narrator seeks to undermine the songstress's authority, suggests that male social anxieties about changing gender roles and power relations are prominent in the narrator's tale. His selfish motives appear to be part of a power play, a wish for his story and performance to prove dominant over that of Josephine.

While Josephine's position as caregiver seems to affirm traditional gender roles, her social influence challenges them. Josephine's domestic responsibilities extend beyond the private realm and into the public, suggesting that a woman plays a powerful, and possibly threatening, social role. Josephine's power is both feared and revered. At the same time that the narrator is in awe of her, he presents her as a destructive force which endangers the folk and leads them into silence and possibly forgetting. Josephine's contradictory qualities suggest an ambivalence about women which perhaps acts as a metaphor for a crisis of masculinity that has been ascribed not only to modernism in general, but also, more specifically, to Kafka's work (not to mention that of Freud).

But whether Kafka shares the viewpoint of his power-hungry storyteller is another matter, one which Gross questions, given that "Josephine" calls attention to the narrator's deceit. Regardless, Josephine remains a maternal figure: she gives the folk a sense of collective identity. Without her, the people risk forgetting their history and identity. In this way, the motherly Josephine enables the mice to be reborn, to feel alive after a long period of emotional and spiritual deadness.

Though one might argue that Freud's creative writer, as well as the artist figure more generally, possesses "feminine" characteristics, gender issues appear less influential to the creative writer. Freud's storyteller, when compared with Josephine, is a more benign figure, whose alluring stories seem primarily, though not entirely, therapeutic for their audience. Though Freud's essay does not give much heed to the creative writer's sex, it should be noted that "The Creative Writer" distinguishes between male and female fantasies, the former being dominated by dreams of social power and the latter by sexual urges. Interestingly, "Josephine" appears to demonstrate such a male fantasy for social influence, one which demands that female powers, which pose a threat to men, be eradicated. Anxieties about crowds, unconscious impulses, and changing gender roles thus merge in "Josephine." Though Freud's writings, one could easily argue, express apprehension about shifting gender relations, the creative writer, like the psychoanalyst, seems to maintain an authoritative male status.

Conclusion

While Freud appears certain about the nature and the effect of the creative writer's art on listeners and readers, the qualities of Josephine's theatrics are more obscure. It is perhaps in this greater mystery that Josephine becomes a more foreboding character. While the creative writer's work clearly is made of language, Josephine's artistic medium is difficult to impossible to define. As discussed previously, whether Josephine's presentation is music, a song, whistling, or nothing at all remains unclear; the ambiguous nature of her act reflects the impossibility of understanding her performance. While Freud offers readers a theoretical frame in which to analyze and make sense of human experience, Kafka gives little hope for such human understanding. These texts hereby reflect seemingly divergent reactions to modernity: on the one hand, the desire to make meaning of experience, and on the other, a frustration with such attempts, which oftentimes prove futile. While Freud's explanation of human needs and desires offers a clearer and perhaps more satisfying explanation of human needs and feelings, "Josephine" provides few, if any, definitive thoughts.

Whether we are to leave Kafka's story believing in the benefits or in the dangers of women—or of men—in the public sphere remains difficult, if not impossible, to determine. However, the text does make clear that the narrator, and probably the mouse folk, experiences anxiety about the social role that Josephine plays, the political power that she may possess, and the insecure sense of self and life meaning with which the mouse culture grapples. It is perhaps the puzzling power and allure of Josephine that she, like the creative writer and the unconscious mind, becomes a threatening figure.

At the same time that "Josephine" leaves many questions unanswered, what does remain clear in the story is that performance is intrinsic to our social, political, and emotional lives. Moreover, attempts to explain the theatricality of everyday life will likely prove dissatisfying, since performance, like human and emotional experience, often defies rational thought. While the mice's hypnotic state during Josephine's musical acts soothes a people that lacks and longs for a sense of collective identity and history, the folk's somnabulism makes it vulnerable to a threatening world and a possibly ill-intended songstress. Whether performance presents more good or more harm to a given society and its people remains unclear. But despite such limitations of language and narrative, Kafka's narrator, like the creative writer, tells his story, gesturing toward a human impulse, and perhaps even a need, to find in stories ways of understanding human, social, and emotional experience, however useful or limited those explanations may be.

As "Josephine" closes with the narrator's simultaneous erasure and remembrance of Josephine, the reader hopefully departs from this reading recalling not only the songstress, her listeners, and the recorder of her performance, but also by noting the writer, Kafka, who stands behind yet another curtain for yet another viewer, the reader. The artist and her spectators, like society and its members, cannot end the production of performance, nor should they attempt to do so. What individuals and social groups *can* do is attempt to remain aware of art's powerful influences on individuals and collectives, even though theatricality's effects may not always be humanly recognizable or comprehensible. If the reader increases her awareness of her theatrical world, perhaps the writing of "Josephine" has been a worthwhile presentation.

Notes

1. See Theodor W. Adorno, "Notes on Kafka," in *Prisms*, trans. Samuel and Shierry Weber (Cambridge, MA: MIT Press, 1981), 246; E. V. Calin, "From Ellipsis into Silence in Contemporary Literature," in *Expression, Communication and Experience in Literature and Language*, (London: Modern Humanities Research Association, 1973), 259–62; Joan Ramon Resina, "Gesture: Kafka's Means to Silence," *International Fiction Review* 15:1 (Winter 1988): 14–20; Roberta Weninger, "Sounding Out the Silence of Gregor Samsa: Kafka's Rhetoric of Dyscommuniciation," *Studies in Twentieth Century Literature* 17:2 (Summer 1993): 263–86.

2. Franz Kafka, "Josephine, the Singer; or, The Mouse Folk," trans. Willa and Edwin Muir, in *Franz Kafka: The Complete Stories*, ed. Nahum N. Glatzer (New York: Schocken Books, 1971), 360–76; "Josefine, die Sängerin oder Das Volk der Mäuse," in *Sämtliche Erzählungen*, ed. Paul Raabe (Frankfurt on Main: Fischer Taschenbuch Verlag, 1991), 172–85.

3. See, for example, Theodor Adorno, "Freudian Theory and the Pattern of Fascist Propaganda," in *The Culture Industry: Selected Essays on Mass Culture* (London: Routledge, 1991), 132; and Julia Kristeva, *Tales of Love* (New York: Columbia University Press, 1987).

4. Sigmund Freud, "The Creative Writer and Daydreaming," trans. David McLintock (New York: Penguin Books, 2003), 23–34; "Der Dichter und das Phantasieren," in *Gesammelte Werke: Chronologisch geordnet*, ed. Anna Freud et al. (London: Imago Publishing Company, 1940–1987), 212–23.

5. Mathew Olshan ("Franz Kafka: The Unsinging Singer," in *Modern Jewish Mythologies*, eds. Glenda Abramson and Eli Yassif [Cincinnati, OH: Hebrew Union College, 1999], 174–90), and Jürgen Egyptin and Dietrich Hoffman ("Ostjüdische Anklänge in Kafkas Erzählung *Josefine, die Sängerin* oder Das Volk der Mäuse," in *Ide: Informationen zur Deutschdidaktik*, 2 [2001], 49–65) have made connections between the mouse folk and the Jewish people. Both cultures may be described by lost traditions, histories, and cultures and by collective persecution. As Thomas Nolden and Vivian Liska suggest in the introduction to *Contemporary Jewish Writing in Europe* (Bloomington: Indiana University Press, 2008), the large number of exiled and displaced Jews had contributed to a diversity of diasporic traditions (xvii).

6. Friedrich Wilhelm Nietzsche, *The Birth of Tragedy*, trans. Walter Kaufmann (New York: Vintage Books, 1967); *Die Geburt der Tragödie. Bibliothek der deutschen Literatur*, microfiche (Munich: Saur, 1990–1994), box 20, fiche 9199.

7. Ann Smock, *Double Dealing* (Lincoln: University of Nebraska, 1985), 91–118; J. P. Stern, "Franz Kafka on Mice and Men," in *Paths and Labyrinths: Nine Papers Read at the Franz Kafka Symposium Held at the Institute of Germanic Studies on 20 and 21 October 1983*, ed. J. J. White (London: Institute of Germanic Studies, University of London, 1985), 141–55.

8. Smock, 96.

9. Jacques Lacan, "Symbol and Language," *The Language of the Self* (Baltimore: The Johns Hopkins University Press, 1956).

10. Thomas Vitzthum, "A Revolution in Writing: The Overthrow of Epic Storytelling by Written Narrative in Kafka's *Josefine, die Sängerin oder Das Volk der Mäuse,*" *Symposium* 46:4 (Winter 1993): 269–78.

11. Vitzthum quotes the original German text. I have used quotes from the English translation of "Josephine" for consistency within the body of my chapter.

12. Deborah Harter, "The Artist on Trial," *Deutsche Vierteljahrschrift für Literaturwissenschaft und Geistesgeschichte* 61 (1987): 155; Vitzthum, 271.

13. James Rolleston, *Kafka's Narrative Theater* (University Park and London: Pennsylvania State University Press, 1974), 134.

14. Margot Norris, "Kafka's Josefine: The Animal as the Negative Site of Narration," *Modern Language* 98:3 (April 1983): 366–83 (esp. 382).

15. The original German *ruheloser* might also be translated as "quiet-less," and underscores the text's play with the themes of sound and silence.

16. Norris, see note 14; Ruth Gross, "Of Mice and Woman: Reflections on a Discourse in Kafka's Josefine, die Sängerin oder Das Volk der Mäuse," *The Germanic Review* 60:2 (Spring 1985): 59–68.

17. Norris, 380.

CHAPTER 10

The Power of the Look: Franz Kafka's "The Cares of a Family Man"

Esther K. Bauer

In one of the aphoristic texts published posthumously under the title "He," Franz Kafka wrote, "He fights against fixation by his fellow men. Man can see, even if he were infallible, only that portion of the other, for which the power and the nature of his look are sufficient. He has, like everybody, yet to the extreme, the urge to limit himself to how the look of men has the power to see him."[1] About Kafka and his works Walter Benjamin maintained, "He was pushed to the limits of understanding at every turn, and he liked to push others to them as well."[2] Read together, these two quotations pinpoint the dilemma of some of Kafka's best-known characters. These protagonists fail to fathom the nature of the other's look and the expectations it raises for them, while their own looks turn out to be inadequate tools for understanding and defining the other and the world. Consequently, the protagonists struggle to find their places in the world and eventually disappear or die, as do, for instance, Karl Rossmann in *Amerika: The Missing Person*, Josef K. in *The Trial*, K. in *The Castle*, and Georg Bendemann in "The Judgment." Despite its minimalist plot and its small cast, Kafka's story "The Cares of a Family Man" is a comprehensive study of the dynamics of the look and its power.

Since its first appearance in 1919 as part of the collection *A Country Doctor*, "The Cares of a Family Man" has become one of the most analyzed of Kafka's shorter works. A first-person narrative told entirely from the perspective of the family man mentioned in the title, the story presents the eponymous figure's attempts to make sense of the only additional character, a very vaguely described creature named Odradek, and of their predominantly silent relationship. Since its initial publication, the majority of readings have concentrated on solving the enigma of the Odradek figure.[3] Heinz Hillmann, however, suggests that the family man is the story's actual main character, since his musings and reactions reveal more about himself than about Odradek.[4] Two more recent studies by Hansjörg Bay and Verena Ehrich-Haefeli, respectively, focus on the figure of the family man as well and read the story within the discourse of the alien other (*das Fremde*), interpreting Odradek either as an outside intruder into a familiar sphere, or as the repressed forcing its way back from the family man's unconscious.[5] Both maintain that the narrator's unsuccessful attempts to integrate Odradek into existing social or psychological structures cause his "cares."[6]

The absence of large gestures and dramatic exchanges characterizing Kafka's story emphasizes the impact Odradek's mere presence or absence and actual or presumed look have on the narrator. This chapter draws on works by Jean-Paul Sartre, Jacques Lacan, Kaja Silverman, and Michel Foucault to analyze the play of look and counterlook linking the narrator and Odradek. It shows that in Kafka's work, the look is the site where the search for knowledge and the search for power intersect, and it reveals the key role assigned to the look in the construction of the self and in the definition and protection of the main character's social identity. Building on the notion of the alien other as a phenomenon that can render the familiar questionable,[7] this analysis shows how the appearance of a little creature such as Odradek can shake the family man's image of himself and of the world.[8] These findings help explain why Odradek, whom Detlef Kremer calls "a figure that is none,"[9] is particularly suited for a discussion of structures of power, the look, and identity, and concurrently highlights the subversive potential of literature and art.

Although this nonfigure does not do anything except to appear and disappear randomly in the narrator's house, it exercises a certain, unclearly defined power over him. The family man's obsession with Odradek is rooted in his desire to control this intruder in his house, whom he sees as a threat. However, instead of deterring this perceived threat, all attempts to grasp Odradek physically or intellectually fail and only increase his subversive effect, and eventually the family man becomes aware of the limits of his own power. Since the use of the definite article in the original German title suggests that the narrator represents an entire social group or role,[10] his failure to control the situation can be read as a critique of the role of the family man in general and, taking into account his important position in society, as a critique of the sociocultural order that provides these structures.

Throughout German history, the so-called *Hausvater* or *pater familias* represented the entire family, including servants and unmarried employees of the family business, in all social, financial, and legal matters. As husband, father, and employer, he owned everything that belonged to "his" house; his children and employees needed his consent regarding their education, careers, and marriages, and the head of the household was also responsible for the family members' religious and spiritual well-being. As the lowest-ranking representative of the authoritarian state (*Obrigkeitsstaat*) and in control of the family as the smallest unit of this state, the family man stood for an entire value system which he was expected to uphold and protect—a value system that is usually summarized under the term *bourgeois*.[11] Kurz writes, "The name suggests patriarchy and cozy security. . . . 'Family man'—that means security, comfort, control, independence, superiority, rule of 'his' house."[12] However, in the nineteenth and early twentieth centuries, social and economic changes resulting from industrialization, the women's movement, and World War I, among other phenomena, together with the diminishing influence of religion on everyday life, undermined the old order and gradually weakened patriarchal authority.[13] Thus, the family man faces the challenge of Odradek's unexplained presence in his house at a time when his role is already under attack.[14]

Kafka dedicated the *Country Doctor* collection to his father Hermann, the one family man he probably knew best. Franz Kafka wrote that his father always seemed to live in "fret and worry."[15] It has become a mainstay of Kafka research that the author experienced his father as tyrannical, insensitive, and overbearing, and that his fear of being unable to live up to his father's expectations caused enormous pressure and feelings of guilt for the writer throughout his life. In his famous *Letter to His Father*, Kafka admits that "my valuation of myself was much more dependent on you than on anything else,"[16] and that every act and every exchange and relationship with other people were overshadowed by his father's views. Kafka had internalized his father's suspicions about him to a degree that they were at work even when the father was absent.

This psychological situation reflects Freud's description of the "superego" and also shows similarities to Jeremy Bentham's *Panopticon*, which Michel Foucault discussed in the context of nineteenth-century bourgeois culture in *Discipline and Punish*. An architectural model for the economical constant surveillance of a large number of people, as in prisons, mental asylums, schools, or factories, the panopticon's goal is to create an environment where the inmates always *could* be watched, but never know when or even if they are watched. Since the guards' presence or absence is beyond the inmates' control and is invisible, they assume this presence all the time and behave accordingly—that is, they follow the rules. According to Foucault, this structure's goal is "to induce in the inmate a state of conscious and permanent visibility that assures the automatic functioning of power."[17] Escaping the panoptic power would require the inmate to fight him- or herself:

> He who is subjected to a field of visibility, and who knows it, assumes responsibility for the constraints of power; he makes them play spontaneously upon himself; he inscribes in himself the power relation in which he simultaneously plays both roles; he becomes the principle of his own subjection. By this very fact, the external power may throw off its physical weight; it tends to the non-corporal; and the more it approaches this limit, the more constant, profound and permanent its effects.[18]

This panoptic power relation is not based on person-to-person contact, but is a "real subjection . . . born from a fictitious relation,"[19] which is structured around bodies and looks. Comparing the power dynamics between Odradek and the narrator with those described in Foucault's analysis of the panopticon, reveals that Kafka put the fictional family man into a situation that is similar to his own in his relationship with his father, as he described it in the *Letter to His Father*, and, at the same time, that represents the opposite of the role typical for the family man of the nineteenth and early twentieth centuries.

The family man finds himself in a panopticon-like setup, since Odradek does not submit to any fixed temporal or spatial structure, and his nimbleness makes it impossible to catch him. The family man cannot foresee when and where he will encounter Odradek, who prefers the spaces in-between, on the margins: "He lurks by turns in the garret, the stairways, the lobbies, the entrance hall."[20] Spaces that lead somewhere and can open up or connect to the unexpected, are very familiar to Kafka readers, especially from the three novels.[21] In addition, the narrator never knows when Odradek is in his house or even whether he ever leaves it: "Often for months on end he is not to be seen; then he has presumably moved into other houses; but then he inevitably returns to our house."[22] Since Odradek is extremely small, his invisibility is no definite proof that he is not present, and the narrator's use of "presumably" (*wohl*) marks the idea that Odradek moves between houses as a mere assumption. Instead of exercising control over this creature, the narrator runs into Odradek accidentally in his own house, and hence his power as master of the house can be challenged by this intruder at any moment. Consequently—and already the title of the story lets readers assume this—Odradek (the "cares") is on the narrator's mind constantly. In his diaries, Kafka described cares as "the impossibility of making calculations."[23] Odradek's random appearances have made the family man an object of the little creature's panoptic look, an "inmate" in his own house.

The degree to which the narrator experiences this unpredictability as destabilizing is conveyed already in the story's first two paragraphs. In an attempt to reassure himself that Odradek is not a mere fantasy of his, but does exist, the family man turns to "common knowledge," yet only to end up betraying himself and the reader with a circular argument. He draws on existing linguistic studies into the etymology of the name *Odradek*, which are based on the assumption of a nonarbitrary connection between the signifier and the signified, and which deliver contradictory and inconclusive results as to the meaning of the name and hence the nature of this creature. More important, though, the family man considers the fact that such studies have been undertaken as confirmation of Odradek's existence: "No one, of course, would occupy himself with such studies if there were not a creature called Odradek."[24] What is meant as reassurance for the reader as much as for himself turns out to be a circular argument, stating that there are such studies because Odradek exists, and that Odradek must exist because there are such studies. The fact that the family man, a representative of rational, enlightened thought, reverts to such weak reasoning betrays his fragile position and his inability to recognize himself as the main oppressive force in the power relation in which he sees himself.

His reasoning turns out to be similarly ill-forced when he tries to convince himself and the reader that there *must* be a successful approach to understanding Odradek and thus to gain control over him. He claims that since Odradek does not show any signs of being broken, he must be "complete" (*abgeschlossen*) as he is.[25] In the family man's world, being complete is synonymous to having meaning and purpose, and therefore, even if Odradek *seems* meaningless—"the whole thing looks senseless enough"[26]—his supposed wholeness guarantees meaning and hence the possibility of being interpreted and eventually integrated into reality.

Convinced that Odradek exists and possesses meaning, the narrator tries his own approaches to unlocking this "riddle." His detailed description of Odradek's appearance combines analysis and analogical reasoning, breaking up Odradek into small, nonthreatening parts and situating this fragmentary creature in reality by comparing him to a combination of common everyday objects: "a flat star-shaped spool for thread," "thread," "a small wooden cross-bar," and another "small rod."[27] Odradek, however, is not *made* of these parts, but only *appears* like them "at first glance."[28] In fact, throughout this almost scientific description the family man uses repeatedly comparisons, the subjunctive mode, and qualifiers such as "at first glance" and "to be sure,"[29] betraying that he can convey only a very subjective and imprecise impression of Odradek's appearance. This vagueness stands in the way of any empirical insight into this creature. When the family man ends his description with the remark that "the whole thing can stand upright as if on two legs,"[30] this is a first hint that he might suspect that the whole is more than the sum of its parts, that Odradek has some human or at least animate quality, and that the attempt to reduce him to a number of inanimate parts prevents the more holistic understanding that the family man is looking for.

As if he were afraid of what a relationship with such an animate creature might entail, the narrator continues treating Odradek as an object for yet another paragraph, referring to him as "this construction" and "the whole thing."[31] Yet prominently situated at the beginning of the fourth paragraph, the narrator's use of the personal pronoun "he"[32] marks the shift to the assessment of Odradek as a living, intelligent creature. This shift is needed for the narrator's attempt to communicate with the little visitor. The fact that he treats Odradek like a child ("Of course, you put no difficult questions to him, you treat him—he is so diminutive that you cannot help it—rather like a child")[33] betrays the family man's desperate need to control this situation. However, just like the ideal guard in the panopticon, Odradek declines the narrator's invitation for a conversation, and thus for intellectual or emotional exchange beyond the provision of his name and of a vague piece of information concerning his address, "No fixed abode."[34] He escapes all attempts to grasp him physically or intellectually and stays "discreet" or "locked" (abgeschlossen).[35]

Once the narrator realizes that he cannot integrate Odradek into his worldview and fully understand him, he defines the creature as the Other, as that which is not part of the given order but intrudes from the outside and has to be fought off. The family man's observation that Odradek seems unaffected by the passing of time and does not show any signs of aging or wear confirms the creature's outsider role. In a culture that is genuinely aware of the finitude of the human lifespan and holds that all beings have an obligation to work toward fulfilling their purpose until they die, the family man's categorical rejection of the idea that Odradek's existence might have any purpose is synonymous to excluding him from the system while concurrently proposing his immortality. This conclusion lacks a solid basis and reveals the narrator's labeling Odradek as the Other as a defense mechanism to protect his time's values and order and hence his own position.

Kafka knew this tendency of the typical family man only too well, since he had repeatedly endured his own father's tirades against himself and anybody else who seemed not to fit into the given structure or submit to Hermann Kafka's control, be it his own children, their potential spouses, or their friends. Yet instead of ending his story with such a "realistic" turn, Kafka presents his readers with an alternative conclusion. Perceiving his dominant position challenged, the narrator develops further his thoughts about the purpose of life, and begins to wonder about his own as well as future generations' mortality. In the end, the notion of Odradek's immortality, and hence the likelihood of children and grandchildren finding themselves challenged by him in the family house, is "*almost* painful"[36]—that is, it is actually *not* painful. Odradek's presence has obviously prompted the narrator to accept certain phenomena in his world that escape his control and whose mere existence questions the given order. This newly found openness—"He obviously does not harm anyone"[37]—cannot eliminate the family man's "cares," but it gives them a less threatening quality and might open the door for more tolerance.

The narrator is obviously the main "bearer"[38] of the panoptic power situation that exists as a result of Odradek's appearance. Yet the question remains how this creature affects the family man so deeply, and what mechanisms are at work when the latter feels looked at. From the narrator's description it is not clear whether Odradek actually has eyes to see and is thus capable of looking in the traditional sense. However, as Jean-Paul Sartre maintains in *Being and Nothingness*, the look and its effects are completely independent of the actual presence of a watching person or a set of eyes:

> Every look directed toward me is manifested in connection with the appearance of a sensible form in our perceptive field, but contrary to what might be expected, it is not connected with any determined form. Of course what *most often* manifests a look is the convergence of two ocular globes in my direction. But the look will be given just as well on occasion when there is a rustling of branches, or the sound of a footstep followed by silence, or the slight opening of a shutter, or a light movement of a curtain.[39]

The French philosopher develops a definition of the look based on the effects it has on the one looked at, most importantly the change of roles from subject to object and the reorganization of the perceived individual's world.

The moment one becomes aware of being looked at, one becomes aware of oneself as an object, and encounters the Other, "the *one who looks at me*,"[40] as a subject. When not looked at, one is at the center of a world which is organized around one and in which one is absorbed. The Other's look initiates a "disintegration"[41] of the object's world and a spatial and temporal recentering of its components around the new, looking subject, which results in a feeling of "alienation"[42] for the object: "With the Other's look the 'situation' escapes me. . . . *I am no longer master of the situation.*"[43] In addition, the look makes the object aware of itself: "I see *myself* because *somebody* sees me."[44] Thus the look transforms the object and its world, and it makes the object aware of the fact that its world is not the only world, but that there are other worlds, whose organizations reflect the Others' possibilities and freedom. However, the look not only broadens the object's horizon by confronting it with a different perspective on itself and the world, but it also evokes feelings of fear and shame in the object—shame because it recognizes itself as "this degraded, fixed, and dependent being which I am for the Other,"[45] and fear because it realizes the Other can limit it by integrating it into the Other's world. The only way to protect a subject against becoming an object is the objectivation of the Other, the preemptive or reactive integration of the Other into the subject's world by the look. This, however, establishes a very fragile situation:

> Thus the Other-as-object is an explosive instrument which I handle with care because I foresee around him the permanent possibility that *they* [individuals who compose the Other in its object state] are going to make it explode and that with this explosion I shall suddenly experience the flight of the world away from me and the alienation of my being. Therefore my constant concern is to contain the Other within his objectivity, and my relations with the Other-as-object are essentially made up ruses designed to make him remain an object. But one look on the part of the Other is sufficient to make all these schemes collapse and to make me experience once more the transfiguration of the Other.[46]

Sartre's work on the look sheds new light on Odradek's impact on the family man and the latter's efforts to understand this creature. The narrator's reaction betrays that the discovery of Odradek in his house is analogous to the feeling of being looked at (i.e., the notion that something is different about one's world, although there are no measurable, empirically verifiable changes). Thus it is less Odradek's form or his actions, but merely his perceived presence, that triggers the cares of the family man and makes him feel as if he is losing control of his world. His efforts to define Odradek are attempts to push the creature back in the object role and to thus regain the role of subject for himself. The family man tries "to look back," to reverse the direction of the look, but his efforts always refer him back to himself. Since, as the discussion of the panoptic nature of Odradek's look has shown, the narrator is both the agent and the recipient of the look, he is incapable of escaping this optical power relation by concentrating on Odradek.

Eventually, the narrator does turn to himself for answers, as the introduction of the pronoun "I" in the final paragraph shows. This change in focus allows the family man to overcome his fear and shame, and results in a less negative attitude toward Odradek and toward the notion of another world different from his own. In order to understand this change in attitude, it will be helpful to take a closer look at the phenomenon of "anamorphosis" as discussed by Jacques Lacan, and Kaja Silverman's notion of the "dominant fiction" and her application of this idea to Lacan's work.

Silverman describes as *dominant fiction* "'the world,' or that which generally passes for reality" in a society.[47] Although many aspects of the dominant fiction are subject to change depending on historical and cultural context, there are certain concepts that exist across cultures and times, and Silverman maintains "that the dominant fiction's most rudimentary binary opposition is that distinguishing masculinity from femininity; its most fundamental equation is that of penis and phallus; and its most central signifier is the family. All the other elements of a given dominant fiction are articulated in relation to these core terms."[48] From the very beginning of his story, Kafka evokes these core elements as they shaped early twentieth-century Western European culture with the term "family man." And with Odradek the writer created a character who subverts each of these categories.

For more than half of the story, the family man refers to Odradek exclusively with the neuter pronoun. This seems appropriate since his description of the little creature does not allow for any assumptions about Odradek's gender. The name *Odradek* itself, as well as the various objects to which the family man compares his parts, are all gender neutral.[49] Nevertheless, once the narrator considers Odradek an animate being, he consistently uses the masculine pronoun "he" without ever questioning this gender designation. This is even more surprising since Odradek's size prompts the family man to explicitly treat him like a child (i.e., as an individual that is traditionally considered part of the mother's feminine sphere). Himself a product of the gender matrix of his time, the family man takes for granted that a creature that moves around freely and can intrude into his house and test his power must be masculine. The fact that the family man assigns Odradek's gender based on the creature's power and independence reveals the degree to which the bourgeois perception of relations is organized along gender lines, and at the same time stresses the arbitrariness of this gender distinction.[50]

When Silverman claims that the "fundamental equation" of the social order is that of penis and phallus, she refers back to Lacan's concept of the symbolic order of language. According to Lacan, every human being has to enter language to designate the self by saying "I" and thus to become a member of culture. Yet entering language means submitting to its rules, which Lacan calls the law of the father, the name of the father, or the phallus. These terms designate the center of the symbolic order that determines and stabilizes the entire structure, and Lacan's terminology points to the patriarchal nature of language and hence of Western culture in general. The Lacanian phallus is not the same as the penis, but is the center of the language structure, and thus nobody can have or be the phallus. The false equation of phallus and penis is the basis of the male dominance of culture, of what Silverman calls the dominant fiction, and the family man's power as a representative of the patriarchal order rests to a large degree on this equation. The fact that the nonhuman, tiny Odradek exercises power over the family man, questions this alleged link between penis and phallus.[51] Against this background, the family man's efforts to control Odradek through language by speaking about him and his name, and by trying to make Odradek speak about himself, appear as attempts to integrate him into the phallocentric, symbolic order of language, which the narrator considers *his* order.

Odradek's presumed refusal to enter the patriarchal order is reflected in his preferred spaces. The actual house has been considered a crucial symbol of the traditional ideal of the German family, and as such also of the family man's responsibility and power.[52] Odradek's avoidance of those spaces within the house that represent different aspects of family life—for instance, the kitchen that stands for nurturing, the living room representing community, or the bedroom as the place of procreation and thus the generational order—emphasizes the notion of him as an intruder. In these places, he would have to take on a role within this system—most likely that of guest—and submit to the rule of the head of the household.

Despite his initial irritation, the narrator begins to accept the existence of this figure, whose mere appearance challenges the basic ideas and values of his life. Lacan's and Silverman's discussions of the perspectival construction called anamorphosis offer an approach to this change in attitude. Anamorphosis allows objects, when looked at from the typical position for viewing perspectival images (i.e., standing in front of the image at a position equidistant from the right and left sides), to appear strange and distorted. The viewer can decode these objects only when looking at them from a specific yet unusual angle. However, from this unconventional perspective, the objects surrounding the anamorphosis and the viewer—the rest of the scene—are barely recognizable. It is the individual viewer's position that determines whether he or she sees the anamorphotic or the surrounding objects as distorted, and thus what the viewer sees and eventually what effect this has on him or her. Thus the anamorphosis constrains the viewers, since it requires that they take a certain point of view in order to understand it. Lacan himself draws a connection to Cartesian subjectivity, and Kaja Silverman, tracing his argument, writes:

> [Lacan] points out . . . that the position in relation to which the conventional perspectival image comes into focus . . . is closely connected . . . to a Cartesian notion of subjectivity. . . . Since, when we occupy that point, everything seems to radiate out from our look, any painting organized in relation to it encourages us to enact that form of *méconnaisance* which is, for Lacan, the visual equivalent of the *cogito*.[53]

Eventually, anamorphosis makes the viewer aware of his or her look as it "undoes the *méconnaisance*"[54] by denying access to a part of reality. At the same time, the desire to decipher the anamorphotic object results in a reversal of the roles of subject and object. In order to identify the distorted object, the viewer has to give up the conventional position as the center of the visual experience. The object seems to look at the viewer, who, in return, feels like an object (i.e., as if he were part of the anamorphotic construction). This loss of the subject position evokes a feeling of lack in the viewer, which, according to Lacan, triggers desire.[55]

Odradek's appearance in the family man's house has an effect comparable to that of an anamorphosis. Thus, for most of the story, the narrator looks at Odradek from the conventional position of a representative of bourgeois values and norms, who expects the people and objects in his world to be measurable and to have a purpose. All the narrator's attempts to integrate Odradek into the bourgeois world, and to bring him under his control, are eventually expressions of his desire to preserve the world as he knows it and thus to protect his *méconnaisance*. Since the family man cannot fathom Odradek from this point of view, Kafka's story depicts him as torn between his desire to protect his privileged position, and his desire to give up the conventional perspective despite his fear in order to "see" Odradek.

This change in perspective takes place once the narrator recognizes that he has lost his subject role in this visual encounter and has become the object of Odradek's look. The desire to understand Odradek and at the same time to regain the subject role drives the narrator to a change in what he looks at and how he looks at it. Following the direction of Odradek's look, the look of the anamorphosis, the family man turns his attention toward himself and his reaction to the intruder and to his world. This change in the object of his look is marked by the use of the personal pronoun "I" throughout the last paragraph.[56] At this point, however, the narrator no longer looks from the point of view of the insider, of the one who controls this world, but from the outside, as someone who understands that this particular world is just one among many others and that the fragility of his own position in it renders the notion that it might be *his* world rather questionable.[57]

As different aspects of the dominant fiction, the very sanction for his role, are undermined, it is only natural that eventually the family man comes to think about his own mortality as the ultimate limit of his influence. Confronted with Odradek's potential immortality, this inevitable final loss of control at first upsets the family man, as the tone of his thoughts reveals: "Am I to suppose, then, that he will always be rolling down the stairs, with ends of thread trailing after him, right before the feet of my children, and my children's children?"[58] Yet instead of undertaking further attempts to control Odradek, the family man, though with some difficulty, comes to accept that he cannot control everything—that he is not, in Lacan's terms, at the center of the symbolic order. What began as a defense of the only world the narrator knew and could imagine, by the end of the story has turned into a first step toward acceptance and tolerance of otherness.

The narrator's look at Odradek has become what Silverman, building on work by Freud and Roland Barthes, calls "productive."[59] Barthes distinguishes between two looks: one that stays within the limits and follows the rules of the dominant fiction, and one that is directed away from this position at the cultural center. The ability for such visual deviation from the norm, Barthes suggests, "resides in memory."[60] According to Freud, visual stimuli are unconsciously and preconsciously classified depending on existing memories before they are consciously perceived and eventually integrated into existing mnemic structures. Therefore, any attempts to change the look would have to affect the unconscious and the preconscious. Silverman defines the productive look as one that to some degree can see beyond or next to the socially and culturally sanctioned: "productive looking necessarily entails . . . the opening up of the unconscious to otherness."[61] At the same time, instead of incorporating the seen into the subject's "own" and thus confirming the ego, this look wants to see that which may not validate but question or even negate the ego, and that may lead to a displacement of the ego in the memory. Silverman writes about productive looking: "It would factor into my mnemic operations not only what resides outside the given-to-be-seen, but what my *moi* excludes—what must be denied in order for my self to exist as such. It would, in short, introduce the 'not me' into my memory reserve."[62] Since this way of looking cannot be achieved by sheer willpower, it needs other prompts such as aesthetic works, which provoke the individual to leave the point of view at the center.[63]

This concept of art is reflected in the effect Odradek has on the family man. He makes the narrator look "beyond" what is culturally accepted, and, even more significant, makes him look at himself differently and eventually modify his understanding of society and of his own role. Thus the narrator's look at Odradek becomes a place where power, knowledge, and identity are negotiated, and in the end becomes productive in the sense that it allows the family man to move beyond his own limits. This change in attitude distinguishes the family man in this story from the many other family men in Kafka's *œuvre*, who defend their positions ruthlessly, even if this leads to the loss of their own sons—for instance, the fathers in "The Judgment" and *The Metamorphosis*, and the many father figures in Karl Rossmann's life. While those reflect central aspects of Kafka's experience with his own father, the narrator of "The Cares of a Family Man" is presented as a potential alternative to the traditional head of the family, a figure willing to tolerate strangeness and to move beyond his narrowly defined role.

Conclusion

Odradek turns out to be the perfect catalyst to trigger the family man's deviation from the norm: on the one hand, this uninvited visitor does not show "the urge to limit himself to how the look of man has the power to see him,"[64] and thus does not fulfill the narrator's expectations in regards to any human or animate being; on the other hand, Odradek is too strange and unfamiliar a figure for the family man to know or even guess the creature's expectations of him. Odradek's power rests in his mysterious nature: as the family man cannot foresee any of Odradek's actions, his own (re)actions lose their teleological coherence and seem futile. As he begins to feel the loss of purpose in his encounters with Odradek, the family man becomes aware of his own expectations toward himself and the world, and of their narrowness. His gradual acceptance of Odradek's existence and presence in his house is a first step toward a more tolerant worldview that looks beyond the cultural screen. At the same time, the Odradek figure, and with it the entire text, may have a similarly "productive" effect on the readers. As a first-person narrative, "The Cares of a Family Man" draws the readers into the hermeneutical process of deciphering Odradek and has them experience the narrator's struggles and doubts vicariously. Thus, Kafka not only pushed the limits of his readers' imagination but also their comfort with contemporary culture, and may potentially have provoked some productive looking of their own.

Notes

1. "Er wehrt sich gegen die Fixierung durch den Mitmenschen. Der Mensch sieht, selbst wenn er unfehlbar wäre, im anderen nur jenen Teil, für den seine Blickkraft und Blickart reicht. Er hat, wie jeder, aber in äußerster Übertreibung, die Sucht, sich so einzuschränken, wie ihn der Blick des Menschen zu sehen die Kraft hat." Franz Kafka, "'Er'—Aufzeichnungen aus dem Jahre 1920," in *Beschreibung eines Kampfes: Novellen, Skizzen, Aphorismen aus dem Nachlaß*, ed. Max Brod (Frankfurt: Fischer Taschenbuch Verlag, 1998), 220 (my translation).

2. Walter Benjamin, "Franz Kafka: On the Tenth Anniversary of His Death," in *Illuminations*, ed. and intr. Hannah Arendt, trans. Harry Zohn (New York: Harcourt, Brace & World, 1968), 124.

3. Often with etymological studies into the meaning of the word "Odradek" as a starting point (Verena Ehrich-Haefeli, "Bewegungsenergien in Psyche und Text: Zu Kafkas 'Odradek,'" *Zeitschrift für deutsche Philologie* 109:2 [1990]: 242; Wilhelm Emrich, *Franz Kafka* [Bonn: Athenäum, 1958], 92–93; Heinz Politzer, *Franz Kafka, der Künstler* [Frankfurt: Fischer, 1965], 152–53), scholars have interpreted the family man's speculations and observations of Odradek within a philosophical-religious (Jörg Kühne, *"Wie das Rascheln in gefallenen Blättern": Versuch zu Franz Kafka* [Tübingen: Rotsch, 1975]; Kurt Weinberg, *Kafkas Dichtungen: Die Travestien des Mythos* [Bern: Francke, 1963], 118–23), metaphysical (Emrich, *Franz Kafka*, 93–95; Politzer, *Franz Kafka*, 153–56), existentialist (Dietger Bansberg, "Durch Lüge zur Wahrheit: Eine Interpretation von Kafkas Geschichte 'Die Sorge des Hausvaters,'" *Zeitschrift für deutsche Philologie* 93 [1974]: 257–69; Heinz Hillmann, "Das Sorgenkind Odradek," *Zeitschrift für deutsche Philologie* 86 [1967]: 197–210; Herbert Kraft, *Mondheimat: Kafka* [Pfullingen: Neske, 1983], 157; Gerhard Kurz, *Traum-Schrecken: Kafkas literarische Existenzanalyse* [Stuttgart: Metzler, 1980], 85–102; Gregory B. Triffit, *Kafka's "Landarzt" Collection: Rhetoric and Interpretation* [New York: Peter Lang, 1985], 171–75), or psychoanalytic-feminist (Astrid Lange-Kirchheim, "Das Ewig-Weibliche—*Die Sorge des Hausvaters*: Franz Kafkas Erzählung psychoanalytisch-feministisch gelesen," in *Proceedings of the 11th International Conference on Literature and Psychology in Sandberg [Denmark], June 1994*, ed. Frederico Pereira [Lisbon: Istituto Superior de Psicologia Aplicada, 1995], 119–32) context. Some approach Odradek with the help of Marxist theory of commodities and alienation and Heidegger's phenomenology of the referentiality of equipment (*Zeug*) (Max Bense, *Die Theorie Kafkas* [Köln: Kipenheuer & Witsch, 1952], 63–67), while others read him as a caricature of modern machines (Politzer, *Franz Kafka*, 153–54), a chiffre of Freud's "Uncanny" (Jürgen Born, "Erscheinungsformen des Anderen in Kafkas Erzählungen: 'Ein altes Blatt' und 'Die Sorge des Hausvaters,'" in *Die Vielfalt in Kafkas Leben und Werk*, ed. Wendelin Schmidt-Dengler and Norbert Winkler [Furth im Wald: Vitalis, 2005], 183–85) or of modern art and aestheticism (Richard T. Gray et al., *A Franz Kafka Encyclopedia* [Westport, CT: Greenwood Press, 2005], 255; Kühne, *Wie das Rascheln*, 70–73), as a critique of paternal power (Allen Thiher, "A Country Doctor," in *Franz Kafka: A Study of the Short Fiction* [Boston: Twayne, 1990], 68–79), or as a metaphor for Kafka's "The Hunter Gracchus" fragment (J. M. S. Pasley, "Two Kafka Enigmas: 'Elf

Söhne' and 'Die Sorge des Hausvaters,'" *Modern Language Review* 59:1 [1964]: 76–81) or the literary work in general (Kurz, *Traum-Schrecken*, 100–102).

4. Heinz Hillmann, "Das Sorgenkind Odradek." See also Kurz, *Traum-Schrecken*, 92. Following Hillmann's lead, several studies point out that the narrator's step-by-step approach to comprehend Odradek presents an interpretive effort similar to the reader's own when faced with this rather enigmatic story (Gray et al., *A Kafka Encyclopedia*, 254; Günter Saße, "Die Sorge des Lesers: Zu Kafkas Erzählung *Die Sorge des Hausvaters*," *Poetica* 10 [1978]: 262–84; Sonja Dierks, "Odradek," in *Es gibt Gespenster: Betrachtungen zu Kafkas Erzählungen* [Würzburg: Königshausen & Neumann, 2003], 54–60).

5. Hansjörg Bay, "Kafkas Tinitus," in *Odradeks Lachen: Fremdheit bei Kafka*, ed. Hansjörg Bay and Christof Hamann (Freiburg: Rombach, 2006), 44–55; Ehrich-Haefeli, "Bewegungsenergien."

6. Unless noted otherwise, English translations of Kafka's "Die Sorge des Hausvater" are quoted according to the following edition: Franz Kafka, "The Cares of a Family Man," in *The Complete Stories*, ed. Nahum N. Glatzer, trans. Willa and Edwin Muir (New York: Schocken, 1971), 427–29. Occasionally, I provide a more literal translation to better support my argument. In those cases, the German original will be provided in a note.

7. Bay and Christof Hamann, "Einleitung," in *Odradeks Lachen*, 11.

8. Saße, "Die Sorge des Lesers," 277.

9. "eine Figur . . . die keine ist." Detlef Kremer, *Kafka: Die Erotik des Schreibens. Schreiben als Lebensentzug* (Frankfurt: Athenäum, 1989), 166 (my translation).

10. Saße, "Die Sorge des Lesers," 270–71.

11. Bay, "Kafkas Tinitus," 45.

12. "der Name suggeriert patriarchalische Herrschaft und behagliche Sicherheit. . . . 'Hausvater': das meint also Sicherheit, Geborgenheit, Übersicht, Selbständigkeit, Überlegenheit, Herrschaft über 'sein' Haus." Kurz, *Traum-Schrecken*, 92 (my translation).

13. Karin Hausen, "Die Polarisierung der 'Geschlechtscharaktere'—Eine Spiegelung der Dissoziation von Erwerbs- und Familienleben," in *Sozialgeschichte der Familie in der Neuzeit Europas*, ed. Werner Conze (Stuttgart: Klett, 1976), 363–93; W. H. Riehl, *Die Naturgeschichte des Volkes als Grundlage einer deutschen Sozial-Politik*, vol. 3: Die Familie (Stuttgart: Cotta, 1889), 119–72. Most likely Kafka wrote "The Cares of a Family Man" during the last week of April 1917, which marked the final days of a very productive phase (Hartmut Binder, *Kafka—Kommentar zu sämtlichen Erzählungen* [München: Winkler, 1975], 230). In December 1916, his four-year epistolary exchange with his fiancée Felice Bauer had virtually ended, and the positive effect of this crisis on his writing (Gray et al., *A Kafka Encyclopedia*, 7) may have confirmed for Kafka how unsuited he himself probably was for the role of family man. Further proof that he was not the "master of the house" type was his role in the Prager Asbestwerke Hermann & Co., an asbestos factory that Kafka founded with his brother-in-law Karl Hermann in 1911 and co-owned. Well into the twentieth century, many factory owners considered their industrial plants, including their workers, extensions of their houses and themselves father figures in this environment (Hans-Ulrich Wehler, *Deutsche Gesellschaftsgeschichte*, vol. 3: Von der "Deutschen Doppelrevolution" bis zum Beginn des Ersten Weltkriegs 1949–1914 [München: Beck, 1995], 725–29). Kafka's "attempt to imitate his own fa-

ther as a successful entrepreneur" (Gray et al., *A Kafka Encyclopedia*, 222) failed due to a lack of genuine interest in the factory, and the eventual liquidation of the asbestos factory in 1917 may have reminded Kafka of the fact that he was not cut out for this role.

14. Bansberg, "Durch Lüge zur Wahrheit," 258.

15. Franz Kafka, *Letter to His Father—Brief an den Vater*, trans. Ernst Kaiser and Eithne Wilkins (New York: Schocken, 1976), 23.

16. Kafka, *Letter to His Father*, 93.

17. Michel Foucault, *Discipline and Punish: The Birth of the Prison*, trans. Alan Sheridan (New York: Vintage, 1995), 201.

18. Foucault, *Discipline and Punish*, 202–3.

19. Foucault, *Discipline and Punish*, 202.

20. Kafka, "The Cares of a Family Man," 428.

21. Gilles Deleuze and Félix Guattari, *Kafka: Towards a Minor Literature*, trans. Dana Polan (Minneapolis: University of Minnesota Press, 1986), 72–74.

22. "Manchmal ist er monatelang nicht zu sehen; da ist er wohl in andere Häuser übersiedelt; doch kehrt er dann unweigerlich wieder in unser Haus zurück." Franz Kafka, "Die Sorge des Hausvaters," in *Drucke zu Lebzeiten*, ed. Wolf Kittler et al. (Frankfurt: Fischer Taschenbuch Verlag, 2002), 283 (my translation).

23. Franz Kafka, *The Diaries 1910–1923*, ed. Max Brod (New York: Schocken, 1976), 369. Kafka's remark here resonates with Friedrich Nietzsche's and Martin Heidegger's idea that indeterminacy and unpredictability are the sources of anxiety. At least from the seventeenth century onward, natural science has been oriented toward providing security by elevating humanity to the position of lord and master of nature. This is accomplished by fixing the indeterminacy of a dynamic nature in stable concepts that make possible predictions about future natural states. Kafka suggests that the project of universal predictability and control is bound to fail. As Heidegger might say, we therefore live in a situation where anxiety can beset us at any time.

24. Kafka, "The Cares of a Family Man," 428.

25. Kafka, "Die Sorge des Hausvaters," 283 (my translation).

26. Kafka, "The Cares of a Family Man," 428.

27. Kafka, "The Cares of a Family Man," 428. See also Emrich, *Franz Kafka*, 93; Saße, "Die Sorge des Lesers," 275.

28. Kafka, "The Cares of a Family Man," 428.

29. Kafka, "The Cares of a Family Man," 428.

30. Kafka, "The Cares of a Family Man," 428.

31. "dieses Gebilde," "das Ganze." Kafka, "Die Sorge des Hausvaters," 283 (my translation).

32. Kafka, "The Cares of a Family Man," 428.

33. Kafka, "The Cares of a Family Man," 428.

34. Kafka, "The Cares of a Family Man," 428.

35. Kafka, "Die Sorge des Hausvaters," 283 (my translation). The German word *abgeschlossen* has several meanings, including locked, finished, complete, isolated, and self-contained, that readers familiar with German would all be aware of.

36. "*fast* schmerzlich." Kafka, "Die Sorge des Hausvaters," 284 (my italics and translation).

37. "Er schadet ja offenbar niemandem." Kafka, "Die Sorge des Hausvaters," 284 (my translation).

38. Foucault, *Discipline and Punish*, 201.

39. Jean-Paul Sartre, *Being and Nothingness: An Essay on Phenomenological Ontology*, trans. and intr. Hazel E. Barnes (New York: Philosophical Library, 1956), 257.

40. Sartre, *Being and Nothingness*, 257.

41. Sartre, *Being and Nothingness*, 255.

42. Sartre, *Being and Nothingness*, 263.

43. Sartre, *Being and Nothingness*, 265.

44. Sartre, *Being and Nothingness*, 260.

45. Sartre, *Being and Nothingness*, 288.

46. Sartre, *Being and Nothingness*, 297.

47. Kaja Silverman, *The Threshold of the Visible World* (New York: Routledge, 1996), 178. On the concept of the dominant fiction, see also Kaja Silverman, *Male Subjectivity at the Margins* (New York: Routledge, 1992), 15–51.

48. Silverman, *The Threshold*, 178.

49. Astrid Lange-Kirchheim defines "yarn, spool, thread as having a feminine connotation" ("Zwirn, Spule, Faden [sind] weiblich konnotiert"; Lange-Kirchheim, "Das Ewig-Weibliche," 122 [my translation]) and as referring back to Ariadne. However, the "flat star-shaped spool for thread" (Kafka, "The Cares of a Family Man," 428) is probably not a spinning utensil, but rather one of the small cardboard stars that hold thread and that Kafka must have been familiar with from his father's store. During Kafka's time, thread and star-shaped spools were equally likely to be found in a housewife's sewing basket and at a (usually male) tailor's studio.

50. Kafka's decision to make Odradek male may have been influenced by the fact that figures of Jewish folklore and mysticism like the wandering Jew or the Golem, whose appearances were equally unpredictable, were male. Kafka wrote "The Cares of a Family Man" in Alchimistengasse in Prague's old Jewish quarter around the Old-New Synagogue, where supposedly the remains of the Golem were left by Rabbi Löw. In 1915, Gustav Meyrink's fantastic novel *The Golem* was published, and it is very likely that Kafka was familiar with this work.

51. Jacques Lacan, *Écrits*, the first complete edition in English, trans. Bruce Fink in collaboration with Héloïse Fink and Russell Grigg (New York: Norton, 2005), 220–31, 575–84.

52. Riehl, *Die Naturgeschichte des Volkes*, 276–303. Kafka himself very much cherished the idea of a house of his own. This becomes obvious from the following remark that refers to the small medieval house on Alchimistengasse in Prague, which Kafka rented together with his sister Ottla from November 1916 to April 1917 and where he wrote most of the *Country Doctor* stories, including "The Cares of a Family Man" (Gray et al., *A Kafka Encyclopedia*, 6–7): "It is something very special to have a house of one's own, to keep the world out by locking the door—not of a room, not of an apartment, but of a house" (Franz Kafka, *Letters to Felice*, trans. James Stern and Elisabeth Duckworth, ed. Erich Heller and Jürgen Born [New York: Schocken, 1973], 542). Thus, to a certain degree, Kafka was a family man himself when he wrote the story (Binder, *Kafka—Kommentar*, 231).

53. Silverman, *The Threshold*, 177.

54. Silverman, *The Threshold*, 177.

55. Lacan and Silverman both refer to Hans Holbein the Younger's painting "The Ambassadors" (1533) in their discussions of anamorphosis. This painting shows two men standing on either side of a two-tier set of shelves holding various objects representing the arts and sciences during their time. In the foreground, at the bottom of the painting, is a strange, distorted object that spectators can only identify as a skull when looking at the painting from the very far right. Unless they recognize the skull, viewers lose an important dimension of the work—namely, the notion of vanity, which, in turn, is supposed to challenge the idea of humans mastering the world with the help of science and the arts exclusively.

56. In Kafka's early story "Wedding Preparations in the Country," the main character, Eduard Raban, reflects on this change from the impersonal "one" to "I": "And so long as you say 'one' instead of 'I,' there is nothing in it and one can easily tell the story; but as soon as you admit to yourself that it is you yourself, you feel as though transfixed and are horrified" (Franz Kafka, "Wedding Preparations in the Country," in *The Complete Stories*, ed. Nahum N. Glatzer [New York: Schocken, 1971], 53).

57. Bay, interested in the figure of the intruder, writes about "The Cares of a Family Man": "The figure of the intruder becomes the key element of an experiment, with the help of which Kafka directs the look on the unfamiliar back to his own culture" ("Die Figur des Eindringlings wird . . . zum entscheidenden Moment einer Versuchsanordnung, mit deren Hilfe Kafka . . . den Blick auf das Fremde zurückwirft auf die eigene Kultur"; Bay, "Kafkas Tinitus," 43 [my translation]).

58. Kafka, "The Cares of a Family Man," 429.

59. Silverman, *The Threshold*, 180.

60. Silverman, *The Threshold*, 182.

61. Silverman, *The Threshold*, 184.

62. Silverman, *The Threshold*, 185.

63. Marc Lucht demonstrates that Kant, in his *Critique of Judgment*, anticipated the notion that art and literature provide experiences with the capacity to broaden our perspectives on the world and ourselves. Marc Lucht, "Towards Lasting Peace: Kant in Law, Public Reason, and Culture," *The American Journal of Economics and Sociology* 68:1 (2009): 313–15.

64. See note 1.

CHAPTER 11

Four Hands Good, Two Hands Bad

Tom Tyler

> Plato had defined Man as an animal, biped and featherless, and was applauded. Diogenes plucked a fowl and brought it into the lecture-room with the words, "Here is Plato's Man." In consequence of which there was added to the definition, "having broad nails."
>
> Diogenes Laertius, *Lives of Eminent Philosophers*[1]

In Kafka's short story "A Report to an Academy," a chimpanzee named Rotpeter, who has been educated to the level of an average European, finds himself in something of a dilemma:

> Honoured members of the Academy! You have done me the honour of inviting me to give your Academy an account of the life I formerly led as an ape [*äffisches Vorleben*]. I regret that I cannot comply with your request to the extent you desire.[2]

Rotpeter explains that although only five years have passed "since I was an ape [*Affentum*]," and that he can recount something of his capture, his incarceration, and the training and personal exertion that lead to his becoming human, of his time in the forests of the Gold Coast he can say nothing.[3] The door through which he passed has now closed, and the strong wind that blew after him from his past is today no more than a gentle puff that plays about his heels. Rotpeter tells the honored members of the Academy that "your life as apes, gentlemen, insofar as something of that kind lies behind you, cannot be farther removed from you than mine is from me" and that "what I felt then as an ape I can represent now only in human terms."[4] Rotpeter is now a human before he is an ape.

Rotpeter, like the members of the Academy he is addressing, classifies himself as a human being. The modes of existence peculiar to apes are now unreachable, left far behind in the distant past of an inaccessible ancestry. Rotpeter affirms Bataille's suggestion that "nothing, as a matter of fact, is more closed to us than this animal life from which we are descended."[5] It is the precarious nature of the classification of human beings, along with the question of temporal preeminence on which it so often depends, that I would like to consider in this chapter. Clearly demarcated categories have always been a problem for the taxonomist, of course. Plato is by no means alone in having had to revise a definition following an impertinent intervention, and Darwin himself complained of the difficulties he experienced, the "undefined & unanswerable" questions with which he tussled, whilst at systematic work.[6] No one has highlighted the problematic character of the questions that haunted Darwin and his fellow systematists quite so concisely, or with such flare, however, as Borges.

Borges's well-known essay "John Wilkins' Analytical Language," first published in 1942, describes several attempts to construct a universal language—that is, a language in which each word defines itself.[7] Such a language would, as Borges put it, speculate on "the words, definitions, etymologies, and synonymies of God's secret dictionary." Borges mentions the system proposed in 1850 by one C. L. A. Letellier, in which "*a* means animal; *ab*, mammalian; *abo*, carnivorous; *aboj*, feline; *aboje*, cat; *abi*, herbivorous; *abiv*, equine," and so on. He recounts a similar example from Wilkins's own "undoubtedly ingenious" system: although the English word *salmon* tells us nothing, "*zana*, the corresponding word, defines (for the person versed in the forty categories and the classes of those categories) a scaly river fish with reddish flesh." Borges is alarmed by some of Wilkins's categories and divisions, however: the whale becomes, for instance, "a viviparous, oblong fish."[8] The "ambiguities, redundancies, and deficiencies" of Wilkins's system recall, he suggests, a certain Chinese encyclopedia:

> In its distant pages it is written that animals are divided into (a) those that belong to the emperor; (b) embalmed ones; (c) those that are trained; (d) suckling pigs; (e) mermaids; (f) fabulous ones; (g) stray dogs; (h) those that are included in this classification; (i) those that tremble as if they were mad; (j) innumerable ones; (k) those drawn with a very fine camel's-hair brush; (l) *etcetera*; (m) those that have just broken the flower vase; (n) those that at a distance resemble flies.[9]

A distinctive kind of disorder manifests here within the heart of the encyclopedic system. In his discussion of Borges's text, Foucault distinguishes the confusion of the merely incongruous from the true turmoil of the heteroclite.[10] The former is apparent in the unusual juxtaposition of creatures listed by Eusthenes when he declares, "I am no longer hungry. . . . Until the morrow, safe from my saliva all the following shall be: Aspics, Acalephs, Acanthocephalates, Amoebo-cytes, Ammonites, Axolotls, Amblystomas, Aphislions, Anacondas, Ascarids, Amphisbaenas, Angleworms, Amphipods, Anaerobes, Annelids, Anthozoans." Ordinarily these creatures would certainly not be found together, but that they might meet on the site of Eusthenes' saliva, as they do in his list, is at least a theo-retical possibility. The disorder of Borges's "Heavenly Emporium of Benevolent Knowledge" is another matter. Here the "fragments of a large number of pos-sible orders glitter separately in the dimension, without law or geometry, of the *heteroclite*."[11] Each of the categories belongs to a different system. There is not even the possibility of a common locus where the creatures could convene, and yet the continuity of the alphabetical sequence obliterates the distances between the categories. The disorder here is the internal incoherence of the paradox.

Heteroclite systems are, Borges suspects, inevitable. Universal languages, and indeed all attempts at classification, do not and cannot hold because "there is no universe in the organic, unifying sense of that ambitious word."[12] In short, "there is no classification of the universe that is not arbitrary and speculative."[13] But, Borges asserts, the impossibility of constructing a perfect taxonomy, of reproducing God's secret dictionary, should by no means discourage us from the attempt. Systems and orders will always be provisional, but that, in itself, is no reason to abandon them. Taxonomy, that branch of biological science concerned with the task of classifying species and other taxa, learned long ago to hypothesize rather than to hypostatize. I will return to this noble endeavor in a moment, but first we must exchange Borges's heteroclite disordering for a little incongruity.

In a rich, inspiring essay titled "Gaps in the Mind," Richard Dawkins works hard to knock down the door that Rotpeter believes to have shut fast behind him.[14] Dawkins describes what he calls "the discontinuous mind," an outlook characterized by the desire to impose inappropriately rigid distinctions on real world continua. Noticing that speciation allegedly occurs by means of infinitesi-mal, gradual variation, the sophistic lawyer will attempt to argue that, since a member of one species could never give birth to a member of another, Darwin's theory of evolution must surely be at fault. A gap is created where none exists. Dawkins points out that it is convenient for our naming rituals that intermedi-ate species have usually become extinct, but he invokes the case of ring species to demonstrate that this need not be the case. The example he provides is that of the herring gull and the lesser black-backed gull, two quite distinct species which are easy to tell apart and do not interbreed. If you follow the population of herring gulls westward from the United Kingdom, however, to North America, then Alaska, Siberia, across Russia, and back into Europe, the gulls gradually begin to look more and more like lesser black-backed gulls, until, as you reach Britain once more, they *are* lesser black-backed gulls. The gulls comprise a ring species, in which neighboring groups can and do interbreed, all the way around the world, but whose "ends" constitute two distinct species.[15] "Footling debates" which seek to establish sharp divisions where none exist entirely miss the point, and import, of Darwin's discovery.

"The word 'apes,'" Dawkins goes on, "usually means chimpanzees, gorillas, orangutans, gibbons and siamangs. We admit that we are like apes, but we seldom realise that we *are* apes." In fact, humans are African apes and are more closely related to chimpanzees and gorillas than either of those two species are to orangutans. Dawkins proposes a thought experiment to demonstrate that there is no great divide, no impassable doorway, separating human from ape. He suggests that the reader imagine themselves standing on the shore of the Indian Ocean in southern Somalia, facing north. "In your left hand you hold the right hand of your mother. In turn she holds the hand of her mother, your grandmother. Your grandmother holds her mother's hand, and so on."[16] Following this "human chain," we will have hardly started across the width of our home continent before we reach our common ancestor with the chimpanzee. If this "arch-ancestress" then turns east, and takes in her left hand her other daughter, from whom chimpanzees are descended, a parallel chain can be followed all the way back to the coast. The reader will now stand face to face with their modern chimpanzee cousin, to whom they are joined by an unbroken sequence of linked hands. Like a kind of diachronic ring species, there are no gaps in this chain of beings.

Anyone who walked up and down this chain might pass members of *Homo erectus*, *Homo ergaster*, perhaps also *Homo habilis* the "handy man," or even *Australopithecus afarensis*, and other species besides.[17] They would also pass individuals who could not comfortably be classified as belonging to any particular species. These individuals can be considered members of "intermediate species" only to those gazing down the line with the benefit of taxonomic hindsight. This hindsight is necessarily based on historical contingencies such as the matter of which species flourished, which became extinct, and which left the fossil remains on which modern classification depends.[18] The true importance of Darwin's work was not that he demonstrated the origin of any species, but that he showed just how specious the notion of species can be.[19] But to whatever species these individuals did or did not belong, all were African apes.

Dawkins' line-up ends with a single individual, a contemporary cousin standing opposite the reader, but there is in fact more than one species of chimpanzee. Chimpanzees (*Pan troglodytes*) have been known to the Western world since at least the seventeenth century. In 1699, the comparative anatomist Edward Tyson, a distant relative of Darwin's, published "The Anatomy of a Pygmie," his account, accompanied by superb anatomical drawings by William Cowper, of his dissection of a juvenile chimpanzee.[20] Tyson's stated objective was to demonstrate that "the pygmies, the cynocephali, the satyrs, and sphinges of the ancients" were actually apes or monkeys, not men, and that his own subject comprised the connecting link in the great chain of being between animal and man. He depicted his pygmy standing upright, supported by a walking stick on account of his failing health.[21] It was not until the early twentieth century that a second species of chimpanzee was identified. In 1928, a skull, previously thought to be that of a young chimpanzee, was recognized as belonging to an adult, albeit one with an especially small head. The following year the subspecies *paniscus* was announced, which, a few years later, was reclassified as a new species.[22] The name was simply a diminutive of the genus name, *Pan*, and the "new" species is often called the "pygmy chimpanzee." In fact, it is only the skull that is smaller, and the build slimmer than the common chimpanzee's body.[23] The origin of the preferred name for this ape—bonobo—is unknown, and may well have derived from a misspelling on a shipping crate.[24] The common and the pygmy chimpanzee are closely related, and the one has in the past often been confused with the other, but that they constitute separate species is now officially recognized.

It does not matter, for the purposes of Dawkins's demonstration, whether the *Pan* we face is a *troglodytes* or a *paniscus*: humans are as closely related to the one as the other. There is an alternative conclusion we might draw from his observations, however, regarding the nomenclature of the African ape family. As has often been noted, humans are genetically extremely close to chimpanzees, sharing 98.4 percent of their DNA.[25] The physiologist Jared Diamond has pointed out that willow warblers and chiffchaffs share less than this, at 97.4 percent, and yet are placed together in the same genus, *Phylloscopus*. And the red-eyed and white-eyed vireos, two North American birds, both belong to the genus *Vireo* while sharing only 97.1 percent DNA.[26] In short, were we to apply the same criteria to the great apes as we do to these other species, humans and chimpanzees would be acknowledged as members of the same genus. Diamond's argument is based on cladistics, the school of taxonomy that depends on the objective criteria of genetic distance between species, rather than traditional or phenetic classification systems which rely on subjective evaluations of the relative importance of anatomical or behavioral traits.[27] Since the genus name *Homo* was proposed first, then, according to the rules of taxonomic nomenclature, it must take priority. Diamond thus argues that "there are not one but three species of genus *Homo* on Earth today: the common chimpanzee, *Homo troglodytes*; the pygmy chimpanzee, *Homo paniscus*; and the third chimpanzee or human chimpanzee, *Homo sapiens*."[28] The African ape facing us on the coast of the Indian Ocean is a chimpanzee, though she is not a *Pan* at all but a fellow *Homo*.

It was the Swedish naturalist Carl Linnaeus who devised both the taxonomic ranking method and the binomial system of nomenclature still used today. Characterized by his contemporaries as a second Adam, Linnaeus set himself the task of giving true names to the Earth's creatures and thereby accurately representing the order of nature.[29] His work constituted an attempt to peek at God's secret dictionary. In the Linnaean system, which quickly replaced a bewildering, hetero-clitic assortment of competing classificatory methods, each species is designated by two Latinate names, the first generic, the second specific.[30] Linnaeus's mas-terwork, his *Systema Naturae*, began with the primates, and indeed with humans (genus *Homo*), whom he divided from the apes (genus *Simia*).[31] More than a cen-tury before Darwin, however, Linnaeus found himself wrestling with undefined and unanswerable questions of taxonomy:

> I demand of you, and of the whole world, that you show me a generic character—one that is according to generally accepted principles of classification—by which to distinguish between Man and Ape. I my-self most assuredly know of none. I wish somebody would indicate one to me. But, if I had called man an ape, or vice versa, I would have fallen under the ban of all ecclesiastics. It may be that as a naturalist I ought to have done so.[32]

In fact, Linnaeus had himself complicated this categorization of man and ape. He divided the genus *Homo* into two species, *Homo sapiens* and *Homo trog-lodytes*. The former, also called *Homo diurnus*, comprised various subspecies or races, including *Homo americanus*, *Homo europaeus*, and even *Homo monstrosus*, a miscellany of oddities including the Patagonian giant, the dwarf of the Alps, the monorchid Hottentot, and others. *Homo troglodytes*, identified as *Homo nocturnus*, was a creature reported by travellers to exist in Africa and Asia, about whom Linnaeus recorded that

> [i]t lives within the boundaries of Ethiopia (Pliny), in the caves of Java, Ambiona, Ternate. Body white, walks erect, less than half our size. Hair white frizzled. Eyes orbicular: iris and pupils golden. Vision lateral, nocturnal. Life-span twenty-five years. By day hides; by night it sees, goes out, forages. Speaks in a hiss. Thinks, believes that the earth was made for it, and that sometime it will be master again, if we may believe the travellers.[33]

According to Colin Groves, this golden-eyed anthropoid included "some undoubted orangutans and possibly chimpanzees."[34] Some of the great apes, at least, counted as *Homo*.

Jared Diamond does not mention Linnaeus's early primate classification. In suggesting, however, that even today's cladistically inclined taxonomists are an-thropocentric, and that "the lumping of humans and chimps into the same genus will undoubtedly be a bitter pill for them to swallow," he is surely correct. The impetus to isolate humans within their own genus betrays a heteroclitic humanism that goes beyond mere incongruity. Nevertheless, Diamond continues, "there is no doubt . . . that whenever chimpanzees learn cladistics . . . they will unhesitatingly adopt the new classification."[35] That is, we might add, whenever *we* learn to accept the new system of classification. Despite the speciousness of species, despite the lack of clear gaps in the continuum, despite the fact that we cannot read God's dictionary, we need not cease the attempt to keep compiling and revising systems of classification. The impossibility of penetrating the divine scheme of the universe should not, Borges asserts, dissuade us from devising our own schemes, even if it is clear that they are provisional.[36] The very nature of classifications, like dictionaries, is that they must be supplemented and amended.

Changing the names of species is nothing new. As we saw, *Pan paniscus* has changed name once already, and Groves lists forty-seven different names by which the several subspecies of ape now subsumed under *Pan troglodytes* have been known since the time of Linnaeus.[37] The operative principles of the International Code of Zoological Nomenclature require that an existing genus name must take priority over any subsequently proposed names. Diamond abides by these rules when he proposes that, although humans should be considered "the third chimpanzee," the genus name *Homo* should be adopted for the three species: *Homo* dates back to the official starting point for zoological nomenclature, the tenth edition of the *Systema Naturae*, published in 1758, whereas *Pan* was not employed as a genus name until 1816.[38] There is a danger here, however, of reduplicating the same anthropocentrism which Linnaeus decried in himself when he imprudently separated man and ape. His very description of the genus *Homo* was in fact the phrase *nosce te ipsum* ("know yourself").[39] Reclassifying chimpanzees as humans suggests once more that humans are in some sense prior to, or preeminent among, the great apes. This is the temporal priority of Rotpeter and Bataille, whereby humanity comes first. Our objective should not be to welcome a few new, privileged members into the charmed circle of human affairs.[40] If we wish to avoid this first and foremost anthropocentrism, it is vital that we find a different way to amend our primate nomenclature.[41]

The genus name of the chimpanzee comes from the Greek god of shepherds and their flocks, Pan (Παν).[42] Depicted with a human torso but the hindquarters, beard, and horns of a goat, the god was a lustful deity, pursuing nymphs and maenads around Arcadia while accompanied by his lascivious satyrs. Legends have long persisted of the prurient ape, and Linnaeus used the name *Satyrus* for one of the species of his genus *Simia*.[43] The name *Pan* is usually taken to have derived from the Indo-European root *pa* (to pasture), but an ancient Homeric hymn to Pan, chanted at religious festivals, suggests an alternative etymology. It tells that the gods gave him the name that they did because, as a rowdy child, full of merry laughter, he delighted them all (from *pantes*, meaning "all").[44] It is most appropriate, then, that this name should apply to *every* one of the species within our chimpanzee genus. But if humans should take the genus name *Pan*, what of their specific name?

In his *Anatomy of a Pygmie*, Tyson wondered whether it might be more appropriate to describe his chimpanzee as "Quadru-manus" rather than "Quadrupes."[45] Buffon, who was well acquainted with Tyson's text, and critical of Linnaeus's inclusion of *troglodytes* within the genus *Homo*, would go on to use the terms "quadrumanous" and "bimanous" of ape and man in his *Nomenclature of the Apes*.[46] It was not until 1795, however, that Johann Friedrich Blumenbach came to employ these two terms in a specifically classificatory sense. In the third edition of his *On the Natural Varieties of Mankind*, Blumenbach suggested that, despite the pioneering work of "the immortal Linnaeus," his *Systema Naturae* was now more than sixty years old and in need of revision. Accordingly, and despite protesting that "I am very far indeed from that itch for innovation which afflicts so many of the moderns," he proposed a new taxonomy of his own.[47]

Blumenbach rejected naturalists' long-established commitment to the continuity or gradation of nature, the chain of being which had still held Tyson captive, and argued instead that there are large gaps between classes and genera of creatures. He proposed ten distinct orders of mammalia, the first of which, the Bimanus, included only the genus *Homo*.[48] He argued that man's unique, erect stature gives him "that highest prerogative of his external conformation, namely, *the freest use of two most perfect hands*." The anthropomorphous animals, the apes, monkeys, and lemurs, however, have on their hind feet a second thumb, not the great toe which is given to man alone. As such they ought not to be considered either bipeds or quadrupeds, but belong in a distinct order of their own, the Quadrumana.[49] Only humans are fully bipedal,[50] a posture made possible precisely by the lack of hands on their hind extremities. It is not, as Heidegger has argued,[51] the hand which distinguishes human beings, but the fact that they have only two of them. With his two new orders, the Bimanus and the Quadrumana, Blumenbach thus definitively separated humans from all the other great apes, a taxonomic distinction that has persisted to the present day. The distinguishing feature of the human chimpanzee is the fact that members of the species do not have four hands, like the majority of the other primates, but a pair. Appropriating Blumenbach's term, but tempering the rigidity of the divisions he described by recalling Dawkins's chain of beings joined by their hands, humans might then best be considered *Pan bimanus*.

In considering the question of ape and human from the perspective of cladistics, my proposed revision breaks the taxonomic imperative of temporal preeminence. *Homo* came first according not only to the author of Genesis, but also to that second Adam, Linnaeus. What justification could be offered for this willful itch for innovation? In retaining and, indeed, extending the use of *Homo*, I have suggested, the rules of nomenclature manifest, in this instance, as a form of anthropocentrism. Linnaeus himself acknowledged that, as a good naturalist, he should have done otherwise. This anthropocentrism is a kind of self-centeredness—a species of narcissism, a species-narcissism. The fact that humans did not evolve from, but continue to be, apes need not, of itself, prevent their being self-centered, of course. Indeed, Derrida has suggested that one will *always* narcissistically reappropriate the other in one's own image:

> I believe that without a movement of narcissistic reappropriation, the relation to the other would be absolutely destroyed, it would be destroyed in advance. The relation to the other—even if it remains asymmetrical, open, without possible reappropriation—must trace a movement of reappropriation in the image of oneself for love to be possible, for example. Love is narcissistic.[52]

What we think of as "nonnarcissism" is in general "but the economy of a much more welcoming, hospitable narcissism." "Narcissism! There is not narcissism and nonnarcissism; there are narcissisms that are more or less comprehensive, generous, open, extended."[53] There is, we might say, more than one self-image in which the other might be cast, and with which one might fall in love. Man (*Homo*) might well be erased as a distinct genus, like a crude taxon sketched in the sands of genealogical time, but this does not draw to a close all possible forms of narcissism. It is true that Derrida himself will not, "for a single moment," take it upon himself to contest the thesis of a rupture or abyss "between those who say 'we men,' 'I, a man,' and what this man among men who say 'we,' what he *calls* the animal or animals."[54] There will always be gaps in the mind, and such a disregard for difference would simply be "too asinine." The point, however, is that this is not the *only* difference, the only abyss or gap or rupture. Derrida has given his attention, he says, not just to difference, but to *differences*, to *heterogeneities* and abyssal *ruptures*. Rotpeter chooses to narrate his history, to recount his particular kind of being, by stressing a single difference, but there are other tales he might have told. To follow Derrida, the autobiographical animal, one final time, we might choose to ask:

> Where then *are we*? Where do we find ourselves? With whom can we still identify in order to affirm our own identity and to tell ourselves our own history? First of all, to whom do we recount it? One would have to construct oneself, one would have to be able to invent oneself without a model and without an assured addressee. This addressee can, of course, only ever be presumed, in all situations of the world. But the schemas of this presumption were in this case so rare, so obscure, and so random that the word "invention" seems hardly exaggerated.[55]

The seemingly incongruous claim that humans are chimpanzees is made possible not by a listing of names, like Eusthenes' inventory of edible snakes, but by the construction of an inclusive taxonomic hierarchy. The individual organisms comprising any given taxon belong, necessarily, to multiple categories. The *bimanus* belong to the genus *Pan*, the family Hominidae, the order Primates, the class Mammalia, the phylum Chordata, and the kingdom Animalia. Derrida suggests that there are "little narcissisms" and "big narcissisms," and here, in the component classes of our nested taxonomic schema, we can identify multiple differences, heterogeneities and ruptures, and therefore assorted scales of self-image. In addition to these incongruously inclusive narcissisms, however, there are many more asymmetrically heteroclite clusters we might move to appropriate. The individual *Pan bimanus* who was Jorge Luis Borges, for instance, was (1) male; (2) middle-class; (3) married; (4) included in the current classification; (5) *etcetera*. Mapping genealogical and evolutionary categories will not exhaust what an individual was, is, or might become, and the politics of adjectives and articles requires that the being inclined to see itself as human pay due care and attention to the parts of speech employed in claims to self-identity. Where the substantive tends to define and delimit, the adjective permits a more inclusive multiplicity of relations. One might choose, then, to acknowledge one's *animal* being rather than to be *an animal*, to see oneself as *mammalian* rather than *a mammal*, to prefer *ein äffisches leben* or even *ein Affentum* to "life as an ape," and perhaps, even, to be *human* rather than *a human being*.[56] The provisional, presumptuous classifications we choose to invent will be, as Foucault, Borges, and Derrida well knew, both incongruous and heteroclite, but no less productive for all that.

I began with Kafka's tale of an ape, but there is another, more appropriate story with which to end *this* report to an academy. Pierre Boulle opens his most famous novel with Jinn and Phyllis, "a wealthy leisured couple," who are holidaying in space "as far as possible from the inhabited stars."[57] They spend their time sailing their solar-powered spacecraft and taking pleasure in one another's company. By chance, they intercept an old-fashioned message in a bottle, which, as they read it, becomes the main body of Boulle's novel. Jinn and Phyllis shake their heads in disbelief as they complete the manuscript, which reports the trials and tribulations of an astronaut, one Ulysse Mérou, who has been stranded on a world populated by rational chimpanzees, gorillas, and orangutans, a veritable planet of the apes. "A likely story," says Jinn, which shows only that "there are poets everywhere, in every corner of the cosmos, and practical jokers too." And so, in the closing words of the novel,

> [Jinn] let out the sail, exposing it to the combined rays of the three suns. Then he began to manipulate the driving levers, using his four nimble hands, while Phyllis, after dismissing a last shred of doubt with an energetic shake of her velvety ears, took out her compact and, in view of their return to port, touched up her dear little chimpanzee muzzle.[58]

Rotpeter appears at first to be an ape, but it soon becomes clear, if his repeated protestations are to be believed, that he is now human. Jinn and Phyllis, on the other hand, we assume to be human, right up until the point at which their quadrumanous limbs and chimpanzee muzzles reveal them to be apes. Rotpeter *is* still an ape, however, despite his cultured ways. He tells us that "the first thing I learned was to give a handshake; a handshake betokens frankness,"[59] but it is clear from his report that he has not been entirely forthright with his captors, trainers, and audience. From the moment he realized that there was only one way out of his confinement, his assumption of human ways has been an elaborate and effective performance.[60] Is Rotpeter lying about his anthropocentric amnesia? Who can say? But his well-groomed fur and tail betray the fact that he remains an ape.[61] Rotpeter *presents* his report as a human, but he is in fact a chimpanzee, just as Jinn and Phyllis seem to be human while *reading* the astonishing account on which they have stumbled, only to turn out to be chimpanzees. And so it is with this report, offered to my presumed addressees, the honored members of the academy. Our lives as apes are not so far removed, and do not lie behind us.

Notes

This chapter was first published in *Parallax* 38: "Animal Beings" 12:1 (January–March 2006): 69–80, and is reproduced by permission of Routledge/Taylor and Francis.

1. Diogenes Laertius, *Lives of Eminent Philosophers*, trans. R. D. Hicks (Cambridge, MA: Harvard University Press, 2005), 2:43 (VI:40).

2. Franz Kafka, "Report to an Academy," in *The Complete Stories*, ed. Nahum N. Glatzer (New York: Schocken, 1971), 250–59 (258, 250). Rotpeter refers to himself as an ape in his report, but is identified by a third party specifically as a chimpanzee in an earlier fragment of Kafka's story; Kafka, *Complete Stories*, 260.

3. Note that Kafka's adjective and adjectival noun—*äffisches* ("apish") and *Affentum* ("ape existence")—become substantives in translation. I will return to this presently.

4. Kafka, "Report to an Academy," 250, 253.

5. Georges Bataille, *Theory of Religion*, trans. Robert Hurley (New York: Zone, 1989), 20.

6. Charles Darwin to Asa Gray, 29 November 1857, in *The Correspondence of Charles Darwin*, ed. Frederick Burkhardt and Sydney Smith (Cambridge: Cambridge University Press, 1990), 6:493.

7. Jorge Luis Borges, "John Wilkins' Analytical Language," in *Selected Non-Fictions*, ed. Eliot Weinberger, trans. Esther Allen, Suzanne Jill Levine, and Eliot Weinberger (New York: Penguin, 1999), 229–32.

8. Borges, "John Wilkins' Analytical Language," 230–32; John Wilkins, *An Essay Toward a Real Character and a Philosophical Language* (London: Gellibrand & Martin, 1668), 142, 415, 132.

9. Borges, "John Wilkins' Analytical Language," 231.

10. Michel Foucault, *The Order of Things: An Archaeology of the Human Sciences,* trans. Alan Sheridan (London: Routledge, 1994), xi–xxi (preface).

11. Foucault, *Order of Things,* xvi, xvii.

12. Borges, "John Wilkins' Analytical Language," 231.

13. In her own discussion of Borges and Foucault, Carol Adams reproduces a heteroclite disorder all the more startling for the fact that it is familiar. The rationale behind the everyday categories by which nonhuman animals are organized is, she demonstrates, "the arbitrary logic of the oppressor"; see Carol J. Adams, *Neither Man nor Beast: Feminism and the Defense of Animals* (New York: Continuum, 1994), 188–90.

14. Richard Dawkins, "Gaps in the Mind," in *The Great Ape Project: Equality Beyond Humanity,* ed. Paola Cavalieri and Peter Singer (London: Fourth Estate, 1993), 80–87.

15. Dawkins, "Gaps in the Mind," 81–82. These birds represent the classic example of a ring species, and have been much discussed. The essential point concerning the mutability of species is in no way compromised by recent research which suggests that the gulls do not, in fact, comprise a ring species; see Dorit Liebers, Peter de Knijff, and Andreas J. Helbig, "The Herring Gull Complex Is Not a Ring Species," *Proceedings of the Royal Society Biological Sciences,* Series B 271:1542 (7 May 2004): 893–901. Liebers and colleagues suggest that the gulls may soon *become* a ring species, as lesser black-backed gulls expand ever westward (899). For an alternative ring species, see the Asian green(-ish) warbler (*Phylloscopus trochiloides*), whose populations circle the Tibetan plateau; Darren E. Irwin, Staffan Bensch, and Trevor D. Price, "Speciation in a Ring," *Nature* 409:6818 (18 January 2001): 333–37. On the history and unstable integrity of the ring species concept, see Darren Irwin, Jessica H. Irwin, and Trevor D. Price, "Ring Species as Bridges Between Microevolution and Speciation," *Genetica* 112–113 (2001): 223–43.

16. Dawkins, "Gaps in the Mind," 82–84.

17. There is considerable debate as to which species of the genus *Homo* were ancestors of modern humans and which were "cousins" who had diverged from the ancestral line. For a lively discussion, see Jonathan Kingdon, *Lowly Origin: Where, When, and Why Our Ancestors First Stood Up* (Princeton, NJ: Princeton University Press, 2003).

18. Dawkins notes that it is sheer bad luck that the intermediates have died out, and that it would take "only a handful of intermediate types to be able to sing: 'I've bred with a man, who's bred with a girl, who's bred with a chimpanzee'"; "Gaps in the Mind," 85. On the ethical consequences of such a hybrid, see Richard Dawkins, "The Word Made Flesh," *Guardian,* 27 December 2001, Science section, 13, www.guardian.co.uk/science/2001/dec/27/genetics.medicalscience (accessed 15 June 2009).

19. For an excellent discussion of the subtleties of the concept of species, and the problems of accurately representing descent graphically, see Daniel Dennett, *Darwin's Dangerous Idea* (London: Allen Lane, 1995), 85–103 (chapter 4). See also John Dupré's discussion of the distinction between species considered as units of evolution and species considered as units of classification, which argues for the pragmatic utility of the latter over the former; John Dupré, "In Defence of Classification," in *Humans and Other Animals* (Oxford: Clarendon Press, 2002), 81–99.

20. Edward Tyson, *Orang-Outang, sive Homo Sylvestris: or, The Anatomy of a Pygmie Compared with That of a Monkey, an Ape, and a Man* (London: Thomas Bennet and

Daniel Brown, 1699). Nicolaas Tulp's earlier account of an "Indian satyr," in 1641, has been taken as a description of a chimpanzee (Huxley) or a bonobo (Reynolds), but now seems most likely to have been an orangutan. See Nicolaas Tulp, *Observationes medicae* (Amstelredami: Apud Henricum Wetstenium, 1641), 3:56, 271; Thomas Henry Huxley, *Evidence as to Man's Place in Nature* (London: Williams and Norgate, 1863), 8; Vernon Reynolds, "On the Identity of the Ape Described by Tulp 1641," *Folia Primatologica* 5 (1967): 80–87; H. D. Rijksen and E. Meijaard, *Our Vanishing Relative: The Status of Wild Orangutans at the Close of the Twentieth Century* (Dordrecht: Kluwer Academic, 1999), 421–27.

21. For an illuminating critique of Tyson's text, see Stephen Jay Gould, "To Show an Ape," in *The Flamingo's Smile: Reflections in Natural History* (New York: Norton, 1985), 263–80. The skeleton of Tyson's chimpanzee can be seen in London's Natural History Museum today.

22. For a fuller account of the ignominious events surrounding the discovery of *paniscus*—both Harold Coolidge and Ernst Schwarz claimed credit—see Mary and John Gribbin, *Being Human: Putting People in an Evolutionary Perspective* (London: Dent, 1993), 4–5; or Frans de Waal and Frans Lanting, *Bonobo: The Forgotten Ape* (Berkeley: University of California Press, 1997), 5–6.

23. Gribbin and Gribbin, *Being Human*, 18.

24. There is a town called Bolobo in the Democratic Republic of the Congo (formerly Zaire), the only nation in which this endangered species has survived; de Waal and Lanting, *Bonobo*, 7.

25. The figure of 1.6 percent divergence in human and chimpanzee DNA refers to corresponding synonymous (functionally relatively unimportant) DNA sites. The figure actually rises to 99.4 percent for nonsynonymous (functionally much more important) DNA sites; see Derek E. Wildman et al., "Implications of Natural Selection in Shaping 99.4 Percent Nonsynonymous DNA Identity Between Humans and Chimpanzees: Enlarging Genus *Homo*," *Proceedings of the National Academy of Sciences* 100:12 (10 June 2003): 7181–88. On the caution that must be exercised in drawing conclusions from such figures, see Steven Pinker, *The Language Instinct: The New Science of Language and Mind* (London: Allen Lane, 1994), 351.

26. Jared Diamond, *The Rise and Fall of the Third Chimpanzee* (London: Vintage, 1992), 19–21.

27. Diamond, *Third Chimpanzee*, 14–21; Colin Tudge, *The Variety of Life* (Oxford: Oxford University Press, 2000), 33–62 (chapter 3), esp. 49–51; Colin Groves, *Primate Taxonomy* (Washington, DC: Smithsonian Institution Press, 2001), 3–14, 303. However, see also Tudge's "neolinnaean impressionist" argument for retaining traditional great ape nomenclature (485–92).

28. Diamond, *Third Chimpanzee*, 20–21.

29. Peter Harrison, "Linnaeus as a Second Adam? Taxonomy and the Religious Vocation," *Zygon* 44:4 (December 2009): 879–93; Raymond Corbey, *The Metaphysics of Apes: Negotiating the Animal-Human Boundary* (Cambridge: Cambridge University Press, 2005), 45.

30. See Harriet Ritvo, *The Platypus and the Mermaid and Other Figments of the Classifying Imagination* (Cambridge, MA: Harvard University Press, 1997), esp. 1–50 (chapter

1). Linnaeus's method of nomenclature, first proposed in 1749, was often accepted even when his classifications were not; see 51–84 (chapter 2).

31. Carl Linnaeus, *Systema Naturae per Regna Tria Naturae Secundum Classes, Ordines, Genera, Species, cum Characteribus, Differentiis, Synonymis, Locis*, tenth edition (Holmiae: Laurentii Salvii, 1758), 20–29, www.biodiversitylibrary.org/bibliography/542 (accessed 15 June 2009). *Systema Naturae* was first published in 1735; on the development of Linnaeus's classification of man and ape through successive editions, see Douthwaite, *Wild Girl, Natural Man*, 15–17.

32. Linnaeus to J. G. Gmelin, 14 February 1747, in Edward L. Greene, "Linnaeus as Evolutionist," *Proceedings of the Washington Academy of Sciences* 11 (31 March 1909): 25. Agamben argues that Linnaeus *does* identify a means to distinguish man—the ability to recognize himself as human; see Giorgio Agamben, *The Open: Man and Animal*, trans. Kevin Attell (Stanford, CA: Stanford University Press, 2004), 23–27 (chapter 7).

33. Quoted in Ramona Morris and Desmond Morris, *Men and Apes* (London: Hutchinson, 1966), 134–35; Linnaeus, *Systema Naturae*, 24.

34. Groves, *Primate Taxonomy*, 40.

35. Diamond, *Third Chimpanzee*, 21.

36. Borges, "John Wilkins' Analytical Language," 231.

37. Groves, *Primate Taxonomy*, 303–7. For a lively survey of the history of primate taxonomy, and the colorful characters who fill it, see 39–49.

38. Groves, *Primate Taxonomy*, 303.

39. Linnaeus, *Systema Naturae*, 18, 20.

40. Dawkins says as much in his qualified endorsement of the Great Ape Project; see "Gaps in the Mind," 87.

41. I discuss varieties of anthropocentrism, including "first and foremost," in "Like Water in Water," *Journal for Cultural Research* 9:3 (July 2005): 265–79 (esp. 273–78).

42. De Waal and Lanting, *Bonobo*, 6. The common name, "chimpanzee," is the name for this ape in Angola, south-central Africa.

43. On the history of the virile ape, see Morris and Morris, *Men and Apes*, 53–82 (chapter 3); H. W. Janson, *Apes and Ape Lore in the Middle Ages and the Renaissance* (London: Warburg Institute, 1952), 261–86 (chapter 9).

44. Robert Graves, *The Greek Myths*, revised edition, two volumes (Harmondsworth, UK: Penguin, 1960), 1:102; *Oxford Classical Dictionary*, third edition, s.v. "Pan"; *Homeric Hymns, Homeric Apocrypha, Lives of Homer*, ed. and trans. Martin L. West, Loeb Classical Library 496 (Cambridge, MA: Harvard University Press, 2003), 198–203 (19).

45. Tyson, *Anatomy of a Pygmie*, 13.

46. This was the fourteenth volume of Buffon's colossal *Natural History*; see John C. Greene, *The Death of Adam: Evolution and Its Impact on Western Thought* (Ames: Iowa State University Press, 1959), 179–82.

47. Johann Friedrich Blumenbach, *On the Natural Varieties of Mankind (De Generis Humani Varietate Nativa)*, trans. Thomas Bendyshe (New York: Bergman, 1969), 150–52.

48. Ibid., 151–52.

49. Ibid., 171–72. Blumenbach's dissertation was first published in 1775, when he argued that apes should be considered quadrupeds; see 86–87. He did not propose the order Quadrumana until the third edition of 1795.

50. Blumenbach discounts "the manati, birds (especially the penguins)," and "the lizard *Siren*"; ibid., 87.

51. See Jacques Derrida, "Geschlecht II: Heidegger's Hand," in *Deconstruction and Philosophy: The Texts of Jacques Derrida*, ed. John Sallis (Chicago: University of Chicago Press, 1987), 161–96; Tyler, "Like Water in Water," 269–73.

52. Jacques Derrida, "There Is No *One* Narcissism (Autobiophotographies)," in *Points . . . Interviews, 1974–1994*, ed. Elisabeth Weber, trans. Peggy Kamuf et al. (Stanford, CA: Stanford University Press, 1995), 199.

53. Ibid.

54. Jacques Derrida, "The Animal That Therefore I Am (More to Follow)," trans. David Wills, *Critical Inquiry* 28:2 (Winter 2002): 398.

55. Jacques Derrida, *Monolingualism of the Other; or, The Prosthesis of Origin* (Stanford, CA: Stanford University Press, 1996), 55–56.

56. On the appeal of a "quantitative, continuously distributed morality," which we might, if space allowed, ally with an adjectival ethics, see the closing paragraphs of Dawkins, "Gaps in the Mind," 87; and David Wood, "Thinking with Cats," in *Animal Philosophy*, ed. Peter Atterton and Matthew Calarco (London: Continuum, 2004), 129–44 (esp. 215n42): "Our capacity to appreciate the other's suffering is not in these cases an anthropocentric projection at all. It is instead a mammalocentric or biocentric projection. It is not as humans that we feel physical pain, but as 'animate organisms.'"

57. Pierre Boulle, *Monkey Planet*, trans. Xan Fielding (Harmondsworth, UK: Penguin, 1975), 7.

58. Ibid., 174. The novel was, of course, made into a spectacularly successful and critically acclaimed film, *Planet of the Apes*, starring Charlton Heston, in 1968. The narrative fulfills the dream of Linnaeus's *Homo troglodytes*, who believed, we will remember, "that the earth was made for it, and that sometime it will be master again."

59. Kafka, "Report to an Academy," 251.

60. Rotpeter is, in fact, at pains to point out that his accomplishment was a matter of necessity rather than choice: "I repeat: there was no attraction for me in imitating human beings; I imitated them because I needed a way out, and for no other reason"; Kafka, "Report to an Academy," 257. On Rotpeter's wily imitation, see Margot Norris, *Beasts of the Modern Imagination: Darwin, Nietzsche, Kafka, Ernst, and Lawrence* (Baltimore: Johns Hopkins University Press, 1985), 65–72.

61. Kafka, "Report to an Academy," 252. Apes, unlike most monkeys, are in fact tailless.

CHAPTER 12

Who Identified the Animal? Hybridity and Body Politics in Kafka's "The Metamorphosis" and *Amerika* (*The Man Who Disappeared*)

Melissa De Bruyker

In Kafka's oeuvre, presupposed borders that separate humans from animals are constantly crossed: whereas animals have human pasts and memories or display a human-like way of reasoning, animal characteristics are ascribed to human characters as well. The combination of human and animal features presents a form of hybridity.[1] Hybrids are characters combining human with animal features.[2] The representation of the hybrid functions as the explicit manifestation of a textual problem development and is embedded within the text's overall narrativity. More specifically, Kafka's stories create an overlap between seemingly natural categories in order to question the different ways in which naturalness (an epistemological notion) and human (an anthropological notion) are defined within their narrated realities. According to Böschenstein, the animal character is, from an historic and ideological point of view, "a sign for a particular relation between human and animal."[3] Hybrids signal a crisis situation in which distinctions between human and animal, notions like subjectivity and humanity and modes of observation are at stake. Whenever Kafka's protagonists draw the attention to these hybrid constellations, they point out the questionable position of individuals in social life.

In the following, I want to find out how animal and human characteristics are intertwined and how focalization techniques—shifts between the inside of characters (reasoning) and references to the outside (animal or human bodies)—help the reader to develop hypotheses about the narrative role of hybrids (for instance, by alluding to ways of seeing and being). Moreover, Kafka's imaginary worlds have an argumentative function: they help the reader to understand the social crisis of the protagonists by "contextualizing" the image of the hybrid. Especially the evocation of external observations superseding the perspective of the protagonist as well as characteristics of spaces and topics related to body (such as procreation, gender, and food) specify the hybrid constellation of human and animal within a problematic social context. Hybridity thus also signals a contested boundary between social norms and the individual.[4] It is not a coincidence that its effects are predominantly visualized through the body. Since the Enlightenment the human body has been defined "materially," with respect to its unique physical and psychological features, its difference from animals, its improvability and position within a society striving for progress. The body has become a metaphoric border between the self and society. Kafka's hybrids show how individual bodies and existing ideological borders are at stake.

Remarkably, in "The Metamorphosis" and *Amerika*, characters are associated with animals through different degrees of *identity*—namely, through overlap or by the mere suggestion of a similarity. These works will therefore also be compared with respect to the way in which they apply the technique of hybridity. The parameter identity addresses the (often disregarded) role of the reader. (S)he ultimately is the instance who turns words into images and is hence able to reflect on how the hybrid animal is created—identified—in Kafka's fictional realities.

"The Metamorphosis" (1915)[5]

Gregor is called a "gigantic insect" (89), a form of animal life as far removed from human appearance as thinkable. In the famous opening scene the body is still recognizable because its single parts can be identified: back, head, belly, legs, and body size (he will be able to reach for the door lock). The possessive pronoun "his" identifies Gregor with this body. Deviations from human characteristics are rendered through adjectives specifying the nouns: "brown," "armor-plated," "stiff arched," and "pitifully thin" (89).[6] The structured intertwinement of adjectives and nouns helps the reader realise that the hybrid is a rhetorically created effect.[7] The composed image shows how modifications of human characteristics are at the origin of the transformation. Moreover, "human" is shown to be culturally predetermined since the body parts refer to cultural notions: labor (back), mind (head), procreation and sin (belly), femininity (absence of a phallus), and a human upright position (legs). When these physical characteristics disappear, Gregor will be expelled from social life. Here he is already lacking his masculinity.[8] As I will show, femininity often signals social changes in Kafka's works.

Gregor's ease suggests that his transformation is something one can expect within the framework of laws and conditions of narrated reality. We indeed learn that the new body definitely disrupts the bond between Gregor and his family, a bond that was already endangered in the past.[9] His animal appearance derives from social influences that determine what is considered human or animal. In this story, the family (a mediator between the individual and society) is chosen as the concrete context in which the transformation takes place. Gregor's and the other family members' definition of what is normal and human (in opposition to animal) constantly change and clash. The hybrid's further evolution tells us something about evolving ideas, ideologies, and scenarios of normality. Pfeiffer claims that no reasons are given why Gregor changes into an enormous insect.[10] Harzer places the story in a "hermeneutical vacuum."[11] Specific reasons are indeed hard to find since they imply an interpretation of what the hybrid character is and what it stands for. "The Metamorphosis," however, focuses on (political, familial, psychological, and so forth) discourses as creating images, identities, and notions of being, rather than on being itself.

In the opening scene we find further motivations for the problematic tension between animal and human. The verb "to wave" disrupts the passivity evoked by "found," "was lying," and "could see" (89). It denotes an unclear sight (caused by an internal bodily defect) or expresses that by viewing something mobile a fixed image cannot be produced (cause lies outside the body). Still, a bug naturally has a limited sight and relies on other sensory impressions to detect objects. Also, moving its legs is what an insect normally does when lying helplessly on its back. "Waving" hence presupposes the human capacity of clear vision and refers to a transitional phase in which the animality forced on Gregor is still mingled with his subjective will to distinguish according to internalized human standards. The two (for humans, distinctive) animal characteristics are not only connected through the insect's body but also causally: the independently moving legs go hand in hand with Gregor's impaired vision and set off his further transformation into an animal body (e.g., his sight grows blurry). Gregor attempts to reclaim and protect his body over and over again, not feeling shocked and adopting its animal logic, and also by preserving his unifying human will and awareness of his previous body and life sphere. Still, his problematic perception implies an ominous psychonarrative comment. His deteriorating eye problems go hand in hand with his altered state within the world and upset his otherwise monotonous life.[12] Similarly, "helpless" not only signals the lack of firm ground beneath his feet but also its consequence, the protagonist's instability from this moment onward. The defective body forming a border between mind and external space can be related to Gregor as well as to expectations within his surroundings. The interaction between character and space is, in other words, made explicit through the body and additionally stressed by means of allusions to natural biotopes and biocentric discourse (cf. infra).[13]

The innumerable legs lie at the origin of the conflict between Gregor and the world. Their number and movement not only lead to blindness and helplessness but also to uncovering. The blanket on top of Gregor's belly—his vulnerable spot—threatens to fall off.[14] Pfeiffer speaks of the "personification" of the blanket and describes the difficulty of holding onto Gregor.[15] Still, precisely the threat of losing coverage means that this dynamic is not part of Gregor. He will undergo a process of uncovering even though his body itself—the fragmented beetle-like creature but also the phantasm of the coherent human body—remains elusive. The body has been symbolically affected. It cannot be recovered after a lifetime of physical determination and definition by familial norms, such as the obligation to wear clothes and repress sexuality. Gregor hopes that the transformation will have passed when he reawakens. Still, precisely the shape of his new body keeps him from going back to sleep. He soon crawls around, crisscrossing over walls and ceiling. His many legs symbolize an awkward dynamic, while the exploration of his mobility distinguishes him further from his social context.

Because of his persistent human-like thinking, Gregor repeatedly draws the attention to hybridity whereas his family members spurn his definite change into an animal. Even though his sister Grete seems to be trying hard to facilitate his new existence, as one would do for a brother according to family discourse, she also triggers his animal instincts by giving him rotten cheese (108). The removal of furniture has a similar effect: Gregor learns to exploit his animal mobility.[16] Remarkably, the text silences the family's motivations that underlie their actions and utterances. Hochreiter believes that Grete opens the window in order to get some fresh air (in).[17] The idea that a smell of decay makes breathing unbearable suggests that Gregor's perspective might be limited. He may even lack common sense and a sensitivity toward others or, vice versa, his ideals, behaviour, and notion of physical appearance may have become outdated. From the point of view of oppressive familial structures, it is not surprising that Gregor has transformed into an indefinable insect-like creature. A pet (cat, dog, or even mouse) could still be linked to the family home. Bugs, on the contrary, lacking both sight and insight, need to be extinguished.

As the story evolves, Gregor's surroundings are explored. When Gregor's sister and mother are removing pieces of furniture from his room, the latter suddenly catches sight of him: "[She] took a step to one side, caught sight of the huge brown mass on the flowered wallpaper, and before she was really conscious that what she saw was Gregor, screamed" (119). The protagonist is reduced to a shapeless brown spot that disturbs the bright flowery wallpaper. His legs, belly, and head are no longer mentioned. The already fragmented hybrid body is expelled from human categorization. On the basis of people's habit of decorating walls with pictures of relatives, celebrities, or kings, walls can be read as microcosmic landscapes of familial and institutional power. The living room, for instance, is decorated with a picture of Gregor wearing his army uniform. Gregor's bedroom wall much rather resembles an animal or plant biotope, especially after the only trace of human culture—the picture of the woman—has disappeared. Remarkably, Gregor and his mother perceive the wall in totally different ways. Whereas Gregor situates the frame against an empty wall, his mother perceives flowery wallpaper. He focuses on the wall's relief created by the picture; she distinguishes a multitude of colors on a flat wall. Gregor singles out the picture; the mother's look situates him against a larger background. What separates their observations literally and symbolically is the frame. Precisely because the protagonist fearfully covers the frame, he blends in with the background. If we interpret the wallpaper as a reference to rich plant life,[18] then the protagonist turns out to be an unprotected primitive creature with a limited insight into its dangerous environment. Moreover, when the mother does not immediately recognize her son, the present is abruptly set off against the past. One gets the feeling that Gregor cannot catch up with the family's sense of time. His apparently retarded rhythm seems to have resulted in his counterevolutionary transformation. In the course of Gregor's transformation, bits and pieces of characters' reactions and of much-telling spatial characteristics seep through. The reader could have difficulties identifying with a larger picture by the time Gregor dies, especially if (s)he were to ignore the inimical or self-preserving acts of his family members. Only after his death, when focalization shifts external to his viewpoint, does one fully realize his limited view. The protagonist is then perceived as a lifeless thing; the hybrid constellation of human and animal has disappeared.[19] All that is left of the protagonist in his already emptied-out room is a dry shell reminiscent of a cocoon rather than of a human being.

The metaphor of the cocoon is anticipated by the lady in fur. Her picture offers a typical case of pictorial narration. The photograph is a symbiosis of womanhood and the sexual connotations of the bedroom. The image is the only object Gregor tries to save: "[He] quickly crawled up to it and pressed himself to the glass, which was a good surface to hold on to and comforted his hot belly" (118). Heat signals a state of anxiety and stress.[20] Gregor's belly—his soft spot—seems to be in need of relief. The verb "to hold on to" expresses his need to stick to what he values. The fact that he framed the picture a while before his transformation hints at its role in the transformation tale: "the picture which he had recently cut out of an illustrated magazine and put into a pretty gilt frame" (89). Gregor's father is a fervent reader of newspapers; he himself reads magazines. Newspapers evoke an alertness to social change of which Gregor, however, fails to take notice. Framing and portrayal introduce a state of iconography that eventually turns against the creator of the frame. The protagonist's fixed ideas and schedules take over and destroy him.

Scholars have explained the furriery as a symbolic reference to pubic hair and Gregor's act as a copulative gesture.[21] Still, he is not represented as explicitly noticing the erotic nature of the image. The sexual is also evoked through the reference to his belly,[22] the seductiveness of the woman,[23] and the implicit biocentric concept instinct. Sexual connotations remind the reader of the words "nakedness" and "uncovering" used to structure the story. By covering the picture, the main character uncovers himself to his family members although he normally hides underneath a sofa or blanket. His act introduces a state of nakedness that contrasts with the lady's, for she remains covered with skin. Gregor does not seem to realize what he does. He evokes enlightened notions such as pity, compassion, and love as well as the heroic attempt to save the damsel in distress known from fairy tales and mythology. These acts and feelings, however, turn out to be short-sighted and all but universally applicable. At the same time, the breakdown of humane and heroic notions ironically counters the bourgeois ideal of the enlightened society. This failure is depicted as a natural evolution through allusions to Darwin's struggle for life. A shiny bourgeois lifestyle, however, needs to be upheld in order to hide this ideological restructuring.

The scene with the lady in fur shows how the dominant male body is over-ridden by the woman. Whereas one could assume that this *femme fatale* is kept by rich men (a scenario of high culture), her body substitutes for the inside of a skinned animal (a scenario of natural competitiveness). Gregor conceives of women as objects which he always failed to conquer either because he went too quickly or too slowly: in addition to "a chambermaid . . . a sweet and fleeting memory," there is also a "cashier . . . whom he had wooed earnestly but too slowly" (125). Whereas his rapid conquering opposes the notion of female fragility, his slowness cannot satisfy an eager *femme fatale*. By framing women and reducing them to types, he obviously tries but always fails to get a grip on them. His reduction of women is compensated for by the narrative enlargement of women in narrated society. Enlargement relates to their number, body size, power over men, food, and birth. In other words, women (especially servants) control body dynamics. In the family household, female servants carry out tasks like cleaning and cooking. Remarkably, these characters foretell the end of ancient familial structures since the father, mother, and daughter themselves become servants in social institutions. Gregor is immediately affected by the acts of cleaning and cooking, even though his personal habits do not change: the food on the breakfast table seems as tasty as always, but his tastes appear to have changed. Moreover, Gregor is covered with dust and finally shovelled away like dirt by the cleaning lady. In other words, the family house and its physical dimensions (hygiene and feeding habits) have been interiorized by Gregor. When the family undergoes radical changes, their effects are rendered visible through Gregor's body.

Grete replaces Gregor within the family.[24] The depicted lady, who according to the protagonist's mindframe is the public female opposed to the familial type Grete, is covered with a dead animal that had to die in order to turn her into this sexual icon. The protagonist's growing powerlessness over the framed picture runs adjacent to the lack of the attribute that prevails in the magazine: the fur. He desiccates like a dead insect, a cocoon that can neither be worn nor produce an offspring. Already his fascination for an idealized image lacking concrete physical substance offered little hope for real procreation. Sexuality can accordingly be read as an act intended to produce ideological offspring. The pornographic character of the picture additionally stresses the inappropriateness of Gregor's sexual preference. Even though he appears as an insect-like creature, a competing parasite feeding upon his social decay is introduced: his sister Grete. Gregor turns out to be a mere recipient of power and is emptied out in the course of the story. A relation between Grete and Gregor, however, cannot save him because of the incest taboo.[25]

It only appears paradoxical that Gregor, who tries to suppress animal instincts to satisfy his family, is ultimately rejected. He supposed that his sister would appreciate being sent to the conservatory but he was wrong. Similarly, he mistook her talent that, through the lack of interest of the three tenants, is shown to be mediocre according to ruling standards.[26] Their beards are reminiscent of prophets or the three wise men foretelling the birth of a new era. By the end of the story Grete has turned into a sexualized being and is liberated from the frameworks of her brother's ideals: "She had bloomed into a pretty girl with a good figure" (139). He thought of her as a *femme fragile* and as a sister, whereas she overrides the difference Gregor set with the *femme fatale* and the public sphere outside the family. Her body is depicted by means of the natural image of blossoming. The image refers back to the flowery wallpaper from which the brown stain has been removed. When Grete says, "You must just try to get rid of the idea that this is Gregor" (134), she also reverses the servile attitude she displayed initially. She no longer thinks about what she could do to help Gregor but blames him for not noticing what is best for the family.[27]

The reason Gregor leaves his beloved picture is the sudden fainting of his mother, whom he worryingly follows into another room. Duttlinger argues that "Gregor's performance as model son and soldier prefigures his transformation into the monstrous other of his ideal."[28] Still, Gregor remains loyal to his parents, sister, employer, and country. On the one hand, when he was out in the wide world, his wish was to be at home.[29] He did not wish to explore the world. On the other hand, his absence has estranged him from what was really going on at home.[30] He never questioned where his money went, and assumed that there was no money left from his father's business. He wrongly suspected that he would have to remain a merchant for another five years before his family would be able to cope without him. He has become lost between ideological or cultural shifts, on the one hand, and spatial or national evolutions, on the other, the reciprocal relations of which have shifted. The private sphere, functioning as a social mediator, has changed as a result.

Competing animal characterizations of power representatives show Gregor's resistance to his disembodiment. The firm's porter, for example, is described as "a creature of the chief's, spineless and stupid" (91). "A creature" and the lack of backbone and intelligence seem more appropriate as his own description.[31] Gregor's ideal is to be intelligent and brave like a soldier whereas he finds the porter lacking in these respects. Still, the chief's clerk is a servant of the actual power, the law. His supposed incapacity to reflect combines with a clear act of identification according to new rules: "That was no human voice" (98).[32] When seeing Gregor, the prosecutor can only "utter a loud 'Oh!'" (100) thus visualizing his need to distance himself from this Other. Surprisingly, Gregor's voice itself does not horrify him, only the observable proof of the transformation does. "Voice" also means opinion or rumour. Perceiving is thus associated with ideas and the right to speak up. The visual identification of voice with reality (Gregor's appearance and uncovered belly) seems to be upsetting the prosecutor and erases all possibility of communication. The text thus indicates that not the voice itself—Gregor's thinking—but narrated reality has altered.[33] Just as he is caught up in his own worries, he never considers leaving the house, as the powerful prosecutor manifestly does. The main character only gets to know his body by gradually activating its parts. Physical accidents, however, visualize confronting insights and psychological violence.[34] He observes the hospital on the other side of the street that could heal his defective body, but it is out of his reach. He is trapped inside the family house and its regulations.

Amerika (1927)[35]

In this novel the relation between the human and the animal is rendered neither through the protagonist's eyes nor by means of his own body. On the contrary, the protagonist Karl Rossmann seems barely perspectivized: his observations show no traces of ideological discourse and the animal seems to exist independently in the narrated world of the past. Moreover, the story is not situated within a place familiar to the protagonist, not even in one single place. Once in America, Karl will undertake several journeys to finally end up in the Oklahoma World Theater. The encounter with various cultures and lifestyles—a narrative tendency anticipated by Gregor's estrangement from his environment—is thus repeated over and over again. The difference in narrative composition is linked to the way in which the animal—in this case, a small hare—is used and developed in *Amerika*. The hare is situated in the narrated past where it was observed by the protagonist. It is not physically or psychologically linked to the focalizer but only is observed. The animal is embedded in Karl's memories and evoked when he observes a writing desk at his American uncle's home:

> He had pulled her to him, until he felt her against his back, and he had drawn her attention to various more subtle manifestations by

loud shouts, say a rabbit that was alternately sitting up and making to run in the long grass at the front, until his mother put her hand over his mouth and presumably reverted to her previous dullness. Of course the desk hadn't been designed to recall such things, but the history of inventions was probably full of such vague connections as Karl's memory. (30)

The desk reminds Karl of a mechanically operated nativity scene which he once saw in Europe.[36] In the narrated past the protagonist pulls his mother close as if he wants her to see from his lower physical standpoint or from his perspective. Also, this text plays with different levels of perception, in this case high and low. We do not learn whether his mother actually sees the hare: "say" indicates that a mere hypothesis is given; we only know that she is not pleased with Karl's excitement. The enigma pervading the anecdote continues in the narrated present. It is told that Karl's memorization processes and the history of inventions resemble each other with respect to their mutual lack of comprehensibility. However, this means that if we understand why this memory is narrated and what the hare alludes to, we can also comprehend the events in the narrated present. Past and present are rhetorically intertwined. The word "unclear" indicates that fixed ideological borders are challenged; inventions create innovative ways of living and observing.

The reader may feel tempted to compare Karl with the hare because he is a privileged observer; he is the one who is attentive. Their mutual status as children enforces this parallel. This hare is said to be little, whereas hares are more typically large, comparatively speaking. The characters' height explains their physical viewpoint but implicitly presents a comment upon their mutual status as childish outsiders in the narrated world. Even at the end of the novel, Karl is still called a child. Moreover, like the hare, Karl also will strive for an alternation between high and low positions. Still, there is no explicit identifying link between the human and the animal. This distance continues throughout the novel. The protagonist does not turn into the animal. On the contrary, disconnected characteristics of the hare reverberate throughout the novel. They only form a meaningful web if the reader associates Karl with the hare. Fictional reality generally turns out to be more complicated in this novel. It is crowded with big people, huge spaces, and fast traffic. These overwhelming shapes, sizes, numbers, and movements stress the diminutive nature of the individual. Also, polarizations between generations and the sexes affect the way in which the body is represented.

In this novel we are not informed about how characters think. When Karl formally introduces himself to the maid Therese, she reacts in a manner almost to reject him: "as though by telling her his name he'd become a little stranger to her" (93). Unlike Gregor, Karl is not confronted with an animal in the present but in the past, where already his own "physical" mother did not seem to support her son. His current status is the result of an intensified though less conspicuous process of animalization. Memorization means the evocation of a thought or habit that surfaces in new rigid social circumstances where it creates confusion: "Karl himself hadn't actually been idle in the hotel, but he had had no notion of work such as this" (133). Karl tries to deal with new situations in new places by viewing them within previous frameworks but proves unable to live up to constantly changing conditions. As a result, he also disappoints the cook of the hotel. Because of her profession (feeding the guests), Grete Mittelbach can be regarded as one of the most powerful people in the hotel. The hotel comes across as an enlarged family house: it is crowded with father and mother figures but, at the same time, it is anonymous and resembles a whole society. Karl remains stuck in familial comparisons and a natural body logic that negatively affect his reputation in the narrated world.

The hare's eye-catching behavior makes Karl first shriek with amazement before his mother reacts to it on grounds that remain suggestively linked to the animal's symbolic meaning. On the one hand, "alternately sitting up" (*Männchen machen*) means that the hare stands on its two hind legs, thus assuming a human-like position. The animal switches between the human and the nonhuman. On the other, "seeing little men" (*Männchen sehen*) means that one is crazy. The hybrid animal makes the movements (*macht Männchen*) and, as a result, Karl sees *Männchen*.[37] His observation could be defined as mad if we relate him to the hare's disruptive behavior. The text does not introduce doubt as to whether the hare is real but about whether it is appropriate to see it. The Christian play forms an explicit discursive background dominated by Christian figures and family rhetoric.[38] The hare does not seem compatible with this scene. With respect to its animal side the hybrid hare embodies Otherness (it also deviates from the typical Christian animals). As human it presents an unwelcome addition to the category human. Through the mother, the hare's hybridity gains a rhetorical depth. She feels ashamed because of her noisy child (a realistic social motivation), and she rejects the hare that appears when people lack Christian devotion (a monoreligious motivation)[39] or she reacts to the hare's unfamiliar connotations (an intercultural motivation).

By focusing on the hare, Karl breaks the visual connection with the family scene and advances his own exile. In German superstition this animal functions as a reference to Jewishness, and in Christian religion it is interpreted as a demonic symbol.[40] Not only is the opposition between the two religions important, but also the introduction of superstition as an unofficial discourse implies a shift in meaning of the German term and hints at a double—or changing—social moral. What does "German" mean in a widening international context: is it related to a shared language, country, or religion? The thought of unofficial discourse also explains why the protagonist fails to comprehend what is happening around him. He only filters out what is obvious and institutionalized. Interestingly, the hare is considered to be an unclean animal in Jewish culture as well. As a consequence, the hybrid hare also embodies a conflict that—via superstition as the domain of intercultural imagination—is shown to have its origins in different cultural conceptions of normality.

East-West oppositions visualize a process of growing estrangement that goes hand in hand with superficial identification, such as through naming. The difference between Eastern and Western European Jews can be read as an allegory for discursive contradictions in general. The horizontal movement resulting from Karl's journeys proves to be incompatible with the vertical actions of himself and the hare. Similarly, traces of his old social habits continue to be vivid on the American continent where they turn out to be impractical. Karl's movements literally seem futile because of the high buildings and outstretched streets surrounding him. Fingerhut explains, "[Kafka] lets his protagonist observe and act according to the European standard" (my translation).[41] When the nativity play—a microcosmic ideological design of society—is described as nearly breaking down ("halting," 30; German, *stockend*[42]), outdated discourse and the phenomenon of secularization are brought to the fore. The old man turning the wheel evokes the idea of decay. At the same time, the scene indicates that the human body has its limitations and defects and warns against the tale of unlimited progress. Scholars argue that America stands for rapid industrialization.[43] This historical connotation not only stresses how every need to hold on to known cultural images is undermined. Because of its massiveness, America can be associated with a discourse of typical modernist nervousness springing from the suppressed body and its natural limitations.[44]

Allusions to the hare specify the hybrid constellation of human and animal features. The *Dictionary of German Superstition* explains that the hare's blood was ritually used when a couple desired to have a baby son.[45] Karl is sent away by his parents because he has made the maid Johanna Brummer pregnant with a son.[46] The (German) Johanna introduces the breakdown of traditional (Jewish) family life. The fact that she seems to have been trying to seduce Karl for a long time refers to the hare as a symbol for a mysterious Jewish attractiveness.[47] Karl turns out to be affected by the consequences of the identification between him and the hare. He is sent to America because he has unknowingly introduced the forbidden themes of Jewishness, sexuality and illegitimate offspring, into the traditional Rossmann household. Even more, an unidentified desire moves on the story: "Because this desire is not form, but unlimited progress, a process."[48] The protagonist appears to be the continuous victim of unknown desires and changes that go on behind his back. Anderson believes that the protagonist desires to be on the road. Still, the main character bears the consequences of desires; he constantly must move. His only development is his growing similarity to the hare; he is the victim of reification and body politics that rely on cultural representation.

Karl gains support from authoritative female characters in the novel who constantly try to integrate (educate) him. Interestingly, the number of female characters who stand for modifying powers and discourses increases throughout the novel. Their number and power—such as Brunelda and her fickle commands[49]— may hint at the grown rapidity with which powers take over. They also point toward an increased social indecisiveness since no male character seems to create a definite (familial) hierarchy. A possible logical reason for women's mediating function is that only the female body is capable of engendering offspring, and it embodies cause and consequence. Familial life is definitely out of the question once the already decadent Brunelda has become a prostitute. A bourgeois framework of moral laws is used to narrate this breakdown. The impression that parental power cannot be installed explains Karl's lasting position as an infant and his inability to take responsibility as a father. When he is looking at the spectacle of the election from Brunelda's balcony, only men move onto the street, whereas women and children remain behind. On the street political battles are being fought between hypocritical male election candidates. The relation between men and women, as Karl knows it, seems to be totally out of balance.

After the Brummer scandal Karl's mother put the salami in his suitcase, where it remains hidden. The salami seems to allude to food as a means to gain strength as well as to the phallus. It is mentioned that the salami's smell has pervaded all of the objects in the suitcase: "that the Verona salami . . . had imparted its smell to everything in the suitcase" (67).[50] Often in modern literature sensual impressions like smells enlarge our knowledge of characters and of textual reality in general. The popular castration motif indicates Karl's loss of power but the salami nevertheless leaves traces behind. Hence he continues to display an inappropriate diligence which Delamarche rather sees as a foolish obligingness. The process of weakening is intensified when the French Delamarche and the Irish Robinson eat the salami. In Jewish culture, it is forbidden to eat the hare's flesh.[51] The two Europeans thus act against Jewish beliefs and erase the protagonist's past in the East. As opposed to "The Metamorphosis," conflict in this novel is not an explicit bodily phenomenon but is only perceptible on the level of symbolic allusions to the body. Karl is at the center of the narrative focus where different scenarios and discourses intersect and where an implicit fertility narrative is created. It starts with attractiveness, leads to the baby son, and necessitates a symbolic castration. In a machine-like way, images start to procreate independently.

The text evokes the hare image at later points as well. The word "hare" derives from the Old High German *haso* and is interpreted as "jumper"— *Springer*—in several languages.[52] The word *Häßchen* anticipates the scene in

Brunelda's quarter where it is said that Karl, probably because he is exhausted, takes pointless high leaps that make him lose time.[53] Even though Karl could be tired because he has undertaken such a long journey, the hare motif also explains his exhaustion. In German superstition the testicles of the hare are recommended as a sleeping drug. Karl's leaping prevents him from running fast, but it also expresses his urge to combine a high and a low viewpoint, which ultimately renders him fatigued. Before, Karl could still move up and down as a lift boy at Hotel Occidental although he did not get an overview of the machine's functioning. Brunelda will only allow him a view from up on the balcony. The reader who tries to understand people's weird reactions toward Karl has in fact identified with an implicit immanent audience that has vaporized in an atmosphere of inimical intentions and polarizations. Whereas empty and emotionless observing characterizes the protagonist from the start, a transforming society is suggested through the combination of his empty perspective, and changes in the constellation of objects and persons surrounding him.[54]

Karl anxiously attempts to hide his mysterious body "in order to remain covered up to the neck" (92). After having been assaulted by Brummer, Karl avoids making the same mistake. Remarkably, the rape scene shows that he has no consciousness of what has happened to him.[55] This can be read as an allusion to his childlike status. It at the same time indicates that he is unable to define and understand his repressed body. By covering his body, he creates a physical and psychological barrier between him and the world. In several ways, *Amerika* refers back to "The Metamorphosis." Like Gregor, also Karl has problems focalizing: "The bridge . . . trembled if you narrowed your eyes" (74).[56] Moreover, whereas Gregor is compared to a brown spot, Karl can be associated with the motif of the black hole.[57] At the end of the story his suitcase appears as an emptied out space. The objects in his suitcase carry his memories. Apparent familial connections between them, however, gradually disappear so that also their ideological value finally vanishes. After having been stripped of ideological, normative, and psychological connotations, the human is shown to be an empty recipient, a mere theater player.

Conclusion

Kafka's texts subvert the direct link between words and images. They visualize the effects and implications of discursive conflicts by staging the hybrid. The hybrid's evolution and changing contexts specify this crisis situation. Kafka's texts stage notions of animal and human that both turn out to be socioculturally determined and highlight discursive imagery (e.g., iconic body representation). Even though "The Metamorphosis" and *Amerika* have in common narrations of their protagonists' encounter with hidden social norms, they also differ with respect to the degree of identification between human and animal and the ideological characteristics of their narrated worlds. Remarkable is the decrease in concrete animal characteristics when there is an increase in superstitious and ideological elements. Moreover, I have suggested that we can read hybrids as indicators of evolving sociopolitical conflicts within a widening European context. The characters are depicted within concrete traditional contexts (family and a combination of family and continent) that seem to be evolving. *Amerika*, however, shows a widening spatial context (American continent versus family house) and a distant temporal origin of the transformation (in the past versus overnight). Furthermore, the two stories recount the ideological rewriting of history and the loss of individual bodies: Gregor is rendered anonymous in the family history and Karl is swallowed by the theatre, obliterating his procreative position in the family saga. These processes are stressed by the way in which focalization evolves throughout the stories. In the case of "The Metamorphosis," focalization grows external to the protagonist, whereas in *Amerika*, Karl is characterized by an empty perspective and sheer diligence from the beginning.

Interestingly, Kafka's stories stage immanent audiences who observe and turn away from hybrid animals in order to decrease complexity or reach a stage of apparent rational (human) behavior. Especially in "The Metamorphosis," the chief's porter is compared to an illness-spreading insect. In *Amerika* immanent audiences seem to have totally disappeared in the narrated present. This reduction of obvious positioning is announced by the fact that Karl's biological mother did not want him to individualize. Not only animal features are less apparent in this novel, but also external hostility is less explicit.

In the two stories, the body and its characteristics, such as clothing, nakedness, eating, and sweating, form a central motif. By turning to physical characteristics Kafka points toward the body as a boundary between the contested self and the outside world. It is not surprising that the motif of the back plays an important role in Kafka's works. Gregor's back is quite literally pierced by the apple. The grudge held against Karl not only suggests that he fails to observe what is being told behind his back, but his unperceivable problem also temporarily lies behind him in the past. Whereas motivations for punishment are least remarkable in "The Metamorphosis," its motivational body structure is most obvious: Gregor and the bug nearly overlap; an insect needs to be eradicated. In *Amerika*, motivational structures are hard to perceive and seem to be absent in the protagonist's mind. They are gradually disappearing—along with Karl's personal objects. Immediate motivation, however, lies at hand: Karl apparently disobeys orders.

In the two texts, the responsibility to feed (a female task) shifts from mothers to servants. In "The Metamorphosis," the maid takes care of nutrition; in *Amerika* the head cook has command over the American hotel's catering, whereas Brummer ruled over the household in Europe. Next to this empowerment of servants, the male protagonists cannot just sit down and eat. Gregor eagerly watches the breakfast table but gets none; Karl has to serve breakfast to Brunelda instead of being served. This affects the ideal of the strong and healthy male body.

Showing one's body means that an image of it can be produced and installed. Kafka's protagonists fear pain and immediate confrontations with the body. The body is hurt when it is not used according to familial rules and to its new shape, or when the body is uncomfortably pushed to the wall in order to avoid physical abuse. Even more, the body is often sweating. It signals that covering clothes and uniforms are inappropriate for a particular climate but also that the protagonist's activities are unnatural within narrated reality. The natural distinction between animal and human and the experience of pain turn out to be matters of appropriateness.

Kafka carries out a search for the human but ends up with empty ideological frameworks. He uses an apparently simple writing style in which familiar discourses and scenarios of normality (such as the Darwinian, psychoanalytical, scientific, familial) shimmer through. Still, his texts never perform an identification between the narrated world and these discourses. They show how the enlightened design of man has been reclaimed in several discourses over and over again. All that is left are hollow constructions, since the notion of humanity—meant to differentiate between human and animal—has become lost in conflicting discourses. The so-called body is disembodied.

Notes

1. I define hybridity as the combination of conflicting features (e.g., human-animal) within the boundaries of a represented object or character. Next to hybrid images I point out verbal hybridity caused by ambiguous words or overlapping ideological discourses that sabotage a straightforward production of images. This double approach builds on postcolonial theory (H. K. Bhabha's concept of the "third" space) and M. Bachtin's polyphony theory that make a similar distinction between visual and verbal hybridity. Cf. Christin Galster, *Hybrides Erzählen und hybride Identität im britischen Roman der Gegenwart* (Frankfurt: Lang, 2002).

2. Harzer and Norris use similar descriptions (*Menschen-Tier* and *Tiermenschen*). Friedmann Harzer, *Erzählte Verwandlung* (Tübingen: Niemeyer, 2000), 132; Margot Norris, "Sadism and Masochism in Two Kafka Stories: 'In der Strafkolonie' and 'Ein Hungerkünstler,'" *MLN* 93:3 (1978): 430–47, 433.

3. Cf. "ein Zeichen für eine bestimmte Relation von Mensch und Tier." Renate Böschenstein, "Tiere als Elemente von Hofmannsthals Zeichensprache," *Hofmannsthal-Jahrbuch* 1 (1993): 137–64, 157.

4. Cf. Szondi's characterization of early modernism based upon the epic subject and the tension with the outside that arises from a grown orientation toward the inside. Peter Szondi, *Theorie des modernen Dramas* (Frankfurt: Suhrkamp 1967), 70–71.

5. Franz Kafka, "The Metamorphosis," *Kafka, Franz, 1883–1924: The Complete Stories* (New York: Schocken, 1971), 89–139. References to the novel are given in the main text.

6. Cf. Christopher M. Schmidt, *Interpretation als literaturtheoretisches Problem* (Frankfurt: Lang, 2000), 159f, 167f.

7. Koelb has already indicated the rhetorical function of realism: "[B]oth fantasy and reality are presented in the fictions as rhetorically structured." Clayton Koelb, *Kafka's Rhetoric: The Passion of Reading* (Ithaca, NY: Cornell University Press, 1989), 119. Pfeiffer suggests that Gregor *is* a bug—and is not just being compared to a bug—which according to him leads to the destruction of the metaphor. Joachim Pfeiffer, *Franz Kafka: Die Verwandlung. Brief an den Vater* (München: Oldenbourg, 1998), 13. Jahraus remarks that the "extended metaphor" (*fortgeführten Metapher*) is demetaphorized (*entmetaphorisiert*) in the course of the story. Oliver Jahraus, *Kafka: Leben, Schreiben, Machtapparate* (Stuttgart: Reclam, 2006), 223. Textual rhetoric, however, urges the reader to ask why Gregor has transformed—and is still transforming—thus delaying the act of identification. Instead of taking the hybrid as an interpretable symbol, I point out the gaps in identities. I show how assumed self-reflexive "symbols" stay logically connected to the textual world and its immanent audiences. Anderson ("self-referential clues," 185) and Müller (*ein meta-literarischer und selbstreferentieller Text*) have a form of self-reflexivity in mind that is related to the author and not to textual features. Beate Müller, "Die grausame Schrift: Zur Ästhetik der Zensur in Kafka's 'Strafkolonie,'" *Neophilologus* 84 (2000): 107–25, 108, 118f. Cf. Mark M. Anderson, *Kafka's clothes. Ornament and Aestheticism in the Habsburg Fin de Siècle* (Oxford: Clarendon Press, 2002).

8. Cf. Ann-Sophie Lehmann, "Das unsichtbare Geschlecht. Zu einem abwesenden Teil des weiblichen Körpers in der bildenden Kunst," in *Körperteile: Eine kulturelle Anatomie*, ed. Claudia Benthien and Christoph Wulf (Reinbek: Rowohlt, 2001), 316–38.

9. Cf. Oliver Jahraus, *Kafka*, 225, 233.

10. Joachim Pfeiffer, *Franz Kafka*, 13.

11. Friedmann Harzer, *Erzählte Verwandlung*, 171.

12. His room presents a remnant of his previous well-known environment and transforms internally.

13. Cf. Margot Norris, *Beasts of the Modern Imagination: Darwin, Nietzsche, Kafka, Ernst, & Lawrence* (Baltimore: Johns Hopkins University Press, 1985).

14. The belly is described in terms of illness: it itches at the beginning and aches further on in the story. Also, the penetration and infection of his protective back shields belong to the terminal illness metaphor.

15. Joachim Pfeiffer, *Franz Kafka*, 60–61.

16. Also, the fact that the father throws apples at him when/because he is running over the floor (instead of crawling on the walls), and the fact that Grete opens his window could be read as attempts to make him change his attitude or leave the house.

17. Susanne Hochreiter: *Franz Kafka: Raum und Geschlecht* (Würzburg: Königshausen & Neumann, 2007), 138.

18. Cf. Anderson, *Kafka's Clothes*, 127.

19. Schmidt distinguishes between the isotopies "human," "animal," and "thing," and between "discursive" and "narrative isotopies." Schmidt, *Interpretation*, 159–73 and 132–33.

20. Also, the liftboys' uniforms are soaked with sweat in *Der Verschollene*. Since heat and sweating are often associated with uniforms, we can assume that Gregor's armor refers to a uniform as well. It literally keeps him from actively fulfilling his former army ideals. Löw explains the impenetrable armour as a symbol for the male body that is distinguished from the female procreative body. Martina Löw, "Der Körperraum als soziale Konstruktion," in *Geschlechter-Räume*, ed. Margarethe Hubrath (Köln: Böhlau, 2001), 211–22, 216. Gregor transgresses gender borders and symbolically gives birth to the new powerful female. Cf. Ryan's discussion of uniforms; Michael P. Ryan, "The aggregate character in Kafka's 'In der Strafkolonie,'" *Symposium* (2002): 213–27, 217–18.

21. Anderson (*Kafka's Clothes*) is an important exception. He thematically links "Die Verwandlung" to an intertext: Leopold von Sacher-Masoch's story "Venus in Furs" (1880).

22. Cf. Joachim Pfeiffer, *Franz Kafka*, 84.

23. Cf. Oliver Jahraus, *Kafka*, 241. Cf. R. K. Angress, "Kafka and Sacher-Masoch: A Note on the Metamorphosis," *MLN* 85:5 (1970): 745–46, 746.

24. Cf. Nina Pelikan-Straus, "Transforming Franz Kafka's 'Metamorphosis,'" *Signs* 14:3 (1989): 651–67, 652, 654.

25. The hybrid is constantly defined against its social background—as a brother, son, lover, office employee, soldier—and as such negated. The emptying out of familiar roles highlights an evolving context. Jahraus remarks that the personal narrative mode is diminishing as Gregor's position within the family weakens. Oliver Jahraus, *Kafka*, 229.

26. According to Norris, musical talent equals influence and power. Margot Norris, "Kafka's Josefine: The Animal as the Negative Site of Narration," *MLN* 98:3 (1983): 366–83, 372.

27. The family functions as a historically connoted motif. The breakdown of arranged marriages in the Habsburg Empire was partly responsible for the empire's political downfall. Changes in sexual and matrimonial conduct are reflected within the story's family constellations. Whereas the house of the Samsa family becomes smaller, Grete's marriage possibilities become larger. Gregor's numerous legs and fragmented belly shield can be related to Habsburg's many states that were falling apart after World War I. His infected back shields are meant to keep the legs and belly rings together. His incapacity to move adequately is reminiscent of Habsburg's retarded economical growth. The fur cap, stole, and muff can be read as allusions to Hungarian dress code too.

28. Duttlinger, *Kafka and Photography* (Oxford: Oxford University Press, 2007), 109.

29. Ingeborg Scholz, *Franz Kafka: Analysen und Reflexionen* (Hollfeld: Beyer, 2003), 37.

30. Cf. Jahraus points out the tension between Gregor's familial and economic responsibilities. Jahraus, *Kafka*, 235.

31. The description of the prosecutor ("so partial to ladies," 102) presents another exchangeable feature.

32. In German: "'Das war eine Tierstimme,' sagte der Prokurist." Franz Kafka, "Die Verwandlung," in *Drucke zu Lebzeiten: Kritische Ausgabe* (Frankfurt: Fischer, 1994), 113–200, 102. I would prefer the translation "prosecutor" instead of "chief clerk" (102).

33. Gregor's transformation reminds one of Herder's definition of "human" as a two-legged creature standing upright. Johann G. Herder, *Ideen zur Philosophie der Geschichte der Menschheit*, vol. 6 (Frankfurt: Deutscher Klassiker Verlag, 1989), 112.

34. Cf. Friedmann Harzer, *Erzählte Verwandlung*, 129. This implies that the story is not solely about Gregor and his emotions, even though Binder very meticulously illustrates how his viewpoint pervades the story. Hartmut Binder, *Kafkas "Verwandlung": Entstehung, Deutung, Wirkung* (Frankfurt: Stroemfeld/Roter Stern, 2004), 205–62.

35. Franz Kafka, *Kafka, Franz, 1883–1924: Amerika* (*The Man Who Disappeared*) (New York: Schocken, 2002). References to the novel are given in the main text.

36. The writing desk already appeared in "Die Verwandlung": Grete believes that the desk obstructs Karl's free movement. Because of its ability to hold and separate objects, the writing desk can be associated with political organization and cultural memory.

37. The previous German words are quoted from Franz Kafka, *Amerika (Der Verschollene)* (Frankfurt: Fischer, 1982), 58.

38. The optical movement between foreground and background is typical of Kafka's protagonists. Hybrid spatial images can be found throughout *Der Verschollene*. Cf. Melissa De Bruyker, *Das resonante Schweigen: Die Rhetorik der erzählten Welt in Kafkas Der Verschollene, Schnitzler's Therese und Walsers Räuber-Roman* (Würzburg: Königshausen & Neumann, 2008), 118f.

39. One story in German superstition in particular links the hare to Christianity. A man goes out to hunt on a Sunday morning. He fails to shoot a hare whereas he usually never misses. Instead of running away, the hare sits on its hind legs, thus imitating a human. The scared hunter goes home and promises never to go hunting again during the Holy Mass. www.reifenberg-online.de/geister.htm.

40. Hermsdorf argues that Kafka already got interested in the theme of Jewishness in 1911 and 1912. Klaus Hermsdorf, *Kafka: Weltbild und Roman* (Berlin: Rütten & Loening, 1961), 141. We can, however, distinguish between stories in which focalization bears the traces of the hybrid background of a writer and texts that refer more explicitly to Jewishness (e.g., through connotations of words, symbols).

41. Karlheinz Fingerhut, "Erlebtes und Erlesenes—Arthur Holitschers und Franz Kafkas Amerika-Darstellungen: Zum Funktionsübergang von Reisebericht und Roman," *Diskussion Deutsch* 20 (1989): 337–55, 351.

42. Quoted from Franz Kafka, *Amerika*, 58.

43. Cf. Walter H. Sokel, *Franz Kafka: Tragik und Ironie. Zur Struktur seiner Kunst* (München and Vienna: Langen-Müller, 1964), 247–48, 311–29. Cf. Karlheinz Fingerhut, "Erlebtes und Erlesenes," 342. Cf. Dieter Heimböckel, "'Amerika im Kopf': Franz Kafkas Roman *Der Verschollene* und der Amerika-Diskurs seiner Zeit," *DVjs* 77:1 (2003): 130–47.

44. Greiner and Metz were the first to actualize the topic of Jewishness in this story with a specific focus on the East-West discrepancy. They show how moving West actually implies a shift toward the East. Bernhard Greiner, "Im Umkreis von Ramses: Kafkas *Verschollener* als jüdischer Bildungsroman," *DVjs* 77:4 (2003): 637–58. Joseph Metz,

"Zion in the West: Cultural Zionism, Diasporic Doubles, and the 'Direction' of Jewish Literary Identity in Kafka's *Der Verschollene*," *DVjs* 78:4 (2004): 646–71.

45. Hanns Bächthold-Stäubli, *Handwörterbuch des deutschen Aberglaubens*, vol. 3 (Berlin: Walter de Gruyter GmbH & Co., 2000), 1521, 1523.

46. The word "horse" (*Ross*-Mann) stands in close connection to the name *Brummer* ("horsefly"). Heinz Politzer, *Franz Kafka: Der Künstler* (Frankfurt: Suhrkamp, 1978). Animals introduce specific animal scenarios used to narrate evolutions in the relations between characters and social classes. Whereas horses reflect prestige in a pre-war society, they lose their value in a technical American society where people drive cars or trams. Karl's situation is definitely deteriorating after he has been violated by a horsefly. Horses are strong animals whereas the protagonist is childlike and weak. "Rossmann" is, however, Karl's family name and he is sent away by his family because of the illegitimate child he has with Brummer.

47. *Handwörterbuch des deutschen Aberglaubens*, 1524.

48. "Denn das Verlangen ist nicht Form, sondern unbegrenzter Fortgang, Prozeß." Gilles Deleuze and Felix Guattari, *Kafka, Für eine kleine Literatur* (Frankfurt: Suhrkamp, 1976), 14.

49. The fact that Brunelda is depicted as an extremely fat woman could be explained as a reference to her power (cf. Pelikan-Straus, "Transforming," 658). However, her power grows dangerously, putting an end to her sexual attractiveness. Liebrand points out the mess and clutter in her apartment, which reminds us of Gregor's room. Claudia Liebrand, "Die verschollene (Geschlechter-)Differenz: Zu Frank Kafkas Amerika-Roman," *Literatur für Leser* 20 (1997): 143–57, 147.

50. In German *mitteilen* also means "to convey a message."

51. *Handwörterbuch des deutschen Aberglaubens*, 1505.

52. *Handwörterbuch des deutschen Aberglaubens*, 1504.

53. In German: "zeitraubende und nutzlose Sprünge." Franz Kafka, *Amerika*, 284.

54. A previous version of the text shows how Karl leaves behind everything he had been taught on arrival in the harbor of New York. During their journey overseas the travellers are not supposed to light a fire—that is, to illuminate and think. Still, they disobey, thus keeping part of their memories intact.

55. The metaphor of the Immaculate Conception is evoked in the description of stains on the liftboys' uniforms and shown to be a lost ideal. Karl's ignorance of sexuality (e.g., when making Johanna pregnant) also puns on Immaculate Conception as an ideological notion separated from the bodily self.

56. The original German version reads as follows: "Die Brücke . . . erzitterte, wenn man die Augen klein machte." Franz Kafka, *Amerika*, 144. The expression *klein machen* refers back to Karl's smallness and shows that being little is not just a physical but also a mental and observation-related characteristic.

57. Cf. Anderson, *Kafka's Clothes*, 112.

CHAPTER 13

The Portrait of an Armor-Plated Sign: Reimagining Samsa's Exoskeleton

Dean Swinford

Classifying and Depicting Insects: Fairchild and Kafka

Attempts to uncover the identity of Gregor Samsa in Franz Kafka's "The Metamorphosis" have tended to follow two trajectories.[1] The first, concerned with the literal representation of a nonhuman body, has focused on the best way to classify or describe that body, leading critics to wonder if Gregor actually is an insect and, if so, what kind. The second path, less concerned with the specific features of the protagonist's body, seeks to understand and interpret the significance not so much of the body itself, but of the transformation it represents.

Vladimir Nabokov's well-known lecture on the novella features an extended consideration of the former and leads to the conclusion that the vermin "belongs to the branch of 'jointed leggers' (Arthropoda), to which insects, and spiders, and centipedes, and crustaceans belong."[2] Nabokov, "elected to the Cambridge Entomological Society" for his work on butterflies, is better suited than most to comment on the interstices of fiction and entomology.[3] This interest in the invertebrate world explains his consideration of the physical features, and corresponding taxonomic categorization, of Samsa's body. Indeed, after establishing the creature's phylum, Nabokov moves to the next biological grouping, class. The key to understanding Samsa's class is an accurate appendage tally: if the numerous legs "mentioned in the beginning mean more than six legs, then Gregor would not be an insect from a zoological point of view."[4] Making the assumption that six legs are sufficient to call numerous, Nabokov concludes that, of the various classes of Arthropods, Samsa "is an insect," and moves to the next piece of this cladistic quandary, identifying the kind of insect, which he describes not as a cockroach, but as a very broad "brown, convex, dog-sized beetle."[5]

On the other side of the interpretive spectrum, the exact qualities of this body have little significance. Instead, the phrase Kafka uses to denote this body, consisting in German of a pair of words beginning with the prefix "un," suggests, as Stanley Corngold points out, something uncanny, "not-this, not-that—a paradox, a creature not even of dust."[6] The continued interest in the symbolic significance of this ghostly body animates what José B. Monleón describes in *A Specter Is Haunting Europe: A Sociohistorical Approach to the Fantastic*, as "the great number of psychological interpretations" of the work.[7] Monleón sees the tension between the narrative's representation of supernatural events and the realistic language used to express these events as indicative of a greater cultural transformation best described as a process wherein new technologies transformed the tangible society produced by industrialization "into a more ethereal world."[8] Monleón describes the significance for modernity of "invisible" technologies such as X-rays and electricity not just in terms of lived reality, but also as contributing to the elevation of the fantastic as a literary and artistic mode. To this end, the fantastic "acquires meaning in its historical trajectory."[9] The genre signifies through its representation of monstrosity in ways that reveal the "apprehensions . . . attached to the specific characteristics of capitalist society."[10]

Around the same time that Kafka imagined an insect enlarged and interposed in the life of a modern family, the American naturalist David Fairchild devised a macrophotographic technique that allowed for magnified frontal and side views of insects. This altered perspective presented a new world in such a radical way that Fairchild titled his 1914 book showcasing this new photographic approach *Book of Monsters* in an effort to emphasize the disconcerting effect of this refiguration of the kinds of insects commonly found in a yard or garden. Published by the National Geographic Society, the book contains "a collection of . . . a few of the small-sized monsters which inhabit the tall grass, the flower garden and vegetable garden, the pines and oaks of a place in the woods of Maryland."[11] However, as Fairchild notes, "if you compare these photographs with those to be found in most books on insects, you will find that they differ in several particulars."[12]

The increased magnification made possible by Fairchild's photographic equipment forces his audience to reconsider the appearance of insects in a way that highlights their menacing modernity, emblematized through Fairchild's text, fixating as it does on their mechanical features and alien behavior as well as the continual threat they pose to the welfare of industrial human society. The more recent popularity of insect documentaries such as *Microcosmos* and *Alien Empire* builds from the representation of another world first made possible by Fairchild's invention. The combination of image and text in the *Book of Monsters* results in a refiguration, or re-presentation of the insect as a living creature and as a signifier or motif in search of meaning.

This refiguration has important implications for attempts to understand the historical development of allegorization as well as the significance of Kafka's use of a magnified insect protagonist for the fantastic as a modern genre. Fairchild's presentation of insects in the *Book of Monsters* parallels the refiguration and magnification of the misunderstood insect in "The Metamorphosis." As Nabokov points out, while Kafka did not see "that beetle any too clearly," Samsa's corporeality has a strong bearing on his thematic significance.[13] The trope of the magnified insect, as revealed through a comparison of Kafka and Fairchild, signifies as an image responding to and made possible by the unreason of the modern. The biological specifics of the exoskeletal shell speak to the significance of this text as a response to modernism and as an important landmark in the development of fantastic literature. The appearance of similar tropes in Fairchild's work also serves to demonstrate the interconnection of literary and scientific modes of expression and the extent to which each of these respond to cultural developments that exist outside of the text. Fairchild's development of macrophotographic techniques and representation of insects in his *Book of Monsters*, when read in conjunction with "The Metamorphosis," reveals the extent to which visual and conceptual readings of Samsa's form overlap. The linguistic emphasis of critical interpretations including and influenced by Stanley Corngold's *Kafka: The Necessity of Form* informs an assessment of the primarily visual disruption created by Samsa's body, which Corngold refers to as Kafka's "opaque sign."[14]

Interpretation of "The Metamorphosis" has historically deemphasized the form of Samsa's body in relation to the various concepts it purportedly signifies. This interpretation has resulted in a hermeneutics that overlooks the bug in pursuit of its elusive significance. The body of Kafka's protagonist, often incised from the text, its own corporeality disregarded, finds itself inserted into an equation intended to produce meaning. This equation, while variously construed as hermeneutic allegorical unraveling or the determination of a linguistic relationship, has viewed Samsa (from above) as a sign, a signified in search of a signifier. The hermeneutic task somehow implied, or necessitated, by Kafka's work extends to a theory of interpretation which even repudiates the task itself. As Theo Elm indicates in "Problematisierte Hermeneutik zur 'Uneigentlichkeit' in Kafkas Kleiner Prosa," "Kafka's historical position between traditional idealism and the modern rejection of ideology is indicated by the epistemological problems raised in his texts. As their truth remains hidden to the reader he is called upon, rather than extracting a 'message' to reflect on his failure to find one."[15] The labor of this interpretive task, and the question of whether or not this interpretation can yield an answer, has led critics away from a consideration of the form being interpreted. Thus, Mark M. Anderson observes in *Kafka's Clothes: Ornament and*

Aestheticism in the Habsburg Fin de Siècle that "since the story's initial publication in 1915, few if any readers of 'The Metamorphosis' have wished to recognize Gregor Samsa's metamorphosed body as an aesthetic form."[16] Instead, Anderson argues that "For Kafka's early public, the bug was simply too repulsive, and was explained away with allegorical notions like 'alienated labor' or 'unconscious self-loathing.'"[17] The arguments regarding Gregor's physical form culminate in Stanley Corngold's "The Metamorphosis of the Metaphor," which denies Gregor's very corporeality. Instead, he is to be regarded as a linguistic and rhetorical cipher: the indeterminate relationship between monster and human results in a "mutilated metaphor, uprooted from familiar language."[18] The instability of Samsa's form, on a linguistic level, parallels the instability of Samsa's own experience. The reader's "unsettling" attempts to mediate the "indeterminate, fluid crossing of a human tenor and a material vehicle" create a metaphoricalink between reader and protagonist.[19] This metaphorical link, however, eschews the dialectical relationship of metaphor. The tenuous relationships result in "opaque sign[s]" that both deny and assert meaning.[20]

This linguistic relationship is not specific to "The Metamorphosis." The same relationship between metaphor and speech can also be found, for example, in a prose piece titled "The Intricate Story of Shamefaced Lanky and Impure in Heart" that Kafka included in a letter to Oskar Pollak. This piece describes an encounter between a fashionable, well-dressed dandy and Lanky, an awkward figure who knits grey socks for the peasants. The "impure" dandy spews forth words that Kafka describes as "'fine gentlemen with patent-leather shoes and English cravats and glistening buttons.'"[21] These words, besides being described as adorned in the fashionable accoutrements of the day, climb onto Lanky. They then violently move across his body, eventually "work[ing] their way into his ears."[22] The words, like the dandy, are not clothed: they are clothing. While empty on the inside, their exteriors hold meaning. The relation between signifier and signified indicative of metaphor is elided. The signifier signifies only its temporary existence. Anderson, building on Corngold's thesis, then dismisses the "allegorical notions" that populate analysis of "The Metamorphosis" and other works by Kafka.[23] As such, the opaque sign is, itself, significatory of the set of social circumstances from which Kafka wrote. The sign, the insect protagonist, is a product of a particular set of social circumstances, and is not a marker of stable, referential meaning.

Anderson points out that "allegory," defined in his usage through a one-to-one relationship between sign and meaning, does not adequately express the complexity of Kafka's text. Here, the simplicity of readings that point to Samsa's metamorphosis as a literalization of the plight of alienated labor or of unconscious self-loathing denies Kafka's rhetorical complexity. Implicit in Anderson's dismissal of such readings is their own Marxist and psychoanalytic agendas.

Furthermore, Anderson refers to the inability of such readings to recognize the "aesthetic form" of Gregor's body. Anderson indicates that its indeterminable but unmistakably grotesque shape is, itself, an expression of aesthetics. While the exact shape of the body is unclear, it serves to signify that which is unpleasant, grotesque, and, viewed from the standpoint of the urban bourgeoisie, unnatural. Anderson's assertions on the aesthetic value of the insect body help to recontextualize Gregor Samsa's body as an allegorical signifier through an understanding of allegory informed by critics such as Franco Moretti, Paul de Man, and Fredric Jameson, who stress that the mode does not necessarily entail a one-to-one correspondence of image and meaning.

Criticism that has read the text allegorically has done so in order to propose Samsa's identity as emblematic of, among others, the oppressed worker or the enraged id. A reconsideration of Samsa's insect form requires, instead, a conception of modern allegory as a polysemic discursive mode in keeping with Franco Moretti's examination of this mode in *Modern Epic*. Kafka's narrative belongs to a trajectory that connects the fabulistic imagination of the allegorist to the indirect association of signifier and signified at work in surrealism and magic realism. At the same time, the supersized insect, construed as both signified and signifier, impels a reexamination of the process of signification at work in "The Metamorphosis." The mystery of the insect body propels the continued tendency toward allegorical readings of the work. Mabel Moraña makes a similar observation in *Kafka: Procesamiento de "La Metamorfosis,"* noting that "In Gregor, the body appears as a machine for a photographic process: this is the plastic characterization of his interior and circumstances, the opposite of his previous being."[24] The significance of the body lies in the "photographic process" by which it produces meaning.[25] Here, Moraña gives an active role to the body itself. It is not merely interpreted by others; instead, its significance stems from what she terms the "mystery of the body," defined as a process that "operates as an insurmountable mediation that interrupts every possibility of communication" between Samsa and the other characters of the story.[26] Because of the unfamiliarity of the trope, its natural unnaturalness, Gregor's body functions as the ideal emblem of the nefarious linguistic multiplicity, the unsettling of perspectives, often attributed to the story.

In other words, critics should not ignore the fact that "The Metamorphosis" is, on the most literal level, about a bug. The textual clues provide minimal support for speculations regarding the actual type of insect represented. While one of the servants, an old widow "whose strong and bony frame had enabled her to survive the worst a long life could offer," addresses Samsa as "old dung beetle," he makes no response, denying her the ability to fix his identity.[27] However, we are not to doubt her accuracy in classification.[28] She is the only character to actively, and repeatedly, gaze at Samsa. After accidentally seeing Gregor one morning, she never fails to "open the door a little for a moment, morning and evening, to have a look at him."[29] There is no reason to disbelieve her assessment of Gregor as a dung beetle, or scarab.[30] Such a classification, by extension, connects the insect of "The Metamorphosis" to a species that has particular mythic significance.

Genotypic classification in and of itself, however, does not fully solve the riddle of Samsa's identity, primarily because his identity is continuously negated through the course of "The Metamorphosis." Critics do agree that Samsa is clearly engaged in an antithetical relationship with the culture of family and work. He is initially concerned that he will miss a business appointment. Secondarily, he worries about his family's reaction to his inability to reach the appointment. From this point, criticism has moved toward the allegorical interpretations frequently derived from Samsa's social circumstances that Anderson regards as so derivative. At the same time, the widow's prognosis validates a focus on the body. Her response to his form reveals the shock produced by the intrusion of a fantastic element into a narrative otherwise concerned with the social preoccupations of literary realism.

The widow sees Samsa and identifies the monstrous form she confronts with the much less threatening life form it resembles. In this way, her predicament as observer parallels Fairchild's. His book is, on the most basic level, presented as a field guide aimed at helping readers identify insects and, to this end, offers fairly complete coverage of the phylum Arthropoda. At the same time, his representation of insects as monsters impels an identification of the familiar that is mediated through the shock produced by the unfamiliar. The widow identifies the insect, but cannot disconnect her identification of a familiar form from her amazement. In the text, she "stood there in amazement."[31] Furthermore, Samsa's body provokes this astonishment. She sees a familiar form that has been magnified to an unnatural size. She identifies Gregor as a creature, and not as an idea. This direct encounter with the insect seems at odds with attempts to reduce Samsa's transformation to a linguistic puzzle. In Corngold's thesis, "The Metamorphosis" testifies to the crisis of signification. This reading, while seemingly distanced from a binary de-allegorization of the text, posits Gregor's form as a sign able to be divided into a stable concept and a referential meaning. It is an "opaque sign" engaged in a relationship with at least one set of signifieds. The Sausserean language serves to distance Kafka's tale from the phenomenological realm of things and experiences.

More significantly than the mere aesthetic unpleasantness of Samsa's form, the uncertainty and promise provided by the supersized insect as a fundamentally visual trope pit the "monstrous vermin" in a dialectical relationship with the early twentieth-century world of fiscal and filial obligation.[32] Quite simply, the insect is and is not in the story. Samsa alternates between hiding from his sister and displaying himself, like the fur-coated pin-up, on the wall. The specific descriptive details trace and erase the shape of the bug.

The initial published version of "The Metamorphosis" featured an illustration selected by Kafka. It does not feature an insect waving its slathering mandibles at the viewer. Instead, it shows "a man in a dressing-gown, agitatedly starting up from a sofa in a narrow room, covering his horror-stricken face with his hands, as if aghast at a nightmare."[33] When the publisher, Kurt Wolff, told Kafka that he had commissioned the artist Ottomar Starke for the frontispiece of the first edition of "The Metamorphosis," Kafka immediately replied, "It occurred to me . . . that [the artist] might want to draw the insect itself. Please, not that—anything but that! . . . The insect itself cannot be drawn. It cannot even be shown in the distance."[34] Kafka's explicit instructions that the insect not be shown have been referenced by a number of critics. In *Franz Kafka: Die Verwandlung. Eine Interpretation*, for example, Jürg Schubiger stresses the inexact composition of Gregor's body.[35] Schubiger points out that Gregor's form, weight, and actions result in an impossible combination. In this way, Samsa's insect body does not quite fit the unproblematic realism so characteristic of the rest of the narrative. Quite simply, Samsa's head, as determined by his ability to observe actions in the apartment, is too agile for the plate-armored head segment of a standard beetle. At the same time, his body cannot be so heavy as to require two men to move it and so lithe as to cling freely to the walls and the ceiling. As a result, the information provided about Gregor's body "does not provide a rounded image of a living being but rather amounts to a mere inventory of possible forms of behavior, which come into their own only within concrete situations but which, however, must be discounted if the creature is to be truly characterized as an insect."[36] Based on the details of Gregor's corporeality, Schubiger draws the conclusion that "Gregor's bodily data should not be misunderstood as facts; rather, we have the case here of bodily-posed questions and answers in the beetle's dialogue with the world."[37]

In "*The Metamorphosis*: The Long Journey into Print," however, Hartmut Binder concludes that Schubiger's project "is not successful," and stipulates that "it is wrong to draw the conclusion . . . that . . . Kafka wanted to prevent the metamorphosed being from being visualized as a representational whole."[38] Binder points out that the foundation of Schubiger's thesis is useful. Instead of regarding the insect as an object, a sign somehow distanced from the remainder of the text, but holding the key to its interpretation, we are to consider the gaze of the insect itself. The beetle's dialogue with the world forces us to consider perspective and the progressive integration of Gregor's human consciousness and beetle form. However, Binder faults Schubiger with ignoring the fundamentally subjective perspective offered by the insect-human hybrid. While Schubiger eschews interpretations that stop at the first sentence of "The Metamorphosis," his own interpretation cannot surpass an attempt to validate Gregor's body as an objective form possible in a realistic narrative. Binder, on the other hand, asserts that "the insect represented by Kafka is a mélange of bug and beetle and—possibly—cockroach. It was designed to lend reality to his narrative intentions, even if a creature constructed like it cannot be found in the empirical world."[39] Binder then considers the body as something that does not need to obey the rules of insect biology necessary for a realistic bug in all manners but size. Instead, he concludes that "such a being is every bit as imaginable as any fabulous beast, especially as his physical build does not display any self-contradictory characteristics."[40] Binder's assessment of Gregor as a fabulous beast built from the bodily components of recognizable creatures connects the visual, tangible character of Gregor's form and the allegorical otherworldliness of this form. In other words, an assessment of the form of the protagonist cannot be distinguished from an assessment of the form of the narrative.

Kafka and the New Fantastic: Adaptation and Transgression

Kafka's attention to the content of the illustration, paired with the desires of the editors to feature the insect, asserts the visual nature of the text. The unsettling of visual expectations parallels the semiotic uncertainty of deciphering Samsa's form. It is, above all, the power of Gregor's body to signify as icon, image, and motif. The significance of this image at the center of the text also serves to animate discussions seeking to classify this text.

Tzvetan Todorov's statement regarding Kafka that "his entire world obeys a dream-like logic without fatiguing, which has nothing to do with the real" epitomizes the logic of the modern allegory.[41] The final chapter of Todorov's *The Fantastic: A Structural Approach to a Literary Genre* poses questions, most specifically regarding Kafka's "The Metamorphosis," which are not easily answerable given the constants of Todorov's formulation of the fantastic. He acknowledges the limitations of the fantastic and consciously separates the chapter "Literature and the Fantastic" from the remainder of the text with the statement "our passage through the Fantastic is finished."[42] At the point when the fantastic has been successfully defined, Todorov begins to dismantle this definition or, rather, to indicate that the fantastic is a historically limited category.

In this chapter, Todorov accounts for the wide distinction between the aesthetics of the nineteenth and twentieth centuries. He connects these aesthetic distinctions to the scientific attitude of each age. For Todorov, "the nineteenth century transpired, it is true, in a metaphysics of the real and the imaginary, and the literature of the fantastic is nothing but the bad conscience of this positivist era."[43] He postulates a firm division between nineteenth-century fantastic literature and the literary fantastic made possible by an era transformed by technology. The influence of a scientific mind-set results in readers who "can no longer believe in an immutable, external reality, nor in a literature which is merely the transcription of such a reality."[44] Here, Todorov refers to the emergence of the fantastic as a direct result of a worldview promulgated by the positivist era. However, the fantastic, despite its claims to the ascendancy of the imagination, "posits the majority of a text as belonging to reality—or, more specifically, as provoked by reality."[45] As he documents the impossibility of the fantastic within a present without access to "an immutable, external reality," Todorov presents Kafka's "The Metamorphosis" as the most prominent "narrative of the supernatural in the twentieth century."[46]

Todorov applies the rules of the fantastic, as articulated earlier in his book, to "The Metamorphosis," and finds them insufficient to contain the narrative. Todorov attempts to define the fantastic as genre by concentrating primarily on thematics. The term "fantastic" indicates the relation of a narrative to ambiguity. In the fantastic narrative, the mysterious exists, is confronted, but is never entirely explained as either mysterious or misinterpreted ordinary event. Essentially, "the rule of the genre implies that the ambiguity be maintained."[47] In his definition of the fantastic as genre, Todorov indicates that, in the same way that the characters of fantastic narratives approach but never arrive at the fantastic, narratives themselves approach but never arrive at the pure fantastic. The various subdivisions of the fantastic (including the uncanny, the fantastic-uncanny, the fantastic-marvelous, and the marvelous) provide a fairly comprehensive set of possibilities which gravitate beyond the explicit ambiguity of the fantastic.

The possibilities provided by the subdivisions of the fantastic are exhausted and overwhelmed by Kafka's narrative. The primary distinction stems from the transition between natural and supernatural. Todorov's categories of the fantastic begin with the natural. Indeed, this clarifies his assertion that the fantastic, as genre, is limited by its relation to nineteenth-century positivism. In the fantastic, the natural is both a clearly defined and uncontested category. The fantastic is achieved through the hesitation of a protagonist in the face of the unnatural, or supernatural. The protagonist seeks to remain within the confines of the natural. However, the narrative of the supernatural in the twentieth century, its form guided by "The Metamorphosis," is based on the "*adaptation* which follows the inexplicable event and which characterizes the transition from the supernatural to the natural. Hesitation and adaptation designate two symmetrical and converse processes."[48]

While Todorov designates hesitation and adaptation as both symmetrical and converse in the context of his argument, the terms he uses seem to refer entirely to the action of the protagonist. In the fantastic, the protagonist hesitates before the supernatural; in this new category which extends beyond the fantastic, the protagonist adapts. This adaptation removes the supernatural veneer from what is essentially a natural, or possible, event. The protagonist neither hesitates nor wonders at the possibility of the laws governing a world where natural and supernatural are no longer clearly designated categories.

However, Todorov clearly distinguishes this new narrative, or this new relationship of the subject and the un/natural, from the marvelous. While the marvelous is, like Todorov's description of "The Metamorphosis," characterized by nonreaction to the supernatural, the relation between the natural and the un-natural is entirely different in these two types of narrative. Todorov maintains that "the marvelous implies that we are plunged into a world whose laws are totally different from what they are in our own and in consequence that the supernatural events which occur are in no way disturbing."[49] This distinction becomes key in consideration of the limits of the natural and if, indeed, Kafka's narrative is explicitly a product of the twentieth century.[50]

The key component of Todorov's argument regarding the relation between Kafka's narrative and the marvelous stems from his attempt to distinguish Kafka's narrative from allegory. He denies "The Metamorphosis" the status of allegory, arguing that while "one might certainly suggest several allegorical interpretations of the text . . . the text itself offers no explicit indication which would confirm any one of them."[51] Todorov's definition of allegory here, of course, is clearly indebted to the split between allegory and symbol promulgated by nineteenth-century critics and poets interested in elevating the latter over the former. However, as Todorov indicates, Kafka's narrative (and, by exten-sion, other twentieth-century narratives of the supernatural) moves beyond the constraints of the fantastic, itself a genre undergirded by nineteenth-century aes-thetic presuppositions. Todorov's own use of allegory, so informed by the same nineteenth-century givens which he attempts to bridge in this final chapter of his consideration of the fantastic, must also be subject to revision.

Todorov hints at the clear distinction between interpretation in Kafka and in traditional allegory. He mentions that "it is often said of Kafka that his narra-tives must be read above all *as narratives*, on the literal level. The event described in 'The Metamorphosis' is quite as real as any other literary event."[52] Indeed, his emphasis of the phrase "*as narratives*," followed by his clarification of this as a reference to the literal level, evokes the four levels of traditional allegory.

Furthermore, as Gavriel Ben-Ephraim notes in "Making and Breaking Meaning: Deconstruction, Four-Level Allegory and 'The Metamorphosis,'" "in Kafka's handling of transformation it is striking that allegory begins precisely where metaphor ends, the obliteration of Gregor's humanity also obliterates the ground for a figurative equation between a man and a bug."[53] Ben-Ephraim ties this "erasure of the human" to Kafka's choice of protagonist and to the philo-sophical implications for readers.[54] To this end, Kafka's symbolism "allows the presentation of non-images or anti-images, metaphor in the process of negating itself. Kafka can thus capture the uncapturable in effaced forms and stilled voices, examples of the collapse of being."[55] The expression of allegory in the text begins with the initial metaphor of the story. This initial metaphor, and the world it constructs, helps to distinguish the fantastic from the new fantastic.

But the symmetrical and converse relationship between hesitation and adaptation remains problematic. As Todorov uses these terms, we are led to believe that these refer only to the action of the protagonist. The protagonist in the fantastic narrative hesitates at the beginning. He is like a frightened child in a fun house, skulking by the front door until pushed in by the ticket-taker. There is a clear distinction between the protagonist and the supernatural event which he inevitably confronts. The protagonist is not of the supernatural. The protagonist is, as Todorov explains, rational and logical, despite his innate fear of an order which exists beyond the limits of rationality and logic. The supernatural event, on the other hand, is an intrusion of the supernatural into a clearly defined natural order. Todorov posits the distinction between hesitation and adaptation and this seems to refer only to the protagonist's hesitation, or the protagonist's adaptation to the rules governing a new world. His analysis represents the tie between the protagonist's identity and the transformed circumstances of setting that distinguish the features of the new fantastic evident in Kafka from those of the nineteenth-century incarnation of the genre, wherein the protagonist is never transformed by the supernatural. The "tension experienced between the 'supernatural' events . . . and the meticulous, 'realistic and natural' language that gives them form" produces a kind of unreason emblematized through transformation.[56] The title of Kafka's story and Todorov's analysis of this particular story as indicative of the shape of the new narrative of the newly configured supernatural (out of Kafka's other works, only *The Castle* receives a brief mention) point to the necessity of transformation. The transformed genre, like the body of the transformed protagonist, presupposes an interaction between protagonist and environment that is absent in earlier fantastic narratives.

Todorov's treatment of *The Castle*, however, is of particular interest to this discussion of the permeable boundaries between protagonist and environment which demarcate this new expression of the fantastic impulse. Likewise, Todorov's mention of *The Castle* contrasts directly to Deleuze and Guattari's discussion of the significance of Kafka's protagonists. Todorov transitions to *The Castle* after referring to Sartre's assertion that "there is now only one fantastic object: man. Not the man of religions and spiritualisms, only half committed to the world of the body, but man-as-given, man-as-nature, man-as-society, the man who takes off his hat when a hearse passes, who kneels in churches, who marches behind a flag."[57] Sartre creates a contrast between the characteristics of the modern citizen, his actions purportedly governed by progress and economy, and the fantastic. Todorov concurs here. This automatic man "is precisely the fantastic being" whose existence necessitates that "the fantastic become the rule, not the exception."[58] This protagonist transforms and is transformed by setting.

The identification of the reader with the protagonist is absent in this genre beyond the fantastic. The fantastic included a "hero with whom the reader identifies [as] a perfectly normal being," but the new genre features a "central character who becomes 'fantastic.'"[59] Interestingly enough, Todorov includes quotes around the term fantastic only here. Even the term, in bold face and presented as an adequate title for an entire genre throughout much of this book, does not quite signify the change in character precipitated by this new kind of literature.

In *Kafka: Toward a Minor Literature*, Deleuze and Guattari, on the other hand, contend that the opposite relation between reader and protagonist adequately expresses the criteria of the new literature precipitated by Kafka. Above all, they do not believe that the animal protagonists of Kafka's earlier stories can adequately express the relation between man and society that Kafka also deals with in *The Castle*. For Deleuze and Guattari, "Gregor's deterritorialization through the becoming-animal fails [in that] the acts of becoming-animal cannot follow their principle all the way through." They wonder if, in fact, "the animals [are] still too formed, too significative, too territorialized."[60]

Deleuze and Guattari address Kafka's selection of animal protagonists in the early tales and assert that the vehicle provided by the animal protagonist is inherently limited. Instead, the resolution of the conflicts first sensed by the animals "can be really expressed only in the novels, in the attempts at novels, as the third component of the machine of expression."[61] Their speculations on the possible success of "a novel about the bureaucratic world of ants or about the Castle of the termites" express a preference not just for a particular narrative form, but for the novel in its concrete dominance.[62] Deleuze and Guattari demonstrate their belief in the value of the novel primarily because of its role in the twentieth century as the dominant form of narrative, and, as Lukács argues throughout *The Theory of the Novel*, a vehicle itself formed to accompany the developing consciousness of a specific social assemblage.[63]

Their assertion that "the becoming-animal was not rich enough in articulations and junctions" hinges on an assessment of the character as well as the genre housing that character.[64] This statement about the limits of the becoming-animal can also be read as an indictment of the fabulistic narratives that include such creatures as characters. This line of reasoning implies a valuation of the realistic novel at odds with Todorov's assessment of the significance of the new fantastic inaugurated by Kafka and further developed by writers such as Borges and Calvino. Deleuze and Guattari state that these hypothetical Kafka novels would have equated his work with Čapek's, whose *War with the Newts* also relies on the disorienting effect produced by a meeting of animals and humans.[65] They surmise, somewhat derogatively, that, in this situation, "[Kafka] would have written a science fiction novel."[66] Their criticism seems to be with the clear objective of Čapek's work, and implies a valuation of genres that presupposes a transcendent value to the novel. But as Ivan Klíma, the contemporary Czech author, notes in "Čapek's Modern Apocalypse," Čapek's creative work "attempted to provide a philosophical explanation for the antagonisms that were repeatedly plunging the world into crisis."[67] While Deleuze and Guattari discuss the peculiar advantages and struggles of the minor literature, they devalue Čapek's philosophical and aesthetic struggle against very real threats to the individual posed by "uncompromising and aggressive ideologies which sought to reduce even the most complex problems and conflicts to the simplistic language of slogans."[68] Furthermore, their viewpoint that "Kafka's principal animal tales were written just before *The Trial* or at the same time as it, like a sort of counterpoint to the novel which liberates itself from all animal concern to the benefit of a much higher concern" implies that all animal protagonists are identical, and that the form of these tales is not related to the forms of their protagonists.[69] The "higher concern" that they speak of, the place of the individual in a complex and changing society, implies the value of political questions over concerns regarding the limits of the human. The criteria that Deleuze and Guattari prefer are those same textual characteristics called into question so acutely by Kafka's postmodern descendants.

For Todorov, on the other hand, the metamorphosis that produces Gregor, the insect-human, is significant because this literary metamorphosis echoes the realities of the outside world. Todorov asserts that the metamorphosis in Kafka's text "will have consequences for the technique of the genre."[70] This seems like a bold prediction: while the transformation in Kafka's text is significant, it is not the first time that a literary character has been changed into an animal. However, as Todorov's discussion of Sartre suggests, this new genre has itself surfaced in the midst of an overwhelming questioning of categories of natural and unnatural themselves. The new fantastic stems from a uniquely modern worldview, where adaptation, a recent concept, begins to coincide with transgression, a seemingly outdated concept. To this end, transformation does not result in any kind of spiritual transcendence. Instead, transformation is reduced to a process of bodily adaptation made necessary by increasingly degraded physical and social environments.

Kafka's use of narrative emphasizes the totalizing world-change characteristic of this new fantastic. In "The Metamorphosis," Gregor quickly adjusts to the limitations imposed by changes in physical form. As soon as Gregor awakes, he is aware of his new form, which is made up of his "armor-plated back . . . domelike brown belly . . . [and] numerous legs . . . wav[ing] helplessly before his eyes."[71] Gregor's difficulties in moving are not caused by his disbelief regarding his new body, the various features of which, ranging from his numerous legs to "the itching place which was surrounded by many small white spots the nature of which he could not understand," are described in great detail, but by his inability to adjust to the very real possibilities and limitations imposed by his new form.[72] Here, Kafka uses a technique Gerald Prince terms a "reality effect" to expand beyond the limits of novelistic realism, despite the customary use of such an effect to connote the real in a manner that "characterizes realistic narrative."[73] Whereas the fantastic as genre is signaled by astonishment at details which contradict a predetermined natural, "The Metamorphosis" is built from this lack of astonishment. The impossible, or unnatural, one day made both possible and natural, is calmly accepted without surprise. Like the hooded figures in M. C. Escher's *Ascending and Descending*, eternally and simultaneously ascending and descending an impossible stair structure, Samsa accepts his own seemingly impossible body structure, and reacts without questioning the possibility of his situation, or the structural possibility of his own physical form. Instead, he sets to work, forcing toothless jaws around the doorknob.

The metamorphosis that, for Todorov, "will have consequences for the technique of the genre," is a metamorphosis which is only apparent through the physical transformation of the protagonist.[74] The details of Gregor's body, themselves expanding as Gregor accepts his animal body over his human consciousness, help to redetermine the relation of character to object so central to Kafka.

Visualizing the Monstrous

Fairchild draws our attention to and magnifies our encounter with insects and other arthropods in order to explore philosophical questions more pertinent to humans. Fairchild's book exemplifies, through the perspective of the photos and the syntax of the text, a rendering of the natural as fantastic. To begin, Fairchild repeatedly personifies insects, turning them into active agents pitted against man. Like Kafka, Fairchild simultaneously humanizes and dehumanizes the insect-machine. For Fairchild, "man's own real struggle for the supremacy of the world is his struggle to control these tiny monsters."[75]

Fairchild begins the book with a frontal view of a wolf spider, which, while not an insect, belongs to the phylum Arthropoda (figure 13.1). In his meditations on the image, Fairchild evokes a variety of scenarios more likely to be encountered in the kind of expressionistic fables created by Kafka or Fritz Lang, including cannibalism, the doppelgänger specter of a spider meeting its own outgrown exoskeleton, and the distinct possibility that a supersized wolf spider would subsist on human flesh.

In his discussion of this frontal view of a mature male spider, Fairchild directly connects the individuality so prized by Western culture, itself made up of "a thousand generations of beings," to the fundamental isolation of creatures

Figure 13.1.   Fairchild's Wolf Spider

which are seemingly identical. Fairchild confronts the alien view of a wolf spider, legs bristling, its many eyes peering at the camera, with a philosophical question: "[I]s it not probable that we cling so dearly to the idea of our own existence as individuals that we forget we are only halves of a whole, and that the whole itself is only a fraction of that vague living something spread out over the earth, moving in millions of places at once which we call a living species?"[76] While his question seems broad and entirely unanswerable, it highlights the role of the magnified animal image in this philosophical speculation. Fairchild derides spiritual explanations for existence, remarking that "it is no wonder we fall back on mysticism whenever we try to explain it."[77] Instead, Fairchild, like the modernists, seeks to explain existential quandaries without resorting to sentimentality.

For Fairchild, and for Kafka, the image of the supersized insect operates as an agent capable of representing the dialectic of individual identity and social uniformity explored so intently by writers and artists confronted by the disjunction between the fading illusion of natural harmony and the more hostile realism of the mechanized city. The language of mechanization motivates Fairchild's discussion of the spider:

> The male spider seems peculiarly to be just a tool in the machinery of descent, merely a carrier of the male germ cells which, whenever, and not before, they come into contact with their female counterparts, start into activity the marvelous growth which results in new individuals similar to itself.[78]

The spider is a mechanized unit, a metonymy certainly exacerbated by the machine-like appearance of a hardened shell, but also a unit with a limited purpose.

The use of the magnified and otherworldly insect body as the form for exploring these kinds of questions allows Fairchild and Kafka to avoid the binarism of traditional allegory. Kafka's use of this motif allows him to collapse the daemon, an agent that can be thought of as a kind of embodied machine, and the locus of his "quest." As Angus Fletcher points out, the allegorical agent moves through an external landscape designed to edify the protagonist through his/her completion of tasks. The completion of these tasks, in both medieval allegory and contemporary science fiction, results ultimately in a union of the successful agent with the divine. By defeating the frail impulses of the bodily nature, the personified Goodman prevails, and the personified virtues prepare a machine or device to whisk the protagonist to some version of paradise. Fletcher focuses on the machine as the ideal allegorical motif because it literalizes this process of transcendence. The machine is an allegorical motif that, as material form, manifests the movement of the agent.[79]

Kafka's narrative, however, does not permit this free movement of the agent. There is no sacred place or "cosmic center . . . free from contamination."[80] Or is there? Gregor's room reeks of a squalor that calls to mind the unsavory hotel rooms he frequented as a traveling salesman. The cramped interior of the apartment serves as a microcosm of the gray city outside the window. But as Gregor's vision fades, and his appetite diminishes so that he is no longer even attracted to rancid milk, he becomes the inhabitant of an environment that is both pure and repugnant: his own shell. This shell, moreover, is both agent and locus. In the traditional allegory,

> the allegorist can develop a sort of mental space, in which by concentrating the thought of the hero on a given object, that hero seems to be placed *in* a symbolic center. Besides being places, the sacred, isolated *locus* can take the form of consecrated talismanic objects, or consecrated moments of time. Our notion of allegorical ornament requires such a reduction of the universal genus to the universal species, of kosmos in its macrocosmic sense to kosmos in its microcosmic sense. We find precisely this. Kosmos becomes the "sacred detail." Despite its small-scale magnitude it can substitute for any much greater and more obvious symbol of the center.[81]

In Kafka's narrative, the allegorical ornament is the sacred loci. Samsa's body operates as the site of this commingling of macrocosmos and microcosmos, cosmological terms signifying the outer universe and the human sphere. This relationship in traditional allegory creates a series of top-down correspondences between the macro- and microcosmoi. This linear relationship parallels the always forward movement of the allegorical hero. However, the supersized insect specifically, as an allegorical, and highly visual, motif only possible by the early twentieth century, further disrupts this relationship. The photographic technique employed by Fairchild, for example, allows the peculiar details of the insect form to become the "sacred details" that enable this meditation on microcosmos and macrocosmos. However, the validity of the linear strata, the movement from micro to macro so central for traditional allegory (evident, most prominently, in Erich Auerbach's "Figura") is questioned by this motif that likewise reverses notions of micro and macro.

The insect, the infinitesimal, the insignificant, becomes magnified as an object and as a presence. Gregor's body (which itself moves from being too heavy for two men to carry to being so light that it is swept out of the room with a broom) emits a gravity that impacts his family. They ignore him, but cannot ignore his body, even as he slowly conceals himself in an exoskeleton that prevents him from moving beyond his room. Eventually, even his vision fades, perhaps his compound eyes coated in chitinous cataracts. The hero moves toward a cosmos even more micro than the human sphere; at the same time, it is closer to the macrocosmos, which, in keeping with Kafka's mystical inclinations, exists but remains inexpressible. This form, then, is particularly attuned to Gregor's doubt and emotional and physical stasis: "Franz Kafka's allegories are just as concerned with doubt, which is intellectual, as they are with emotive ambivalence; or rather, with him the ambivalence of feeling becomes intellectual as well."[82] Fletcher connects Kafka's use of allegory to the psychological peculiarities, as detailed in Freud's "Notes on a Case of Obsessional Neurosis" exacerbated by corporate culture. We can also consider this from a narratological standpoint in order to understand how this particular motif impacts and reflects Kafka's use of allegory as a symbolic mode.

The ambivalence of feeling that Fletcher speaks of becomes, also, ambivalence toward movement. We have already noted that Samsa is alone in his exoskeleton. The exoskeleton externalizes what, for mammals, should be internal. At the same time, what was internal serves to restrain and encage. The paradox at the very root of the placement of human consciousness in exoskeletal form results in a collapsed allegory that "show[s] no diminishing, [but] only a confusion . . . of the semantic and syntactic processes of double or multiple-leveled polysemy."[83] The increased irony, or paradox, which Northrop Frye details in *Anatomy of Criticism* in relation to narrative form and content, manifests itself as well in the selection of motif.

Of course, this is not to imply that Kafka was an entomologist, or was able to distinguish between hymenoptera and coleoptera or even between a spider and an insect. The words Kafka uses to describe Samsa as vermin and pest have particular connotations when applied to people. The significance of this use of the insect, however, lies in its magnification. The placement of the supersized insect in the human environment allows this particular motif to engage the multileveled polysemy so significant to the contemporary use of allegory.

The key element of this magnification is also a resignification. The magnified insect also means something different than the regular bug. The common denotative meanings of insect, roach, and vermin are likewise called into question by what is, above all, a new motif. This relationship between the nonmagnified insect, the magnified insect, and the modern individual removes the magnified insect from the interpretive dyad that characterizes the relationship between worker and nonmagnified insect.

Kafka's metamorphosis of these traditional narrative forms parallels the metamorphoses that drive Kafka's narrative. "The Metamorphosis," like many of Kafka's narratives, moves toward stasis. The shape of the story comes from the events of the first page, which overshadow the significance of the events that follow. Indeed, the conclusion of the story is written in the first paragraph. Like the many fragments and false beginnings which populate Kafka's notebooks, "The Metamorphosis" is a paraphrastic parable. To use the terms popularized by Gérard Genette in *Narrative Discourse*, the transformation, both proleptic and analeptic, cancels itself out.[84] It is proleptic in that the transformation, the main "action" of the story, occurs before the story. The transformation, an indeterminate, but highly complex, set of events occurs, like the actual transformation of a beetle from a grub, in the amorphous larval state of unsettling dreams. Grete's own transformation, at the end of the narrative, constitutes the inverse moment anticipated by Gregor's transformation. The abstract-machine suggested by Deleuze and Guattari results in a series of possibilities stemming from these reciprocally canceling actions. But Deleuze and Guattari's interpretation of the text creates a binary relationship between these two actions. Gregor's transformation anticipates, forces, and is canceled out by Grete's. Likewise, Grete's transformation, which occurs outdoors, and after Gregor's body has been disposed of by the cleaning woman, lies outside of the narrative. "The Metamorphosis" is written, perhaps with the tattooing device used in "In the Penal Colony," on Gregor's exoskeleton.

These textual and metatextual metamorphoses parallel Fairchild's evocation of actual insect metamorphosis in the *Book of Monsters*. He treats this topic through a discussion of the development of *Allorhina nitida*, the June beetle, a species not that dissimilar in appearance from Nabokov's sketch of Kafka's dog-sized beetle. Fairchild provides two images: one is a side view of the June beetle, the other a side view of its larva. The passage that accompanies the image of the larva, an elongated gelatinous mass, provides a detailed account of the physiological changes that occur in the cocoon:

The change begins; each organ goes to pieces, disintegrates, becomes a mass of disconnected cells, so that the body filled with these, becomes, as it were, a bag of mush. This mushy fluid has been likened by entomologists to the disintegrated tissues which inflammation causes in our own bodies. If, then, you should slit it open at this stage, you would find no alimentary canal, no salivary glands, no muscles, simply a thick fluid, with here and there a thicker lump, that is attached at certain places to the inside of the sac wall. These lumps are formed of groups of active cells which were not disintegrated in the general breakdown of the muscle tissue, and these form the nuclei around which the new creature is to be built. These groups of cells grow rapidly, feeding on the fluid mass of broken-down tissue much as a young chick inside the egg feeds on the yolk, and builds up the whole complicated structure of the winged beetle, which seems to have no possible relation to the white grub out of whose body it was made.[85]

The extensive remodeling of the organism begins at the cellular level. The mature beetle and its larva differ in terms of both their exterior and interior structure. Fairchild describes the stages of this formation, pausing only to relish in the grotesqueness of the goo from which the beetle emerges. But the actual larva, or its transformation, does not lead to the allegorization of the insect form found elsewhere in the text.

The entry that accompanies the image of the mature *Allorhina nitida*, however, becomes linked to the very foundations of rationality underlying modern science-based culture:

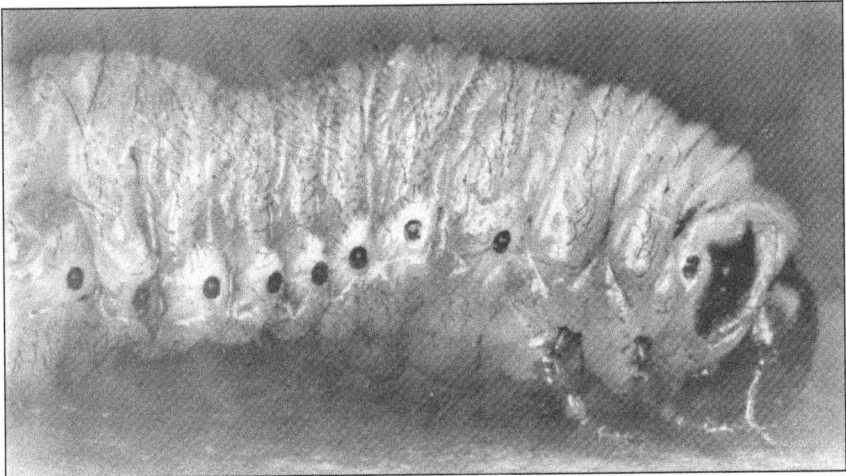

Figure 13.2. The June Beetle Larva

In looking at these two strange beings . . . we cannot feel confident that science has gone very far in giving us the reasons for the things we see. They seem no more alike than fish and tortoise or bird and quadruped and yet, before our very eyes, in one brief year, the one turns into the other. This beetle dies, and leaves behind a hundred little cells, parts of its own body and the body of its mate. These paired cells, the fertilized eggs, grow rapidly into the form of the clumsy, helpless grub which feeds upon the leaves, only to break up and form themselves again into this armor-plated creature of the beetle world. There must be something as radically wrong with our individualistic ideas of today as there was with the conception of a flat world which prevailed before the time of Columbus. Perhaps if we stop trying to think of these manifestations of beetle life as individuals and think of them as parts of one great organism scattered over the surface of the earth, these striking differences will seem no stranger to us than do the difference in the various stages of a flower's life. The beetle forms inside the grub and the tulip flower bud forms inside the bulb. If tulip flowers could fly, we should then have the strange spectacle of the opening of the scale-covered tulip bulb and the coming forth of the gorgeous colored flower which sailed away to shed its seeds in someone else's garden. I think that this is the way we must look at it if we would get a clear idea of this strangest of phenomena, metamorphosis.[86]

Fairchild's extension of the discussion of insect development to individuality seems, at first glance, ill-founded and out of place. All creatures, from humans to the flying flowers he evokes at the end of this passage, arise from the splitting of fertilized cells. His meditation on these far-flung themes forms the subtext of the *Book of Monsters*. While it does classify and describe in sufficient scientific detail the life processes of insects, this book, like "The Metamorphosis," serves as an iconic narrative. Furthermore, this iconic narrative, or story of a symbol, develops a new symbol which fills the void.

This particular icon, the supersized insect, fills a visual, philosophical, and linguistic void. There seems to be no textual clue to explain Fairchild's rhetorical move from insect metamorphosis to individualism. The phrase "armor-plated creature of the beetle world" does suggest that the beetle is otherworldly and warlike. Unlike other animals equally equipped for the struggles of daily existence, the beetle resembles the most destructive of human machines. Magnified, Fairchild's beetles share an aesthetic kinship with the rudimentary tanks that metamorphosed into the panzer divisions of World War II.

We are to view the beetle as alien because its very life-cycle pits it beyond the realms of human understanding. The world of the beetle is more akin to the aesthetic model promulgated by the futurists than by the nascent bourgeois comforts at the heart of a humanism which was under attack, both literally and

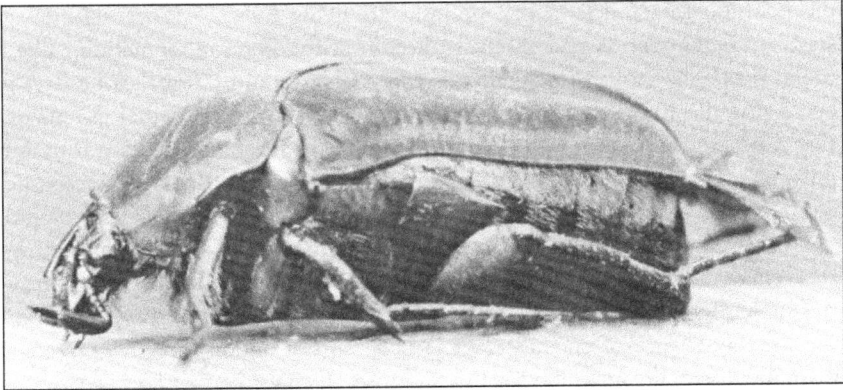

Figure 13.3. The June Beetle

metaphorically, by the twentieth century. The pan-identity of the beetle stems from an unchanging instinct. The beetle does not need another of its species to realize its own beetleness. But, unlike human social institutions, the beetle world is totalizing, and unchanging.

The exoskeleton becomes a barrier that confuses intelligence and instinct. Is it really the beetle world, the world of animal instinct, that is so unchanging and complete? Or is it the human world of reason that devastates and oppresses the subtle whims of instinct? This paradox hints at the features of the supersized insect which render it so useful as an expression of the modern condition. Unlike the robot or machine, which externally resembles the insect, the insect constantly "transform[s] intelligent acts into instinctive acts."[87] E. L. Bouvier, a French entomologist writing in the early twentieth century, makes this statement in *The Psychic Life of Insects* in a discussion of the adaptation of insects in relation to instinctual traits. He cites Henri Bergson here to clearly distinguish the animal from the human:

> Among animals, invention is never more than a variation on the theme of routine. Locked up within the habits of the species, the animal succeeds, no doubt, in broadening these by its individual initiative; but it escapes from automatism only for an instant, just long enough to create a new automatism. The gates of its prison close as soon as opened; dragging on its chain, it merely succeeds in lengthening it. With man consciousness breaks the chain.[88]

Bouvier then traces the paths of the articulates and the vertebrates to "an obstacle . . . that doubtless almost checked the progress of animal life."[89] Bergson sees this obstacle as the shell: "The animal which is shut up in a citadel or in a coat of mail is condemned to an existence of half-sleep. It is in this torpor that the Echinoderms and even the mollusks are living today."[90] The evolutionary stasis of Echinoderms and mollusks becomes, for Bergson, something like a moral flaw. The "torpor" of their existence calls to mind Gregor's long days of occupying the stimulus-deprived niche under his bed. Bergson then points out that fishes and insects moved beyond the mollusks through the motivating impulse of active life. The language Bergson uses closely parallels the characteristics of Gregor's active life as a salesman: "In both groups the inefficiency of the protective envelope was compensated for by an agility that enabled them to escape their enemies and also to take the offensive and to choose the place and time of the encounter."[91] The inefficiency of the shell, shed by animals eager to choose the time and place of encounters, enacts a transformation directly counter to Gregor's. Here, the antediluvian fish and insects, concerned with efficiency and punctuality, are not becoming-animals, but becoming-capitalists.

Conclusion

The contrast between the realm of the insect and the human exists also at the level of sensory perception. As an allegorical trope, the supersized insect serves as more than a form which is regarded by a human observer. Instead, the insect-human also has access to a heightened range of sensory perception. The gaze of the insect-human peers back into the lens of the compound camera. The creation of the insect-human, both in literature and in scientific photography, opens up this new position, this new monstrous position from which an observer can observe humanity.

A desire for the perceptive faculty of an insect and the desire to perceive an insect eye to eye are analogous. Fairchild's *Book of Monsters*, fittingly, ends with an evocation of this desire: "What a world this would be to us had we microscopic vision. A thousand times as many beasts to look at, a thousand times as many things to see and understand."[92] How do we read Fairchild's desire for microscopic vision? What does he mean by it? There are two immediate possibilities. The first is that he wishes humans possessed the magnifying power made possible by his camera. Our vision, not telescopic but microscopic, would necessitate a constant meditation on the microcosmos. Thus attuned to the microcosmic, we would find "a thousand times as many things to see and understand."[93] These things, though, would be gathered quite close. The second possibility is that microscopic vision refers to the visual capabilities of the microcosmic. The beasts of the microcosmos view one another with microscopic vision. If we saw as they see, then we would gain in understanding. These two possibilities are one and the same. While Fairchild's macrophotographs do not show insects broken into facets, as they would be from an insect's perspective, they visualize the insect while at the same time mimicking the visual capabilities of the insect.

The supersized image of the insect allows us to both "see" the insect and to "see like" the insect for the first time. Fairchild's technique, like Kafka's use of the insect-agent, is an attempt to look at and to look like the creatures of the microcosmos. Both Kafka and Fairchild, responding to a corporate and mechanized culture, fixate on the insect as a site of resistance and inquiry. The supersized insect, furthermore, has frustrated Kafka critics interested in the generic classification of "The Metamorphosis" precisely because of the paradoxes inherent in the form. The bug is often linked to binary allegorical meaning. However, we must distinguish the nonmagnified insect from the supersized insect. The supersized insect, or the insect magnified and explored through the development of the biological sciences in the late nineteenth and early twentieth centuries, resignifies as an allegorical motif characterized by interpretive multiplicity.

This motif engages the primary ideological concerns of the new fantastic—in particular, the role of the supernatural in an increasingly denatured world—in ways unavailable to purely artificial or mechanical motifs. David Fairchild's long-neglected book of insect photographs, then, allows us to read Kafka's "The Metamorphosis" not just as an allegory of the effect of modern work on the individual, but also as an expression of the fundamental conflicts between the modern world and the natural.

Notes

1. I would like to thank Nancy Corber of Fairchild Tropical Garden in Miami, Florida, for her help. All images from Fairchild's *Book of Monsters* are courtesy of the Fairchild Tropical Botanic Garden Archive.

2. Vladimir Nabokov, *Vladimir Nabokov Lectures on Literature*, ed. Fredson Bowers (New York: Houghton Mifflin, 2002), 258.

3. Brian Boyd, *Vladimir Nabokov: The American Years* (Princeton, NJ: Princeton University Press, 1993), 66.

4. Nabokov, 258.

5. Ibid., 258, 259.

6. Franz Kafka, *The Metamorphosis*, trans. and ed. Stanley Corngold (New York: Bantam, 1986), xix.

7. José B. Monleón, *A Specter Is Haunting Europe: A Sociohistorical Approach to the Fantastic* (Princeton, NJ: Princeton University Press, 1990), 12.

8. Ibid., 81.

9. Ibid., 138.

10. Ibid., 139.

11. David Fairchild and Marian Fairchild, *Book of Monsters: Portraits and Biographies of a Few of the Inhabitants of Woodland and Meadow* (Washington, DC: National Geographic Society, 1914), 7.

12. Ibid.

13. Nabokov, 259.

14. Stanley Corngold, *Franz Kafka: The Necessity of Form* (Ithaca, NY: Cornell University Press, 1988), 56.

15. Theo Elm, "Problematisierte Hermeneutik zur 'Uneigentichlichkeit' in Kafkas Kleiner Prosa," in *Die Deutsche Parabel: Zur Theorie Einer Modernen Erzählform*, ed. Josef Billen (Darmstadt: Wissenschaftliche Buchgesellschaft, 1986), 322 (translation mine).

16. Mark M. Anderson, *Kafka's Clothes: Ornament and Aestheticism in the Habsburg Fin de Siècle* (Oxford: Clarendon Press, 1992), 124.

17. Ibid.

18. Corngold, 59.

19. Ibid., 56.

20. Ibid.

21. Anderson, 58.

22. Ibid.

23. Ibid.

24. Mabel Moraña, *Kafka: Procesamiento de "La Metamorfosis"* (Montevideo: Fundación de Cultura Universitaria, 1975), 9 (translation mine).

25. Ibid.

26. Ibid.

27. Franz Kafka, "The Metamorphosis," in *The Sons*, trans. Willa and Edwin Muir (New York: Schocken Books, 1989), 96.

28. Indeed, her attempt to classify Gregor as species, paired with his denial of this classification, calls to mind the social parasitism found in some insect species. Various species of beetle, for instance, fool ants into providing for them. In *Journey to the Ants*, E. O. Wilson notes that "many socially parasitic beetles and other insects, a majority of which are radically different in shape and size, have mastered the art of acquiring the colony odor or the attractive scent of an art larva." In describing this arrangement, Wilson paraphrases another entomologist, William Morton Wheeler: "It is as though a human family were to invite gigantic lobsters, midget tortoises, and similar monsters to dinner, and never notice the difference." This description of social parasitism eerily parallels the relationship between Gregor and his family. E. O. Wilson and Bert Hölldobler, *Journey to the Ants: A Story of Scientific Exploration* (Cambridge, MA: Harvard University Press, 1994), 123.

29. Kafka, 96.

30. A reading of Samsa as a dung beetle connects "The Metamorphosis" to earlier insect narratives. While insects "have long been powerful spiritual symbols," tales featuring insectoid protagonists, Clarke suggests, are more prevalent in the postmodern era. Bruce Clarke, *Allegories of Writing: The Subject of Metamorphosis* (Albany: State University of New York Press, 1995), 84.

31. Kafka, 96.

32. Ibid., 3.

33. Roy Pascal, "Kafka's Parables: Ways Out of the Dead End," in *The World of Franz Kafka*, ed. J. P. Stern (New York: Holt, 1980), 118.

34. Allan Blunden, "A Chronology of Kafka's Life," in *The World of Franz Kafka*, ed. J. P. Stern (New York: Holt, 1980), 22.

35. Jürg Schubiger, *Franz Kafka "Die Verwandlung": Eine Interpretation* (Frankfurt: Atlantis Verlag, 1969), 27–40.

36. Jürg Schubiger, *Franz Kafka "Die Verwandlung": Eine Interpretation* (Frankfurt: Atlantis Verlag, 1969), 27–40, quoted in Hartmut Binder, "*The Metamorphosis*: The Long Journey into Print," in *The Metamorphosis*, ed. Stanley Corngold (New York: Norton, 1996).

37. Ibid.

38. Binder, "*The Metamorphosis*: The Long Journey into Print."

39. Ibid.

40. Ibid.

41. Tzvetan Todorov, *The Fantastic: A Structural Approach to a Literary Genre*, trans. Richard Howard (Ithaca, NY: Cornell University Press, 1975), 181.

42. Ibid., 165.

43. Ibid., 168.

44. Ibid.

45. Ibid.

46. Ibid., 168, 169.

47. Ibid., 183.

48. Ibid., 171.

49. Ibid., 171–72.

50. Mark M. Anderson's *Kafka's Clothes*, for example, stresses Kafka's debt to decadent aesthetics. Anderson points out that, for many interpretive methodologies, Kafka's writings, "rooted in no particular culture or period . . . seemed to be meant for all cultures, thus providing an example of the hermetic, autonomous, sui generis modern artwork that apparently validated these very formalist, ahistorical methodologies." Anderson seeks to "reveal the traces of fin-de-siècle ornament" in Kafka's mature work (from 1912 onward) in order to historically contextualize Kafka. Anderson, 10, 15.

51. Todorov, 172.

52. Ibid., 172.

53. Gavriel Ben-Ephraim, "Making and Breaking Meaning: Deconstruction, Four-Level Allegory and 'The Metamorphosis.'" *The Midwest Quarterly* 35 (1994): 450–68.

54. Ibid.

55. Ibid.

56. Monleón, 102.

57. Todorov, 173.

58. Ibid.

59. Ibid., 174.

60. Gilles Deleuze and Félix Guattari, *Kafka: Toward a Minor Literature*, trans. Dana Polan (Minneapolis: University of Minnesota Press, 1986), 16.

61. Ibid., 37.

62. Ibid., 38.

63. Georg Lukács, *The Theory of the Novel*, trans. Anna Bostock (Boston: MIT Press, 1974), 56–70.

64. Deleuze and Guattari, 38.

65. Karel Čapek's *War with the Newts* and *R.U.R.* are particularly important for their political, generic, and aesthetic significance. Čapek is credited with influencing both

science fiction and contemporary political satire. Likewise, the use of collage, and the presentation of newspaper reports, advertisements, and scientific treatises in *War with the Newts* foreshadows the textual interplay so crucial to the postmodern aesthetic.

66. Deleuze and Guattari, 38.

67. Karel Čapek, *War with the Newts*, trans. M. and R. Weatherall (Evanston, IL: Northwestern University Press, 1996), x.

68. Ibid., xv.

69. Deleuze and Guattari, 15.

70. Todorov, 174.

71. Kafka, 53.

72. Ibid., 54.

73. Gerald Prince, *A Dictionary of Narratology* (Lincoln: University of Nebraska Press, 1995), 80.

74. Todorov, 174.

75. Fairchild, 5.

76. Ibid., 47.

77. Ibid.

78. Ibid.

79. We have only to consider Alain de Lille's *Anticlaudianus*, where the virtues both construct and instruct, or the various quests in science fiction novels for some mysterious energy source to allow the heroes to escape the treacheries of the forbidden planet, to see this correlation between built form and successful spiritual and moral edification.

80. Angus Fletcher, *Allegory: The Theory of a Symbolic Mode* (Ithaca, NY: Cornell University Press, 1964), 213.

81. Ibid., 214.

82. Ibid., 227.

83. Ibid., 230.

84. Gérard Genette, *Narrative Discourse: An Essay in Method*, trans. Jane E. Lewin (Ithaca, NY: Cornell University Press, 1990), 40.

85. Fairchild, 115.

86. Ibid., 113.

87. E. L. Bouvier, *The Psychic Life of Insects*, trans. L. O. Howard (New York: The Century Co., 1922), 357.

88. Ibid.

89. Ibid., 358.

90. Ibid.

91. Ibid., 359.

92. Fairchild, 247.

93. Ibid.

CHAPTER 14

Extraterrestrial Kafka: Ahead to the Graphic Novel

Henry Sussman

Amid the Flows

There is always something out of the world, by which we probably mean radically weird and inexhaustible, about Kafka. The weirdness arrives in broad strokes and tiny splashes. It encompasses the earthshaking fictive premises of *The Trial* (*Der Prozess*), "The Metamorphosis" ("*Die Verwandlung*"), and "The Burrow" ("*Der Bau*"), which have given rise to innumerable extensions and adaptations in fantastic literature, science fiction, and the graphic novel, but also such specific touches as the servants' uniforms in *The Castle* (*Das Schloß*) and the hum of the castle telephone system. Often in Kafka's writing, there is no greater weirdness than a minor detail. Or a creature that may not exactly be human but that thinks and generates discourse, not only obscuring the boundaries between the human and the animal but inquiring, at the most elemental level, into the nature, qualities, domain, and pertinence of consciousness and cognition.[1]

We can watch in bemused awe as the overarching skew and strangeness in his fiction ricochet beyond his written corpus into entire orders of speculative and conceptual derangement. I think in particular of the degree to which Kafka's writing, more than any other single factor, occasions Deleuze and Guattari's notion of deterritorialization,[2] a general category of social and psychic alienation and displacement amid global flows of money, goods, migration (some forced), sexual traffic, and signs (the latter accorded the same status by the mega-trope of flow); amid current hegemonic incursions by war machines on a greater than continental scale. Deterritorialization, of which Kafka is the exemplary visionary and poet, is for Deleuze and Guattari always the consequence of a crisis of encoding and decoding that has resulted in mutations.

> The modern theory of mutations has clearly demonstrated that a code which necessarily relates to a population, has an essential margin of decoding: not only does every code have supplements capable of free variation, but a single segment may be copied twice, the second copy left free for variation. In addition, fragments of code may be transferred from the cells of one species to those of another, Man and Mouse, Monkey and Cat, by viruses or through other procedures. This involves not translations between codes . . . but a single phenomenon we call surplus value of code, or side-communication. . . . Every code is affected by a margin of decoding due to these supplements and surplus values—supplements in the order of a multiplicity, surplus values in the order of a rhizome.[3]

This sample passage, in which Deleuze and Guattari begin to characterize deterritorialization as the aftermath of a crisis in the transmission of a program or code, is redolent of the overarching wish spanning their combined project: to place an array of cultural, biological, semiological, and sociopolitical processes, all involving the transfer and decoding of signs, in parallel. The great enigma still hovering at the outreaches of their combined project is whether the exchanges of language, on the Lacanian symbolic order, comprise one flow among others, translate unproblematically into movements of goods, money, and bodily fluids, say, or whether, as deconstruction would have it, language is the very possibility of all the movements or exchanges.[4] This cataclysmic learned negotiation is left for another treatment, one less invested in the graphic novel.

But the lines immediately above set the stage for a dynamic in which deterritorialization experienced in a putative outside, that is tangibly and substantially, occasions a scrambling or reconfiguration of the codes programming the immanent behavior and possibility of the affected entities, whether individuals, communities, or biological species:

> Nomadic flows or waves of deterritorialization go from the central layer to the periphery, then from the new center to the new periphery, falling back to the old center and launching forth to the new. The organization of epistrata moves in the direction of increasing deterritorialization. . . . Not only are physical particles characterized by speeds of deterritorialization . . . but a single chemical substance (sulphur or carbon, for example) has a number of more or less deterritorialized states. The more interior milieus an organism has on its own stratum, assuring its autonomy and bringing it into a set of aleatory relations with the exterior, the more deterritorialized it is. That is why degrees of development must be understood relatively. . . . Deterritorialization must be thought of as a perfectly positive power that has degrees and thresholds (epistrata), is always relative, and has

reterritorialization as its flipside or complement. An organism that is deterritorialized in relation to the exterior necessarily reterritorializes on its interior milieus.[5]

Kafka emerges as the poet and prophet of deterritorialization in his relentless pursuit of the collapse of regimes of order and the radical mutations these constitutional crises occasion at the infrastructural level. This meticulous pursuit, all the more outrageous and horrifying in its precision and realism, may track Gregor and his social world after he has suddenly and radically switched species, flipping out (or into) our beloved giant insect with alien genetic coding, or the colonial war machine after its instrument of torture, whose program is indistinguishable from the power and justice claimed by the Judaic god, has totaled itself. The aftermath of the devastating crisis of incomprehensibility, of superannuation at the level of code, well-illustrated when Gregor as family secret is lured by his sister's playing into the public eye of the boarders, is invariably a frenetic effort of scrambling and improvization (as in jazz) within the sphere of the immanent or underlying operating system.

Institutional and Typographical Architectures

Kafka is the avatar, prophet, and bureaucrat of an alterity and resulting waves of deterritorialization that are complexly too unmotivated and unremitting ever to be resolved, rationalized, domesticated, territorialized, or disciplined in the academic sense. So unremitting are the conditions of unabashed strangeness and architectural disorientation that Kafka infuses into his characters and the predicaments besetting them that he trespasses terrestrial limits, not only rendering national boundaries of language and culture tenuous, but circumventing the notion and economy of globalization before it achieved currency.

It has long proven more fruitful to think of Kafka as an atelier or worksite of textual programming rather than as a specific author, producer, or franchiser of a limited or closed body of works. The existing "complex art-games"[6] that Kafka disfigures in the process of inventing others can surely walk, and in many cases do so, far afield, not in the mechanized march of iterability but in the improvised postures of modern dance.

This is ultimately a retracing of Kafka's cosmic journey, into fields remaining disturbingly open, even if they have been charted. Among the multiple distinctive features of his fictive and inscriptive landscapes, we want to focus on his spatial disorientation, the sordid involution of his architectural settings; on the prepossessing failure of the communications media and traffic systems that his domain encompasses; and on the blurred gender lines on which his human, animal, and mythological creatures interact, taking each other's places and forming hybrids difficult to place, perhaps, but inexhaustible in their suggestiveness. Kafka's uncanny architecture, decisive as it was to the twentieth-century imaginaries of literature and the visual arts, incorporates the threshold between the human and the animal, under his administration a particularly active and generative interface.

The cumulative effect of the calculated weird effects coinciding in this field and defining it is a relentlessly open frontier or borderline, one that has never been and never will be completely filled in. It is the paradoxical openness of architectural involution and interspecies hybridization that delineates the hinge between the global and the extraterrestrial. The Baedeker to this realm might well begin with the following blueprint of one of the court's installations, though it would surely go on to catalogue Mr. Pollunder's house, the superhighway on the way to Ramses, and the image and structure of the castle:

> "Just look at this waiting room." It was a long passage, a lobby communicating by ill-fitting doors with the different offices on the floor. Although there was no window to admit light, it was not entirely dark, for some of the offices were not properly boarded off from the passage but had an open frontage of wooden rails, reaching, however, to the roof [*denn manche Abteilungen hatten gegen den Gang zu statt einheitliche Bretterwände bloße, allerdings bis zur Decke reichende Holzgitter*], through which a little light penetrated and through which one could see a few officials as well, some writing at their desks, and some standing close to the rails peering through the interstices at the people in the lobby [*und durch die Lücken die Leute auf dem Gang beobachteten*]. There were only a few people in the lobby.[7]

Kafka's architectural blueprints to the court are ambiguous to the fullest degree: here the language of structural description and the rhetoric of bureaucratic organization and rule become indistinguishable from one another. The court lobby itself combines intrusive panoptical monitoring—the civil servants can peer down at its current occupants—with a ramshackle architectural inefficiency: the incomplete compartmental walls allow whatever illumination might enlighten this rendition of the law accidentally to filter through. The space of this particular installation is made unbearably oppressive both by a dearth of windows and by the sunlight that the windows do permit, because they refuse to open. This may well be a nightmare from the perspective of all the room's fictive users, yet it also presents a visual artist, whether of the comics variety or not, with a rich opportunity.

Since all spaces in the novel, even the church where the pivotal parable of the doorkeeper is read to Joseph K. as his ultimate sentence, "belong to the Court," it is no surprise that protagonist has wandered into a setting with similar features when he rushes up a residential staircase past child prostitutes, some with physical deformities, for his consultation with the artist Titorelli, who delivers a semiotically knowing playback of his legal fiasco.

> When he reached the third floor he had to moderate his pace, he was quite out of breath, both the stairs and the stories were disproportionately high, and the painter was said to live quite at the top, in an attic. The air was stifling; there was no well for these narrow stairs, which were enclosed on either side by blank walls, showing only at rare intervals a tiny window very high up [*Auch war die Luft sehr drückend, es gab keinen Treppenhof, die enge Treppe war auf beiden Seiten von Mauern eingeschlossen, in denen nur hier und da fast nach oben kleine Fenster angebracht waren*].[8]

Yet this now characteristic architecture is most disturbing in its complete coincidence with regimes of power, discipline, and punishment. Kafka's architectural blueprint extends into the organization and strategic operations of the law as a system of philosophical speculation that has eventuated into its practicality, its tangible application. The narrative's tangential remarks on the law, delivered by a wide range of its knowing insiders, men and women, privileged cognoscenti and peons, thus hovers on the cusp between Kant's first and second *Critiques*:

> The ranks of officials in this judiciary system mounted endlessly, so that not even the initiated could survey the hierarchy as a whole [*Die Rangordnung and Steigerung des Gerichtes sei unendlich und selbst für den Eingeweihten nicht absehbar*]. And the proceedings of the Court were generally kept secret from subordinate officials; consequently they could hardly ever quite follow in their further progress the cases on which they had worked; any particular case thus appeared in their jurisdiction often without their knowing whence it came, and passed from it they knew not whither.[9]

In this passage, architectural survey and description have made a sharp swerve into sociological mapping. The upper echelons of power in this social system are as remote and inaccessible as the Kantian transcendental, whether in its "good" emanation, as the highest authority, purified by detachment and disinterest, or in its malevolent configuration as barren nature, retaining at all times the potential of devastating outbreaks against humanity. The hierarchy of officials, in this passage, ascends toward an utterly desolate and unforgiving *human* polar region.

Galactic Mood Climates

Our tracking of Kafka's meteoric and commodious swerves toward the universe of fantastic literature and the graphic novel begins in the panoply of dimensions in which Walter Benjamin set his virtual simulation, in *The Arcades Project* (*Das Passagen-Werk*), of nineteenth-century Paris. What is astonishing about this print medium website of more than we could possibly wish to know or attend to about Paris as the portal and capital city of global modernization is that Benjamin would even attend to its modal parameters, the backdrop of cosmic ennui, inscribed in sources extending from Balzac's *Human Comedy* to Baudelaire's lyrics to Meryon's misty engravings to Grandville's galactic cartoons. It is against this backdrop of world-weary fatigue that the culture of the moment works up a voracious appetite for the cornucopia of new commodities and entertainments, and an overall addiction to sensory overload that, Benjamin argues, through a display of textual materials rather than logic, are the mainstays of European modernity.

> Only someone who has grown up in the big city can appreciate its rainy weather [*Städtiaches Regenwetter mit seiner ganz durchtriebenen Lockung*], which altogether slyly sets one dreaming back to early childhood. Rain makes everything more hidden, makes days not only gray but uniform. From morning until evening, one can do the same thing—play chess, read, engage in argument—whereas sunshine by contrast shades the hours and discountenances the dreamer. The latter, therefore, must get around the day with subterfuges—above all, must rise quite early, like the great idlers, the waterfront loafers and the vagabonds. The dreamer must get up before the sun itself. [D1a,9][10]

> Blanqui's last work [*Critique sociale*, 1885], written during his imprisonment, has remained entirely unnoticed up to now, so far as I can see. It is a cosmological speculation. Granted it appears, in its opening pages, tasteless [*abgeschmackt*] and banal. But the awkward deliberations of the autodidact are merely the prelude to a speculation that only this revolutionary could develop. . . . In fact the cosmic vision of the world which Blanqui lays out, taking his data from the mechanistic natural science of bourgeois society, is an infernal vision. At the same time it is a complement of the society to which Blanqui, in his old age, was forced to concede victory. What is so unsettling is that the presentation is so lacking in irony. It is an unconditional surrender [*eine vorbehaltlose Unterwerfung*], but it is simultaneously the most terrible indictment of a society that projects this image of the cosmos—understood as an image of itself—across the heavens. With its trenchant style [*sprachlich von sehr starker Prägung ist*], this work displays the most remarkable similarities both to Baudelaire and Nietzsche. (Letter of January 6, 1938, to Horkheimer) [D5a,6][11]

> In the idea of eternal recurrence, the historicism of the nineteenth century capsizes. As a result, every tradition, even the most recent, becomes the legacy of something that has run its course in the im-

memorial night of the ages. Tradition henceforth assumes the character of a phantasmagoria in which primal history enters the scene in ultramodern get-up [*in modernster Ausstoffierung*]. [D8a,2][12]

Life within the magic circle [*Bannkreis*] of eternal return makes for an existence that never emerges from the auratic. [D10a,1][13]

Benjamin's weather central for nineteenth-century Paris, or twentieth-century Berlin, for that matter, combines the resignation and making do of rainy days, often an edifying experience of self-discovery and interpersonal intimacy, with the programmed inevitability of the Nietzschean *ewige Wiederkehr*. On those seemingly lost days of climatic infelicity, locating their cultural capital city in the nineteenth century, play joins up with fatalism. These are days of improvised activities, trivial pursuits, and silly games. They are also the ideal moment for breaking the comic book collection out, with its piled leaves of disintegrating newsprint.

It does not surprise us that in Convolute C Benjamin plumbs to the foundations of Paris's vertical configuration, where he encounters ancient springs, sewers, metro tunnels, and the dungeons (under the Châtelet in Victor Hugo's phantasmagoria of *Les misérables*), where slave labor for the Mediterranean galleys was sequestered and the argot-song born, or that in Convolute F he assembles the textual materials illuminating iron and glass, the new smart materials liberating function from form in architecture and urban planning and allowing both the buildings (e.g., the grand train stations, the Eiffel Tower) and the infrastructure (e.g., railroad tracks) to usher in production, consumption, movement, and acceleration on an unprecedented scale. We might find it a little bit odd, but marvelous, that Benjamin devotes Convolute B to fashion—not only as a paradigmatic consumer industry of the age but as the very model for the evolution of culture in time, even if by the end of this mixed portfolio of materials he incriminates himself by suggesting that women persisted later in anthropological history than men in their horizontal positions for perambulation and related functions.

Reports on the *démolitions de Paris* by Baron Haussmann, contemporary prospectuses for major development projects, statutes regarding the employment of *filles publiques*, reports on the political swings occasioned by such events as the uprisings of 1848 and the Commune, modern-day speculations on architecture and public transportation and related topics by Le Courbousier, Georg Simmel, Sigfried Giedion, and Sigfried Kracauer: all these comprise the *matériel* and camera angles that we would expect to be followed by Benjamin's unabashedly cinematographic critico-historical *Photoapparat*. "Method of this project: literary montage. I needn't *say* anything. Merely show" (*Ich habe nichts zu sagen. Nur zu zeigen*) [N1a,8].[14] Yet *The Arcades Project* takes no less seriously—and documents no less tangibly—dimensions of modernization of a far different nature: its tempos, moods, even its collective dreams. In this much more speculative outreach, Benjamin demonstrates his solidarity with an ongoing Frankfurter Schule project whose simultaneous purviews would be phenomenological, anthropological, mass psychological, and multimedia as well as historical, literary, critical, psychoanalytical, and sociological. The literary montage that informed critique brings about effects a near-simultaneous panning from one of these discursive frameworks or perches to the next. In this virtually simultaneous overload of contrasting perspectives, the materials of *Das Passagen-Werk* allegorically enact the desperate temporalities of expansion, consumption, and perception of the historical moment. (Marx's core passages on the simultaneity of industrial manufacturing process from *Capital*, volume I, are among the materials of Convolute K [K3.1–2].) In daring to assemble the moment's collective dream or in reconstructing its distinctive moods and mood swings, Benjamin displays a more democratic receptivity to incompatible or minority reports on the megaphenomenon of modernization than we are inclined to under our contemporary division of labor of professional academic subspecializations. Which hip psychoanalytical critic engaged in spinning out the present-day dream-phantasmagoria do you know who currently entertains Jung? Benjamin certainly did.

The modal parameters of modernization, as they are assembled and extrapolated above all in Convolute D but also elsewhere, incorporate boredom, sublime world-weariness, indeed exhaustion in general, set within an urban landscape engulfed by clouds and other atmospheric downers. The externally projected sociopsychological scene of depressive "learned helplessness"[15] is undergirded, as Benjamin's extracts chronicle, by a manic release always about to break out. We can indeed argue that the nineteenth-century visual precedents to the *noir* aesthetic are the visual objective correlative to this collective mood of urban Parisian funk: that is, a depopulated urban landscape, ripe for the solitary wanderings of the *flâneur*, the somber tone of which is accentuated by clouds and other soft visual filters, on the verge of an outbreak of the grotesque. (For the sake of the present discussion, why don't we define the modern grotesque as the atmosphere of always immanent invasion specifically of the city by the monsters, other mutants, and extraterrestrials accessed by scientists and other scholars whose insider knowledge and duty calls them to the very brink of the Kantian transcendental? Baudelairean spleen in this sense incorporates the troubled expectation that Frankenstein's monster is going to wander into Paris from the Swiss Jura as an advance party to mutants such as postnuclear Japan's Godzilla.)

Time Regained in Graphic Panels

The foregoing has hopefully established, from a number of related sectors or screens, that Kafka traveled well into the populist literatures of comics art and fantastic fiction—despite his solid bourgeois upbringing, the small cadre of Prague intellectuals with whom he interacted, and the learned erudition in clear evidence throughout his writings. While there are a variety of formats of literary and intellectual history allowing us to trace such influences, the challenge before us is to appreciate the unrelenting, ongoing openness of the particular open that Kafka configured for twentieth-century culture, the specific ways in which it remains a screen on which turbulent and autopoietic cultural force fields can still be charted. Key factors in this demonstration are the meticulous detail that Kafka infused into his serial portraits of strangeness, whether the furrows on Sortini's forehead or the conflation of mechanics and semantics programmed into the penal colony execution machine, and the rather original techniques by which he realized spatial disorientation. We should bear in mind, though, that Kafka's entirely deranged spatial maps ultimately segue into a time frame at once definitively open and unachieved, in which motion stutters, like the shutter on a movie camera, between definitive arrest and open-ended continuity. This is a temporality in which repetitions are mutations, in which motion vacillates between time-lapse photography and slow motion, in which the outlines of the body multiply into the shadows of an image endlessly retaken and retraced. The temporal possibilities that Kafka opened up for fiction form a Bermuda triangle with Marcel Duchamp's "Nude Descending a Staircase" and the odd temporal solutions found by the contemporary *bande dessinée*. This is something other than the magisterial, but also monstrous and deeply unsettling *reprise* that Proust fashions for his cosmic plan of remembrance and inscription in *Le temps retrouvé*, even if Proustian melancholy and recollection claim a significant role in the demographics of mood that Benjamin extracts and assembles. Kafka's truest extraterrestriality consists in the yet persistent openness in which mutations can still be scored within his permutations of alterity, the compulsive involution of his spatial zones, and the time frame of a motion never quite realized and never quite virtual.

The architectural implications of the court in Kafka's *The Trial*, its involuted passageways, spatially compromised compartments, and unmarked conduits to the halls of greatest power find a native land in the domain of sequential graphic narrative. Benjamin has, once again, through his immersion into the *matériel* of modernization and his insistence on a history discovering its truth only amid the flash of dialectical tensions impinging on the present, accessed the nineteenth-century visual sources, above all Grandville and Charles Meryon. Benjamin, in his pivotal Baudelaire Convolute (J), cites Gustave Geffroy on the atmospheric features of this latter artist's urban landscape translating particularly well into the graphic novel:

> I have rarely seen the natural solemnity of an immense city more poetically reproduced. Those majestic accumulations of stone; those

spires "whose fingers point to heaven"; those obelisks of industry, spewing forth their conglomerations of smoke against the firmament; those prodigies of scaffolding 'round buildings under repair, applying their openwork architecture, so paradoxically beautiful, upon architecture's solid body; that tumultuous sky, charged with anger and spite; those limitless perspectives, only increased by the thought of all the drama they contain;—he forgot not one of the complex elements. [J2,1][16]

Comics art is constantly beset by the demand to open up panoramas of "mystery and the imagination" within a medium constantly conforming to the constraints and architecture of frames and framing. Kafka and theoretically astute twentieth-century comics art intersect at the framework where his parody of power, elaborating through fictive figuration not only the antinomies but also the absurdities of the law and its banal abuses as they derive from a universe of speculation (perhaps best exemplified by Kant), segues into the cartoonist's unremitting struggle against the law of the frame, its structure, and its sequence. One could argue, then, that the architecture of Kafka's castle as well as court is already comics art embedded into the medium of discursive fictive narrative.

The comics artist, on the other hand, is a master in the laws and gymnastics of the line. Against the narrative imperatives of discernible sequence and developments, she orchestrates a shibboleth between the line as principle of continuity and assertion and the line as trace of physical accident. All comics art registers itself as the slapstick collision, evidenced in Kafka's "A Common Confusion" ("*Eine alltägliche Verwirrung*"), for example, between the linear logic and progressive constructions of speculative thinking and the accidents of the line as an above all physical phenomenon or Deleuzian "line of flight."

Because we are dealing here with structural affinities between some of Kafka's investigations along the time-space-language discontinuum in fictive narrative art and some of the exigencies imposed on comics artists by their very medium, it is no surprise at all that the traits of Kafka's extraterrestrial investigations migrate well to very different graphic settings, whether the illustrative style of the old classic comics, the *cités obscures* of the Belgian *bande dessinée*, or the rich, if slightly maudlin, New York cityscapes of Ben Katchor. The migratory range of the grotesque urban climate and aesthetic documented in *The Arcades Project* and elaborated throughout Kafka's novels extends well beyond the print medium. This comes home with particular force when we trace the impact of the Belgian *cités obscures* on the recent French Canadian contribution to big-time, full-length animation, *The Triplets of Belleville*.[17]

I'm going to begin this demonstration of the endurance and scrambling of nothing more persistent than a distinctive climate or mood of inscription with the comics art of Ben Katchor, whose daily strips for the *Jewish Daily Forward* furnished the material for such volumes as *Julius Knipl Real Estate Photographer* and *The Beauty District*. My point here is that even in a framed and paneled world of muted and restrained realism, one accentuated tangibly by the daily fluctuations in the real estate market, the allegorical melancholy of nineteenth-century Paris can persist and the uncanny involutions of Kafkan architecture find an extension. Indeed, Katchor exploits the somber style in which he depicts the neighborhood settings of the purely local and small-scale real estate transactions that take place there as the ho-hum, customary backdrop to the relentless productions of his wit. Knipl surveys, along Ornamental Avenue, "that broad, tree-lined thoroughfare originating at Beukelson Circle," in the section leading off *The Beauty District*, such public architecture as "a monument to the inventor of pickled herring," "Arterial Hall, a legitimate surgical theater," "the Halitosis Society and the Museum of Insect Art," and "the Municipal Laxitive Garden and the Katsigh Collection of Worn Shoes and Broken Laces."[18] It is true that some modest introduction into the world of perverse humor might be useful for the full appreciation of these jokes, but the effect that Katchor achieves is their flashing up, akin to the Benjaminian dialectical image in Convolute N of *The Arcades Project*, against the backdrop of the drab urban surroundings.

There is, in other words, a thread in the graphic novel leading it back to the Parisian arcades when its delivery mode is realism and its subject even real estate. This point is already evident on the cover of *Julius Knipl Real Estate Photographer*[19] (figure 14.1), whose perspective is sweepingly panoramic. As Knipl enters a crowded Brooklyn intersection from stage left, his gaze continues a visual pan initiated by the elevated tracks and station in the upper right-hand corner. His gaze has moved from the urban density in which Katchor has initiated the panel leftward toward a horizon still largely open. Comics art's affinity for panoramic sweeps through the horizontal panels of comics gutters plays a decisive role in the very design of *The Beauty District*, the sequel to *Julius Knipl*. The front inside cover is at first glance a continuous montage of three continuous street fronts, ending with a left-hand structure in which Sensum's Symmetry Shop sits atop the Synthetic Apriori Corp., whose storefront signage advertises "Mindwork," but it also encompasses a collage element: two theater tickets peer out from the strip of 1950s fold-out real estate snaps. The back endpaper to the volume (figure 14.2) fully exploits the collage motif initiated at the front. Here a theater seating plan, a perfume sample-strip (this is the beauty district), and a waterproof urban map are affixed to a photo of the street gutter running alongside the rightmost block of storefronts. Katchor thus appropriates to his particular practice of the graphical novel the visual tradition of collage, both in the multiregister fragmented surfaces of Cubism and in the playful assemblages of Surrealism. It is nigh impossible to overestimate the centrality of Surrealism to Benjamin as the aesthetic sensibility and *technē* most closely accompanying the jarring collisions of the modern cityscape and approximating the disjunctions of allegory. Louis Aragon's *Paris Peasant* (*Paysan de Paris*) may well serve as *The Arcades Project*'s preeminent contemporary fictive talisman, not only in shuttling between the centrally located Parisian arcades and the artists' colony gathered at the periphery around such sites as the Parc des Buttes Chaumont and the Canal St-Martin: its narrative is structured by the Arcades's architectural configuration, by the linear progression of boutiques, the parallelism between storefront and covered passageway, and the vertical layering of legitimate and illegitimate business zones. It is no accident, then, that Katchor's collage in the endpapers of *The Beauty District* is of a type strikingly similar to that incorporated by Aragon into his exemplary urban-surrealist novel, whether consisting of the ads spliced onto the pages of fictive exposition[20] (figure 14.3), or the engravings of the official buildings and monuments of the nineteenth *arrondisement*, reproduced into the narrative with perfect typographical fidelity (figure 14.4).

Yet the play of architecture—its fantastic exaggeration, its emergence from linear structures of the sort schematized in blueprints, the modal shadows, canyons, and clearings cast by the profiles of skyscrapers—is even more decisive to the Belgian *bande dessinée* than to Katchor's atmospheric evocations of the real estate market. And if Katchor's productions hold Kafka at bay as an implicit demiurge of its relentless maudlin wit, he is an in-your-face business partner of the Schuiten brothers, Luc and François, who, sometimes with and sometimes without Benoît Peeters, invent the apocalyptic and grotesque urban landscape to which I refer. Of particular interest to the pursuit of Kafka into the popular visual media are two long-standing and multifarious series of comics art volumes produced by these artists, *les cites obscures* and *les terres creuses*. Both of these in turn fall under the marvelously sordid rubric, *les humanoïds associés*. It may be asserted without a hitch that Kafka is in serious cahoots with these comics artists, both as a supplier of narrative themes and as an unofficial city planner. The conceptual gutter or margin of humanoids holds itself invitingly open to the multifarious animal experimentation (cognitive, narratological, characterological) that Kafka implanted within a literary framework.

Who but Kafka could have inspired the Schuitens's postnuclear holocaust tale—titled *Carapaces*—of two lovers who, too hungry for direct contact, strip off their prophylactic carapaces—this is a fable deriving from the age of AIDS—only to be devoured by the insects who now dominate the world[21] (figures 14.5 and 14.6)? Kafka's Gregor has indeed been fruitful and multiplied. The central image is no longer his quite particular shell but the mutant exoskeleton so dominating the biosphere that the remaining human stragglers are forced to devise a parallel covering for themselves.

Moving into an explicitly urban environment, the denizens of the *cités obscures* devote considerable labor and newsprint to chronicling their own projects and initiatives, generating a massive archive filled with the blueprints and textual remains of the various themed and styled architectural sites. The internal archivists of the *cités obscures* are good businessmen as well: compilation volumes based on the most striking graphics from each prior book can be added to the series. Unapologetic BD fans will snap them up. We meet Kafka as well (not to mention the Melville of "Barnaby the Scrivener") in the pages of *L'archiviste*,[22] specifically in the figures of the stooped-over archivists who, amid the mad symmetry of a Borgesian library done shabby, transfer disintegrating volumes of architectural plans from one crumbling floor of the archive to the next (figures 14.7 and 14.8).

With respect to the grotesque architectural setting of these volumes, the key point to bear in mind is the rich interface between Kafka's conceptual and rhetorical dismantling of the law and the graphic novel's capability to tease out, elaborate, and structurally analyze the infrastructures as well as exoskeletons of buildings and other constructed spaces. We can achieve an appreciation of the full richness of registers of signification, rhetoric, and performance embedded by this medium in the act and material of writing not merely by interposing a comic book in the place of what the examining magistrate had been reading during the Joseph K.'s notorious preliminary hearing on a Sunday, a porn novel titled "How Grete was Plagued by her Husband Hans" (*"Die Plagen, welche Grete von ihrem Manne Hans zu erleiden hatte"*).[23] This is the title Joseph K. comes on a week after the initial deliberation, when he approaches the dais of justice.

It will be hopefully apropos to note once again that it is precisely at the law of the line that the authoritarian and closed systems of the law, whether in *The Trial*, or the commandant's parodic Mosaic law in "In the Penal Colony" (*"In der Strafkolonie"*)[24] segue into the hyperdetailed architectural schemata that have been within the range of lithography and the print media for many decades now. The line is the mark or scoring where the ideational elements of communications and the accidents of physical linearity converge. The sheer arbitrariness of the line, which I can make swerve anywhere I want to on the reasonably flat two-dimensional *tabula* before me, snuffs out the mannered distinctions between conceptualization and materiality, between reflection and graphic arbitrariness. The attenuated materiality of the line, its unmarked swerves between word and sentence formation and the semantic burden this bears and unmitigated visual accident preempts a full range of the exasperating confusions, between media and meaning, between message and unintended resonance, taking up so much of critical-exegetical deliberation. It's far less absurd than you think to imagine that the Kafkan examining magistrate's "actual" pulp reading was a comic book.

To the degree that I myself have stepped out of the attorney's role in the utterly spurious and corrupt court of Kafkan law, let me begin to rest my case.

Exhibit 1: The case of an architectural virus, a cube form, that erupts and madly proliferates in *The Fever of Vrbicande* (*La fièvre d'Vrbicande*), something like killer weed, within the architectural projects of one Eugène Robick, imploding them from within[25] (figure 14.9). The virus is another mutation filtering into the world of utopian-apocalyptical graphics from the world of AIDS. Robick, whose name resonates well with Rubik's Cube, a mind-bending geometrical puzzle in its ascendancy when these volumes were produced, is yet another advanced male protagonist in this literature who always ends up paired with the much younger female possessor of pornographic aura. Yes, indeed, another fertile field of exploration in the law of the line, particularly in its open-ended graphic *flânerie* over the smooth space of the page, are exquisite effigies of fantasized sexual objects, whichever genders or modes of dress and other aspects of presentation are mitigated by fashion. The graphic novel, by way of Husserl's assignment of a pivotal role to auto-affection as a constitutive element of personal experience and Derrida's subsequent appeal to auto-affection as the very dynamic of representation's effect and power in the face of the absence of the signified, thus encompasses an irreducible pornographic dimension, as the *auteurs* of the Belgian *bande dessinée* make sure to remind us at every turn.[26]

Now the cube virus, in *The Fever of Vrbicande*, is relatively more primitive, more closed, in terms of contemporary systems theory: more analog, in terms of Anthony Wilden's *System and Structure*.[27] The graphics artists thus establish a tension between the style of their phantasmatic intervention and the structural elements into which their own graphic arabesques break down.

Yet exhibit 2 will demonstrate that their ultimate loyalty is to the phantasmagoria that can indeed be summoned forth, in conjunction with suggestive theories of representation, from the graphic line. An interior landscape from the volume entitled *The Tower* (*La tour*) refers explicitly to some of Escher's most notorious graphic tricks.[28] We look down from our perch in the antiquated gothic tower, but all at once we are also glimpsing architectural shapes head on, which are in turn on a Möbius strip with other elements we are staring at from below (figure 14.10). Kafka's own explorations of temporal-spatial anomalies are notorious, not only the trip village to village in "A Common Confusion" lasting, in separate transversals, ten minutes, ten hours, and "practically . . . an instant," but also the wild juxtaposition of divergent paces of activity in *Amerika* and *The Castle*. I think particularly of how excruciatingly long it takes the aged paterfamilias of the Barnabas family, in the latter novel, to cross the parlor all the while that K. marvels at Barnabas's sleekness and gains an introduction to his ostracized family.[29] As the present demonstration continues and we all begin to tabulate further instances of Kafka's centrality to contemporary popular phantasmagoria, it becomes increasingly evident that the grotesque flank of contemporary comics art, including the hilarious antics of R. Crumb, may be well characterized as Kafka made graphic.

Comics art, at the same time that its radical combination of framed enclosure and open-ended panoramic perspective initiates very serious explorations of represented space, also maintains a vividly operatic relation to time. Exhibit 3, our last from the Belgian *bande dessinée*, details how a theoretically motivated comics art deals with its own status, in Scott McCloud's terms, as "sequential fiction."[30] The title of *Nogegon* is a long palindrome, suggesting a closed feedback loop.[31] The volume details some work Nelle, an artistic as well as pornographic model, does for a master of a futuristic art medium, "arttrace." By leaping from a balcony to the ground in a simulated flying posture, Nelle allows her image both to be fragmented, photographically dissected into the separate moments of her fall, and to bring sculpture into a new paradigm of poetic fluidity. Nelle's leap, captured in multiple outlines like the cinematic image, claims a noble source in twentieth-century visual experimentation: nothing less than Marcel Duchamp's nude negotiating a downward staircase.

We don't really need to go into the rapport that Nelle enters with her artistic master when the relationship turns personal. Through this fantasy, the comics art of the Belgian *bande dessinée* indicates the horizon of its own rapport to time, imagining the acceleration of its progressive sequence of frames until it achieves a blur, the sustained continuous trace of movement in space. It is no accident that Convolute Y of *The Arcades Project*, "Photography," becomes an overall survey of the technology of image-transfer made possible by nineteenth-century innovations.[32] It may not anticipate arttrace, but it encompasses, in addition to photography, the phenakistiscope, the pantograph, the physionotrace, and photosculpture (indeed, it is the latter of these technologies that probably most closely approximates the futuristic master's sculptures).

At the moment when comics art theorizes its possible relations to time, it acknowledges with renewed commitment its status as writing or trace. It is precisely when the graphic mark achieves the contours of a continuous if blurred profile that the possibility of graphic narrative is born. There is a tedious repetitiveness to the necessity of moving along the gutter from one framed image to the next, perhaps born of the splenetic rainy days of the Second Empire in Paris. But *flânerie* in the city, or strolling along the boutiques of the arcades, the linear progression from one visual frame to the next, reaches toward the acceleration of cinema and all the manipulations that can be achieved through montage. The graphic novel knows that it is cinema in the making, or already in the happening, on the page. Through the blurred extension of figures such as Nelle, at once fast-forward graphics and freeze-frame, comics art reveals its status as a cinema that has invaded and taken over reading, the private experience of the defile of words, icons, and other signifiers along the gutters and other passageways of the screen or page.

Conclusion

Through their graphic effigies, cultural programmers stake out the very climate of writing: its parameters; the laws of the line, panel, and gutter; its enabling and disabling conditions. Graphic fiction may be read as a weather map of inscriptive possibilities from one historical moment or epistemological configuration to another.

This becomes quite clear in the encounter that Leo Leonhard and Otto Jägersberg stage, in *Rüssel in Komikland*,[33] between shapes and characters emerging from Hieronymus Bosch's apocalyptic landscapes and the outrageous pastels dominating contemporary advertising and other forms of hard sell. Indeed, the shapes that Rüssel and Schrüssel assume and the landscape through which they wander derive from a specific Boschean apocalyptic work, "The Garden of Earthly Delights," a comics-art translation of which Leonhard and Jägersberg insert late in the volume[34] (figure 14.11). The tale of *Rüssel in Komikland* is a simple one: two characters in every sense of the word, Rüssel and Schrüssel, every bit "animal" as they are "human," wander further and further from their home in an environment reminiscent of late medieval/early Renaissance Flemish landscape painting, depicted in a severe style of monochromatic etching, until they encounter Flabby Jack, a knock-off of Disney's Goofy, but with the outrageous hair of the 1970s and the unmistakable residue of profound recent chemical experiences (figure 14.12). They are flown in a helicopter called the "Red Pill" to *Komikland* while Flabby Jack sleeps off some of the toxins still circulating in his blood system. There they meet bubblegum executive Al Bosso, dressed in the costume of a 1930s Mafia don but speaking the patois of aggressive capitalism under conditions of expansion so rapid that it becomes blurred (figure 14.13). This is Al Bosso's discourse:

> We need to feature the Chinese. This is our new market. The Chinese should be chewing bubblegum, the devil with them. That's what we need to push, so that the stock goes up. Chop chop! BANG! BANG! [*Wir müssen die Chineschen fietschern. Das ist die neue Markt für uns. Die Chinesen sollen Babbelgamm kauen, zum Geier. Da müssen wir zuschlagen, daß die Aktien steigen, racker, racker, ZACK, ZACK!*][35]

The overall didactic thrust of this volume is a warning about the cultural environmental impact of voracious global capitalism and the creeping Americanization of global mass culture, which has the effect of sweetening the pill. But what powers this line of thought and critique is above all a multiregistered and multifaceted contrast of styles: first between the narrative density and rich mythological and allusive traditions underscoring European culture, as embodied in the paintings of a Bosch or a Poussin and the utter bluntness of U.S. mass culture of the 1960s and 1970s, devoid precisely of a sequential history of modulation and qualification. And *Rüssel in Komikland* orchestrates this cultural divergence above all in a visual sense: through the screaming contrast between the intricate etching of the Brueghels or Dürer and the extreme pastels and blurry shapes colonizing the late capitalist mind by way of psychedelic culture. This is not to suggest that living in a Brueghelian apocalypse of hyperactive mass superego would be any more edifying than kowtowing to the staccato business orders of Al Bosso. But through the medium of graphic narrative, Leonhard and Jägersberg have brilliantly seized on an opportunity to couch a sociopolitical and critical argument in the most vivid visual terms.

We need to remember that psychedelic humor, achieved with or without the deployment of chemical substances, is another by-product of Kafka's imaginative intervention. I'm arguing nothing less than that the extraterrestrial expanse cleared open by Kafka's literary dismantling of the prevailing systems of law and authority is in fact a drug with chemical aftereffects. Kafka's out-loud readings from *The Trial* and "The Metamorphosis" kept his close circle of friends in stitches. This laughter did not require the stimulation of hemp or hashish. In certain of its emanations, the dawning of the extraterrestrial may cast an ominous shadow, but it is only a rollicking, furious, and unremitting Nietzschean laughter that resounds in the open cleared out by critique and the radical deployment of aesthetic variation.

Notes

1. The present chapter arises in the specific context of work on Kafka's animals I wrote many years ago. See, above all, "The All-Embracing Metaphor: Reflections on Kafka's 'Der Bau,'" in *Glyph 1: Johns Hopkins Textual Studies* (Baltimore: Johns Hopkins University Press, 1977), 100–131, reprinted in *Franz Kafka: Geometrician of Metaphor* (Madison, WI: Coda Press, Inc. 1979), 147–81. I glossed other of Kafka's animal studies, including "A Crossbreed" and "Josephine the Singer; or, the Mouse Folk," in *The Trial: Kafka's Unholy Trinity* (New York: Macmillan, 1993), x, xii, 6, 10, 15, 26, 36, 40–43, 70, 103, 107, 118.

It turns out that Kafka's experiments on the threshold between the human and the animal exerted a tremendous figurative and conceptual influence across the breadth and depth of the philosophical project Gilles Deleuze undertook in conjunction with the liberation psychoanalyst Félix Guattari. We would expect this in relation to their key notion of deterritorialization (see note 2). But Kafkan animality can also be discerned at work, decisively, in the background of such pivotal notions as nomadic flow, smooth and striated space, becoming-death, the pack, and the body without organs. In these connections, see *A Thousand Plateaus*, trans. Brian Massumi (Minneapolis: University of Minnesota Press, 1987), 149–62, 174–76, 232–309, 380–94.

2. For this notion specifically in relation to Kafka, see Gilles Deleuze and Félix Guattari, *Kafka: Toward a Minor Literature*, trans. Dana Polan (Minneapolis: University of Minnesota Press, 1986), 13–15, 18–21, 35, 58, 67–68, 85–88. For a general introduction to this term, see their *A Thousand Plateaus*, 32–33, 40, 54, 61, 65, 70, 87–88, 91, 99–100, 109, 112, 117, 129, 134–35, 172, 174–91, 219–21, 291–92, 301–3, 306–7, 333–37, 345–48, 353, 432–34, 508.

3. Ibid., 53.

4. An absolutely decisive passage where Deleuze and Guattari meld semiotics with their mega-trope of flow is to be found near the outset of *A Thousand Plateaus*: "An assemblage, in its multiplicity, necessarily acts on semiotic flows, material flows, and social flows simultaneously. . . . There is no longer a tripartite division between a field of reality (the world) and a field of representation (the book) and a field of subjectivity (the author). Rather, an assemblage establishes connections between certain multiplicities drawn from each of these orders" (*A Thousand Plateaus*, 22–23).

5. Ibid., 53–54.

6. A term for aesthetic innovation and recalibration I devised in reference to Ludwig Wittgenstein's construction, "complex language-games." See my *The Aesthetic Contract: Statutes for Art and Intellectual Work in Modernity* (Stanford, CA: Stanford University Press, 1997), 165–67.

7. Franz Kafka, *The Trial*, trans. Willa and Edwin Muir (New York: Schocken Books, 1974), 63. German citations refer to Franz Kafka, *Der Prozess*, ed. Max Brod (Frankfurt: Schocken Verlag, 1965), 80.

8. Kafka, *The Trial*, 141; *Der Prozess*, 170.

9. Kafka, *The Trial*, 119; *Der Prozess*, 144.

10. Walter Benjamin, *The Arcades Project*, trans. Howard Eiland and Kevin McLaughlin (Cambridge, MA: Harvard University Press, 1999), 104; the German citation derives from Walter Benjamin, *Das Passagen-Werk*, in *Gesammelte Schriften*, ed. Rolf Tiedemann (Frankfurt: Suhrkamp Verlag, 1989), v, 1, 159.

11. Benjamin, *The Arcades Project*, 112; *Das Passagen-Werk*, v, 1, 169.

12. Benjamin, *The Arcades Project*, 116; *Das Passagen-Werk*, v, 1, 174.

13. Benjamin, *The Arcades Project*, 119; *Das Passagen-Werk*, v, 1, 177.

14. Benjamin, *The Arcades Project*, 460; *Das Passagen-Werk*, v, 1, 574.

15. See William R. Miller, Robert A. Rosellini, and Martin E. P. Spiegelman, "Learned Helplessness and Depression," and Lyn Y. Abramson, Martin E. P. Spiegelman, and John D. Teasdale, "Learned Helplessness in Humans: Critique and Reformulation," in *Essential Papers on Depression*, ed. James C. Coyne (New York: New York University Press, 1985), 181–219, 259–310.

16. Benjamin, *The Arcades Project*, 321; *Das Passagen-Werk*, 303. The reference is from Gustave Geffroy, *Charles Meryon* (Paris: Floury, 1926).

17. Among the cinematic influences on this production surely numbers Terry Gilliam's futuristically urbane "Brazil."

18. Ben Katchor, *The Beauty District* (New York: Pantheon Press, 2000), 1.

19. Ben Katchor, *Julius Knipl Real Estate Photographer* (New York: Little, Brown, and Co., 1996).

20. See Louis Aragon, *Paysan de Paris* (Paris: Éditions Gallimard, 1953), 41–59, 62–63, 85, 97–98, 109, 111, 113, 121–22, 124–26, 195–204.

21. Luc and François Schuiten, *Les terres creuses: Carapaces* (Geneva: Humanos, 1980).

22. Luc and François Schuiten and Benoît Peeters, *Les cités obscures: L'archiviste* (Brussels: Casterman, 1987).

23. See Kafka, *The Trial*, 52; *Der Prozess*, 67.

24. Franz Kafka, "In the Penal Colony," in *The Complete Stories*, ed. Nahum N. Glatzer (New York: Schocken Books, 1975), 144–45, 161–62; "*In der Strafkolonie*," in *Sämtliche Erzählungen*, ed. Paul Raabe (Frankfurt: S. Fischer Verlag, 1972), 117–18, 133.

25. Luc and François Schuiten and Benoît Peeters, *Les cités obscures: La fièvre d'Vrbicande* (Brussels: Casterman, 1992), 38–39.

26. Derrida's early remarks on auto-affection as an indication of the signified's very power in its absence remain among his most suggestive and illuminating on this representational dynamic. See Jacques Derrida, *Speech and Phenomena* (Evanston, IL: Northwestern University Press, 1973), 68, 78–80, 82–83, 85–86, 95.

27. Chapter 7 of Anthony Wilden's *System and Structure* (London: Tavistock Press, 1972), 155–90, does a splendid job in elaborating the differences between analog and digital communications and the implications of this great divide.

28. Luc and François Schuiten and Benoît Peeters, *Les terres creuses: La tour* (Brussels: Casterman, 1987).

29. Franz Kafka, *The Castle*, trans. Willa and Edwin Muir (New York: Schocken Books, 1974), 40–41; *Das Schloß* (Frankfurt: S. Fischer Verlag, 1965), 47.

30. See Scott McCloud, *Understanding Comics: The Invisible Art* (New York: Paradox Press, 2000), 5, 7–9, 17–22, 59, 65, 68, 88, 107–17, 159, 193, 199, 212.

31. Luc and François Schuiten, *Les terres creuses: Nogegon* (Geneva: Humanos, 1990).

32. Benjamin, *The Arcades Project*, 676, 689–90; *Das Passagen-Werk*, v, 2, 830, 842–43. Also see Mc Cloud, *Understanding Comics*, 108–10.

33. Leo Leonhard and Otto Jägersberg, *Rüssel in Komikland* (Darmstadt: Melzer Verlag, 1972).

34. It so happens that years ago I invoked this very painting—as the insignia of a world in a state of a priori deconstruction—in the reading of Kafka's "The Burrow" referenced earlier. See Henry Sussman, "The All-Embracing Metaphor: Reflections on Kafka's 'Der Bau,'" *Glyph: Johns Hopkins Textual Studies*, reprinted in *Franz Kafka: Geometrician of Metaphor*.

35. Leo Leonhard and Otto Jägersberg, *Rüssel in Komikland* (Darmstadt: Melzer, 1972), 35.

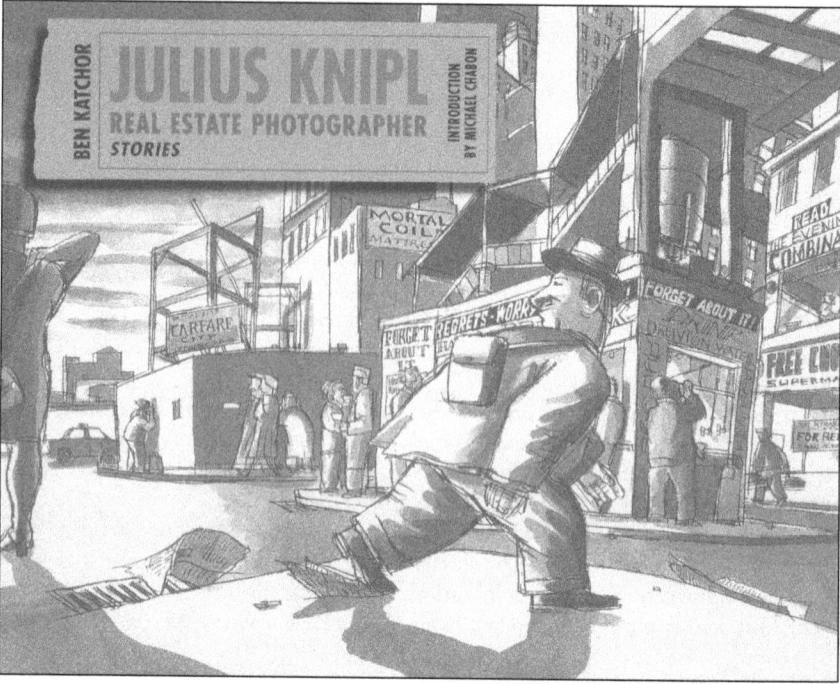

Figure 14.1.   Front Cover, Ben Katchor, *Julius Knipl Real Estate Photographer*

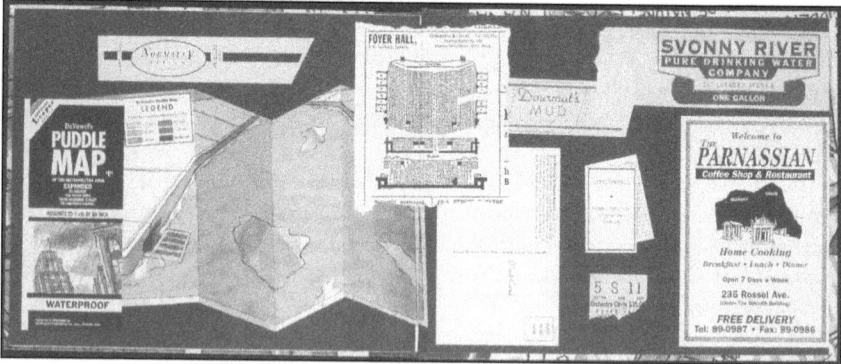

Figure 14.2.   Back Endpaper, Ben Katchor, *The Beauty District*

LOUIS ARAGON

us call forth these enigmas as the mood takes us, as temptation lures us : to the left, the doorway of number 17 and its shadowy staircase are framed by placards which immediately send me into a reverie.

Demon of conjectures, fever of phantasmagoria, pass your sulphurous and nacreous fingers through your tow hair and answer me : who is Prato, and on the first floor with its paradoxical lift what is this agency which I am obstinately convinced must be a vast organization engaged in white-slave traffic. Turn round, and see, there right opposite is the little restaurant where, in our progress towards the depths of the imagination, I find the last traces of the Dada movement. When Saulnier seemed too expensive for us, we used to come here, appeasing our inopportune appetites as best we could with food cooked in rancid coconut oil and with their sharp, unpleasant wine, consumed in a stuffy, vulgar atmosphere. What memories, what revulsions linger around these hash houses : the man eating in this one has the impression he is chewing the table rather than a steak, and becomes irritated by his common, noisy table

– 92 –

Figure 14.3. Louis Aragon, *Paris Peasant*, 92

PARIS PEASANT

PARC DES BUTTES-CHAUMONT

MAP OF PARIS

TOWN HALL AT 3^k 500 S. W.
PORTE D'AUTEUIL AT 10^k 500 W. S. W.
PORTE DE VINCENNES AT 4^k 300 S. S. E.
PORTE DE LA CHAPELLE AT 2^k 700 N. W.
PORTE DE GENTILLY AT 7^k 300 S. S. W.

Finally on the southern face,

19th ARROND^t
BUTTES-CHAUMONT

MUNICIPAL ADMINISTRATION } PLACE
MAGISTRATURE   } ARMAND
                            } CARREL

DISTRICT
POLICE STATIONS
RUE DE TANGER 22 (VILLETTE 73 Q)
RUE DE NANTES 19 (P^t DE FLANDRE 74)

– 165 –

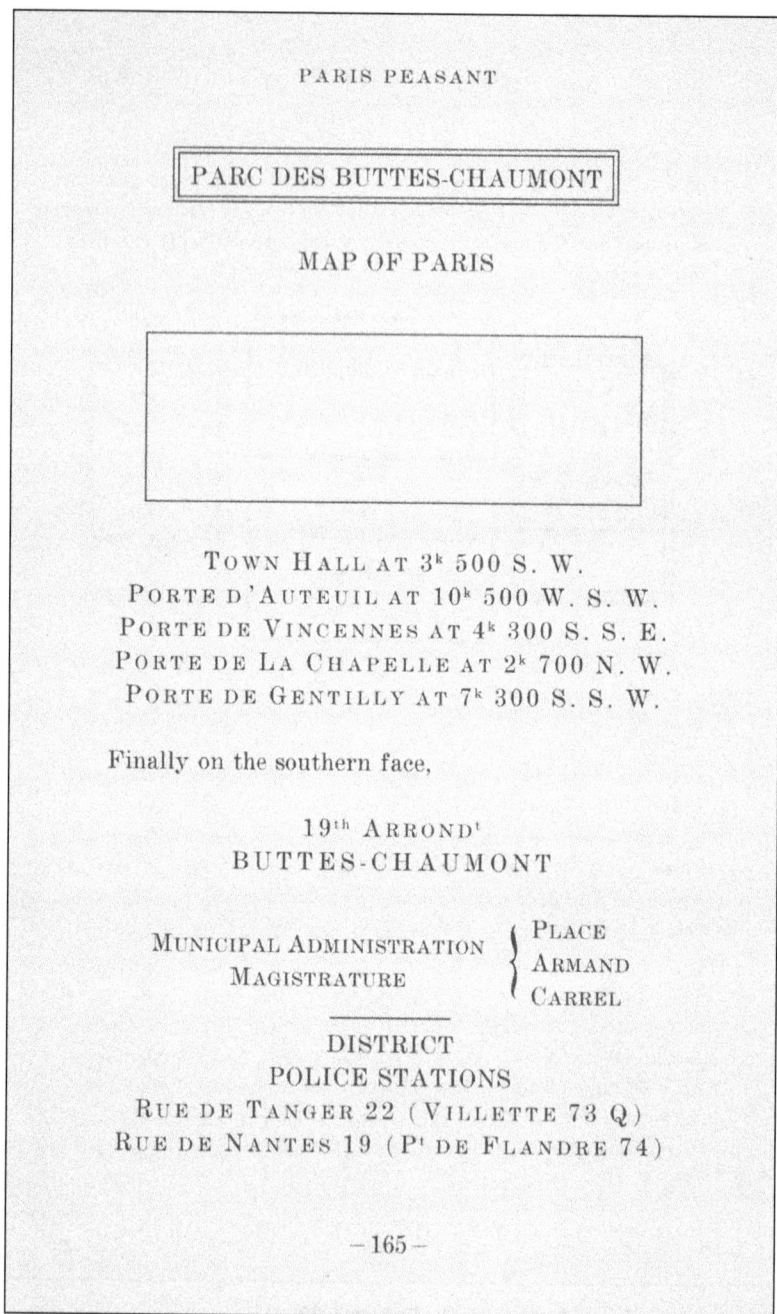

Figure 14.4. Louis Aragon, *Paris Peasant*, 165

Figure 14.5.   Copulation Scene, Luc and François Schuiten, *Carapaces*

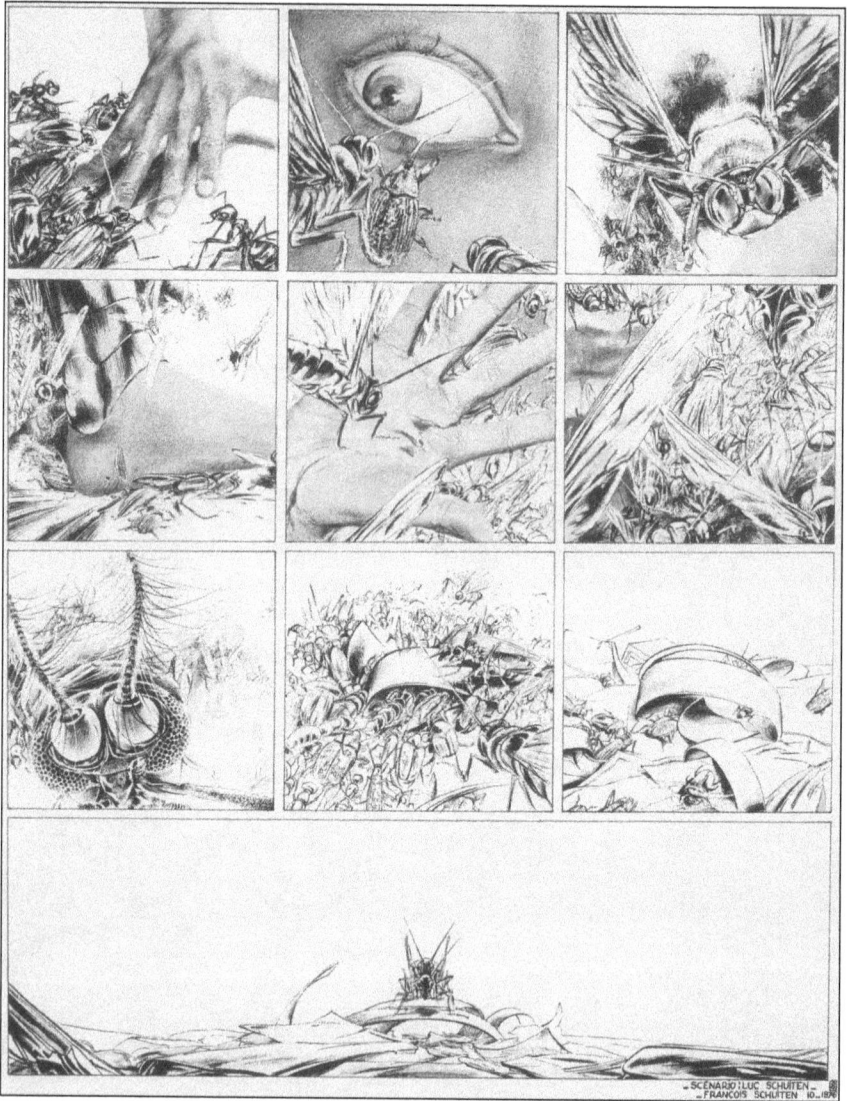

Figure 14.6.   World of Insects, Luc and François Schuiten, *Carapaces*

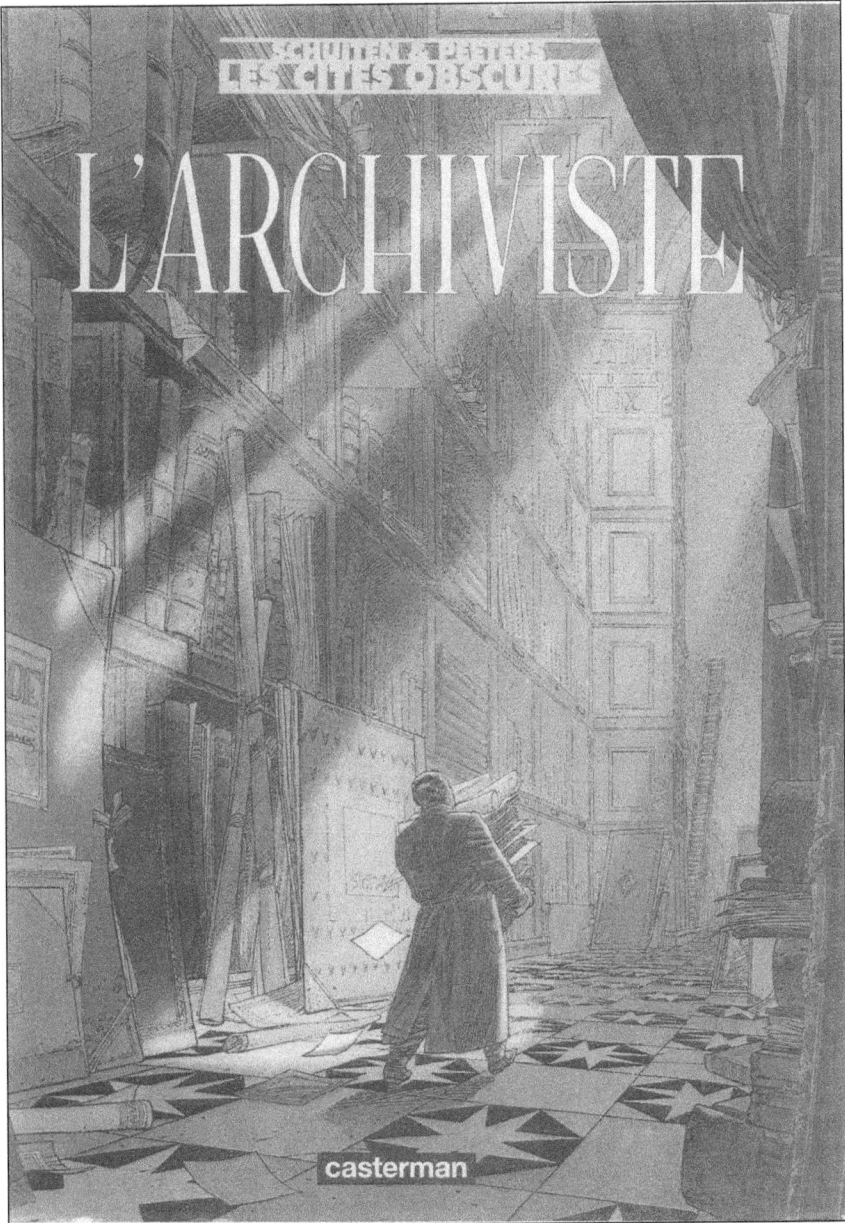

Figure 14.7. Jacket Cover, Luc and François Schuiten and Benoît Peeters, *L'archiviste*

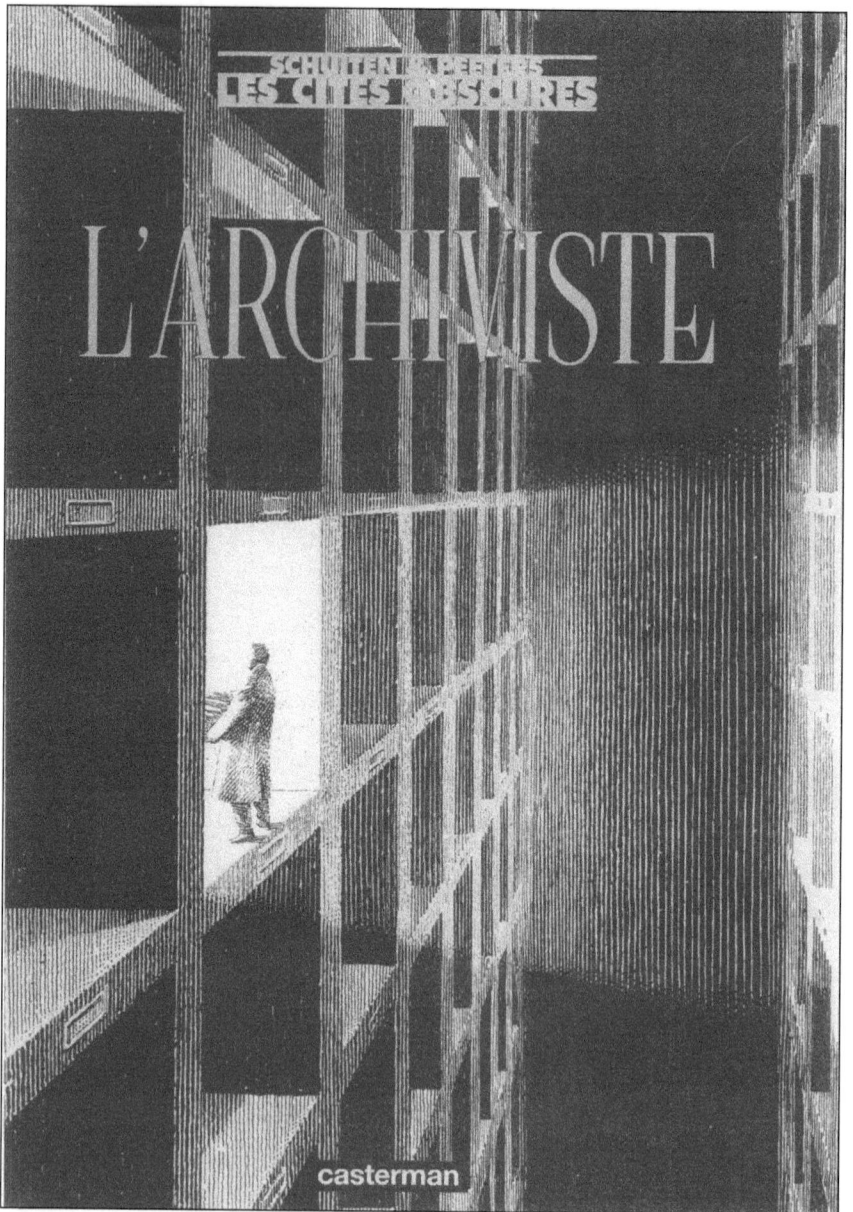

Figure 14.8. Front Cover, Luc and François Schuiten and Benoît Peeters, *L'archiviste*

Figure 14.9. Luc and François Schuiten and Benoît Peeters, *La fièvre d'Vrbicande*, 38–39

Figure 14.10.   Interior Scene, Luc and François Schuiten and Benoît Peeters, *La tour*

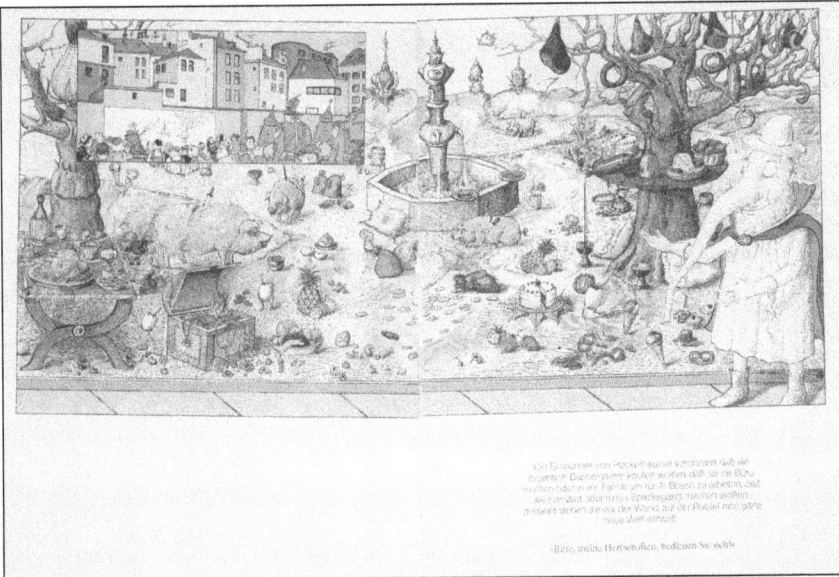

Figure 14.11.   Bosch's "Garden of Earthy Delights," A Comics Art Rendition. Leo Leonhard and Otto Jägersberg, *Rüssel in Komikland*

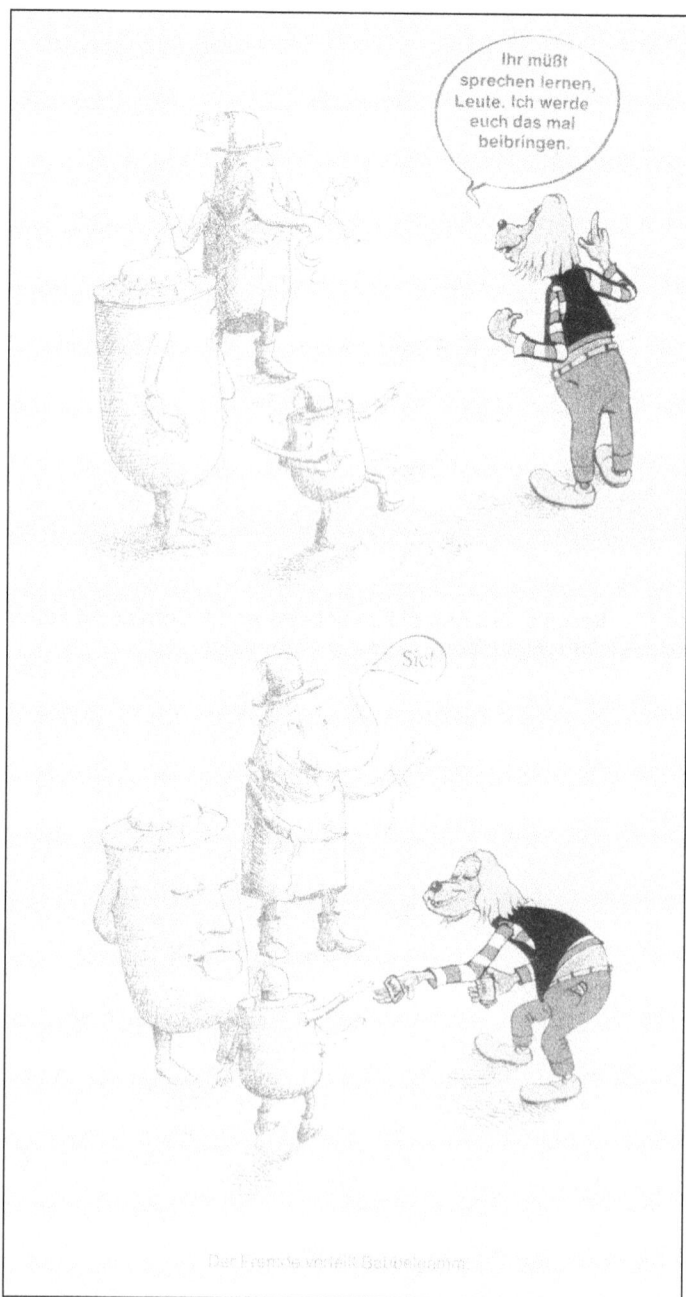

Figure 14.12.   Medieval Line-Creatures Meet Flabby Jack. Leo Leonhard and Otto Jägersberg, *Rüssel in Komikland*

Figure 14.13. Al Bosso Rules. Leo Leonhard and Otto Jägersberg, *Rüssel in Komikland*

CHAPTER 15

Index to Kafka's Use of Creatures in His Writings

Donna Yarri

As far as I know, there is no comprehensive guide to the location of different types of creatures in Franz Kafka's works, and this chapter is meant to provide this kind of guide for his English translations.[1] It is well-known to both readers and scholars of Franz Kafka that nonhuman creatures heavily populate his fiction and nonfiction writings. The previous chapters have provided analyses of some of these creatures, but there are many more that appear in his writings not referenced in this volume. While Kafka's writings principally have to do with the human condition, nonhuman or even cross-human creatures figure prominently in his books, fragments, stories, letters, and diaries. They appear in all of his longer stories, and in about half of his shorter ones. The majority of these creatures, however, are animals. It has frequently been pointed out that the name "Kafka," the Czech version of which is "jackdaw," was a first step "towards Franz Kafka's imaginative identification with insect, ape, dog, rodent—species show names as borrowed as terms of abuse."[2] How these creatures function in Kafka is open to various interpretations. Max Brod, Kakfa's most personal biographer, indicates that the use of animals in particular could represent the separation between God and humans:

> The eternal misunderstanding between God and man induces Kafka to represent this distortion again and again in the picture of the two worlds which can never, never understand one another—hence the infinite separation between dumb animals and men is one of his chief themes in the numerous animal stories which his works contain, not by accident.[3]

But other interpretations have also been put forth. Peter Stine maintains that animals for Kafka "betoken a vulnerable self escaping the coercion of a modern world in which social organization is fate."[4] As the various chapters in this volume indicate, individual creatures are utilized by Kafka in different ways. But regardless of how their use is understood, it is obvious that nonhuman creatures are part of many of his works. While relatively few references to creatures exist in his novels, they abound in his other works.

But what do we mean by Kafka's creatures? There are several different types of creatures, all of which only have in common that they are not fully human. One type is animals themselves, referred to by their normal nomenclature, such as cat, dog, horse, and so forth; he also references unnamed animals, such as the animal in "The Burrow," the species of which we are never explicitly told. Another type of creature is hybrids, which are a combination of different kinds of animals, such as the kittenlamb and Gregor, the young man turned into an insect. Some of these creatures are even inanimate objects that appear to have some kind of autonomy, such as the two bouncing balls in the story "Blumfeld, an Elderly Bachelor." And finally, there are those like the Odradek in "The Cares of the Family Man," in which it is unclear exactly what kind of creature it is.

These creatures are used in different ways in Kafka. Animals are referred to in both his fiction and nonfiction writings simply as part of life. A common example of this in his fictional works is when he refers to horses pulling carriages, or to birds flying, which are simply a part of the world in which the story takes place, or are part of his environment as described in letters or diary entries. An example in one of his nonfiction works—his diaries—recounts Kafka's anxiety about the mice problem in his apartment, and his obtaining a cat to assist with the problem. Animal characters are sometimes used to demonstrate the plight of the animals themselves; one example is Red Peter in "A Report to an Academy" (although there may be other interpretations of this story as well). Thus, animals sometimes possess human characteristics. Creatures are also used in an analogical sense, often interpreted to be understood as representing something about the human condition. Especially in his fictional works, animals have frequently been used to demonstrate the estrangement and isolation of human individuals in this world.

There are difficulties inherent in the task of cataloging creatures in Kafka's writings. As all those who work with Kafka's writings realize, it has been a long and circuitous path to even identify his complete corpus. Kafka never finished his novels in his lifetime; some of his stories have more than one version and often contain fragments, and some are even incomplete. The recent publication of Kafka's reports on workers' accidents that he wrote while working at the Workers' Accident Insurance Institute indicates that the corpus of Kafka, unlike many other writers, is still being refined and standardized.[5] In terms of creating an index, the problems are even more apparent when working in English. Whereas there is now a standard corpus of critical editions of Kafka's works in

German, no such corpus exists in English. While there is a generally accepted list of works in English, there have been different editions and translations of these writings, in which the latter editions contain corrections, often to Max Brod's original editing. In addition, new translators may render the original German words into English differently; for example, in *The Castle*, the word used by one translator may be "hare," whereas another may use "rabbit." Finally, since all of Kafka's English translations are not available online, to discover mention of these creatures in his works, one has to rely simply on the naked eye, so it is possible that a few creature references may have been missed.

Despite these difficulties, the purpose of this essay is to provide a resource principally for scholars of Kafka working in English who are interested in further exploration of Kafka's creatures. In some ways, a German index would be more helpful, since it would include the precise nouns that Kafka actually used, rather than having to rely on translations, some of which translate the German terms differently. As we all know, something is always lost in translation. However, it is hoped that the following guide may assist those who wish to delve deeper into Kafka's use of creatures in his writings. The index provided is generally comprehensive and should provide a useful tool.

This index includes references to all of Kafka's fictional works (many of which were published posthumously by Max Brod), including the complete collection of his stories and parables, and his three novels: *Amerika*, *The Castle*, and *The Trial*. It also includes Kafka's nonfiction writing, including his diaries, his many letters, and even written fragments and aphorisms. As Schocken Books, now under Random House, has the right to all of Kafka's writings, all of the works listed have been published by them. I have included the official body of Kafka's works, inasmuch as it exists in English. Since there have in some cases been multiple editions of some of them, I have listed the precise editions that I have used to create this index.

What is not included is almost as important as what is included. Only creatures listed as nouns (always listed in singular form) are listed but not animals as adjectives; for example, a chicken is listed but not chicken soup. There are not separate entries for subspecies, so that a subspecies is listed alphabetically only within the general species; thus, a sparrow would only appear as a subcategory under bird, whereas page references that use the word "bird" specifically will follow the word "bird." In addition, various terms that are related to a species will be listed with that species; thus, "cattle" and "calf" will be found under the main category of "cow." Generally the singular form of the noun will be listed even if it is found in a plural form; thus, the entry will say "flea" rather than "fleas," unless the word itself is plural, such as cattle. While individual species will be listed, so will generic terms such as "vermin," "creature," and "animal," even if it is clear that it refers to an aforementioned particular species. This occurs even when the term may be referring to an aforementioned animal, including a human. References to religious "creatures"—such as angels, devils, or even God—are not included, since they do not function in the same way in his works as the other creatures. References to animals in writings of others quoted by Kafka are not included. Indirect references, such as to sleigh bells or carriages, which are associated with horses, will not be listed either.

The index is organized in two ways; thus, there are actually two indices. The first contains an alphabetical list of each of Kafka's major works, complete with bibliographic information, with the creature references following in alphabetical order with page references. This is helpful if one wants to explore Kafka's use of animals in particular works. The second simply is an alphabetical list of the references to creatures, and following each reference is an abbreviation to the work in which it is found, along with the page numbers. The abbreviations for each work are listed at the beginning of that section. This index is helpful especially to those who want to explore the use of particular creatures in Kafka.

Index 1: References Listed According to Works of Kafka

Amerika: The Man Who Disappeared. Translated by Michael Hofmann. New York: New Directions Book, 1996.

animal, 71–72; bird, 45—lark, 73, pigeon, 42, swallow, 73; cat, 46, 156—wildcat, 46; dog, 38, 64–65, 154; fish, 79; frog—bullfrog, 161; horse, 32–33, 38, 72, 148, 211; insect—bee, 187, fly, 47, 141, 164; monkey, 121; rabbit, 30; rat, 8, 11; sardine, 82; sheep, 2; shrimp, 102; snake, 85

The Castle. Translated by Mark Harman. New York: Schocken Books, 1998.

animal, 282; beast, 158; bird—canary, 184, cock, 274, crow, 8, eagle, 55, 115–16; cat, 102, 127, 129–30, 133, 139, 162–64—kitty, 129; cow, 39; creature, 132, 283; dog, 46, 250; ghost, 252, 282; horse, 15–16, 101–2, 105–6, 316; insect—blindworm, 55, moth, 283, spider, 289, 303; lamb, 39, 201; rat, 5; snake, 18

The Complete Short Stories. Edited by Nahum N. Glatzer. New York: Schocken Books, 1971.

"Before the Law"

insect—flea, 4

"Description of a Struggle"

bat, 45; bird, 22—duck, 27, vulture, 22; creature, 34; dog—wolfhound, 43; horse, 51; insect—ant, 46, mosquito, 29, spider, 30; squirrel, 23

"The Cares of a Family Man"
  creature, 428; Odradek, 427–29
"The Silence of the Sirens"
  fox, 432; Sirens, 430–32
"Prometheus"
  eagle, 432
"Poseidon"
  Poseidon, 434–35
"The Vulture"
  animal, 443; bird—vulture, 442–43
"A Little Fable"
  cat, 445; mouse, 445
"Home-Coming"
  cat, 445
"The Departure"
  horse, 449
"Advocates"
  fox, 450; mouse, 450; weasel, 450
"The Married Couple"
  fish, 455

Dearest Father: Stories and Other Writings. Edited by Max Brod. Translated by Ernst Kaiser and Eithne Wilkins. New York: Schocken Books, 1954. Includes:
—"Wedding Preparations in Country" (no creature references included here; story found in *Complete Stories*)
—"Reflections on Sin, Suffering, Hope, and the True Way" (contains 105 statements; not clear if this is found anywhere else)
  animal, 37; bird, 36—crow, 37; dog—hunting dog, 38; horse, 38; leopard, 36
—"The Eight Octavo Notebooks" (numbering below represents Max Brod's numbering system, but later named by letters of alphabet; these references match this version of notebooks)
  first notebook: dog—arctic, 50; bird—sparrow, 54; fish, 59
  second notebook: cat, 59
  third notebook: bird—eagle, 84; cat, 79; dog—bitch, 68–69; fox, 72; horse, 86; pet, 82; squirrel, 64
  fourth notebook: bird, 97–99, 107—partridge, 107; horse, 89; snake, 97
  fifth notebook: bird, 111—raven, 109; cat, 109; dog, 115—pug, 115, Great Dane, 115; fish, 109; horse, 113, 116–17; mule, 116
  sixth notebook: bird, 118–20—stork, 119; fish, 119–20; frog, 119; insect—worm, 119–20; mouse, 117–18
  seventh notebook: dog, 126
  eighth notebook: dog—hound, 135; horse, 135

Index 2: References Listed Alphabetically

FEL	*Letters to Felice*
FRG	"Fragments from Notebooks and Loose Pages" (found in *Dearest Father*)
FTR	*Letter to His Father*
MIL	*Letters to Milena*
O	*Eight Octavo Notebooks* (found in *Dearest Father*)
OTT	*Letters to Ottla and Family* (found in book of this title)
PAR	"Paralipomena" (found in *Dearest Father*)
REF	"Reflections on Sin, Suffering, Hope, and the True Way"
T	*Trial*

animal	A: 71, 72; C: 282; CSS: 52, 72, 130, 183–84, 188, 205, 259, 262, 272, 274–75, 347, 353, 398, 408, 426–27, 443; D: 178, 273, 285, 309–12, 348, 362, 384, 451, 473, 484; FAM: 21, 41, 123, 141, 150, 154, 172, 174, 176, 294, 296–97, 326, 338; FEL: 117, 256, 320, 374, 447, 545; FRG: 214, 226, 251, 261, 270, 296–98, 315, 323, 353, 358–63, 368; MIL: 25, 29, 42, 59, 116, 145, 167, 175, 187, 199–200; REF: 37; T: 33
ape	CSS: 250–54, 257–60; FEL: 74, 169, 283; MIL: 74, 169, 283
bacilli	FAM: 146
bat	CSS: 45; FRG: 281
bear	D: 309; MIL: 28
beast	C: 158; CSS: 252, 275, 337, 346–47, 353–54, 358–59, 410, 426–27; D: 311, 318, 412; FAM: 35, 152, 275, 340; FEL: 408; MIL: 104
bird	A: 45; CSS: 22, 226, 340, 379; D: 290, 333, 367, 477; FAM: 13, 232, 341, 417; FEL: 214, 398; FRG: 216, 223–23, 263, 316, 368; FTR: 192; MIL: 21, 55: O: 97–99, 107, 111, 118–20; OTT: 60, 73; PAR: 379; REF: 36
	blackbird, FAM: 72
	canary, C: 184; CSS: 184; D: 104; FEL: 157, 164, 448; FRG: 223
	chicken, D: 79, FAM: 396
	cock, C: 274; CSS: 228; FEL: 419
	fighting cock, FTR: 138
	cockatoo, D: 138
	crow, C: 8; D: 16; FRG: 395; REF: 37
	dove, CSS: 226, 228; MIL: 208
	duck, CSS: 27; D: 338; FAM: 72
	eagle, C: 55, 115–16; CSS: 432; O: 84
	flock, CSS: 366; FAM: 330

lizard	D: 46, 439–40; FAM: 232; FRG: 272; MIL: 21, 29
menagerie	CSS: 274–75
mole	CSS: 168–74, 176, 218; D: 317; FAM: 8, 17; MIL: 140
monkey	A: 121; D: 55; FEL: 288
mouse	CSS: 326, 445, 450—implied, 360–76; D: 142; FAM: 143, 168–69, 171–76, 178, 187; FEL: 64, 109, 160, 491; FRG: 262; MIL: 111; O: 117–18
mule	O: 116
nursling	CSS: 365
Odradek	CSS: 427–29
ox	CSS: 417; D: 126, 141; FAM: 340; O: 16
panther	CSS: 277
parasite	D: 25; FAM: 141, 312, 405
pet	D: 285–86; O: 82
pig	D: 272, 330; FAM: 71, 150, 172, 174, 240–41; FEL: 374; MIL: 205
	swine, CSS: 223; OTT: 19
Poseidon	CSS: 434–35
rabbit	A: 30; D: 478; FRG: 213; O: 30
rat	A: 8, 11; C: 5; CSS: 329, 425–26; D: 83, 310–11, 417, 477; FAM: 117, 172, 316, 322; FEL: 163, 396, 408, 451, 462; FRG: 370; MIL 145; T: 140
	water rat, CSS: 403
sardine	A: 82
seal	FAM: 228
sea-serpent	FAM: 257
sheep	A: 2; D: 237, 363, 380–81; FRG: 213
shrimp	A: 102
Sirens	CSS: 430–32
small fry	CSS: 327–28, 343, 345, 347–49, 353
snake	A: 85; C: 18; D: 104, 363; FEL: 115, 308, 310; FRG: 311; MIL: 59; O: 97
	boa, FEL: 410
	python, CSS: 255
squirrel	CSS: 23; FAM: 243; FEL: 201; FRG: 214, 327; O: 64; OTT: 78
tiger	D: 91; FRG: 291
vermin	D: 22, 199, 211, 398; FTR: 146, 195
weasel	CSS: 450
wolf	CSS: 230; D: 309; FRG: 213
woodlouse	FRG: 299

Notes

1. An encyclopedia for Kafka's works, which is a very comprehensive and helpful source, only has a relatively short entry on "animals" and does not catalogue them anywhere; see Richard T. Gray, Ruth V. Gross, Rolf J. Goebel, and Clayton Koelb, *A Kafka Encyclopedia* (Westport, CT, and London: Greenwood Press, 2005).

2. Ronald Hayman, *A Biography of Kafka* (London: Phoenix Press, 1981), p. 6.

3. *Franz Kafka—A Biography by Max Brod* (New York: Schocken Books, 1937; second enlarged edition 1960), chapters I–VII translated by G. Humphreys, and chapter VIII by Richard Winston), 175.

4. Peter Stine, "Franz Kafka and Animals," in *Contemporary Literature* 22:1 (Winter 1981): 58–80. This is an excellent article outlining developments in Kafka's use of animals in particular stories.

5. This newer publication is not included as a source for the index, primarily because it is unlikely to contain references to creatures as do Kafka's other works.

Index

About the Contributors

Andrea Baer received her PhD in comparative literature from the University of Washington in June 2008, after defending her dissertation, "The Moods of Postmodern Metafiction: Narrative and Affective Literary Spaces and Reader (Dis) Engagement." She specializes in American and German contemporary literature, and her research interests include gender studies, theories of emotion, self-reflexive narrative, and reader response. She is currently pursuing a master's degree in information science at the University of Tennessee-Knoxville with the intention of becoming an academic subject librarian of literature and the humanities.

Esther K. Bauer is assistant professor of German at Virginia Polytechnic Institute and State University (Virginia Tech). She holds an MA in German and English language and literature, and linguistics from the University of Freiburg, Germany, and a PhD in German literature from Yale University. Her area of specialization is in German literature and culture since the mid-nineteenth century, and she has done extensive research on the Wilhelminian and Weimar periods, as well as Expressionist paintings and the nude in art. Her recent research, which extends to contemporary German literature and culture, focuses on questions of subjectivity, gender, desire, and visualizations of bodies. She has published and presented on writers Thomas Mann, Franz Kafka, Vicki Baum, Judith Hermann, and painter Christian Schad.

Melissa De Bruyker is currently working as a postdoctoral fellow at the German department at the University of Ghent, Belgium. She finished her PhD in 2006, and has published on G. Kolmar, A. Kolb, J. Roth, R. Walser, A. Schnitzler, and F. Kafka. Her research interests are nineteenth- and early twentieth-century literature from German-speaking countries, narrative theory, anthropological and epistemological motifs (silence, body, photography, animals), and the link between literary and cultural contexts.

Thomas H. Ford holds a PhD in English language and literature from the University of Chicago. He has taught at the University of Chicago and at the School of the Art Institute of Chicago. He is currently employed by Monash University in Melbourne, Australia, where he is a research associate of the social aesthetics research unit.

Naama Harel is a lecturer at the College for Oriental Languages and Literature of Shanghai International Studies University, China. Her research focuses on literary animal studies, and her published articles deal with anthropomorphism, beast fables, metamorphosis literature, and interspecific liminality. She is also an animal rights activist, and her examination of nonhuman representation in literature is conducted from a critical animal rights viewpoint.

Eleanor Helms is a PhD candidate and alumni dissertation fellow at Fordham University in the Bronx, New York. Her research interests include philosophy of literature (especially theories of authorship), phenomenology, and environmental philosophy. She finds that these interests are helpful in addressing the questions and concerns of environmental philosophy as well as exploring poetic language, imagination, and selfhood.

Hadea Nell Kriesberg is a lecturer in the Division of Interdisciplinary Studies at North Carolina State University, where she teaches courses in applied ethics, particularly science ethics, environmental ethics, and animal ethics. She has written online curriculum materials in the area of research ethics, including the development of a training website for the Office of Research Integrity (ORI) on animal subjects in research. She has presented papers about animals at the annual meetings of the Association for Practical and Professional Ethics and the Society for the Study of Social Problems.

Marc Lucht is visiting assistant professor of philosophy and works as curriculum coordinator in the Center for Peace Studies and Violence Prevention at Virginia Tech. He earned his PhD at Emory University, and has taught philosophy at Rocky Mountain College, the University of Maine, Kenyon College, and Alvernia University. His scholarly work focuses on phenomenology, environmental philosophy, aesthetics, intercultural dialogue, and ways in which humanistic education can contribute to peace. He has published and delivered numerous conference papers on the work of thinkers such as Martin Heidegger, Immanuel Kant, George Santayana, Arthur Schopenhauer, Friedrich Nietzsche, and Leo Tolstoy.

Burkhard Müller was born in Schweinfurt, Germany, and studied German and Latin at Würzburg University. He teaches Latin at Chemnitz Technical University, and is a regular contributor to the *Süddeutsche Zeitung,* mainly as a literary critic. Publications include books on modern German literature, the meaning of history, the shortcomings of evolutionary theory and Christianity, Stephen King, Karl Kraus, and Friedrich Schiller.

Margot Norris is Chancellor's Professor of English and Comparative Literature at the University of California, Irvine, where she teaches modern literature, intellectual history, and theories of narrative. Her book *Beasts of the Modern Imagination: Darwin, Nietzsche, Kafka, Ernst, and Lawrence* was published in 1985. She is also author of a book on twentieth-century war literature titled *Writing War in the Twentieth Century* (2000), and four books on the work of James Joyce.

Tahia Thaddeus Reynaga graduated from Yale College with a BA in English language and literature. In 2004, she was awarded a PhD in critical theory and cultural studies from the University of Nottingham for a dissertation on the phenomenon of self-reflexivity in Kurt Switters's Hanover *Merzbau.* From German Expressionism to Dada in early twentieth-century metaphysics, she has published and lectured on the avant-garde elements of European and American modernism, particularly as read and informed by the philosophies of Henri Bergson and Georg Simmel.

Henry Sussman is visiting professor of Germanic languages and literatures at Yale University. He was educated at Brandeis University (BA) and Johns Hopkins University (PhD), where he studied English and comparative literature. He has published widely, and among his works in literary criticism and critical theory are the following: *The Aesthetic Contract: Statutes of Art and Intellectual Work in Modernity* (1997); *Psyche and Text: The Sublime and the Grandiose in Literature, Psychopathology, and Culture* (1993); *The Trial: Kafka's Unholy Trinity* (1993); *Afterimages of Modernity* (1990); *High Resolution: Critical Theory and the Problem of Literacy* (1989); *The Hegelian Aftermath* (1982); and *Franz Kafka: Geometrician of Metaphor* (1979). He has won research fellowships from the National Endowment for the Humanities, the Rockefeller Foundation, the Fulbright Commission, and the Camargo Foundation. In 1988, he was inducted into the Johns Hopkins Society of Scholars.

Dean Swinford is assistant professor of English at Fayetteville State University. He is interested in the relationship between science and the development of literary genres, a topic he explored in his book *Through the Daemon's Gate: Kepler's Somnium, Medieval Dream Narratives, and the Polysemy of Allegorical Motifs* (2006).

Tom Tyler is senior lecturer in philosophy and culture at Oxford Brookes University, United Kingdom. His published research concerns the use of animals, and the persistent expression of anthropocentric and anthropomorphic assumptions within philosophy and critical theory. He is editor of *Animal Beings* (2006), coeditor of *Animal Encounters* (2009), and author of *CIFERAE: A Bestiary in Five Fingers* (forthcoming).

Donna Yarri is associate professor of theology at Alvernia University. She received her PhD from Southern Methodist University in religious studies, with a specialization in Christian ethics. Her teaching and research interests include medical ethics, the ethical treatment of animals, global issues, and popular culture. She has presented numerous papers and published articles, as well as two books. Her dissertation, "The Ethics of Animal Experimentation," was published in 2005 by Oxford University Press, and she recently coauthored a book titled *God, Science, and Designer Genes*, which was published in 2009. She currently has two forthcoming book projects: *The Sopranos: Exploring TV's Most Infamous Family* (2012), and a coauthored work titled *God, Darwin, and the Origin of Life* (2013), both to be published by Mercer University Press.

www.ingramcontent.com/pod-product-compliance
Ingram Content Group UK Ltd.
Pitfield, Milton Keynes, MK11 3LW, UK
UKHW050041041025
463598UK00017B/136

9 780739 143957